AN INTRODUCTION TO MULTILEVEL MODELING TECHNIQUES

Univariate and multivariate multilevel models are used to understand how to design studies and analyze data in this comprehensive text distinguished by its variety of applications from the educational, behavioral, and social sciences. Basic and advanced models are developed from the multilevel regression (MLM) and latent variable (SEM) traditions within one unified analytic framework for investigating hierarchical data. The authors provide examples using each modeling approach and also explore situations where alternative approaches may be more appropriate, given the research goals. Numerous examples and exercises allow readers to test their understanding of the techniques presented.

Changes to the new edition include:

- The use of Mplus 7.2 for running the analyses including the input and data files at www.routledge.com/9781848725522.
- Expanded discussion of MLM and SEM model building that outlines the steps taken in the process, the relevant Mplus syntax, and tips on how to evaluate the models.
- Expanded pedagogical program now with chapter objectives, boldfaced key terms, a glossary, and more tables and graphs to help students better understand key concepts and techniques.
- Numerous, varied examples developed throughout, which make this book appropriate for use in education, psychology, business, sociology, and the health sciences.
- Expanded coverage of missing data problems in MLM using ML estimation and multiple imputation to provide currently accepted solutions (Ch. 10).
- New chapter on three-level univariate and multilevel multivariate MLM models provides greater options for investigating more complex theoretical relationships (Ch. 4).
- New chapter on MLM and SEM models with categorical outcomes facilitates the specification of multilevel models with observed and latent outcomes (Ch. 8).
- New chapter on multilevel and longitudinal mixture models provides readers with options for identifying emergent groups in hierarchical data (Ch. 9).
- New chapter on the utilization of sample weights, power analysis, and missing data provides guidance on technical issues of increasing concern for research publication (Ch. 10).

Ideal as a text for graduate courses on multilevel, longitudinal, and latent variable modeling; multivariate statistics; or advanced quantitative techniques taught in psychology, business, education, health, and sociology, this book's practical approach also appeals to researchers. Recommended prerequisites are introductory univariate and multivariate statistics.

Ronald H. Heck is professor of education at the University of Hawai'i at Mānoa. His areas of interest include organizational theory, policy, and quantitative research methods.

Scott L. Thomas is professor and Dean of the School of Educational Studies at Claremont Graduate University. His specialties include sociology of education, policy, and quantitative research methods.

Quantitative Methodology Series

George A. Marcoulides, Series Editor

This series presents methodological techniques to investigators and students. The goal is to provide an understanding and working knowledge of each method with a minimum of mathematical derivations. Each volume focuses on a specific method (e.g. Factor Analysis, Multilevel Analysis, Structural Equation Modeling).

Proposals are invited from interested authors. Each proposal should consist of: a brief description of the volume's focus and intended market; a table of contents with an outline of each chapter; and a curriculum vita. Materials may be sent to Dr. George A. Marcoulides, University of California – Santa Barbara, gmarcoulides@ education.ucsb.edu.

Marcoulides • Modern Methods for Business Research

Marcoulides/Moustaki • Latent Variable and Latent Structure Models

Heck • Studying Educational and Social Policy: Theoretical Concepts and Research Methods

Van der Ark/Croon/Sijtsma • New Developments in Categorical Data Analysis for the Social and Behavioral Sciences

Duncan/Duncan/Strycker • An Introduction to Latent Variable Growth Curve Modeling: Concepts, Issues, and Applications, Second Edition

Cardinet/Johnson/Pini • Applying Generalizability Theory Using EduG

Creemers/Kyriakides/Sammons • Methodological Advances in Educational Effectiveness Research

Hox • Multilevel Analysis: Techniques and Applications, Second Edition

Heck/Thomas/Tabata • Multilevel Modeling of Categorical Outcomes Using IBM SPSS

Heck/Thomas/Tabata • Multilevel and Longitudinal Modeling with IBM SPSS, Second Edition

McArdle/Ritschard • Contemporary Issues in Exploratory Data Mining in the Behavioral Sciences

Heck/Thomas • An Introduction to Multilevel Modeling Techniques: MLM and SEM Approaches Using Mplus, Third Edition

AN INTRODUCTION TO MULTILEVEL MODELING TECHNIQUES

MLM and SEM Approaches Using Mplus

Third Edition

Ronald H. Heck
Scott L. Thomas

Routledge
Taylor & Francis Group

NEW YORK AND LONDON

Third edition published 2015
by Routledge
711 Third Avenue, New York, NY 10017

and by Routledge
27 Church Road, Hove, East Sussex BN3 2FA

*Routledge is an imprint of the Taylor & Francis Group,
an informa business*

First Edition published by Taylor and Francis, November 1999
Second Edition published by Routledge, September 2008

Reprinted IBM SPSS output (Figures 2.1–2.2, 3.1, 8.1–8.2, 10.1–10.3) is
courtesy of International Business Machines Corporation, ©SPSS, Inc,
an IBM Company[a]

a. SPSS was acquired by IBM in October, 2009.

Library of Congress Cataloging-in-Publication Data
Heck, Ronald H.
    An introduction to multilevel modeling techniques : MLM and SEM
approaches using Mplus / by Ronald H. Heck and Scott L. Thomas. —
Third edition.
        pages cm. — (Quantitative methodology series)
    Includes bibliographical references and index.
    1. Social sciences—Mathematical models.   2. Social sciences—
Research—Mathematical models.   I. Thomas, Scott Loring.   II. Title.
    H61.25.H43 2015
    001.4′22—dc23
    2014038512

ISBN: 978-1-84872-551-5 (hbk)
ISBN: 978-1-84872-552-2 (pbk)
ISBN: 978-1-315–74649-4 (ebk)

Typeset in Bembo
by Apex CoVantage, LLC

CONTENTS

PREFACE

Over the past decade, multilevel modeling has become a mainstream data analysis tool, emerging from a somewhat niche technique in the late 1980s to a technique now figuring prominently in a range of educational, behavioral, health, and social science disciplines. In this book, we provide an applied approach for utilizing multilevel modeling techniques within these fields and disciplines. Our intent is to develop a basic rationale behind the use of these techniques and to provide an introduction to the process of developing, testing, and interpreting the results of models that facilitate the investigation of hierarchical data structures. Hierarchical (or nested) data structures are defined by the nesting of a lower-level unit of analysis in a higher-level grouping that may itself constitute a separate unit of analysis. Individuals, for example, may be nested in various types of higher-order groupings such as employees clustered within departments and within companies, students clustered within classrooms and within schools, patients clustered within nursing units within hospitals, and repeated measures nested within individuals who may be randomly assigned to various experimental and treatment groups. Single-level analyses of hierarchical data would not be appropriate in most situations because clustering suggests that individuals within groups may be more similar to each other than to individuals clustered within other groups. Treating individuals as if they were separate from their social groupings therefore introduces potential biases in the proper analysis of hierarchical data structures. Along the way in our presentation of multilevel modeling, we provide numerous examples of cross-sectional and longitudinal hierarchical data structures with outcome variables scaled at a range of measurement levels including nominal, dichotomous, ordinal, count, and interval/ratio.

Multilevel modeling provides a variety of new possibilities for asking questions of the data that cannot be adequately investigated using well-known single-level analytic methods such as multiple regression, path analysis, and structural equation modeling. In this volume, we develop two basic classes of multilevel models: multilevel models (MLM) for univariate outcomes, which make use of multilevel regression (and other random-coefficient) techniques, and multilevel models for multivariate outcomes, which make use of multilevel structural equation modeling (SEM). Both approaches come from somewhat different modeling traditions, but they share many similarities, as well as some important differences, for examining hierarchical data structures. Throughout our presentation, we illustrate some often-encountered situations for using each common modeling approach and also explore some situations where one or the other approach may be more appropriate, given the goals of the research. As modeling possibilities for multilevel data become more extensive, these analytic choices can become more consequential in fully investigating theoretical relationships implied in multilevel data structures.

New to the Third Edition

The ideas developed in this book span more than a decade since the original volume. In our second edition, we illustrated how different multilevel modeling approaches (random-coefficient modeling, mixed-effect modeling, hierarchical linear modeling, structural equation modeling) could be subsumed under a more general view of modeling hierarchical data structures using concepts of continuous and categorical latent variables and simultaneous equations (e.g., see Muthén, 2002; Muthén & Asparouhov, 2003). Building on this earlier presentation, our intent in our third edition is to help readers set up, run, and interpret a variety of different types of MLM and SEM cross-sectional and longitudinal models using the multilevel procedures available in Mplus 7.2 (Muthén & Muthén, 1998–2012). We have found this statistical package to be quite adaptable in handling a variety of multilevel data structures (e.g., cross-sectional, longitudinal, cross-classified data), analytic approaches (e.g., univariate and multivariate multilevel regression models, single-level and multilevel latent variable models, mixture models), complex model relationships (i.e., direct, mediating, and moderating effects; reciprocal effects), and types of outcomes (i.e., categorical and continuous observed and latent variables).

We provide a generous collection of Mplus model statements for the various examples we utilize, so that readers may see how to set up and run the models with the software. Readers can work with the various examples provided in each chapter by using the input files and corresponding data, which can be downloaded from www.routledge.com/9781848725522/. The example input files in each chapter reference the corresponding data files. Readers can find more extended coverage of model-building techniques we present in this volume in the *Mplus 7 User's Guide* (Muthén & Muthén, 1998–2012), which is available online from www.statmodel.com. All popular statistical programs tend to evolve over time, and this is true for Mplus as well. We have found over the years that some input files that converged on a solution previously may have to be changed subtly (e.g., changing a model statement, adding or changing start values, fixing an error term) in order to estimate the proposed model. So as estimation procedures do evolve over time, this can have some influence on calculating the model parameters we estimate in our examples throughout this book.

Our new edition, in which more than three-quarters of the material is new or newly revised, emphasizes how these various types of multilevel models can all be subsumed under a more general view of modeling hierarchical data structures using the Mplus latent variable modeling framework (Muthén & Asparouhov, 2011; Muthén & Muthén, 1998–2012). The Mplus program offers wide range of options for dealing with a number of data-related issues such as missing data, power analysis, and the application of sample weights in multilevel contexts.

Changes to the extensively revised new edition include:

- Integrated use of Mplus 7.2 throughout for running the analyses.
- Expanded discussion of the MLM and SEM model-building processes that outlines the steps taken in the process, the relevant Mplus model-building syntax, and tips on how to evaluate the models to make the material more accessible to students.
- Expanded pedagogical program including chapter objectives, boldfaced key terms in each chapter, which are cross-referenced to a glossary at the end of the book, and more tables and graphs that summarize key material to help students better understand key concepts and modeling techniques.
- Numerous, varied examples of the multilevel techniques developed through-out, which make this book appropriate for use in several disciplines such as education, psychology, business, sociology, and health sciences.
- Expanded coverage of introductory material for basic multilevel models with univariate outcomes and multilevel models with longitudinal data structures to help students more easily build simple models with varied data structures.
- Introductions to single-level regression (Ch. 2) and structural equation models (Ch. 5), which are used as building blocks for introducing their multilevel counterparts.
- New section extending two-level SEM to three-level SEM provides readers with a new option for developing latent variable models for three-level data hierarchies (see Ch. 5).

New chapters to this edition include treatments of:

- Three-level univariate MLM and multilevel multivariate MLM models with mediating effects provide readers with further options for investigating more theoretical relationships than simple direct effects (Ch. 4).
- MLM and SEM models with categorical outcomes, which facilitates the spec-ification multilevel models with dichotomous, nominal, count, and ordinal observed and latent outcomes (Ch. 8).

- Multilevel and longitudinal mixture models provide readers with diverse options for thinking about emergent subpopulations of individuals or groups in hierarchical data (Ch. 9).
- The utilization of sample weights, power analysis, and missing data analysis for multilevel data structures provides researchers with guidance on several technical issues of increasing concern to research committees, funding and journal reviewers, and journal editors (Ch. 10).

Organization of the Book

Our first three chapters provide an introduction to basic concepts for utilizing multilevel modeling. In Chapter 1, we locate multilevel modeling within a broader set of univariate and multivariate analyses with various types of data structures. In Chapter 2, we outline a few of the differences between single-level and multilevel models, as well as some basic research issues to consider in conducting multilevel analyses. These include developing a basic modeling strategy for investigating multilevel data structures and considering several technical issues such as model estimation options and sample size requirements. Extensions of this basic multilevel framework to other types of multilevel models are described in more detail in subsequent chapters. In Chapter 3, we develop the basics of the multilevel regression modeling approach (MLM) for continuous univariate outcomes. We provide a series of models to explain variability in a random intercept and random slope across level-2 units. We illustrate how to develop the successive models using Mplus input files and how to evaluate their suitability. We also consider how centering level-1 predictors can influence the interpretation of the model results.

Our middle chapters provide various extensions of modeling cross-sectional multilevel data structures. Chapter 4 extends the basic two-level univariate MLM to a three-level MLM and also develops several extensions of the two-level univariate MLM to include multivariate outcomes. First, we develop a series of models to explain variability in a random intercept and slope across level-3 units. Second, we develop a two-level MLM with multivariate outcomes and extend this multivariate model to investigate a multilevel path model with mediating variable. In this latter type of MLM models, we illustrate how to use the matrix specification in Mplus for specifying multivariate multilevel models. This feature in Mplus opens up a whole range of new modeling relationships (e.g., mediating effects, reciprocal effects) beyond simple direct-effect relationships that form the dominant MLM approach to multilevel modeling. In Chapter 5, we consider further some of the ways in which structural equation modeling (SEM) methods can be integrated with multilevel regression models (MLM) to investigate a wide variety of models containing hierarchical data structures, focusing in particular on incorporating measurement error into the analyses by defining latent constructs through their observed indicators. We first develop a single-level confirmatory factor analysis

(CFA) model with two latent factors. We then consider the nesting of individuals within departments in specifying the CFA model at two levels. Finally, we extend this CFA model to consider the nesting of departments within organizations. In Chapter 6, we extend the multilevel CFA model to examine structural relations between latent variables within and between groups. Multilevel SEM can include combinations of observed predictors and continuous and categorical latent variables, random intercepts and slopes, as well as direct, indirect, and reciprocal effects. We develop a series of models that illustrate some of the possible relationships that can be investigated where structural relationships between latent variables are the major focus of the analyses.

Our latter chapters present other adaptations of multilevel modeling including longitudinal data, outcomes that are categorical observed or latent variables, and latent mixture models. In Chapter 7, we present an introduction to multilevel methods that can be used to examine changes in individuals and groups over time. The MLM approach for longitudinal data makes use of repeated observations for each individual defined at Level 1 with differences between individuals specified at Level 2. This requires multiple subject lines for the repeated measures to define the individual's growth over time in a basic two-level model. In contrast, the SEM approach treats the repeated measures in a manner similar to observed items defining latent intercept and slope factors. Group-level variables such treatment and control groups, departments, or organizations can be defined above the individual growth models using either the MLM or SEM approach. In Chapter 8, we extend some of the previous models presented to consider a variety of modeling situations where categorical outcomes are present. We first develop several multilevel models with binary, ordinal, multinomial, and counts as the dependent variable. We then consider a multilevel factor model where the observed indicators are categorical (e.g., binary, ordinal). In Chapter 9, we present an overview of latent mixture modeling. Mixture models are a special type of quantitative model in which latent variables can be used to represent mixtures of subpopulations or classes where population membership is not known beforehand but, rather, is inferred from the data. Mixture modeling is used to assign individuals to their most likely latent class and to obtain parameter estimates that explain differences between the classes identified. The approach can be applied to both cross-sectional and longitudinal models and can enrich our understanding of heterogeneity among both individuals and groups.

Finally, in Chapter 10, we provide further consideration of important data-related issues associated with modeling individual and group processes embedded in hierarchical data structures. We first provide an introductory discussion of the application of sample weights, focusing in particular on their potential impact at the group level of the study. We next turn our attention to issues related to sample size requirements in multilevel models and corresponding statistical power to detect hypothesized effects. Third, we discuss some common issues related to missing data. We then conclude our presentation with some further thoughts about multilevel modeling.

Intended Audience

One of our goals was to produce a book that would lend itself for use in first- and second-year graduate-level multivariate or multilevel modeling courses—in addition to being a valuable resource for readers with more mature statistical abilities. We assume the reader has a solid grounding in univariate statistics, typical of introductory- and graduate-level statistics courses in multiple regression and analysis of variance (ANOVA) methods. Readers who have also had multivariate statistics will be comfortable with discussions of latent variable (or factor) analysis, multivariate outcomes (e.g., multivariate analysis of variance), repeated measures analysis, and categorical outcomes. Today multilevel modeling techniques are more widely used, but they have not yet been fully integrated into most textbooks on univariate and multivariate analytic methods.

We hope this edition provides a useful guide to readers' efforts to learn more about the basics of multilevel and longitudinal modeling and the expanded range of research problems that can be addressed utilizing the Mplus software program. Ideal as a primary text in multilevel modeling courses or as a supplementary text for graduate-level courses on latent variable modeling (SEM), multivariate statistics, continuous and categorical data analysis, and/or advanced quantitative techniques taught in departments of psychology, business, education, health, and sociology, we hope the book's practical presentation will also appeal to researchers in these fields.

Acknowledgments

We would like to thank a number of people for their help at various stages in producing this third edition—series editor George Marcoulides for numerous discussions, helpful insights, and comments on earlier versions of our multilevel manuscripts; Lynn Tabata for expert help with preparing our final text and subject and author indices; Loring Thomas for editorial assistance at a critical moment; Linda and Bengt Muthén of Mplus for helpful advice regarding multilevel analyses using Mplus over the years; Angela Halliday for supervising the production of the manuscript, and Debra Riegert, who provided guidance, encouragement, and kept us on task. We would also like to thank the reviewers who provided us with invaluable input on the revisions plan including G. Leonard Burns, Washington State University; Laura M. O'Dwyer, Boston College; and one anonymous reviewer. Finally, we would also like to thank our readers and students, who have provided valuable feedback about what works and where we might additionally clarify concepts presented. Although we remain responsible for any errors remaining in the text, the book is much stronger as a result of their support and encouragement.

Ronald H. Heck
Scott L. Thomas

ABOUT THE AUTHORS

Ronald H. Heck is professor of education at the University of Hawai'i at Mānoa. His areas of interest include organizational theory, educational policy, and quantitative research methods. He has published widely on multilevel and longitudinal approaches for investigating school improvement and policy impact. He is the author (with Scott L. Thomas and Lynn Tabata) of *Multilevel and Longitudinal Modeling With IBM SPSS* and *Multilevel Modeling of Categorical Outcomes Using IBM SPSS*.

Scott L. Thomas is professor of education and Dean of the School of Educational Studies at the Claremont Graduate University. His areas of interest include the sociology of education, educational policy, and quantitative research methods. His published work often employs social network and multilevel methods for understanding student access to postsecondary education and curricular pathways to high school and college completion. He is the author (with Ronald H. Heck and Lynn Tabata) of *Multilevel and Longitudinal Modeling With IBM SPSS* and *Multilevel Modeling of Categorical Outcomes Using IBM SPSS*.

1

INTRODUCTION

Chapter Objectives

In this introductory chapter, we present an overview of several conceptual and methodological issues associated with modeling individual and group processes embedded in **clustered/hierarchical data** structures. We locate multilevel modeling techniques within a broader set of **univariate and multivariate methods** commonly used to examine various types of data structures. We then illustrate how choices of analytic method can impact the optimal investigation of the data. This overview foreshadows our further development of these issues and models in subsequent chapters.

Introduction

Over the past several decades, concerns in various fields with conceptual and methodological issues in conducting research with hierarchical (or nested) data have led to the development of multilevel modeling techniques. Research on organizations such as universities or product and service firms presents opportunities to study phenomena in hierarchical settings. Individuals (Level 1) may work within specific formally defined departments (Level 2), which may be found within larger organizations (Level 3), which, in turn, may be located within specific states, regions, or nations. These individuals interact with their social contexts in a variety of ways. Individuals bring certain skills and attitudes to the workplace; they are clustered in departments or work units having certain characteristics, and they are also clustered within organizations having particular characteristics. Because of the presence of these successive groupings in hierarchical data, individuals within particular organizations may share certain properties including socialization patterns, traditions, attitudes, and work goals. Similarly, properties of groups (e.g., leadership patterns, improvement in productivity) may also be influenced by the people in them. Hierarchical data also result from the specific research design and the nature of the data collected. In survey research, for example, individuals are often selected to participate in a study from some type of stratified random sampling design (e.g., individuals may be chosen from certain neighborhoods in particular cities and geographical areas). Longitudinal data collection also presents another research situation where a series of measurements is nested within the individuals who participate in the study.

In the past, researchers often had considerable difficulty analyzing data where individuals were nested within a series of hierarchical groupings. Ignoring such data structures can lead to false inferences about the relations among variables in a model, as well as missed insights about the social processes being studied. Today, however, for studying individual and group phenomena, multilevel modeling is an attractive approach because it allows the incorporation of substantive theory about such individual and group processes into the clustered sampling schemes typical of large-scale survey research. It is steadily becoming the standard analytic approach for research in fields such as business, education, health sciences, and sociology because of its applicability to a broad range of research situations, designs, and data structures (e.g., hierarchical data, cross-classified data, longitudinal data). Multilevel modeling is referred to by a variety of names including random coefficients models, mixed-effects models, multilevel regression models, hierarchical linear models, and **multilevel structural equation models**. This diversity of names is an artifact of the statistical theory underlying multilevel models—theory developed out of methodological work in several different fields. For this reason, there are some differences in the preferences and manner in which the methods are presented and used within various fields. At their core, however, these methods are all integrally related by virtue of their primary emphasis on the decomposition of variance in a single outcome or a multivariate set of outcomes and the explanation of this variance by sets of explanatory variables that are located in different strata of the data hierarchy.

We begin with the principle that quantitative analysis really deals with the translation (or operationalization) of abstract theories into concrete models and that theoretical frameworks are essential guides to sound empirical investigation. Statistical models are not empirical statements or descriptions of actual worlds (Heckman, 2005); rather, they are mathematical representations of behaviors and attitudes believed to exist in a larger population of interest. In other words, our statistical models represent a set of proposed theoretical relations thought to exist in the population—a set of theoretical relationships that account for relationships actually observed in the sample data from that population (Singer & Willett, 2003).

Providing a Conceptual Overview

Multilevel conceptual frameworks open up new possibilities for investigating theories concerning how individuals and groups interact. We refer to the lowest level of the hierarchy (Level 1) as the *micro level*, with all higher levels in the hierarchical data structure as the *macro level*. As an example, we might be interested in defining and examining relationships between individual, departmental, and organizational processes on organizational productivity. A three-level conceptual model might include variables relating to individuals at the micro level (Level 1), departments at Level 2, and organizations at Level 3. We could, of course, define higher organizational levels such as locales, regions, or nations at Level 4 through *k*. From this perspective, the relationships among variables observed for the micro-level units (individuals) in a study have parameters that can take on values different from those of the higher-level units (e.g., departments or organizations). Macro-level variables are frequently referred to as *groups* or *contexts* (Kreft & de Leeuw, 1998). With a contextual model, therefore, one could envision successive levels extending well beyond the organization.

Each of these groupings or levels of context may exert effects on, for example, productivity in the workplace. Outcomes may be influenced by combinations of variables related to the backgrounds and attitudes of employees (e.g., experience, education and work-related skills, attitudes and motivations), the processes of organizational work (e.g., leadership, decision making, staff development, organizational values, resource allocation), the context of the organization, or the cross-level interactions of these variables within the structure of the organization (e.g., size, management arrangements within its clustered groupings). Some of these possible theoretical relationships within and between levels are summarized in Figure 1.1.

Research strategies for dealing with the complexity of the multilevel, or contextual, features of organizations have been somewhat limited historically. Researchers did not always consider the implications of the assumptions they made about measuring variables at their natural level, or moving them from one level to another through **aggregation** or **disaggregation**. This process is summarized in Figure 1.1 with two-headed arrows. *Aggregation*, for example, means that the productivity level of individuals within departments or organizations would be combined to a higher level (e.g., the organizational level). Successive aggregation of variables reduces the variability in productivity within each individual and within each unit to a single organizational-level variable. The comparison is then made between organizations' mean productivity outcomes. Of course, failing to acknowledge the within-group variability present in the data can potentially distort relationships examined between such units leading to what Robinson (1950) called an ecological fallacy.

In contrast, *disaggregation* refers to moving a variable conceptualized at a higher level to a lower level. For example, in a different analysis we may have productivity measured at the organizational level but also have items that express individual employee attitudes and motivation. In this case, we intend to analyze the data at the individual level to see whether employee attitudes influence productivity. If we assign to all individuals the same value on the organizational productivity variable (and possibly other organizational variables such as size), we attribute properties of the organization to individuals. This can also confound the analysis.

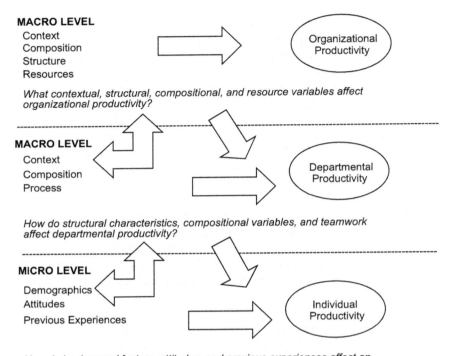

MACRO LEVEL
Context
Composition
Structure
Resources

Organizational Productivity

What contextual, structural, compositional, and resource variables affect organizational productivity?

MACRO LEVEL
Context
Composition
Process

Departmental Productivity

How do structural characteristics, compositional variables, and teamwork affect departmental productivity?

MICRO LEVEL
Demographics
Attitudes
Previous Experiences

Individual Productivity

How do background factors, attitudes, and previous experiences affect an employee's productivity?

FIGURE 1.1 Defining variables and relationships in a multilevel conceptual model.

Examples such as these suggest that analyses conducted exclusively at the micro or macro level may produce different results. Treating individuals as if they were independent of these various organizational groupings ignores the complexity inherent in the data and introduces a potentially important source of bias into the analysis. This is because individuals in a group or context tend to be more similar on many important variables (e.g., attitudes, behaviors) than individuals in different contexts. With hierarchical data, a more complex error structure must be added to account for the dependencies among observations. Such dependencies violate key assumptions of single-level analyses such as **ordinary least squares (OLS) regression** and can lead to underestimated variances and standard errors. This in turn may result in drawing erroneous conclusions about the empirical relationships under consideration (Thomas & Heck, 2001).

As one may surmise, it is important to develop a scheme to place the explanatory variables hypothesized to affect individuals and other types of organizational processes in their proper hierarchical locations. This helps to clarify the organizational, or contextual, level to which they rightly belong. Different sets of variables associated with each level, or cluster, in the data quite likely affect productivity in the workplace. These relationships are indicated by horizontal arrows in Figure 1.1. As the figure indicates, each level within the data hierarchy can suggest different sorts of questions to be asked. For example, at the micro level, we might be interested in how specific individual variables affect employees' productivity. At the organizational level, we might be interested in how the availability of resources explains differences in productivity levels between organizations.

In addition, there are also likely effects that may result from various interactions across organizational levels. These cross-level relationships are shown in Figure 1.1 with arrows that extend from the macro level toward the micro level. More specifically, we might ask how departmental teamwork moderates (i.e., enhances or diminishes) the relationship between employee attitudes and productivity within organizations. In the past, mapping these sorts of relations between groups and individuals has often been problematic—often focusing on single, discrete elements while ignoring the interrelated aspects of larger organizational processes. In specifying this type of cross-level relationship, we can assess how the presence of a feature such as democratic decision making at the department level may coordinate the behavior of individuals within those work units.

One important contribution of multilevel modeling, then, is to allow the researcher to avoid the aggregation (i.e., assigning the same organizational mean to each member) or disaggregation (i.e., treating subjects as independent from their organizational groupings) problem. Developing a conceptual framework of organizational relations can also help the researcher avoid another potential source of bias within the analysis—that of ignoring the different levels of the explanatory (independent) variables. Figure 1.1 also suggests that through examining the variation in outcomes that exists at different levels of the data hierarchy, we can develop more refined theories about how explanatory variables at each level contribute to variation in the outcomes examined in the study. Importantly, where single-level analyses focus on average effects, which are each typically *fixed* at one value for the whole study sample, multilevel modeling procedures open up possibilities for examining how outcome intercepts (means) such as productivity and regression coefficients (slopes) regarding relationships at lower levels of the data hierarchy may vary across higher-order units in the sample.

Analysis of Multilevel Data Structures

As Figure 1.1 implies, decisions about analysis are located within a larger conceptual and methodological framework that begins with research questions and designs, data structures, and methods of analysis (Raudenbush, 1988). For organizational theories in particular, variables must be defined and measured at multiple levels of interest within a data hierarchy. These decisions about a study's conceptualization and conduct are critical to the credibility of the analyst's results and to the study's overall contribution to the relevant knowledge base.

The goal of multilevel analyses may be either prediction or explanation. In the former instance, the focus is more on efficiency of prediction and parsimony of variables included in the prediction equation, while in the latter case, the focus rests more upon the correct specification of a theoretical model under consideration. Our approach toward multilevel modeling takes us generally in the direction of explanation; that is, the researcher formulates a model from theory to explain variability in the outcomes and then tests this model against the data. We call attention to this distinction between explanatory and predictive aims, however, because in predictive studies, variables would be retained in an analysis only if they were statistically significant and dropped simply because they were not. In other words, theory may not enter into decisions about model efficiency.

Because of the nature of the data structures in multilevel models (e.g., individuals nested within groups, resulting in more complex relationship between variables), there seems to be an inherent need for the application of theory to guide the kinds of relationships specified within, between, and across levels. This is because for purely predictive purposes, it would often be more efficient to just ignore the underlying structure of the data. In contrast, in the explanatory approach to modeling (i.e., especially in testing structural equation models), model specification should be carefully considered, and subsequent changes should be made judiciously and with regard to theory. Otherwise, it may be difficult to attach any substantive meaning to the final model.

Contrasting Linear Models

Linear models [e.g., correlation, analysis of variance (ANOVA), multiple regression, path analysis, multivariate analysis of variance (MANOVA), discriminant analysis, factor analysis, *generalized* linear models] have a long tradition in the social and behavioral sciences for bringing meaning to a variety of different data structures. More recently, **structural equation modeling (SEM)**, a modeling approach that combines **latent variables** defined through factor analysis with path models that can specify a variety of direct, mediating, and reciprocal effects, has become a widely used means of specifying common linear models (e.g., ANOVA, MANOVA, multiple regression). Over time, the approach has been adapted to include models with both continuous and categorical outcomes (e.g., Muthén, 1984). A core assumption of these single-level models is independence of errors (Curran, 2003).

We present two types of multilevel models in this introductory text. They have evolved from different conceptual and methodological roots (Mehta & Neale, 2005). Multilevel regression (or random coefficients) models were developed to deal with nested data structures, that is, where errors were not independent because of features of the data set, for example, the sampling of individuals in multistage surveys, the clustering of individuals such as students within classrooms or schools, or repeated math tests nested within individuals over a period time.

The outcomes were primarily univariate, although it is also possible to investigate multivariate outcomes using the multilevel regression approach. SEM represented an extension of factor analysis (i.e., defining latent constructs through measuring observed indicators) and path analysis (i.e., examining **direct and indirect relationships** as well as **recursive and nonrecursive relationships**). As such, it primarily concerned the modeling of multivariate data through correcting one or more latent outcomes and often explanatory variables for **measurement error**, which provided more reliable estimates of effects between variables in the structural portion of the model.

It is easy to see there is usefulness in applying both types of modeling approaches to efforts aimed at examining group and individual processes. On the one hand, in many fields there is interest in examining phenomena that entail the nesting of individuals within higher-order groups. As we have noted, examples include students nested in classrooms and schools, health care personnel nested within clinics or hospitals, employees nested in product and service firms, and voters nested within congressional districts. On the other hand, many investigations of social processes concern the measurement of latent constructs (e.g., leadership, decision-making norms, organizational culture, workplace satisfaction) through their observed indicators and the strength of direct (and indirect) structural processes operating between them at one or more points in time. It is no surprise, therefore, that extending the SEM approach to hierarchical and longitudinal data structures has also been the subject of much research (e.g., Curran, 2003; Grilli & Rampichini, 2007; Hox, 1995; McDonald & Goldstein, 1989; Mehta & Neale, 2005; Muthén, 1991, 1994; Muthén & Muthén, 1998–2006; Rabe-Hesketh, Skrondal, & Pickles, 2004).

This extension has taken some time, however, because of inherent differences in how the data sets and analyses were structured in the random coefficients (multilevel regression) and the SEM approaches—one primary difference being the use of covariance and mean structure matrices that depended on having complete data (obtained through listwise deletion of individuals with partial data) and relatively large sample sizes in the SEM approach. This prohibited the incorporation of random slopes into multilevel SEM until more recently. For longitudinal analyses, intervals between measurement occasions also had to be equally spaced. The introduction of raw data, or **full information maximum likelihood (FIML)** estimation as a means of providing estimates of the model's parameters partially resolved the equal interval problem (Arbuckle, 1996) and eventually led to the ability to model person-specific covariances, which was central to estimating randomly varying slopes using SEM (Mehta & Neale, 2005).

In addition, more recently Muthén (2008) has proposed a variety of hybrid latent variable formulations that include both continuous and categorical latent variables (e.g., latent class analysis, growth mixture analysis, factor mixture analysis). These techniques, which are readily available in the Mplus statistical package (Muthén & Muthén, 1998–2012), expand the manners in which cross-sectional,

TABLE 1.1 Summary of Quantitative Approaches to the Analysis of Organizational Data

Analytic Approach	Example Techniques
Single-level data structure	
1. Univariate (one dependent variable)	correlation, analysis of variance (ANOVA), regression, repeated measures ANOVA
2. Multivariate (two or more dependent variables)	canonical correlation, multivariate analysis of variance and discriminant analysis, factor analysis, path analysis, time series analysis, covariance structure models, other types of structural equation models (e.g., latent curve, mixture, latent class)
Multilevel data structure	
3. Univariate (one dependent variable)	multilevel regression or random coefficients models, variance components models, mixed linear models, time series analysis, growth curve models
4. Multivariate (two or more dependent variables)	multilevel multivariate models, multilevel covariance structure models, other types of multilevel structural equation models (e.g., multilevel latent curve, mixture, latent class)

longitudinal, and hierarchical data structures may be examined in the coming years. As Muthén noted, the latent variable emphasis of SEM actually provides a general modeling conceptual framework that incorporates **random effects** and univariate outcomes in hierarchical settings as one of several types of models [e.g., see also Raudenbush & Bryk (2002), Mehta & Neale (2005), and Muthén & Asparouhov (2011) for further discussion].

In Table 1.1, we locate multilevel modeling within a larger methodological framework of quantitative methods of analysis relevant to social and behavioral research. For ease of presentation, we group the methods by data structure (e.g., single-level versus nested or hierarchical) and number of dependent variables (univariate versus multivariate). Within this larger framework, we can identify four general types of analyses involving (1) single or (2) multiple dependent variables and (3) single-level or (4) nested data structures. In general, these types of quantitative techniques, as well as the various hybrid techniques, can all be subsumed under a broader latent variable framework (Muthén, 2002; Muthén & Asparouhov, 2011).

The choice of analytic strategies and model specification is not a trivial one. More complete modeling formulations may suggest inferences based on relationships in the sample data that are not revealed in more simplistic models. At the same time, however, better developed modeling formulations are also more likely to lead to fewer findings of substance than have often been claimed in studies that employ more simplistic analytical methods (Pedhazur & Schmelkin, 1991). We draw a clear distinction between concerns over model specification limited to the exclusion or inclusion of theoretically relevant variables and model specification related to the mathematical explication of the relationships among those variables. While theory should guide both considerations, the former concern deals with the availability of relevant variables in the data set, and the latter deals with the structure of the data set itself and the choice of modeling approach used to exploit theoretically important relationships presumed to exist in the population. Besides the choices we make about methods of analysis, our inferences may also be affected in practice by limitations of our samples (e.g., size and sampling variation, missing data). It is important to acknowledge that these limitations can also lead to potential biases in our results.

Univariate Analysis

In the remainder of this chapter, we present several examples to illustrate the potential implications of decisions about methods of analysis and data structures that affect the interpretation of results. Another of our guiding principles is that the responsible researcher should consider approaches that are likely to take full advantage of the features of particular data structures and goals of the overall research when making decisions about analytic methods. We illustrate our point about decisions regarding methods of analysis and fully exploiting features of our data with a series of short examples.

For our first example, let's consider a case where the goal is to examine whether gender is related to student achievement. There are a number of different options in Table 1.1 we could choose to analyze the data in this simple proposed model. One way to think about statistical modeling is in terms of an attempt to account for variation in a dependent variable such as student achievement—variance that is believed to be associated with one or more explanatory variables such as gender and other demographic categories (e.g., socioeconomic status, race/ethnicity) or personal attributes measured as continuous variables (e.g., motivation, previous learning). This is analogous to thinking about how much variance in student achievement (R^2) is accounted for by a given set of explanatory variables.

In this case, we might propose that gender accounts for variation in students' test scores. In Table 1.2, we have data compiled on a small random sample of 14 students from a larger study. The data consist of their scores in a reading test, a math test, and

TABLE 1.2 Descriptive Statistics for Example

Variable	Male		Female	
	Mean	SD	Mean	SD
Reading	650.88	37.01	641.50	15.80
Math	679.75	36.54	637.00	15.80
Language	658.13	27.78	631.67	25.57

a language skills test. The data in the table show that females in the sample scored lower than males on each test. For ease of presentation we set aside the issue of whether there are other variables that should also be included in the model to provide a more thorough examination of whether gender differences in achievement would exist after other known variables related to achievement were controlled.

Multiple Regression

We might choose univariate regression to conduct the analysis. Regression analysis employs cross-sectional data that are obtained as individual-level data through random sampling or individual and group data using cluster sampling. Gender would be the independent variable, and each of the tests would represent a single dependent variable. This strategy would require three separate tests and would get at the issue of how gender affects achievement, but in each case, achievement would be described somewhat differently (i.e., math, reading, language). The ratio of the estimate to its standard error (β/SE) can be used to provide a t-test of statistical significance for each of the hypothesized relationships. Assuming the data in the example are single level, the hypothesis tested is that the population from which males and females were selected has the same means for each of the dependent variables. If we examine the regression coefficients between gender and achievement in Table 1.3, we can see that for this small sample, females scored significantly lower than males in math (unstandardized $\beta = -42.75$) but not in reading ($\beta = -9.38, p > 0.05$) or language ($\beta = -26.46, p > 0.05$). If we were to summarize these data, we would likely conclude that gender affects achievement under some conditions but not others.

Analysis of Variance

Another way to think about statistical modeling is in terms of an attempt to decompose variability in the test score into its component parts. For example, if we used a simple one-way ANOVA to investigate the relationships in Table 1.3,

TABLE 1.3 Single-Level Regression Analyses

	Reading		Math		Language	
	Beta	SE	Beta	SE	Beta	SE
Female	−9.375	16.23	−42.75	17.76	−26.46	14.52
SS Between	301.339 (1 df)		6265.929 (1 df)		2400.149 (1 df)	
SS Within	10836.375 (12 df)		12973.500 (12 df)		8672.208 (12 df)	
F-ratio	0.334 ($p = 0.574$)		5.796 ($p = 0.033$)		3.321 ($p = 0.093$)	
p	0.57		0.03		0.09	
R-Square	0.03		0.33		0.22	

we would be testing the similarity of group means for males and females by partitioning the sum of squares for individuals into a portion describing differences in achievement variability due to groups (i.e., gender) and differences in variability due to individuals. In this case, the F-ratio provides an indication of the ratio of between-groups variability (i.e., defined as between-groups mean squares) to within-groups variability (i.e., within-groups mean squares).

To partition the variability in achievement, we disaggregate individuals' raw scores into their deviations about their respective group mean (within-groups variation) and disaggregate the group means from the overall grand mean (between-groups variation). This amounts to a key piece of information in a test of whether the difference in means in reading, for example, between males and females (650.88 − 641.50 = 9.38) in Table 1.2 is statistically significant in the population. As we noted, in Table 1.3 the regression coefficient representing the effect of gender on reading score ($\beta = -9.38, p > 0.10$) also summarizes the difference in means between males and females. As we would expect, the results using one-way ANOVA and multiple regression are consistent although presented in a slightly different fashion.

Multivariate Analysis

As suggested in Table 1.1, multivariate analysis is the more general case of univariate analysis; that is, it facilitates the examination of multiple independent and dependent variables in one simultaneous model. When we chose to examine the relationship between gender and each achievement test separately, our choice of analytic approach would have eliminated the possibility that students' reading scores were also correlated with their math and language scores. The initial correlations (not tabled), however, suggest that reading and math are highly correlated ($r = 0.79$), as are reading and language ($r = 0.76$) and language and math ($r = 0.85$).

Multivariate Analysis of Variance

We could use multivariate analysis of variance (MANOVA) to investigate whether gender affected student achievement more generally (i.e., using reading, math, and language test scores as dependent variables in the same model). The multivariate approach has the advantage of providing an analysis of differences considering all dependent variables simultaneously. It has the effect of controlling for the covariance structure between the dependent variables. Classic multivariate analysis uses descriptive information about means, standard deviations, and correlations (or covariances) to summarize relationships between the dependent variables in the sample initially. A set of means (called a vector, in matrix terminology) replaces the individual means for each achievement score in the model. The hypothesis tested is that the population from which the groups are selected has the same means for all dependent variables. A more sophisticated way to think about this system of three dependent variables is as representing a linear combination of the dependent variables, or a single latent (unobserved) variable that we might call "achievement."

The MANOVA approach can be conceptualized as creating a latent (or underlying) achievement variable defined by a linear weighted function of the observed dependent variables and then assessing whether this function is the same for males and females. The scores on the dependent variables generated by the function can be seen as representing an individual's standing on a latent variable (Marcoulides & Hershberger, 1997). Although the achievement latent variable is corrected for correlations between the set of tests, from the MANOVA analysis we do not get any direct information about how strongly each test is associated with the underlying achievement factor. This information would help us understand how well each separate test contributes to the definition of the latent achievement variable. While we can obtain univariate information (e.g., parameter estimates, standard errors, hypothesis tests) about how predictors affect each dependent variable separately, this violates the multivariate nature of the outcome.

Matrices are important building blocks for both multivariate and multilevel analyses. A **covariance matrix** represents a convenient way to store information about observed variables (e.g., variances and covariances) that can be used to test relationships implied by a statistical model. Mathematical operations (e.g., multiplication or inversion) are performed on the covariance matrix as a way of determining whether a proposed set of relationships comprising a model explains patterns observed in the data. Remember that in the univariate case, the ratio of between-group variability to within-group variability is described by an F-ratio. This provides a test of the significance of difference between the means of two groups. In the multivariate case, there are sets of dependent variables, so a similar test of variability involves decomposing a total sample matrix of **sums of squares and cross products (SSCP)** into a between-subjects matrix and an error (or within-subjects) matrix. The question of whether or not there is significant variability in the outcomes due to groups is then answered with a multivariate test.

Summary measures of the variation that exists within a matrix are called **determinants**. The determinant represents a measure of generalized variance in the matrix after removing covariance. Ratios between determinants (similar to F-ratios) provide a test of the hypothesis about the effect of the independent variable on the linear combination of dependent variables. We can compare the within-groups portion of the variance to the total sample SSCP matrix (between + within matrix) using a ratio of the respective determinants ($|D|$) of these matrices. One statistic often used for testing multivariate hypotheses is Wilks's lambda ($|D_W| / |D_T|$), which can be interpreted as a measure of the proportion of total variability in the outcomes not explained by group differences. It is of interest to note that the univariate case, for a single dependent variable, Wilks's lambda can

TABLE 1.4 Multivariate Analysis of Variance (MANOVA) Results

	Within-Groups SSCP Matrix			Total SSCP Matrix		
	Reading	Math	Language	Reading	Math	Language
Reading	10836.375	10214.750	7594.125	11137.714	11588.857	8444.571
Math	10214.750	12973.500	8535.250	11588.857	19239.429	12413.286
Language	7594.12	8535.250	8672.208	8444.571	12413.286	11072.357

Within determinant = 1.00888×10^{11} Total determinant = 2.27001×10^{11}

Wilks's $\Lambda = 1.00888 \times 10^{11} / 2.27001 \times 10^{11} = 0.444$

be expressed in terms of a ratio of the sum of squares within groups to the total sum of squares (Marcoulides & Hershberger, 1997).

The results of this analysis (Table 1.4) suggest that gender is significantly related to the latent achievement variable (Wilks's $\Lambda = 0.444, p = 0.037$). This result also suggests a conclusion somewhat inconsistent with the previous univariate regression analysis. Assuming that we felt the MANOVA approach was better suited to capture the theoretical relationships of interest in our population, we might then view the univariate regression results as incomplete and suggestive of an incorrect conclusion regarding the relationship between gender and academic achievement.

Structural Equation Modeling

We could also conduct a multivariate analysis with structural equation modeling (SEM). SEM facilitates the specification and testing of models that include latent variables, multiple indicators, measurement errors, and complex structural relationships such as reciprocal causation. The SEM framework represents a generalization of both multiple regression and factor analysis and subsumes most linear modeling methods as special cases (Rigdon, 1998). SEM can be used to address two basic concerns in the example data: development of latent variables and the adjustments for measurement error in estimating these latent variables. As we shall next illustrate, SEM can be used to estimate well-known linear (e.g., ANOVA, MANOVA, multiple regression) models (Curran, 2003).

Defining constructs in terms of their observed indicators is generally the first part of an SEM analysis. This is often referred to as **confirmatory factor analysis (CFA)** since the proposed relationships are specified first and then examined against the data to see whether the hypothesized model is confirmed. This part of the analysis helps support the validity and reliability of proposed constructs through the measurement properties of their observed indicators. In the SEM approach to examining data structures, a smaller set of latent (unobserved) factors is hypothesized to be responsible for the specific pattern of variation and covariation present in a set of observed variables. In a technical sense, when a researcher tests a particular model, restrictions are imposed on the sample covariance matrix

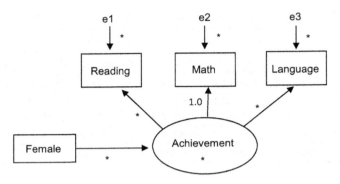

FIGURE 1.2 Parameters estimated in proposed model of gender's influence on student achievement.

summarizing a set of empirical relationships (e.g., factor loadings, factor variances and covariances, residual covariances). Through such restrictions, the relationships observed in the sample data are compared to the restrictions defined through the mathematical model, and any of a number of assessments of "fit" between the data and the implied model can be derived. For example, a matrix of covariances among observed variables may be decomposed into a matrix of factor loadings and a matrix of errors, and the adequacy of the reproduced matrix of implied relationships may be examined against the data.

In the example summarized in Figure 1.2, we can treat the observed tests as if they define a latent achievement factor. Defining latent constructs through several observed indicators helps to address the second concern identified previously: producing more accurate estimates of structural relationships (i.e., regression coefficients) because the achievement factor has been corrected for measurement error. To provide a metric to measure the factor, we typically fix one factor loading to 1.0. In this case, we would also have to assume that the errors for each test do not covary (given our limited sample size). We can then examine whether the achievement results are different for males and females.

The structural model summarized in Figure 1.3 suggests that the three subtests are strong indictors of the latent achievement factor (i.e., with factor loadings ranging from 0.79 to 1.00). High factor loadings indicate that the achievement factor is well measured by the individual tests (i.e., corresponding errors for each indicator will be relatively small). Because we fixed one factor loading (Math) to 1.0, its corresponding standard error is not estimated (i.e., it is not tested for statistical significance). The unstandardized beta coefficient summarizing the effect of female on achievement is −42.73, and the standardized effect is −0.57 ($p < 0.05$). The remaining variance in student achievement unaccounted for by gender is summarized in parentheses (0.67), which implies that gender accounts for 33% of the variance in achievement in this small sample.

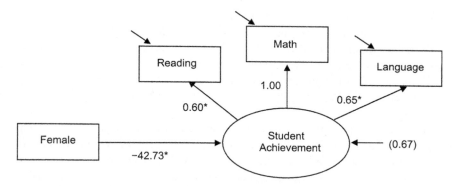

FIGURE 1.3 Standardized and unstandardized (in parentheses) relationship between gender and student achievement (*$p < 0.05$).

Multilevel Data Structures

Multilevel analysis is an extension of these basic types of variance decomposition models that examine within-individual variability and group variability. Clustered data result from the sampling strategies used in large-scale databases, as well as the natural groupings of people within organizations. Because the data structures are hierarchical, people within successive groupings will share similarities that must be considered in the analytic methods. In the decomposition of variance in a student's score into its component parts, as an example, a new goal is to identify the proportion of variance in an outcome that is associated with individuals who are clustered with others in a set of groups (e.g., patients in hospitals, voters in states). People within specific groups may share certain similarities by virtue of their membership in that particular group. As Figure 1.1 indicates, individuals within departments may also be nested within an organization such that individuals in specific departments all share certain similarities, and the departments may also share some operational similarities within each firm.

As we have suggested, analysis of variance methods offer an initial way to examine the variance between individuals and groups. For example, variance decomposition routines in standard statistical packages (e.g., SAS or SPSS) can be used to determine how much of the variability in an outcome lies between individuals, between departments, and between firms. Although ANOVA offers partial answers to some of the questions that can be posed with nested data (e.g., where certain individuals may be nested within one of several experimental groups), the formulation of the multilevel modeling approach has facilitated examinations of variability in an outcome at each of several levels as a function of individual-level variables such as gender, department-level variables such as size or decision-making participation, and organizational-level variables such as climate and workplace expectations for employee productivity. One primary difference is that multilevel models assume that higher-order units are selected at random, and individuals are selected at random within the units. In the ANOVA case, a nested design refers to testing hypotheses similar to interactions but where the levels of the nested variables are not the same for every combination of factors within which they are nested (e.g., where subjects are nested within different levels of a specific treatment).

Our second example is intended to illustrate the advantages of effectively exploiting the hierarchical structure of the data in our analyses. A common limitation of the univariate and multivariate techniques discussed previously is that they are confined to single-level analyses; that is, either individuals are the unit of analysis or groups are the unit of analysis. Because single-level analytic methods are generally based on the assumption that subjects are randomly sampled and thus are independent of each other, this assumption is violated in the case where individuals are clustered within groups. Applying single-level analytic techniques to nested data produces several difficulties including a forced choice over the proper unit of analysis (individuals or groups), trade-offs in measurement precision, limitations in the ways in which the model's parameters are examined, violations related to errors in the prediction equation (i.e., errors should be independent, normally distributed, and have constant variance), and, therefore, missed opportunities to fully investigate the complexity of substantive relationships between people and their social groupings.

Suppose we wish to examine the impact of school quality on school outcomes, controlling for community socioeconomic status. In this example, there are a number of students within each school who are assessed on the same three tests (reading, math, language). We obtain background information on students including their individual socioeconomic status (SES) and age. We also collect data from their schools regarding school quality (i.e., defined as a factor score consisting of several educational process indicators) and community SES (i.e., defined as a z-score representing the proportion of students participating in federal free/reduced lunch). We could, of course, develop separate multilevel models focusing on each univariate outcome. From our previous analyses, we need an approach that will consider both of the correlations between the subtests, and we need to take into consideration the hierarchical data structure as well as the proper definition of the explanatory variables. More specifically, we have student SES defined at the individual level (i.e., a dichotomous variable flagging individuals within low SES according to participation in the federal free/reduced lunch program) and as a student composition variable representing community SES (CSES) at the school level.

In this example, we present results for a sample data set with clustered observations (120 students in 24 schools). The expansion of the data set is necessary to accommodate the more comprehensive specification of the model (i.e., estimating between-group relations). More complex model formulations require that additional thought be given to the ability of the data structure to support the examination of the relationships presumed to be operating in the population. This is a critical point that we revisit in subsequent sections of the book. As readers may surmise, we can make the same type of distinction between univariate analysis and multivariate analysis when the data are hierarchically structured (e.g., individuals clustered in successive groups, repeated measures nested within individuals who are clustered in groups).

Multilevel Multivariate Model

One way to specify the model is to develop a multilevel multivariate model. We can consider the three subtests as a multivariate outcome, that is, with the correlations between the outcomes incorporated into the model similar to MANOVA. In this way, we consider the three outcomes to be observed (rather than defining a latent variable); however, the multivariate formulation will adjust for their correlations. In addition, specifying the model as a multilevel model will adjust the estimates for the clustering of individuals within groups. If we structure the model in this manner, using Mplus, we can decompose the variability in the three observed outcomes into their within- and between-groups components. We specify the multivariate outcomes for individuals at Level 1 and the multivariate outcomes for schools at Level 2. When we do this, there is considerable variation in the tests due to differences between schools. An initial examination of the proportion of variability in outcomes lying between schools indicated considerable variability in this small data set (i.e., 14% in reading, 36% in math, 17% in language). This suggests that a multilevel analysis is warranted.

Figure 1.4 presents the fixed-effect estimates. Readers may notice that the between-groups indicators of achievement in Figure 1.4 are defined as ovals. This is because they are viewed as latent variables between groups and represent the underlying heterogeneity among individuals due to their randomly varying intercepts in the within-group portion of the model.

The solid dots on the within-group outcomes indicate that the intercepts vary randomly across schools; that is, we assume that the means for each test can vary from one organizational setting (i.e., school) to another. That variation can be explained by a set of between-school predictors. We first tested a model with separate effects from the predictors to each outcome specified; however, we found there were no differential effects (i.e., a path was significant to one outcome but not another). Therefore, the model summarized in the figure has *equality constraints* for the predictors (i.e., the estimate is assumed to the same for each outcome). We found that this second model fit the data better than the preliminary model with separate paths to each outcome estimated.

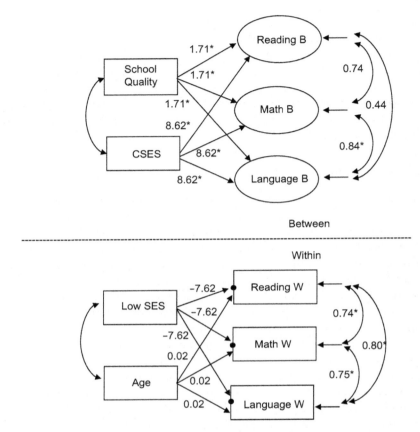

FIGURE 1.4 Multilevel multivariate model with equality constraints ($*p < 0.05$).

Multilevel Structural Model

It turns out that the SEM framework, which emphasizes latent variables, can also be used as a core template for formulating a number of different multilevel models [see Mehta and Neale (2005)]. For example, it is possible to incorporate latent variables into multilevel regression models as a multivariate formulation, although this type of latent variable formulation, however, is not typical in the empirical literature on **multilevel regression modeling**. In Figure 1.5, we present a simple two-level model with a latent achievement outcome specified within and between schools. The figure also indicates that school SES and school quality were significantly related to school achievement; however, the sizes of the school-level coefficients in Figure 1.5 are a bit larger than the estimates in Figure 1.4. This is often the result of correcting the estimates for measurement error (i.e., through defining a latent variable). These corrections yield more accurate estimates of the

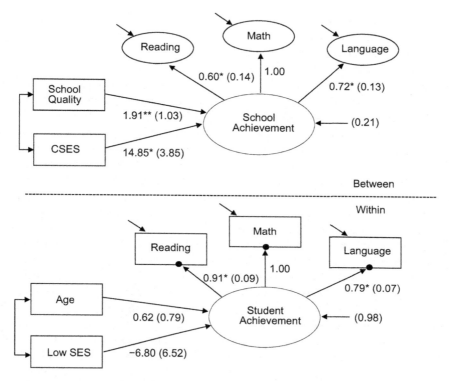

FIGURE 1.5 Multilevel model of individual and school variables' influence on achievement, with standard errors in parentheses (*$p < 0.05$, **$p < 0.10$).

model's structural parameters than is possible in other types of model formulations. (We introduce latent variable models that correct for measurement error in Chapter 5.)

Overall, however, the results in Figures 1.4 and 1.5 suggest that the multilevel, multivariate formulations provide results that are consistent with the complexity of hierarchical data structures. We end with the point that one of the central concepts of the SEM formulation, latent variables, is quite useful in describing other types of statistical models that implicitly utilize the concept of latent, or underlying, components that capture variability among individuals and groups (e.g., MANOVA, discriminant analysis, cluster analysis). Statistical models that use random effects to describe unobserved heterogeneity sources of variation, missing data, finite mixtures, latent classes, and nested data structures (e.g., individuals within groups, repeated observations within individuals) represent other applications of latent variables modeling (Mehta & Neale, 2005; Muthén, 2002; Muthén & Asparouhov, 2003; Raudenbush & Bryk, 2002; Snijders & Bosker, 1999). Although most empirical work with these types of models focuses on continuous latent variables, categorical latent variables (e.g., mixture models, latent class analysis) can also be considered (Muthén & Muthén, 1998–2012). For example, we might conceive of different latent classes of students' growth trajectories, that is, underlying groups of similar trajectories. The latent variable concept can therefore be extended beyond the typical SEM conceptualization of an underlying construct that is measured by a set of observed indicators to account for measurement error. Another possible application is in adjusting observed covariates for possible bias in estimating level-2 slopes through the application of a latent covariate approach (see Muthén & Asparouhov, 2011). Such estimation bias can result from small within-group sample sizes and less similarity on outcomes among individuals within clusters. We illustrate the application of the latent covariate approach briefly in Chapter 6.

By extension, hierarchical models may also be conceived of as latent variable models. As we noted earlier in this chapter, one way to think about this is in terms of estimating randomly varying coefficients (intercepts, slopes) that cannot be directly observed in the data. The random coefficients and residuals (or variability left unexplained by predictors) can be considered as representing the effects of unknown or unmeasured (or latent) variables that, because they are not directly observed, must be inferred from the observed cases sampled to represent the population (Raudenbush & Bryk, 2002; Snijders & Bosker, 1999). In this multilevel SEM formulation, latent variables are used to reflect the sampling procedure correctly, that is, as representing sources of variation at different levels of the hierarchical data structure (Muthén, 2002). Individuals' growth trajectories (and initial statuses) can also be conceived of as latent variables that vary due to differences in both individual and group processes. In the SEM approach to examining individual change, for example, growth modeling with random effects is defined as a form of factor analysis with covariates (Muthén, 2002).

The concept of latent variables is therefore useful in representing both random effects in multilevel models, as well as representing variance components that result from the hierarchical nature of the data. As some have noted (e.g., Curran, 2003; Mehta & Neale, 2005; Muthén, 2002), given identical model formulation, multilevel regression and SEM provide analytically identical solutions in many multilevel applications (e.g., growth modeling) despite slightly different ways of defining and estimating these models (the differences are more reflective of software differences than actual technical differences). SEM does provide some additional possibilities for defining multilevel models that incorporate measurement error in predictors and incorporate various types of hybrid (or mixture) models for continuous and categorical latent variables (Muthén, 2008).

Summary

In this chapter we developed a context for the use of multilevel models in the social and behavioral sciences. This context invokes a framework with four distinct categories of models: single-level univariate, single-level multivariate, multilevel univariate, and multilevel multivariate. We illustrated some of the biases that may result given certain choices about the type of modeling framework chosen for particular types of data structures. In the next chapter we develop a rationale for using multilevel models with various types of data structure in the social and behavioral sciences.

References

Arbuckle, J. (1996). Full information estimation in the presence of incomplete data. In G. A. Marcoulides and R. Schumacker (Eds.), *Advanced structural equation modeling: Issues and techniques* (pp. 243–278). Mahwah, NJ: Lawrence Erlbaum Associates.

Curran, P. J. (2003). Have multilevel models been structural equation models all along? *Multivariate Behavioral Research, 38*, 529–569.

Grilli, L. & Rampichini, C. (2007). Multilevel factor models for ordinal variables. *Structural Equation Modeling: A Multidisciplinary Journal, 41*(1), 1–25.

Heckman, J. J. (2005). *The scientific model of causality*. Retrieved from http://citeseerx.ist.psu.edu/viewdoc/download?doi=10.1.1.142.6006&rep=rep1&type=pdf

Hox, J. J. (1995). *Applied multilevel analysis*. Amsterdam: T.T. Publikaties.

Kreft, I. & de Leeuw, J. (1998). *Introducing multilevel modeling*. Newbury Park, CA: Sage.

Marcoulides, G. A. & Hershberger, S. (1997). *Multivariate statistical methods: A first course*. Mahwah, NJ: Lawrence Erlbaum.

McDonald, R. P. & Goldstein, H. (1989). Balanced versus unbalanced designs for linear structural relations in two-level data. *British Journal of Mathematical and Statistical Psychology, 42*, 215–232.

Mehta, P. D. & Neale, M. C. (2005). People are variables too. Multilevel structural equations modeling. *Psychological Methods, 10*(3), 259–284.

Muthén, B. O. (1984). A general structural equation model with dichotomous ordered categorical and continuous latent variable indicators. *Psychometrica, 49*, 115–132.

Muthén, B. O. (1991). Multilevel factor analysis of class and student achievement components. *Journal of Educational Measurement, 28*, 338–354.

Muthén, B. O. (1994). Multilevel covariance structure analysis. *Sociological Methods & Research, 22*(3), 376–398.

Muthén, B. O. (2002). Beyond SEM: General latent variable modeling. *Behaviormetrika, 29*, 81–118.

Muthén, B. O. (2008). Latent variable hybrids: Overview of old and new models. In G. R. Hancock & K. M. Samuelson (Eds.), *Advances in latent variable mixture models* (pp. 1–24). Charlotte, NC: Information Age Publishing.

Muthén, B. O. & Asparouhov, T. (2003). *Advances in latent variable modeling, Part I: Integrating multilevel and structural equation modeling using Mplus*. Unpublished paper.

Muthén, B. & Asparouhov, T. (2011). Beyond multilevel regression modeling: Multilevel analysis in a general latent variable framework. In J. Hox & J. K. Roberts (Eds.), *Handbook of advanced multilevel analysis* (pp. 15–40). New York: Taylor and Francis.

Muthén, B. O. & Muthén, L. (1998–2006). *Mplus user's guide*. Los Angeles, CA: Authors.

Muthén, L. K. & Muthén, B. O. (1998–2012). *Mplus user's guide* (7th ed.). Los Angeles, CA: Authors.

Pedhazur, E. & Schmelkin, L. (1991). *Measurement, design, and analysis: An integrated approach*. Hillsdale, NJ: Lawrence Erlbaum.

Rabe-Hesketh, S., Skrondal, A., & Pickles, A. (2004). Generalized multilevel structural equation modeling. *Psychometrika, 69*(2), 167–190.

Raudenbush, S. W. (1988). Educational applications of hierarchical linear model: A review. *Journal of Educational Statistics, 13*(2), 85–116.

Raudenbush, S. W. & Bryk, A. S. (2002). *Hierarchical linear models* (2nd ed.). Newbury Park, CA: Sage.

Rigdon, E. (1998). Structural equation models. In G. A. Marcoulides (Ed.), *Modern methods for business research* (pp. 251–294). Mahwah, NJ: Lawrence Erlbaum Associates.

Singer, J. & Willett, J. (2003). *Applied longitudinal data analysis: Modeling change and event occurrence.* New York: Oxford University Press.

Snijders, T. & Bosker, R. (1999). *Multilevel analysis: An introduction to basic and advanced multilevel modeling.* Newbury Park, CA: Sage.

Thomas, S. L. & Heck, R. H. (2001). Analysis of large-scale secondary data in higher education research: Potential perils associated with complex sampling designs. *Research in Higher Education, 42*(5), 517–550.

2

GETTING STARTED WITH MULTILEVEL ANALYSIS

Chapter Objectives

In this chapter, we outline a few of differences between single-level and multi-level models, as well as some basic research issues to consider in conducting multilevel analyses. These include developing a basic modeling strategy for investigating multilevel data structures and considering several technical issues such as **model estimation** and sample size requirements. Extensions of this basic multilevel framework to other types of multilevel models are described in more detail in subsequent chapters.

Introduction

In the past, multiple regression was a popular analytic choice for cross-sectional data typically obtained as individual-level data from simple random sampling or from complex, multistage sampling strategies found in large-scale survey research (e.g., oversampling individuals according to particular demographics nested within neighborhoods). In the latter case, analyses of survey data generally required the application of sampling weights to address oversampling of individual subgroups (e.g., by ethnicity, socioeconomic status). Although analysts were aware of problems due to the clustering of individuals within higher-level units such as neighborhoods, the presence of these effects did not enter directly into the analyses. Prior to the development of multilevel techniques, there were few satisfactory solutions to the problem of defining the unit of analysis properly (e.g., individuals, organizations), although concerns were raised repeatedly (e.g., Burstein, 1980; Kish, 1957; Strenio, 1981; Walsh, 1947) and corresponding approaches were laid out (e.g., Aitken & Longford, 1986; Cronbach & Webb, 1975; Dempster,

Laird, & Rubin, 1977; Goldstein, 1987; Lindley & Smith, 1972; Muthén, 1989, 1991; Schmidt, 1969; Wong & Mason, 1985).

Conceptual and methodological concerns in applying single-level analytic techniques to research with nested data structures over the past several decades led to the development of multilevel modeling. The various terms used to refer to these methods (e.g., multilevel models, hierarchical linear models, mixed-effects and random-effects models, random coefficients models, and covariance components models) are related to their use within different fields of inquiry (Kaplan & Elliott, 1997). The statistical theory underlying these models was developed out of several streams of methodological work including biometric applications of mixed-model ANOVA, random coefficients regression models in econometrics, and developments in the statistical theory of covariance structure models and **Bayesian estimation** of linear models (Bock, 1989; Curran, 2003; de Leeuw & Kreft, 1986; Efron & Morris, 1975; Fisher, 1918, 1925; Goldstein, 1987; Hartley & Rao, 1967; Jedidi & Ansari, 2001; Laird & Ware, 1982; Lindley & Smith, 1972; Mehta & Neale, 2005; Morris, 1995; Muthén, 1989, 1991, 1994; Muthén & Asparouhov, 2011; Rabe-Hesketh et al., 2004; Raudenbush & Bryk, 1986, 2002; H. Rubin, 1950; Shigemasu, 1976; Tate & Wongbundhit, 1983; Wald, 1947; Wong & Mason, 1985).

It is important to emphasize that methodological advances in multilevel modeling are continuing at an impressive pace, so there is still considerable debate over specific issues that have surfaced from initial modeling efforts (e.g., employing various estimation methods under different data conditions, weighting parameter estimates, determining statistical power, analyzing diverse types of data structures). As multilevel modeling objectives and methods become more accepted into the "mainstream" of quantitative modeling, we expect that many of these issues will be resolved and that new issues will emerge.

During the past decade, the intentional and systematic exploitation of hierarchical data structures has become the focus of a number of new multilevel modeling techniques that can be investigated within the general structural equation modeling (SEM) framework. We draw a few distinctions between basic approaches for examining hierarchical data structures.

Currently, there are two basic classes of multilevel procedures. One class is multilevel regression models, typically specified with a single outcome, and focusing on direct effects of predictors on the outcome. The second class is characterized by latent variables, which are defined by observed indicators and direct and indirect effects between variables at different levels of a data hierarchy. Multilevel univariate and multivariate regression models for both cross-sectional and longitudinal data can be conceptualized within the more general multilevel SEM framework, which provides a considerable advance in modeling (Mehta & West, 2000; Muthén & Muthén, 1998–2012). We have made a decision to use the software package Mplus in this edition of the book. One of our goals in presenting these models in Mplus is the ease in which both models with univariate and multivariate outcomes can be incorporated into the general multilevel SEM framework.

In our presentation, we consider the multilevel regression model as a subset of more diverse types of models that can be defined within the SEM framework using Mplus. In practice, however, we note there are some basic differences in the types of models that multilevel regression and multilevel SEM are optimally suited to examine, as well as some key differences in how the data sets are structured to analyze these models and the procedures typically used to estimate the outcomes. We will refer to some of these differences as we work our way through basic multilevel models with univariate and multivariate outcomes in subsequent chapters. In these latter situations, the outcomes obtained and their meanings may be somewhat different. With considerable care taken in terms of defining and estimating the *same* model (i.e., with the same number of estimated parameters and estimation methods), as we would expect, the results obtained are quite close.

From Single-Level to Multilevel Analysis

In a typical single-level regression model, the coefficients describing the intercept and slope are generally considered as fixed values in the population estimated from the sample data. For example, we might hypothesize that socioeconomic status (SES) is positively related to the subject's score on the math test. The resulting model to explain individual i's math achievement outcome can be defined as follows:

$$Y_i = \beta_0 + \beta_1 SES_i + \varepsilon_i \tag{2.1}$$

where β_0 is the intercept, β_1 is a slope parameter, and ε_i represents error in predicting individual outcomes from the equation. The key point about a single-level regression model is that the estimates of the intercept and slope are each fixed to one value that describes the average for the sample.

In Table 2.1 we can see that the average math score for the sample is 55.49. The intercept can be interpreted as the level of Y when X is 0. We note that the meaning of 0 in our example is students' *average* SES status. This is because we

TABLE 2.1 Fixed Intercept and Slope Coefficients

Coefficients[a]

Model	Unstandardized Coefficients		Standardized Coefficients	t	Sig.
	B	Std. Error	Beta		
(Constant)	55.494	1.404		39.536	0.000
SES	5.941	1.888	0.492	3.146	0.004

[a]Dependent Variable: math

recoded the raw SES scores by standardizing them such that the sample mean is 0.0 and the standard deviation (*SD*) is 1.0. It is often useful to recode continuous predictors such as SES in this way, since the intercept can then be interpreted as the expected score for a person whose SES background is equal to the grand mean of the sample. In contrast, if we left SES in a dollar metric, there would likely be no student in the sample with a reported family income of 0 dollars. The slope coefficient (β_1) represents the expected change in math achievement for a one-unit (in this case one *SD*) change in SES. In this case, the regression coefficient describing the impact of student SES on their math achievement is 5.94, which represents the average weight for sample. In Figure 2.1 we have added a vertical line where student SES is 0, which emphasizes that the intercept is defined as the place where the regression line crosses the *Y* axis and the value of the *X* predictor is 0.

From Table 2.1, we can formulate the following prediction equation:

$$\hat{Y}_i = 55.49 + 5.94 * SES,$$

where $\hat{Y}$ indicates the predicted value of *Y* is equal to the estimated intercept plus the coefficient for SES. The slope coefficient suggests that, on average, as student SES increases by one unit (in this case, one *SD*) from the intercept value of 55.49, student test scores goes up by 5.94 points, for a predicted score of 61.43. This is arrived at by multiplying the regression weight by the desired one-unit increase in SES. Similarly, if we wanted to know the predicted score for an individual who was one *SD* below the mean, it would be 55.49 + 5.94 × (−1), or 49.55. If we wanted to know the predicted score for a two-unit increase in SES (i.e., a 2-*SD* increase), we would multiply the regression coefficient by 2, which would yield a predicted score of 55.49 + 11.88, or 67.37. The important point to keep in mind is that in the single-level model both the intercept and the slope estimates are *fixed* (i.e., specified as the same for everyone in the sample).

Figure 2.1 also implies that there is considerable error associated with that prediction, since the actual data points do not all rest on the predicted regression line. Some errors lie above the regression line and some below. The principle of least squares states that the correct regression line is the one that best fits the data points, that is, the line that represents the maximum correlation between the observed and predicted scores for *y*. Model fit is assessed by summing the squared distances of each observed value from the predicted value that rests on the regression line. The distance from the actual data to the estimated regression line is also referred to as the error or **residual** since it expresses the inaccuracy of the predicted model. The further the data points from the regression line, the more prediction error. The line that minimizes the sum of these squared distances (i.e., where the distances are squared to cancel out positive and negative errors above or below the line) is said to fit the data best; hence, the term "ordinary least squares (OLS) regression" (Neter, Kutner, Nachtsheim, & Wasserman, 1996). In the linear regression model, the error term is considered as a random source of variation, which is assumed to

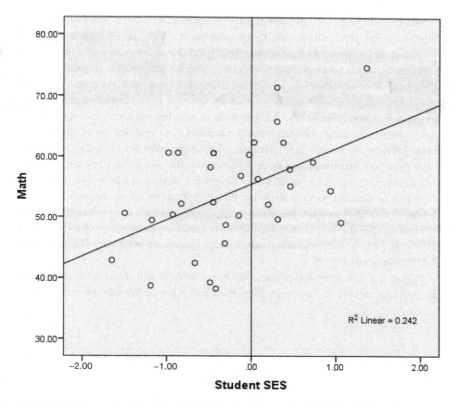

FIGURE 2.1. Regression line describing the fixed intercept (55.49) and slope (5.94) for student SES and math achievement in the sample.

vary independently of X and be normally distributed, with a mean of zero and constant variance across all levels of X.

One measure of fit for this predicted set of relationships is the variance in Y accounted for by X (R^2), which in this case is only about 0.24. This suggests there is considerable error associated with predicting students' math scores from only their socioeconomic status since nearly 76% of the variance in math is left unexplained in this simple model. Possible sources of error could include measurement error (i.e., students' math scores and SES are likely not perfectly measured), sampling error (i.e., the sample likely does not exactly represent the population), and missing variables (i.e., there may be other variables that influence math outcomes) or interact with the relationship between SES and math outcomes. Each of these possible sources of error is itself an important topic in quantitative modeling. Where all of the observed data points sit squarely on the regression line, the prediction would be perfect and the variance accounted for would be 100%.

We use the term "multilevel model" with respect to two separate statistical objectives described within one theoretical model. The first objective concerns inferences made about a model's structural parameters. The second objective of a multilevel analysis concerns inferences about the random variance parameters in the model. Multilevel models encourage researchers to model variability in means and covariance structures across a set of groups that have ideally been randomly sampled from the population. Although the researcher's primary concern is generally with estimating the structural parameters (i.e., referred to as the model's **fixed effects**), in some cases, examining the appropriateness and distribution of these **random intercept** and slope parameters is the researcher's primary interest. In a multilevel model, the math achievement intercept and the SES–achievement slope can be defined to vary as probability distributions across the set of schools. Where single-level analyses focus on average effects, which are each typically *fixed* at one value for the whole sample, multilevel modeling procedures allow outcome intercepts (means) and regression coefficients (slopes) to vary across higher-order units in the study.

Figure 2.2 illustrates the relationship between SES and math achievement for the previous sample of students within their five schools. We can see immediately

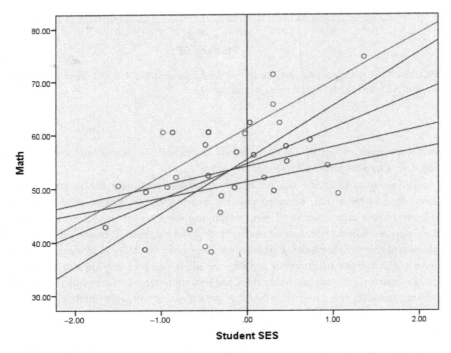

FIGURE 2.2 Random intercepts and slopes in the student sample within five schools.

that a single fixed intercept and slope for the sample would not adequately describe the actual variability present in the figure. In all five schools represented in the figure, we can see that the intercepts are different, and the slope coefficients are all positive; however, the steepness of the lines obviously varies. In this case, the researcher might be interested in estimating the average intercept and the SES effect on math achievement across the schools, as well as how particular schools deviate from the overall average intercept and SES-achievement slope.

These randomly varying intercept and slope parameters are referred to as *random effects* or *random coefficients* from various statistical perspectives. In experimental research, for example, a random effect describes a situation where the treatments (or levels of a treatment) in a study are assumed to represent a sample drawn from a universe of treatments or treatment levels. Because the effect is considered as randomly varying across a universe of treatments, the intent is to make inferences beyond the specific treatment levels included. The effects, therefore, are not assumed to be constant. In contrast, a fixed effect describes the situation where all possible treatments are present in the experiment (Kreft & de Leeuw, 1998). In this latter case, inferences can only be made about the specific treatments used. The effects are considered to be constant and measured without error because all possible cases are included.

Summarizing Some Differences

Our initial discussion of single-level and multilevel regression models suggests some key differences, which we summarize next. In situations where we can determine that there is sufficient variance in an outcome to be explained by variables defined at different organizational levels, multilevel regression models offer a number of advantages, both conceptual and technical, over the previous single-level univariate and multivariate frameworks.

First, multilevel regression analysis provides a more refined environment in which to test these theoretical relationships because the variables comprising the models can be specified at their correct hierarchical levels in conducting the analysis. Unlike a single-level analysis conducted at the individual level, group-level variables such as size can be defined correctly in terms of the number of organizations in the data set as opposed to the number of individuals. One submodel is developed for the variables measured at the individual level; another is developed to specify and explain the distributions for each individual parameter at the group level. The multilevel regression approach therefore provides a single framework that combines information from within and across units to produce more accurate explanations of outcomes (Draper, 1995). It brings together regression equations at the individual level and the group level into a single statistical model. In this manner, the approach allows the comparison of differences between organizations on random parameters after considering differences attributable to their individual members.

Second, unlike the independent, normally distributed residuals in a single-level model, in a multilevel model random error is more complex. The individual-level residuals are dependent within each unit because they are common to every individual within that unit. Moreover, the within-group intercept is assumed to vary across level-2 units, and the strength of a within-group slope such as student SES may also be specified to vary across level-2 units. In this latter case, neither the intercept nor the slope will have constant variances. Optimal estimation of the unknown parameters associated with randomly varying intercepts or slopes can therefore depend on characteristics of the data (e.g., sample size, degree of imbalance in sample sizes of higher-level units, strength of similarity among individuals within units), the type of analysis being conducted, and the measurement scale (e.g., binary, ordered category, continuous) of the dependent variables (Muthén & Muthén, 1998–2006; Raudenbush & Bryk, 2002).

Third, where variability in an outcome is actually present across one or more levels, multilevel regression yields better calibrated estimates of standard errors than single-level analyses. This concerns the extent to which a multilevel model offers an improvement in the precision of these estimates over single-level techniques such as OLS regression. This is important because ignoring the effects of clustering results in smaller standard errors and, because hypothesis tests are dependent on the ratio of a parameter to its standard error, an increased likelihood of finding more significant parameters in the model. Ignoring clustering effects increases the likelihood of making Type I errors (i.e., falsely rejecting the null hypothesis of no effect). In the absence of clustering effects (i.e., where there is little or no similarity among individuals within groups), there is little need (and limited benefit) to perform a multilevel analysis.

Fourth, the multilevel regression approach provides greater flexibility in that a range of models can be specified, from those where only the level of the learning outcome is treated as a random coefficient and the individual-level regression coefficients are fixed (i.e., assumed to have constant variance across units), to ones where some of the regression coefficients of individual-level variables may also be treated as random coefficients that vary across group-level units. In these latter models, the focus is often on how variables at a higher level of the data hierarchy may interact with processes that occur at a lower level (Rousseau, 1985). The presence of this type of moderating effect (often referred to as a cross-level interaction) implies that the magnitude of a relationship observed within groups is dependent on a contextual or organizational feature.

Fifth, in recent years the basic multilevel regression framework has expanded in notable ways to include analyses of dependent variables measured in different ways (e.g., continuous, ordered categorical, binary, counts). In addition to multilevel models that have a univariate outcome (e.g., a general measure of productivity), other useful extensions include the specification of multivariate outcomes for each individual (e.g., using several measures of productivity), models with intervening variables between predictors and outcomes, longitudinal models for examining individual and organizational change, and models with cross-classified data structures.

Sixth, although the SEM approach and corresponding computer software have been widely accepted in the analysis of single-level multivariate data, these techniques have been less frequently applied to analyzing multilevel data structures (Hox, 1995; Mehta & Neale, 2005; Muthén, 1994). This is changing quickly, however, now that SEM software such as Mplus can readily handle hierarchical data structures through solving challenging model estimation issues. Given the increasing flexibility of software programs, it is currently possible to examine many new types of multilevel models using these powerful analytic techniques. As Mehta and Neale note, in the same manner in which SEM improves on multiple regression, multilevel SEM brings advantages of latent variables and more complex path models with direct and mediated effects to clustered data. Multilevel modeling with SEM, which emphasizes latent continuous and categorical variables and path models with direct and indirect effects, has therefore offered a number of extensions to the analysis of hierarchical data in terms of correcting model estimates for measurement error and offering greater facility to define more complex sets of relationships among variables, as well as ways to examine population heterogeneity through various types of mixture model formulations. In contrast, the incorporation of **random slopes**, which was a defining feature of multilevel univariate regression modeling, was challenging to integrate into the multilevel SEM framework, given the latter's traditional emphasis on sample covariance and mean structures, which required listwise deletion of individual cases with incomplete data.

Along with the possibilities presented by multilevel models, often single-level analyses suffice quite well, depending upon the structure and characteristics of specific data sets (de Leeuw & Kreft, 1995). The researcher should always be mindful of the possible nested structure of the data with which he or she is working, but even if the multilevel nature of the data is taken into account, there are a variety of modeling options that can be considered before a choice is made.

Developing a General Multilevel Modeling Strategy

In our presentation, we apply a general strategy for examining multilevel models (e.g., Bryk & Raudenbush, 1992; Heck, Thomas, & Tabata, 2010; Hox, 2010; Raudenbush & Bryk, 2002). Multilevel models are useful and necessary only to the extent that the data being analyzed provide sufficient variation at each level. "Sufficiency" of variation is relative and depends as much on theoretical concerns as it does on the structure and quality of data. To develop this strategy, we provide an illustration of what a simple two-level model to explore a random intercept describing organizational productivity and a random slope describing the effect of employee motivation on productivity might look like. Keep in mind, however, that models become more complex if there are multivariate outcomes, multiple random slopes as outcomes, latent variables, and direct and indirect effects. Each type of addition represents a basic multilevel building block. Of course, there may be times when the analyst might change the specific steps, but, in general, we have found this overall model development strategy works pretty well.

Multilevel regression modeling can be used to specify a hierarchical system of equations that takes advantage of the clustered data structure. Multilevel regression models are typically formulated in two ways: (1) by presenting separate equations for each of the levels in a data hierarchy (e.g., employees, workgroups, departments, divisions, corporations, etc.) or (2) by laying out the separate equations and then combining the equations through substitution into a single-model framework (i.e., either by algebraic substitution into a single equation or by using matrix specification). For readers familiar with the HLM software package (Raudenbush, Bryk, & Congdon, 2004), the HLM approach uses separate equations specified at each level to build the multilevel model. This results in the need to generate separate data sets at each level first (e.g., individuals, classrooms, schools, etc.), which then are "combined" within the software program to make the final data file. The user can neither see nor edit the case-specific contents of this final data set. The separate-equation approach emphasizes how models are constructed, but it tends to hide the fact that modeling slopes results in adding interactions between the random slope and level-2 predictors to the model (Hox, 2010). Most other software packages (e.g., SAS, IBM SPSS, Stata) use single-equation representation (through algebraic substitution), so all analyses can be conducted from within one data set.

Univariate multilevel regression models can be easily adapted to SEM language and matrix specification of Mplus (Mehta & Neale, 2005; Muthén & Muthén, 1998–2012). The general SEM approach emphasizes simultaneous equations used to specify latent variables and their observed indicators, relationships between predictors and latent variables, and relationships between latent variables including possible intervening variables, which are specified through matrix algebra. The specification of several types of matrices (e.g., item loading matrix, item error matrix, factor covariance matrix) represents a convenient way to store a considerable amount of information about model parameters.

We can think of the typical two-level univariate regression model as one of many possible multilevel models that can be specified using the SEM approach, that is, as a model with only direct effects between observed predictors and the outcome. For example, this basic two-level univariate model can be easily extended to include both direct and mediating effects, latent variables, and mixtures. For reference, in Figure 2.3 we provide a simple illustration of the direct-effects type of model that is common in the multilevel regression framework, as well as the simple addition of a mediating variable that can be specified using the multilevel SEM framework in Mplus. In this latter model, the effect of the predictor to the outcome is specified to be indirect (i.e., through the mediating variable) rather than direct. We develop this type of multilevel path model with direct and mediating effects in more detail in Chapter 6.

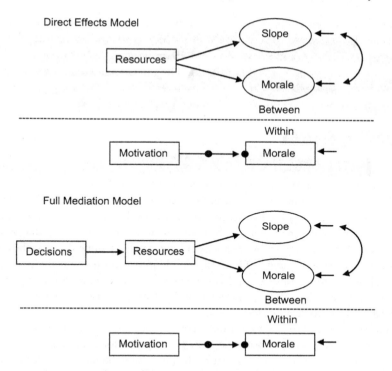

FIGURE 2.3 Comparing direct–effect and mediated–effect models.

As we noted in the first chapter, one important contribution of multilevel modeling is to allow the researcher to avoid the aggregation (assigning the same group mean to each member) or disaggregation (treating subjects without reference to their groups) problem. Developing a conceptual framework of theoretical relations ahead of time can also help the researcher avoid another potential source of bias within the analysis—that of ignoring the different levels of the explanatory (independent) variables. Through examining the variation in outcomes that exists at different levels of the data hierarchy, we can develop more refined theories about how explanatory variables at each level contribute to variation in outcomes.

Step 1: Partitioning the Variance in an Outcome

Partitioning the variance in an outcome into its within- and between-group components is an important first step in determining whether a multilevel analysis is justified. If there were little or no variation in the outcome between higher-level units, there would be no warrant for a multilevel analysis. For a univariate outcome, partitioning variance into level-1 and level-2 components without other predictors in the model allows the researcher to test the validity of this assumption and provides important information about the sources of variation in the outcome variable. The extent of variance that exists between versus within groups (homogeneity of variance) can be described by an **intraclass correlation** (ICC), which is designated with the Greek letter *rho* (ρ). The intraclass correlation refers to the portion of variance that lies between macro-level groups, which will be a part of the total variance in the outcome to be explained. It is defined as

$$\rho = \sigma^2_b / (\sigma^2_b + \sigma^2_w), \tag{2.2}$$

where σ^2_b is the between-group variance and σ^2_w is the within-group variance. The intraclass correlation can also be interpreted as the expected correlation between any two randomly chosen individuals in the same group (Hox, 2002). If it is substantial, it suggests that the groups are relatively homogeneous and, therefore, likely quite different from each other. We note that if our outcome were a latent variable (i.e., defined by several items), we could examine the intraclass correlations for the set of items. This will provide information about the quality of the items used to measure the individual and collective (i.e., group) components of the outcome. We discuss defining multilevel latent constructs with observed indicators in more detail in Chapter 5.

There are at least two ways to think about the relative homogeneity of groups. The first is in terms of the potential remedies required for conducting a conventional single-level analysis of data that are hierarchically differentiated. A common example is the multistage type of sampling strategy used in large-scale surveys (where higher units may first be sampled followed by individuals within these units). The focus in this type of analysis to remedy possible bias due to multistage sampling is on statistical adjustments to yield unbiased estimates of variances and standard errors. Acknowledging the ICC is important because it changes the error variance in single-level regression analyses. When clusters and nontrivial ICCs are present, the OLS regression assumption of independent errors resulting from simple random sampling will likely be violated. This problem results in a downward bias in the estimation of standard errors (i.e., the errors calculated will be too small). Because the statistical test of the significance of a variable (e.g., a *t*-test) is defined as the ratio of the size of its parameter coefficient to its standard error, an underestimated standard error can increase the probability of making Type I errors (i.e., a false rejection of the null hypothesis).

Let's develop this important point a little further. Because statistical tests of model parameters are based on the ratio of an estimate to its standard error, the underestimation of standard errors will often lead to more findings of significance than would be observed if clustering were considered. Suppose in a single-level analysis, we observe that the estimate of the effect of gender on achievement is 4.0 points, and the standard error is estimated as 2.0. This would result in a *t*-ratio of 2.0 (i.e., the ratio of the estimate to its standard error). At a commonly adopted significance level of $p = 0.05$ and a sample size of 500 individuals, the required t-ratio would be 2.0. Suppose the same analysis conducted as a two-level analysis (e.g., individuals clustered in schools) results in an estimated standard error of 2.5. Now when we calculate the t-ratio (4.0/2.5), the result would be 1.6, which would not be significant at $p = 0.05$. Single-level analytic approaches, such as multiple regression, ignore the clustered nature of individuals within higher-level groupings; therefore, in the presence of similarities among individuals within groups, estimated parameters may be biased. We note that there are a number of ways to adjust the single-level analysis for these problems but that these techniques do not allow the researcher to specify presumed effects at different levels of the data hierarchy (Thomas & Heck, 2001).

To address this shortcoming, the second way to think about group-level homo-geneity in hierarchical data is in terms of the opportunities it presents to specify conceptual models designed to operationalize organizational processes at more than a single level. After determining that an outcome varies across units, the analyst can investigate how various within-group and between-group variables explain variance in the outcome at each successive level. Multilevel modeling, then, also contributes to our understanding of hierarchical data structures by allowing the analyst to estimate structural and variance/covariance parameters (e.g., residual variance in intercepts or slopes at Level 2, covariance between inter-cepts and slopes at Level 2) more efficiently and accurately. The complete set of residual variances and covariances is referred to as the model's variance compo-nents (Singer & Willett, 2003).

Notation for a multilevel regression model is consistent with the mixed-effects model formulation of univariate outcome models. Let's consider the case where individuals ($i = 1, 2, \ldots, N$) are nested within a number of level-2 units ($j = 1, 2, \ldots, n$) and are measured on a single outcome. In this initial one-way ANOVA, or "no predictors" model, an individual's score (Y_{ij}) can be thought of as the sum of the individual cluster mean and an individual-specific deviation as follows:

$$Y_{ij} = \beta_{0j} + \varepsilon_{ij}, \qquad (2.3)$$

where we will refer to β_{0j} as the mean of productivity for the jth group, and the Greek lowercase letter epsilon (ε_{ij}) is the residual component for individual i in organization j (i.e., ε_{ij} represents the deviation from the level-2 unit mean for indi-vidual i). Each level-1 error term is assumed to have a mean of 0 and a constant variance σ^2. In a two-level model, level-1 fixed effects are typically expressed as unstandardized β coefficients. *Unstandardized* means the coefficients are in their original metrics. The subscript j indicates that the intercept represents the mean outcome for groups.

Between groups, variation in the average intercept (β_{0j}) is assumed to vary across units:

$$\beta_{0j} = \gamma_{00} + u_{0j}. \qquad (2.4)$$

Level-2 fixed-effect coefficients (which are also unstandardized) are generally expressed as the Greek lowercase letter gamma (γ), which represents the mean value of the level-1 outcome across all level-2 units, and u_{0j} represents the deviation of cluster j's mean from the grand mean of productivity; that is, u_{0j} represents the random intercept effect, which is assumed to have a mean of 0 and constant variance σ^2. Through substituting Equation 2.4 into Equation 2.3 for β_{0j}, we arrive at a single equation, which can be written as

$$Y_{ij} = \gamma_{00} + u_{0j} + \varepsilon_{ij}, \tag{2.5}$$

where ε_{ij} is the level-1 residual variance and u_{0j} is the level-2 random effect, and γ_{00} is the grand mean. The null model therefore provides an estimated mean productivity score for all organizations. It also provides a partitioning of the variance between Level 1 (ε_{ij}) and Level 2 (u_{0j}). Altogether, Equation 2.5 suggests there are three parameters to estimate: the intercept; the between–organization error, or deviation, from the average intercept (u_{0j}); and the individual-level residual, or variation in individual scores within organizations (ε_{ij}). The model represented by Equation 2.5 only partitions variance in Y_{ij} between Level 1 and Level 2 and does not "explain" any of the total variance. The partitioning creates two variance components that are assumed to be independent, one at Level 1, within groups (σ_W^2) and another at Level 2, between groups (σ_B^2). From this, the sum of the variance in Y_{ij} can be rewritten as

$$\mathrm{Var}\left(Y_{ij}\right) = \mathrm{Var}\left(\sigma_B^2 + \sigma_W^2\right) \tag{2.6}$$

The intraclass correlation provides a sense of the degree to which differences in Y_{ij} exist between level-2 units. More specifically, it helps answer the question of the existence or nonexistence of meaningful differences in outcomes between the level-2 units—differences that determine the extent to which the data are hierarchically differentiated and, by extension, encourage the development of helpful level-2 models to explain the variance in Y_{ij}. We note that there is no "magic" cutoff point for what might be suitable variance in Y to conduct a two-level analysis. It depends on the outcome under consideration, the size of the level-2 sample, as well as what is common practice in terms of what other researchers have done in the past in similar situations. Even small ICCs (ρ) can have an impact on significance tests when the number of individuals in a cluster is large (Barcikowski, 1981).

This suggests that it is important to consider the **design effect**, which is a function of both the ICC and the average cluster size (Muthén, L., 1999; Muthén & Satorra, 1995). A design effect (*deff*) quantifies the extent to which the sampling error present in sampling individuals in a sampling design departs from the sampling error that would be expected under simple random sampling (i.e., where each individual had the same chance of being selected). Where clustering is present within level-2 units, individuals will no longer be independent of others selected the same cluster. This lack of independence can lead to more findings of statistical significance than would be expected under conditions of simple random sampling. The design effect is approximately equal the following: [1 + (average cluster size − 1 × ρ)]. As Muthén notes, approximate design effects of less than 2.0 do not appear to result in overly exaggerated rejection proportions at $p = 0.05$ for conducting single-level analyses. So, for example, for an average cluster size of 30 and $\rho = 0.04$, the design effect would be approximately 2.16. For the same average cluster size and a $\rho = 0.03$, the design effect estimate would be approximately 1.87. Certainly, if there is only 1–2% variation in an outcome across units, there will not be much available variance to explain by developing a level-2 model. When we have multivariate outcomes, we can partition the total sample covariance matrix into within-cluster and between-cluster covariance matrices. We develop this latter approach further in Chapter 4.

Step 2: Adding Level-1 Predictors to Explain Intercept Variability

After determining that there is sufficient variance in the outcome to support a multilevel analysis, a second step is often to define a model that can explain variability in the individual portion (Level 1) of the outcome. In its simplest form, the level-1 model is equivalent to an ordinary regression model. Rather than estimating parameters across all N cases in the data set, however, the level-1 model is used to produce estimates within each level-2 unit j in the sample data. The multilevel approach yields a potentially different set of estimates for each level-2 unit.

The level-1 predictors are often referred to as X variables. For each individual i in organization j, a proposed model summarizing the effect of employee attitudes on productivity can be expressed as

$$Y_{ij} = \beta_{0j} + \beta_1 X_{1ij} + \varepsilon_{ij}, \tag{2.7}$$

where Y_{ij} is the observation for the ith individual in level-2 unit j, β_{0j} is the level-1 intercept within unit j, β_{1j} is a level-1 slope for predictor X_{1ij}, and ε_{ij} is error for individual i in organization j. In this case, Equation 2.7 suggests that, within groups, X_{ij} (employee motivation) is related to productivity levels. Readers may recognize that this level-1 model with predictors is similar to a multiple regression model in Equation 2.1, the difference being the subscript j indicates there is a second (group) level included in the model. Within each level-2 unit, ε_{ij} is assumed to have a mean of 0 and constant variance across all levels of X_{1ij}.

If sufficient variation exists within and between the level-2 units, this model can yield a different set of estimates of β_{0j} and β_{1j} for each level-2 unit. Each of the j within-unit models is simply an OLS regression model, where the regression coefficients indicate the effects of level-1 characteristics on a level-1 outcome *within* each level-2 unit. Rather than considering these j models separately, however, we treat them as a system of estimates with an overall mean and variance (averaged across all j level-2 units). The researcher can now treat the level-1 intercept and slope as outcomes in a level-2 model.

$$\beta_{0j} = \gamma_{00} + u_{0j} \tag{2.8}$$

$$\beta_{1j} = \gamma_{10} + u_{1j}. \tag{2.9}$$

Equation 2.8 implies that variation in level-1 intercepts can be described by a school-level intercept (γ_{00}), or grand mean, and a random parameter capturing variation in individual school means (u_{0j}) from the grand mean. Equation 2.9 implies that variability in level-1 slopes can be described by a school-level average slope coefficient (γ_{10}), or grand mean, and a random parameter capturing variation in individual school coefficients (u_{1j}) from the grand mean. These varying level-1 slopes and intercepts, which express the functional relationship between the level-1 outcome and predictor within each level-2 unit, are a distinctive feature of multilevel regression analysis. For each slope and intercept in the level-1 models, the implied between–unit model is:

$$\beta_{qj} = \gamma_{q0} + u_{qj} \text{ for } q = 0,1,2,...,Q, \tag{2.10}$$

where β_{qj} represents the number (Q) of within–unit (j) regression parameters from the level-1 model in Equation 2.7 and γ_{q0} is the mean value for each of the within-unit parameters. Across all level-2 units, then, each β_{qj} has a distribution with a mean of 0 and some variance. Should there exist significant variance in any level-1 coefficient between level-2 units, β_{qj}, multilevel regression gives the researcher the option to model this variance using higher-level variables. Alternatively, the researcher may also specify a common or fixed regression slope for any level-1 coefficient, β_{qj}, that is relatively homogeneous across level-2 units (i.e., by removing the relevant u_{qj} term).

The determination of how to treat each level-1 slope or intercept, as a random or fixed parameter, depends first on the researcher's theoretical framework and, second, on the amount of variance that exists across level-2 units. Should the researcher, based on these criteria, decide to treat any given β_{qj} as randomly varying across level-2 units, a model to explain the variation in β_{qj} would be developed using explanatory variables from Level 2.

Step 3: Specifying Level-2 Predictors to Explain Intercept Variability

The third step is often to specify one or more group-level predictors that can explain variability in the randomly varying intercepts. Often level-1 slopes are first considered as fixed at step 3. Assuming a level-1 model with one predictor, X_1, the level-2 models would appear as follows:

$$\beta_{0j} = \gamma_{00} + \gamma_{01}W_j + u_{0j} \tag{2.11}$$

$$\beta_{1j} = \gamma_{10}, \tag{2.12}$$

where β_{0j} is the level-1 intercept in level-2 unit j; γ_{00} is the mean value of the level-1 outcome, controlling for the level-2 predictor, W_j; γ_{01} is the slope for the level-2 variable W_j; u_{0j} is the random variability for organization j; β_{1j} is the level-1 slope in level-2 unit j; and γ_{10} is its mean value at the group level. Because there is no random effect (u_{1j}) in Equation 2.12, the slope coefficient is therefore fixed to one value for the sample. In contrast to level-1 outcomes, which are based on N individual-level observations, the level-2 estimates specified in Equations 2.11 and 2.12 are based on j unit-level observations.

Figure 2.4 provides an illustration of what the proposed multilevel model of organizational productivity might look like after step 3. In the figure, organizational productivity is defined as an observed outcome (represented as rectangle). The filled dot on the income indicates that the intercept is proposed to vary across organizations at Level 2. At Level 2, because the random productivity intercepts vary across groups, productivity is conceived as a latent variable (depicted with an oval) that represents unknown heterogeneity among individuals in the sample. At the group level, other predictors such as organizational structure (e.g., size), resources, and processes can be hypothesized to explain differences in productivity intercepts between organizations. Short arrows not connected to explanatory variables in the figure are used to represent residual variance in the outcome, that is, variance not accounted for

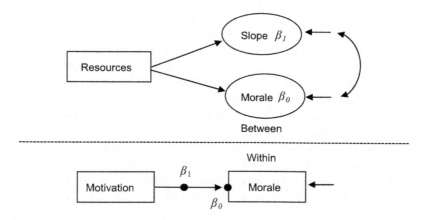

FIGURE 2.4 Proposed two-level model examining a random intercept and slope.

by other variables in the model. As noted in Equation 2.11, in this model, we will propose that employee motivation has an impact on individuals' productivity within organizations, but its variability is fixed at the group level; that is, the relationship is considered to be restricted to the micro (individual) level of the data hierarchy (as shown in Equation 2.12).

It is important to think about the potential consequences of decisions we make about where to place a variable in the data hierarchy on the subsequent analysis. In single-level analyses, we are faced with the problem of whether an individual-level variable such as motivation should be defined as an aggregate, or whether an organizational variable such as resource allocations or decision structure should be defined as an individual-level (disaggregated) measure. If we aggregate a variable like motivation, we miss the likelihood that there is considerable variation within organizations in how their members perceive their motivation individually. In some cases, we may also have predictors that have an individual and a collective component. In that case we could specify motivation as being both an individual variable and a group-level variable. Another example might be a latent variable such as organizational culture. In multilevel models we develop later in the book, we have the option of defining such constructs as organizational culture as a within-unit variable (i.e., as an individual perception) of beliefs, values, and traditions and also as between-unit latent variable (i.e., which captures its collective property at the organizational level) simultaneously. Multilevel modeling therefore provides considerable flexibility in defining predictors and outcomes in ways that avoid the forced choice between aggregation and disaggregation in investigating conceptual models.

Step 4: Examining Possible Variation in Slopes

In addition to examining variability in the levels of outcomes such as productivity between organizations, as a fourth step, we might also wish to investigate variability in the effects of within-organization predictors such as motivation on outcomes. In the typical single-level regression model, the relationship between a predictor such as employee motivation and the Y outcome is estimated as one *fixed* value for the whole sample. This means that regardless of what organization the employees might be in, the regression coefficient (referred to as a *slope*) between motivation and productivity is defined to be the same.

In contrast, in random coefficients or multilevel regression models, we assume that regression coefficients may be different due to features of level-2 units. The concept of slope coefficients that may vary between groups as a function of other observed variables is central to multilevel modeling. Multilevel formulations directly encourage researchers to investigate possible random variation in the effects of within-group variables on outcomes. We treat the regression coefficient describing the impact of employee motivation on productivity as a random effect, which means we can allow its impact on productivity to vary across our sample of organizations. We can then develop an organizational-level model that might explain this observed variation in the slopes across the organizations. Because adding random slopes to the models increases the complexity of the model and therefore its estimation, we suggest focusing only on relationships of theoretical interest rather than conducting a type of "fishing" expedition. Generally, we might think of this fourth step as specific features of the theoretical model that you wish to highlight once you have the basic intercept model defined for both levels. If a random slope is not the particular interest, the interest might be in defining a mediating effect between motivation and productivity, or something of that nature.

Investigating random slopes is often referred to as a slopes-as-outcomes model (Raudenbush & Bryk, 2002), which represents another powerful way that multilevel modeling expands the types of research questions we can ask of the data. We now specify the level-1 slope describing the effect of employee motivation on productivity to vary across organizations. The level-2 slope model can be specified as randomly varying as follows:

$$\beta_{1j} = \gamma_{10} + u_{1j}. \tag{2.13}$$

Step 5: Adding Predictors to Explain Variation in Slopes

In this last step, we typically refine our final two-level model. In the case of investigating a random slope, if we find there is variability in the slope across level-2 units, we can add the cross-level interactions (i.e., the group predictors) to explain variation in the level-1 slopes. We might speculate that particular organizational structures (e.g., perhaps the size of the organization or the presence of participatory decision making) and availability of resources impact the size of the slope coefficient between employee motivation and productivity. In our between-groups analysis, therefore, we would formulate one model to explain differences in levels of productivity variable (i.e., representing intercepts) as a result of the organizational-level predictors (i.e., structure, resources). A second model using the same set of organizational variables can be formulated to explain the variation in the latent employee motivation-productivity slopes between organizations. This model suggests that resource levels may moderate the within-unit (e.g., motivation-productivity) slope:

$$\beta_{1j} = \gamma_{10} + \gamma_{11}W_j + u_{1j}. \tag{2.14}$$

By considering the level-1 and level-2 models as a single system of equations, however, all of the information necessary for estimation of parameters at both levels is provided. We note in passing that we should specify the two models to be similar in terms of predictors, at least initially, and after testing nonsignificant predictors could then be discarded (Raudenbush & Bryk, 2002). Of course, such decisions are best made on the basis of theoretical considerations balanced with model parsimony.

By substitution of Equations 2.14 and 2.11 into Equation 2.7, this system of equations is represented by a single equation in Equation 2.15, and then it is reorganized in terms of fixed effects and variance components in Equation 2.16:

$$Y_{ij} = \beta_{0j} + \beta_1 X_{1ij} + \varepsilon_{ij} \qquad \text{(2.7, repeated)}$$

$$\beta_{0j} = \gamma_{00} + \gamma_{01} W_j + u_{0j} \qquad \text{(2.11, repeated)}$$

$$\beta_{1j} = \gamma_{10} + \gamma_{11} W_j + u_{1j} \qquad \text{(2.14, repeated)}$$

$$Y_{ij} = (\gamma_{00} + \gamma_{01} W_j + u_{0j}) + (\gamma_{10} + \gamma_{11} W_j + u_{1j}) X_{1ij} + \varepsilon_{ij} \qquad \text{(2.15)}$$

$$Y_{ij} = \gamma_{00} + \gamma_{10} X_{1ij} + \gamma_{01} W_j + \gamma_{11} X_{1ij} W_j + u_{1j} X_{1ij} + u_{0j} + \varepsilon_{ij}. \qquad \text{(2.16)}$$

Equation 2.16 indicates that Y_{ij} is generated by two components: the fixed-effect relationships and the stochastic, or probabilistic, relationships captured by the last three variance-component terms.

Two major differences between the ordinary regression model and the multi-level model warrant note. First, in the deterministic component of Equation 2.16, the term $\gamma_{11} X_{1ij} W_j$ represents a cross-level interaction between level-1 and level-2 variables. Essentially, this can be understood as the moderating effect of a level-2 variable on the relationship between a level-1 predictor and the outcome Y_{ij}. Second, in the stochastic component of Equation 2.16, are the random slope and intercept effects variances, $u_{1j} X_{1ij}$ and u_{0j}, respectively, as well as the level-1 residual ε_{ij}. The interaction $u_{1j} X_{1ij}$ is considered to be a random effect, which is defined as the deviation in slope for cases in group j multiplied by the level-1 predictor score (X_1) for the ith case in group j (Tabachnick, 2008). Equation 2.16 suggests seven parameters to estimate. These include four fixed effects (i.e., intercept, within-group predictor, between-group predictor, cross-level interaction), two random effects (i.e., the randomly varying intercept and slope), and the level-1 residual.

In Figure 2.4, we summarize the motivation-productivity slope to vary randomly across organizations using the Mplus diagram specification. The random slope is shown in the figure with a filled dot on the line representing the proposed effect of attitudes on productivity (again suggesting it represents unknown heterogeneity among individuals in the sample). The Greek symbol beta (β), often used to define a regression coefficient, is above the line. The goal of the analysis of slope variability is to determine how features of organizations *moderate* (e.g., increase or diminish) the strength of the within-organization effect of employee motivation on productivity. This type of effect is referred to as a cross-level interaction, which is defined as the potential effects variables at one level of a data hierarchy have on relationships at another level (Hofmann & Gavin 1998; Rousseau 1985).

Hence, the presence of a cross-level interaction implies that the magnitude of a relationship observed within groups is dependent on contextual or organizational features defined by higher-level units. Again, we note that at Level 2, the random slope and intercept are shown as ovals in the figure, which indicates that they are underlying latent variables. As we develop in later chapters, we might also examine possible *mediating* effects (i.e., where a third variable is specified between a predictor and outcome, which may specify how or why the particular effect or relationship occurs).

Specifying Random Effects at Level 2

We also need to consider the covariance structure for level-2 random effects. If only the intercept is randomly varying (u_{0j}), we can specify an identity covariance matrix at Level 2:

$$\sigma^2_{u_{0j}} \begin{bmatrix} 1 & 0 \\ 0 & 1 \end{bmatrix}, \tag{2.17}$$

which suggests there is simply one level-2 variance component, that is, the variance in intercepts for level-2 units (with the covariance of u_{0j} and ε_{ij} assumed to be 0).

If we specify a random intercept and random slope, the level-2 variances in the intercept and slope are specified in the diagonals of the matrix and the covariance is the off-diagonal element, which, because the covariance matrix is a square matrix, only requires either the upper or lower coefficient. If we do not include the covariance term between the intercept and slope (which is the default in Mplus), we would specify a diagonal covariance matrix at Level 2, which has heterogeneous variances in the diagonals and the covariance is fixed at 0:

$$\begin{bmatrix} \sigma^2_{u_{0j}} & 0 \\ 0 & \sigma^2_{u_{1j}} \end{bmatrix}. \tag{2.18}$$

The random intercept and slope effects at Level 2 may also include the covariance between u_{0j} and u_{1j}, which is common to every level-1 observation within each level-2 unit j—a dependency that violates the assumption in ordinary regression of independent errors across observations. Clusters are assumed to be sampled at random from the population, which leads to the assumption of independently and identically distributed random effects. For a given cluster j, we often specify an unstructured covariance matrix of random effects at Level 2 to accommodate the covariance between the random intercept and slope as follows:

$$\begin{bmatrix} \sigma^2_{u_{0j}} & \sigma_{u_{1j}u_{0j}} \\ \sigma_{u_{1j}u_{0j}} & \sigma^2_{u_{1j}} \end{bmatrix}. \tag{2.19}$$

In this example, we have illustrated a couple of common ways that multilevel models facilitate the investigation of relationships between individuals and their social groupings. It is important to develop clarity regarding which explanatory variables are assigned to what level in the analysis. Only with such clarity can these variables be appropriately measured and entered into the analysis in a manner that is consistent with the organizational theory being tested. Multilevel modeling puts the focus squarely on the researcher to use theory beforehand to explain proposed relationships. It is also important to caution, however, that the complexity of most organizational theories cannot be reduced to a single model attempting to explain organizational outcomes. One can always be criticized for omitting a potentially important variable in the analysis. Since all possible causes cannot be included, the problem is reduced to using previous theory to construct a model such that all known, relevant causes are included, while recognizing that this will almost assuredly be incomplete (Marcoulides & Heck, 1993).

The two-level multilevel model can be generalized to three or more levels, depending on the research question being addressed and the structure of a particular set of data. This basic two-level model could be enlarged into a three-level analysis by including employee effects, department effects, and organizational effects. In this example, the researcher would explore the effects of the structural characteristics of organizations on department processes that, in turn, have effects on individual morale. As with the two-level model presented in this section, more complex models allow the researcher increased control over the variation of lower-level parameters and the ability to partition overall variance in the outcome across all levels of analysis. As we suggested earlier, Equation 2.16 containing the fixed effects, level-2 random intercept, slope, and covariance effects, and the level-1 residual can also be expressed in terms of a two-level mean and covariance structure model with random intercept and slope in Mplus using a different type of notation.[1] We develop this specification further in Chapter 3.

Methods for Estimating Model Parameters

Model estimation provides a means of determining the values of a model's unknown population parameters using the sample data. This is one way of determining whether a proposed model represents a plausible representation of the observed data. In other words, does the proposed model help reduce uncertainty surrounding the phenomenon of interest? Of course, the answer to this question is seldom as straightforward as it might appear (Pawitan, 2001).

There are a number of different ways to think about the estimation of unknown parameters. In the past, Bayesian and frequentist schools of statistics developed in response to the problem of uncertainty. For frequentists, the concern was summarizing the distribution of specific observed data and its likely distribution over repeated sampling under similar conditions in the future. In this latter approach, for example, we use concepts such as variability, standard error, t-ratio, p-value,

Type I error, power of a test, and confidence interval to describe our confidence in the likelihood of hypothetically observing similar occurrences of the phenomena in the future (Pawitan, 2001).

For Bayesians, the concern was how probability theory could be used to make statements about uncertain events beyond any specific instance of observed data. In contrast to frequentists' computations, Bayesian computations begin with an explicit statement about a phenomenon's probable occurrence; this probable occurrence (or a prior distribution) can be based on thinking alone rather than an empirical distribution. In this case, if we know nothing about the probability of getting into graduate school, for example, we may say it is evenly distributed between 0 and 1 in the population, just as we might have some empirical information that an individual has a 60% chance of being admitted. For frequentists, the parameter would not have a distribution separate from its observed variability in a specific sample of the population (Pawitan, 2001). In the Bayesian perspective, however, probability is viewed as a subjective uncertainty about the process that produces the data, rather than the relative frequency of occurrence in a population (Raudenbush, 1995).

From the frequentist view, answering questions about the uncertainty of parameters can be addressed rather easily by conducting parameter tests (e.g., examining t-tests, significance levels, and confidence intervals), perhaps increasing the sample sizes to increase the likelihood of detecting effects if necessary, or controlling for a known influence on the outcome. In contrast, however, the truthfulness of a proposed model may always remain to some extent uncertain, owing to the incomplete nature of any model test to describe reality, given the inductive nature of the scientific process. Stated differently, although one may find a model that fits the data quite well, there may be other models that would fit the data the same or better, and, in truth, we often must rely on judgment to determine whether it represents a plausible representation of reality.

Maximum Likelihood Estimation

There are a number of different ways to estimate structural and variance component parameters in multilevel models. In the past, using linear modeling techniques was limited by the fact that only in cases of perfectly balanced sampling designs (i.e., equal group sizes) were closed-form mathematical formulas available to estimate the random variance and covariance components in the model (Raudenbush & Bryk, 2002). When sampling designs are unbalanced, iterative estimation procedures are necessary to obtain efficient estimates. The most common method to estimate multilevel models is **maximum likelihood (ML) estimation** (Dempster, Laird, & Rubin, 1977; Efron & Morris, 1975; Fisher, 1922; Hartley & Rao, 1967; Lawley & Maxwell, 1963; Lindley & Smith, 1972; Raudenbush, 1988). ML estimation provides a means for dealing with the uncertainty present in the observed sample data by finding optimal values for the unknown parameters in a proposed model (e.g., means, regression parameters, variances) using a likelihood function that is based on the underlying sampling distribution of the outcome (e.g., normal, binomial, Poisson). The likelihood function conveys information about unknown quantities. These may be fixed effects (intercepts, regression slopes), randomly varying coefficients, and covariance components.

Software packages for multilevel modeling typically incorporate one or more basic ML approaches as well as numerous variations. One advantage of ML estimation is that it is generally robust to departures from normality with sufficiently large samples and produces asymptotically efficient and consistent estimates (Hox, 2010). A growing body of research (e.g., Chou & Bentler, 1995; Fotiu, 1989; Goldstein, 1986; Hartley & Rao, 1967; Harville, 1977; Hoyle & Panter, 1995; Raudenbush, 1995) suggests ML estimation approaches yield reasonable estimates under a variety of less-than-optimal conditions (i.e., small samples, departure from multivariate normality). ML estimation in Mplus features robust standard errors (MLR) calculated for less than ideal sampling conditions. What constitutes the limits in using these types of corrections in terms of addressing departures from normality, group sample size, imbalance within groups, and model complexity, however, is open to debate (Hox & Maas, 2002; Raudenbush & Bryk, 2002). A second advantage is that ML can be used to estimate models with random variables that are from sampling distributions other than the normal distribution— for example, binomial, multinomial, Poisson, or negative binomial (Muthén & Muthén, 1998–2006; Raudenbush & Bryk, 2002; Stiratell, Laird, & Ware, 1984; Wong & Mason, 1985). When outcome variables are not measured on a continuous scale, other model specification and estimation procedures are used to take the scale of the outcome variables and their underlying probability distributions into account. A third advantage is that for examining the discrepancy between the sample and implied covariance matrices, ML estimation provides a chi-square goodness-of-fit test (Marcoulides & Hershberger, 1997), and other indices are also available that can also be used comparing various models.

Obtaining a set of model estimates involves an iterative process that determines a set of weights for random parameters in the model in order to maximize the likelihood function. The likelihood function provides the probability of obtaining the observed data over a range of possible parameter values that may be almost as likely as the ML estimate (Pawitan, 2001). This allows us to compare the probability of the observed data under different parameter values. The likelihood function allows the parameters in a model to vary while holding everything else constant in the context of finding the set of ML estimates that maximize the likelihood function (Azen & Walker, 2011). For multiparameter models, this is often expressed as the discrepancy between the sample covariance matrix and a model-implied covariance matrix, where a smaller discrepancy implies a stronger fit of the proposed model to the sample data (Marcoulides & Hershberger, 1997).

In reality, since we do not know the population values, we attempt to find values from the sample data for the unknown model parameters that result in a small discrepancy in the likelihood function between the model-implied and sample parameter values. For many types of analyses (e.g., SEM), the sample data are summarized in the sample covariance matrix (and a vector of variable means). Model estimation then proceeds by specifying a set of restrictions on the sample covariance matrix, and the difference between the original sample covariance matrix and the reproduced (or implied) covariance matrix with the restrictions imposed is examined. If one considers the sample covariance matrix to represent the true population covariance matrix, then the difference between the sample covariance matrix (S) and a covariance matrix implied by the proposed model ($\hat{\Sigma}$) should be small if the model fits the data. Different approaches for estimating model parameters can be considered as different ways of weighting the differences between the corresponding elements of the observed and implied covariance matrices:

$$F = (s - c)W(s - c)',\tag{2.20}$$

where s and c are the nonduplicated elements of the observed and implied covariance matrices S and Σ, respectively, arranged as vectors, and W is the weight matrix. For example, if S were a 3×3 covariance matrix, s would be a six-element vector and $(s - c)'$ would contain the differences between these elements in their respective covariance matrices (Loehlin, 1992). If W is an identity matrix, the expression in Equation 2.20 reduces to the sum of the squared differences between corresponding elements of the observed and implied matrix (i.e., the OLS criterion). Generalized least squares estimation (GLS) uses the inverse of the S covariance matrix (S^{-1}). This only needs to be estimated once during the model iteration process. ML estimation uses the inverse of the model-implied covariance matrix ($\hat{\Sigma}^{-1}$), which must be updated at each iteration of the model estimation process until the model converges (if it does converge) and an optimal set of estimates is obtained.

ML estimation entails finding an unknown parameter or parameters for which the probability of the observed data is greatest. Finding the maximum of the likelihood function, or the log likelihood function (which is easier to work with), involves taking the derivative of the function, setting it to zero, and solving for the unknown parameter being maximized. The maximum likelihood estimates are those values of the parameters that make the observed data most likely. The likelihood, or probability, of the data can vary from 0.0 to 1.0, and since this can be a very small number, it is often easier to work with its natural log. This has an additional advantage of making differentiating the likelihood function easier. It turns out that minimizing the log likelihood function amounts to maximizing the likelihood of the observed data (i.e., if the probability of the data = 1, the natural log of it is 0). Either approach therefore leads to equivalent parameter estimates (Wu, West, & Taylor, 2009). Importantly, either approach represents the likelihood of observing the sample data without assuming the validity of any model-implied hypotheses.

The mathematical relationships implied in the proposed model are solved iteratively until the estimates are optimized. Estimation starts with an educated guess of the parameter estimates and requires a computational algorithm to accomplish the iterations. At each successive step, a new set of estimates is obtained and evaluated until the estimates no longer change. The goal of ML estimation is to minimize the log likelihood function by taking partial derivatives of it by the model parameters with respect to the elements of $S - \hat{\Sigma}$. The function looks something like an upside down U. Obtaining the ML estimates involves differentiating each of the implied equations by setting the first derivative to zero and solving for each β coefficient, while the other parameters are held constant. The first derivative of the function is defined as the exact slope at its maximum; that is, it is the slope of a tangent line to the curve at that point (i.e., it is the limit of a sequence of slopes describing the curvature of the function). If the log-likelihood function is well approximated by a quadratic function, its curvature is estimated by the second derivative, which is defined as the change in the slope per unit of X evaluated at the ML estimate. We can ensure the ML estimate is a maximum for the log likelihood function by checking the second derivative. If the second derivative is negative, the critical point is a maximum (Pawitan, 2001). The second derivative also provides information used in estimating the sample variance (Pawitan, 2001).

Minimizing the distance between the implied covariance matrix and the sample covariance matrix can be accomplished by estimating the following fit function with respect to the model parameters:

$$F_{ML} = \log | \hat{\Sigma} | - \log | S | + tr(S\hat{\Sigma}^{-1}) - p + (\bar{y} - \mu)'\hat{\Sigma}^{-1}(\bar{y} - \mu), \tag{2.21}$$

where $\hat{\Sigma}$ is the model-implied covariance matrix, S is the sample covariance matrix, $|.|$ is the determinant of the matrix, "tr" indicates the trace (i.e., defined as the sum of the diagonal elements in the matrix) of the products of the sample and model-implied covariance matrices, and log refers to the natural logarithms of the determinants of the model-implied and sample covariance matrices, given the number of nonduplicated elements (p) in the covariance matrix. The corresponding observed mean structure is defined by $\bar{y}$, which is a $p \times 1$ vector of sample means, and μ represents the $p \times 1$ vector of fitted means.

Full Information ML

One limitation of conventional analyses of covariance and mean structures using ML estimation is that they depend on relatively large samples with complete data. Individuals with **missing data** have to be eliminated from analysis through listwise deletion. This can result in many individuals being excluded, which is likely to result in biasing the estimation of the model's parameters. Where we have missing data, or where there are random coefficients in a two-level model and unbalanced group sizes, we need to model the raw data instead of the estimated covariance matrices. Full information maximum likelihood (FIML) represents an approach based on the raw data (i.e., individual-level data) in the sample, rather than just the sample covariance matrix, or in the case of a two-level model, the within-group and between-group covariance matrices. This approach takes advantage of all *available* data on individuals (including where some individuals may have only partial data). This is why FIML is often referred to as a "raw data" estimation approach (Arbuckle, 1996). This approach represents a sharp contrast from estimation based on the sample covariance matrix, which may biased due to dropping incomplete cases.

As Enders (2001) notes, the FIML method is quite general and can be applied to a wide variety of analyses, including the estimation of means and covariance matrices in the presence of missing data, unequal spacing of observations in studies of individual growth, multilevel models with unbalanced group sizes, and multilevel SEM. If the data are incomplete, the sample covariance matrix is no longer sufficient for estimating the model since its estimation requires listwise deletion of missing cases. With respect to multilevel models, we can think of the unbalanced group sizes as a type of missing data problem, and make use of FIML to estimate the model parameters. Under the notion of data that are missing at random (MAR) and conditional on the data, the assumption is that the individuals with missing data will be the same as those with complete data. This allows the specification of different covariance matrices for individuals depending on the number of observations present for each individual (Mehta & Neale, 2005). For multilevel models, in particular, the EM (expectation maximization) algorithm (Dempster et al., 1977) provided a breakthrough in efficiency for estimating random effects by treating them as "missing data"—that is, the algorithm proceeds by first making guesses about the expected missing values of unknown parameters such as the mean and variance, given the observed data and current estimates of the model parameters. The estimated values are then substituted into the formulas for the ML estimates given the complete data. Each step of the expectation maximum (EM) algorithm increases the likelihood function and, moreover, the estimates converge to the maximum likelihood estimate (Enders, 2001; Raudenbush et al., 2002).

Mplus has a number of different ML-based estimators for use with the EM algorithm, which are differentiated by their approach to estimating standard errors. The ML estimator is appropriate if group sizes are balanced and estimates conventional standard errors and chi-square statistic; standard errors for the MLF estimator are based on first-order derivatives and a normal chi-square statistic; and MLR is based on robust standard errors (calculated with a sandwich estimator) adjusted for nonnormality and is appropriate for unbalanced groups. The MLR chi-square test statistic is asymptotically equivalent to the Yuan-Bentler test statistic (Muthén & Muthén, 1998–2012).

Mplus actually provides four settings to optimize the ML estimates in multilevel models (Muthén & Muthén, 1998–2012). In addition to EM (which optimizes the complete-data log likelihood), there is EMA (an accelerated EM procedure that uses Quasi-Newton and Fisher Scoring optimization steps when needed), Fisher scoring (FS), and ODLL (observed data log likelihood). These can be chosen by specifying the type of algorithm after the model type (ALGORITHM = EM). Fisher scoring is used in some situations because it generally converges rapidly and produces standard errors of all parameter estimates (Longford, 1993).

In the FIML approach, likelihood is computed using individual data vectors. Assuming multivariate normality, the likelihood of a specific response vector for individual i is as follows:

$$F_{FIML} = \frac{1}{N} \sum_{i=1}^{N} (\log|\mathbf{\Sigma}_i| + (\mathbf{y}_i - \mathbf{\mu}_i)' \mathbf{\Sigma}_i^{-1} (\mathbf{y}_i - \mathbf{\mu}_i) + K_i) , \quad (2.22)$$

where $\mathbf{y}_i$ is the vector of complete data for case i, $\mathbf{\mu}$ contains the $p \times 1$ vector of fitted means of the variables derived from the entire sample, and $\mathbf{\Sigma}$ is the $p \times p$ covariance matrix. The determinant and inverse of $\mathbf{\Sigma}$ are based on the variables observed for each case i (Enders, 2001). K_i is a constant that depends on the number of complete data points for case i and is independent of the model parameters ($K_i = \log(2\pi)^* p_i$), where p_i is the number of variables without missing data for case i. It is important to note, therefore, that the notation simply suggests that the dimensions of $\mathbf{y}_i$ and of the associated mean and covariance structures can vary from observation to observation; that is, the approach allows for different amounts of data per individual. FIML produces the model-implied mean and covariance matrices that are contributed for each individual response pattern, resulting in a covariance matrix whose dimensionality depends on the amount of actual data present. In other words, the dimension of the covariance matrix could vary across individuals (Mehta & Neale, 2005). This facility is necessary for utilizing the SEM framework because in modeling random slopes, for example, covariances between variables within groups are a function of some predictor and, hence, must be allowed to vary across groups.

Because FIML uses the raw data as input, it takes advantage of all of the available information in the data. This is opposed to other methods that use the observed covariance matrix, which necessarily contains less information than the raw data. It is important to note that an observed covariance matrix contains less information than the raw data because one data set will always produce the same observed covariance matrix; however, one covariance matrix could be generated by many different raw data sets. The overall fit function for the sample is obtained by summing the n casewise likelihood functions across the sample as follows:

$$\log L(\mu, \Sigma) = \sum_{i=1}^{N} \log L_i. \quad (2.23)$$

Researchers have demonstrated that multilevel regression models with individuals nested within groups can be specified as structural equation models (e.g.,

Mehta & Neale, 2005; Muthén & Muthén, 1998–2006). The approach implies that level-2 clusters are the units of observation and individuals within clusters are treated as variables. This implies that the unbalanced numbers of individuals within groups can be included in the model similar to missing data estimation in typical SEM (Hox, 2010; Mehta & Neale, 2005; Wu, West, & Taylor, 2009). Importantly, FIML estimation based on individual likelihood has afforded greater flexibility in estimating a wider variety of multilevel models with SEM. This includes random slopes and growth models with different measurement time points for individuals [see Mehta & Neale (2005) and Wu et al. (2009), for further discussion]. For example, the missing data estimation capability of FIML facilitates unequal spacing of measurement intervals for individuals in growth curve analysis (Mehta & Neale, 2005; Mehta & West, 2000).

Model Convergence

Through an iterative algorithm such as EM, arriving at a set of final model estimates is known as model convergence (i.e., where the estimates no longer change and the likelihood is therefore at its maximum value). It is important that the model actually reaches convergence, as the resulting parameter estimates will not be trustworthy if the model has not converged. Sometimes increasing the number of iterations will result in a model that converges, but often, the failure of the model to converge on a unique solution is an indication that it needs to be changed and re-estimated. Keep in mind that even if a model converges, it does not mean the estimates are the *right ones*, given the sample data. In the same way, we would not conclude that because we fail to "reject" a model as consistent with the observed data, that it is the only model that would fit this criterion.

Once we have a model solution that converges, we can assess how well the proposed model fits the data using various model fit indices. In general, confirmation of a proposed model relies on a failure to reject the null hypothesis (H_0)—that is, the data are consistent with the proposed model. The desired acceptance of the null hypothesis may be somewhat different for readers who are used to equating rejection of the null hypothesis as acceptance of a proposed, alternative research hypothesis. In contrast to this common use of the null hypothesis, one wishes to accept from the null hypothesis that the model cannot be rejected on statistical or practical grounds. Failure to reject this null hypothesis therefore implies that the proposed model is a plausible representation of the data, although it is important to note that it may not be the *only* plausible representation of the data. The value of the fit function based on the final parameter estimates is used to determine how well the proposed model implied by $\hat{\Sigma}$ fits the observed covariance matrix **S**. As we noted previously, if the value of the log-likelihood function is 0, it suggests the proposed model fits the data perfectly.

For example, ML estimation produces a model deviance statistic (which is often referred to as $-2LL$ or $-2 \times$ log likelihood), which is an indicator of how well the model fits the data. We multiply the log likelihood by −2 so it can be expressed easily as a positive number. Models with lower deviance (i.e., a smaller discrepancy function) fit better than models with higher deviance. If the two matrices are identical, the value of the expression will be 0. The larger the discrepancy function becomes, the worse the fit, which implies less similarity between the elements in the two matrices. We can also look at the residuals (or residual matrix) that describe the difference between the model-implied covariance matrix and actual covariance matrix. Large residuals imply that some aspects of the proposed model do not fit the data well. Nested models (where a more specific model is formed from a more general one) can be compared by examining differences in these deviance coefficients under specified conditions [e.g., see Muthén & Muthén (1998–2012) for more information about comparing models using Mplus]. We will take up this issue of comparing models further in subsequent chapters.

Considerations for ML Estimation

ML estimation requires assumptions about the nature of the sample chosen from the population. One assumption is that model estimation is based on characteristics of multivariate normality present within the sample covariance matrix in order to produce optimal (i.e., consistent and asymptotically efficient) estimates of the population parameters. From a frequentist viewpoint, statistical models depend on distributions of observations in a sample that is assumed to represent a population. Hypothesis tests are conducted based on the probability of a particular result likely occurring within a population over repeated random samplings, given a particular level of error the analyst is willing to tolerate. Of course, in real-life settings, the sample data may depart from normality and, therefore, may not represent the population accurately.

A second assumption is sufficient sample sizes to produce accurate estimates. For estimates of model parameters provided with ML, larger sample sizes reduce the likelihood for error due to imprecision in sampling. ML works optimally where there are large numbers of groups available at Level 2 and where the numbers of individuals within the groups are relatively large and balanced. Under less-than-ideal sampling conditions, there has been considerable debate among methodologists about the efficiency of ML estimation, given the nonnormal features of the groups (e.g., Longford, 1993; Morris, 1995; Muthén, 1994). Where the number of groups available to study is small and the within-groups sample sizes unbalanced, ML estimation may provide biased estimates that understate the between-groups variance and, hence, the group-level coefficients may be misleading (Morris, 1995; Raudenbush, 1995). This is because the group-level slope coefficients are conditional on estimates of the group-level variance. Where residual variance is likely to be underestimated, standard error estimates will be too small and, therefore, a greater likelihood of committing Type I errors exists. One alternative is restricted ML estimation, which can provide better estimates of variance components than FIML, and Bayesian estimation.

Several problems can result from group sample size issues. One is the number of group-level predictors that can be included in the model. Where researchers will often enter many predictors into a single-level regression analysis and remove the ones that are not significant, this strategy may not work very well where there are relatively few groups. Another issue to consider is that the power to detect effects in the population may be minimal, especially for detecting moderate or small effects in group sizes under 100 (e.g., Hox & Maas, 2001). A third issue is that with small samples, ML estimation may provide biased estimates, primarily with respect to the model's random variance estimates (Morris, 1995). Bayesian estimation, which is available in Mplus, provides an alternative estimation approach with small level-2 sample sizes. A fourth issue that can occur is that with multiple random coefficients (e.g., slopes and intercept), it is more difficult to assess the adequacy of the group-level observations against each possible group-level equation because of the increased likelihood of correlated outcomes and multicollinearity, both in the individual- and group-level equations. In some situations, the group-level sample may only be a crude representation of some population, as in a convenience sample. Although researchers may believe there to be a close correspondence between their convenience sample and a real population of interest, this assumed correspondence can be difficult to quantify (Draper, 1995; Goldstein, 1995). Even if the resultant model might fit the data well, the extent to which it could be replicated in other samples would be uncertain. It is also the case that if data are too skewed, linear models may not be suitable; therefore, corrections for standard errors may be suspect anyway. Of course, replicating findings is one manner in which this limitation can be lessened.

A final assumption is that any missing data are missing at random (MAR). MAR implies that the missing data can be a function of both the observed outcomes and covariates in the model. We note that Mplus can provide ML estimation under various conditions of missing data including MCAR (missing completely at random), MAR (missing at random), and NMAR (not missing at random) for continuous, censored, binary, ordered categorical (ordinal), nominal, counts, or combinations of these variable types (Little & Rubin, 2002). For data that do not support the standard of MAR, it is possible to use ML estimation where categorical variables are used to represent indicators of missingness, and where the missingness can be predicted by continuous and categorical latent variables such as in pattern-mixture models (Muthén, Asparouhov, Hunter, & Leuchter, 2011; Muthén, Jo, & Brown, 2003).

We illustrate some of the previous problems discussed with ML estimation with a simple empirical illustration in Table 2.2. In this table, we summarize some results from several random samples drawn from a data set with 13,189 employees nested in 165 organizations using MLR estimation (i.e., appropriate for multilevel models unbalanced sample sizes). Both models have significant level-2 random variation in the intercept and slope. First, we can note that the random samples do a reasonable job of estimating the full model's fixed effects (i.e., intercept $= 15.600$ and

TABLE 2.2 Examining the Effects of Sample Size on Model Parameters Using MLR Estimation

Variables	Sample 1	Sample 2	Sample 3	Sample 4	Sample 5
Random Coefficients					
Between Groups					
Sample size	91	91	67	58	47
Intercept	15.301*	15.208*	15.127*	14.512*	15.744*
Satpay slope	1.236*	1.247*	1.267*	1.321*	1.195*
Within Groups					
Sample size	7500	3500	1000	700	500
Average cluster size	82.4	38.5	14.9	12.1	10.6
Variance Components					
Level-2 slope	0.006*	0.008**	0.004	0.006	0.012
Level-2 variance	1.642*	1.461*	1.758*	2.148*	0.697
Level-1 variance	17.935*	17.986*	18.847*	17.189*	16.576*
Parameters	5	5	5	5	5

Note: $*p < 0.05$; $**p < 0.10$

Estimates for the full model are intercept $= 15.600$; slope $= 1.216$; level-2 intercept variance $= 1.621$; level-2 slope variance $= 0.004$; level-1 residual variance $= 17.682$.

slope $= 1.216$). Regarding random effects, we can see that our random samples with 91 organizations and either 7,500 or 3,500 employees both pick up the two hypothesized random effects (i.e., random intercept and slope). Models with 67 or 58 organizations and 1,000 or 700 individuals, respectively, are able to detect the random variation in level-2 random intercept only, while the last random sample (i.e., 47 units and 500 individuals) does not pick up the level-2 random intercept variance. For this last model, even with an ICC of 0.10, the average cluster size ($n = 10.6$) would produce a design effect under 2.0 $[1 + (9.6 \times .1) = 1.96]$, which, as we noted earlier in the chapter, does not appear to result in overly exaggerated rejection proportions for conducting single-level analyses. As the table suggests, with smaller samples at both the group and individual levels, we can observe that both our ability to detect statistically significant variation in random parameters (an issue of power) and our ability to provide accurate estimates of both fixed and random parameters may become increasingly suspect. This empirical illustration is consistent with Raudenbush and Bryk's (2002) observation that for multilevel models, the number of higher-level units is usually the most important factor in determining whether ML will provide optimal estimates.

Other Model Estimation Approaches in Mplus

While univariate and multivariate outcomes from normal distributions can be estimated with ML using the EM algorithm, in models where the outcomes are from probability distributions other than normal, the multilevel models can be estimated with ML, but numerical integration is required in the computations for estimating the random effects (Asparouhov & Muthén, 2007). Numerical integration is one means of estimating model parameters for models with discrete outcomes; however, for multilevel models, it can be computationally demanding, especially where there are several random effects—that is, they take a considerable amount of time to estimate. Numerical integration is a broad term used for a family of algorithms that are useful in calculating the numerical value of an area under a curve (a term often referred to as quadrature), where the change in Y per change in a unit of X is not linear (as in the case of a dichotomous variable). We note that for curvilinear relationships such as for discrete outcomes, problems of quadrature are much more difficult in estimating model parameters.

For binary and ordered categorical dependent variables, for example, probit or logistic regression models are available in Mplus (and multinomial models for unordered categorical outcomes). For models with latent factors and categorical (rather than continuous) observed indicators, with ML estimation, numerical integration is used with one dimension of integration for each factor (Muthén & Muthén, 1998–2012). To reduce computational time with several factors, the number of integration points per dimension can be reduced for an approximate solution.

Another approach is **weighted least squares (WLS) estimation**. WLS estimation is useful in handling binary, ordered categories, multinomial, and count outcomes, as well as combinations of continuous and categorical outcomes, where estimates of random effects can be estimated using numerical integration (Asparouhov & Muthén, 2007). For models with many dimensions of integration and categorical outcomes, the WLS estimation may improve computational speed. The limited-information WLS method available in Mplus represents a generalization of Muthén's (1984) WLS approach for estimating single-level models. In one simulation study for two-level factor analysis, the multilevel WLS estimator was shown to provide estimates on par with ML for continuous outcomes and to outperform ML for categorical outcomes (see Asparouhov & Muthén, 2007). The Mplus WLS essentially replaces complex model estimation with a more simplified integration approach with one- or two-dimensional integration (Asparouhov & Muthén, 2007).

WLS Estimation

Similar to ML estimation, WLS estimation is also used to minimize the discrepancy between the model-implied and sample covariance matrices; that is, the WLS estimates are the parameter estimates that minimize the fit function. The weight matrix for WLS involves the square of the nonduplicated elements in the sample covariance matrix, so if s were a six-element vector, the weight matrix would be derived from the inverse of a 6×6 covariance matrix (referred to as G) among all possible pairs placed in *s* (Loehlin, 1992). As the sample covariance matrix gets larger, the vector of nonduplicated elements *s* increases rapidly as does the corresponding covariance matrix for WLS estimation. Therefore, WLS usually requires larger sample sizes for efficient estimation (Loehlin, 1992). In a multilevel model, the dimensions of *G* can exceed the number of clusters in the sample (referred to as a singular matrix). In this case, the weight matrix is restricted to be zero for all off-diagonal elements, which is referred to as a diagonal WLS estimator (referred to as WLSM or WLSVM), depending on whether one desires standard errors and mean-adjusted chi-square coefficient that use a full weight matrix (WLSM) or standard errors and mean- and variance-adjusted chi-square coefficient that use a full weight matrix (WLSMV) in order to compare competing models (Asparouhov & Muthén, 2007; Muthén & Muthén, 1998–2012).

Bayesian Estimation

Bayesian estimation provides a contrasting approach to ML for estimating model parameters (Bryk & Raudenbush, 1992; Spiegelhalter, Thomas, Best, & Gilks, 1994) that have recently been incorporated into many multilevel modeling software programs. Bayesian estimation is also available in Mplus, which allows continuous, categorical, and combinations of these variable types, as well as random intercepts, slopes, and missing data. One common use is where there are only a small number of groups available to study. Bayesian estimation involves the incorporation of information about uncertainty from prior knowledge of the distributions of variables. For example, this could be used in providing small-variance priors for parameters that are hypothesized to be small but not exactly zero, as well as problems involving the examination of measurement invariance.

The incorporation of Bayesian analysis in Mplus Version 7 makes it possible to examine multilevel models with many random effects, where ML estimation is unwieldy, or impossible, due to requiring too many dimensions of integration. One way this can be useful is in situations where factor models, for example, may have random factor loadings, which is an important part of studies of measurement invariance across groups and across time, particularly for a large number of groups or time points. Because Bayesian estimation is not conditional on the accuracy of specific point estimates of variances and covariances, it can correct the tendency for ML methods to underestimate variance and covariance parameters in small (or nonrandom) group samples. A disadvantage is that estimates are often unrealistic for units that have few observations (Kreft & de Leeuw, 1998). From a Bayesian perspective, inferences about group-level coefficients are based on prior and posterior distributions regarding the group-level coefficients rather than specific point estimates from the current data set.

Practically speaking, the Bayes approach assumes that all model parameters have prior distributions that can aid in estimation efficiency for examining future data. This prior information may be easier to apply to some parameters (e.g., means, slopes) than to others (e.g., variance and covariance parameters), however. In practice, the choice of prior distributions to employ for estimating variance and covariance parameters can be difficult to describe, since the researcher may have little prior knowledge about them. Bayesian methods of estimation differ from more traditional ML estimation methods according to the extent to which various kinds of prior distributions are incorporated in the analysis on unknown parameters. In the Bayesian approach, all unknown parameters in a model are assumed to have prior probability distributions that generate the data. Because inferences about the regression coefficients are not conditional on specific point estimates as in ML, but rather on comparisons of prior distributions (which may be generated) and posterior distributions, Bayes estimates can often do a better job of accounting for uncertainty in the random coefficients estimates in situations where the data are less than ideal (Morris, 1995; Lindley & Smith, 1972; Smith, 1973). Once new data are incorporated, the prior distribution is revised in light of the combining of new evidence with the previous evidence. As sample size increases, the precision of the estimated sample mean will increase until a point where incorporating previous evidence with new evidence will converge with ML estimation methods.

Since the issue of appropriate model estimation under different types of conditions is not yet settled, when choosing a method of model estimation the researcher should consider the nature of the sampling scheme for Level 2 and the degree of imbalance within those units. Although individuals may be chosen at random within units, they are seldom assigned at random to their existing units. While including a number of individual-level background variables helps us adjust for differences within units before making comparisons across units, every variable added to the model also contributes to its complexity. At some point, having too many variables in the model may actually create problems in modeling and interpreting the meaning of the between-unit differences (Longford, 1993). Accurately modeling the distribution of effects across the sample of level-2 units that may be either nonrandom or may depart from normality, therefore, is generally more of a problem in multilevel modeling than problems presented by the number of individuals sampled within each unit (e.g., Morris, 1995). In actual cases where organizational units are also randomly sampled, the idea of random variation at both levels is very appealing.

A Comparison of Estimation Approaches With Small Numbers of Level-2 Units

What is the case, however, with a small numbers of units? In this example, we will provide one illustration of several alternative approaches to estimate the model's parameters. We will examine a randomly varying level-1 intercept for students' math achievement and slope coefficients of students' SES status on their achievement levels. In this example, the full data set consists of 6,618 students in 123 schools with cluster average cluster size of 53.8. Using MLR estimation again, we obtained an intercept estimate of 661.12, slope estimate of −16.28, and, with variance components of 1246.66 (residual variance Level 1), intercept variance of 233.00, and slope variance of 26.29 (results not tabled).

Now let's suppose instead that we have only a small subset of this data set. In this subset, there are 1,205 students nested in 28 randomly selected schools with sample sizes ranging from 6 to 123. The individual sample size is certainly large enough to obtain efficient estimates. The between-group sample size, however, can be considered quite small and likely to produce considerable parameter bias in the between-group portion of the model. In addition, from our last illustration, we know that we may not be able to detect intercept variance or slope variance at Level 2 (school level). We can use either ML-based estimation methods or Bayesian methods to estimate the model's unknown parameters (e.g., level-1 means or slopes, level-2 fixed coefficients, variance-covariance parameters of level-1 coefficients, residual level-1 variance).

As we have noted, software is now available within several programs that can be used to produce Bayesian estimates (Spiegelhalter et al., 1994). In this small example, we provide a simple comparison of model estimates produced by Mplus (MLR) and HLM (restricted ML) against Bayes estimates produced by Mplus and the BUGS (**B**ayesian inference **U**sing **G**ibbs **S**ampling) project (www.mrc-bsu.cam.ac.uk/bugs). This latter project is concerned with developing flexible software (WinBugs) for the Bayesian analysis of complex statistical models using Markov chain Monte Carlo (MCMC) methods. We note that Bayesian estimation provides a contrasting approach to frequentist approaches; however, they depend on a certain amount of judgment and experience because of the necessity of dealing with prior distributions.

For WinBugs, because estimates of unknown parameters are based on their posterior distributions after the data have been collected, the analyst first has to specify a prior distribution for the group-level intercepts, where we suggest they are normally distributed with random errors that also constitute a random sample of such vectors. In this case, let's say we have a good idea about the sample mean for math achievement. We will make the assumption that it is normally distributed with mean 660 (i.e., since the population mean in the full data set is 661) and relatively small variance. This would suggest that with high precision about the prior mean, we might expect a more reliable estimation of the population mean using the Bayesian estimator (as long as the prior distribution is well known).

In contrast, let's assume we know less about where the actual slope coefficient lies, and so we will assume greater variance in slopes across units in describing its actual position (i.e., less prior precision about the estimation of slope variance). We will guess the impact of low SES on math achievement is about −20.0. We can also provide prior information on other parameters (e.g., errors associated with units), as well as prior information about the level-1 variance in means and covariances between predictors. The price to be paid in using Bayesian estimation in Win-Bugs is that prior distributions have to be specified for all unknown parameters, where it is typical that the researcher may not actually know much about them. As our simple illustration suggests, therefore, the choice of the priors can be very important in affecting posterior distributions (Selzer, Wong, & Bryk, 1996). Gibbs sampling can be used to approximate the posterior density of all unknowns, even those where the corresponding densities have an unknown form (Raudenbush & Bryk, 2002); that is, one can start with initial estimates of the unknown parameters previously described based on RML and use these initial estimates to sample from the full conditionals because each of these has a known form.

For Mplus, Bayesian analysis uses Markov chain Monte Carlo (MCMC) algo-rithms (Muthén & Muthén, 1998–2012), which are used for sampling from probability distributions based on constructing a Markov chain that has the desired distribution as its equilibrium distribution. This process tends to proceed by generating feasible solutions uniformly at random and then remembering the one that works the best so far. By specifying ESTIMATOR = BAYES, a Bayesian analysis will be carried out. In Bayesian estimation, the default is to use two inde-pendent Markov chain Monte Carlo (MCMC) chains. Mplus includes a number of input commands that can be used to change the default number of MCMC chains, the minimum and maximum iterations, the type of point estimation to compute, and the default number of draws from the prior distribution. In our view, Bayesian estimation in Mplus is quite easy to implement and can provide considerable flexibility in terms of assumptions about the model parameters (see the *Mplus 7 User's Guide* for some of these additional possibilities). We do not fea-ture the approach extensively in our introductory presentation in this book, but it remains a viable estimation alternative for a number of modeling situations. We provide the example input file we used for the Mplus Bayesian results in Table 2.3 in the chapter notes.[2]

Table 2.3 presents a comparison of the intercepts, slopes, and variance com-ponents associated with each approach. The ICC for the test is 0.16. The table suggests considerable consistency in estimating the intercept (varying by less than 0.7 point). Here, the estimates are similar likely because the prior information for the Bayesian approach was well known. In contrast, in the example we assumed

TABLE 2.3 Comparison of Intercepts, Slopes, and Variance Components

	WinBugs	Mplus (Bayes)	HLM (RML)	Mplus (FIML)
Math Mean, B_0	669.10	668.75	668.43	669.03
Low-SES Math, B_1	−16.27	−16.29	−17.77	−16.86
Variance Components				
Level 1	1341.00	1340.00	1337.11	1338.95
Level 2	321.60	312.39	272.68	267.66
Level-2 Slope	5.90	47.92	21.86	1.46

ICC = 0.16; Sample Mean = 671.24, SD = 41.84

for the Bayesian approach that little was known about the slope location and variance. Correspondingly, in full model there was a bit more variation in estimating the slope across contrasting approaches (roughly 1.5 points). The level-1 residual variance is quite similar across approaches. For Level 2, however, the Bayesian approach estimates the variance as considerably larger than the ML approaches. Notice also the differences in estimating the variability in slopes. For the Bayesian approach these results can depend on the sorts of choices made in specifying the model.

No definitive results should be drawn from this analysis. Its purpose is merely to suggest that researchers have to be cautious in interpreting results from small data sets because of the likelihood of underestimating parameter dispersion. This can lead to errors in interpreting the effects of between-group variables (i.e., both *Type I* and *Type II* errors). The Bayesian approach offers considerable advantages with small data sets, but analysts should be aware that the efficiency of the estimates can depend considerably on the information available about prior parameters. Without this information, the estimates may not be much better than those produced by other approaches (and could actually be worse).

Summary

It is clear that multilevel models can be used to investigate a variety of organizational and educational research problems. They can be an important analytical tool for researchers when they are used to test models guided by strong substantive theory. In the next chapter, we provide more detail about the mathematical models underlying the basic single-level and multilevel regression models.

Notes

1. A two-level measurement model with latent variables at each level can be specified as follows:

$$Y_{ij}^* = \nu_B + \Lambda_W \eta_W + \Lambda_B \eta_B + \varepsilon_W + \varepsilon_B \tag{A2.1}$$

where y_{ij}^* is a vector of observed indicators, ν_B is a vector of latent factor means, Λ is a matrix of factor loadings, η is a vector of latent variables, and ε is a matrix of residuals contained in covariance matrix Θ. Factor loadings, latent factors, and residuals can have within-group and between-group components. The two-level structural model can be specified as follows:

$$\eta_{ij} = \alpha_j + B_j \eta_{ij} + \Gamma_j x_{ij} + \zeta_{ij}^{(2)}, \tag{A2.2}$$

where α_j represents a vector of level-2 random effects, B is a matrix of regression coefficients, η is a vector of latent variables, Γ is a matrix of regression coefficients for observed covariates (x) and ζ represents errors in equations at each level, which are normally distributed with mean of 0 and some variance, and are contained in covariance matrices Ψ_W

and Ψ_B. Since our specified model is relatively simple, we can specify the level-2 model with random intercept (η_{0j}) and slope (η_{1j}) as follows:

$$\begin{bmatrix} \eta_{0j} \\ \eta_{1j} \end{bmatrix} = \begin{bmatrix} \alpha_1 \\ \alpha_2 \end{bmatrix} + \begin{bmatrix} 0 & 0 & 0 & B_{14} \\ 0 & 0 & 0 & B_{24} \\ 0 & 0 & 0 & 0 \\ 0 & 0 & 0 & 0 \end{bmatrix} \begin{bmatrix} \eta_{0j} \\ \eta_{1j} \end{bmatrix} + \begin{bmatrix} \zeta_{0j} \\ \zeta_{1j} \end{bmatrix}, \Psi_B = \begin{bmatrix} \psi_{11} \\ \psi_{21} & \psi_{22} \\ 0 & 0 & 0 \\ 0 & 0 & 0 & 0 \end{bmatrix}. \tag{A2.3}$$

At Level 1, we simply have the level-1 residual for the outcome:

$$\Psi_W = \begin{bmatrix} 0 \\ 0 & \psi_{22} \\ 0 & 0 & 0 \\ 0 & 0 & 0 & 0 \end{bmatrix}. \tag{A2.4}$$

This suggests eight parameters to estimate (two level-2 intercepts, two level-2 structural effects, three level-2 random variances and covariance, and one level-1 residual variance. This specification can be confirmed in the Tech1 output from Mplus, which indicates eight parameters to estimate.

Specification Within Groups

PSI

	S	MORALE	X1	W1
S	0			
MORALE	0	1		
X1	0	0	0	
W1	0	0	0	0

Specification Between Groups
ALPHA

	S	MORALE	X1	W1
	2	3	0	0

BETA

	S	MORALE	X1	W1
S	0	0	0	4
MORALE	0	0	0	5
X1	0	0	0	0
W1	0	0	0	0

PSI

(Continued)

	S	MORALE	X1	W1
S	6			
MORALE	7	8		
X1	0	0	0	
W1	0	0	0	0

2. We provide our input file below.

TITLE: Two-level Bayesian Estimation Example Ch.2;
DATA: FILE IS C:\program files\mplus\ch3 ex3.dat;
            Format is 1f3.0,1f4.0,1f2.0;
VARIABLE: Names are schcode totmath lunch;
            Usevariables are schcode totmath lunch;
            Missing are .;
            within = lunch;
            CLUSTER IS schcode;
define: center lunch (grandmean);
ANALYSIS: TYPE = twolevel random;
            Estimator is bayes;
            algorithm = GIBBS;
            POINT = Median;
            FBITERATIONS = 2000;
            PRIOR = ;
Model:

            %Between%
            totmath;
            s;
            %Within%
            s | totmath on lunch*−12;
OUTPUT: TECH1;

References

Aitken, M. & Longford, N. (1986). Statistical modeling issues in school effectiveness studies. *Journal of Royal Statistical Society (Series A), 149*, 1–43.

Arbuckle, J. (1996). Full information estimation in the presence of incomplete data. In G. A. Marcoulides & R. Schumacker (Eds.), *Advanced structural equation modeling: Issues and techniques* (pp. 243–278). Mahwah, NJ: Lawrence Erlbaum Associates.

Asparouhov, T. & Muthén, B. O. (2007). *Computationally efficient estimation of multilevel high-dimensional latent variable models*. Proceedings of the 2007 JSM meeting in Salt Lake City.

Azen, R., & Walker, C. M. (2011). *Categorical data analysis for the behavioral and social sciences*. New York: Routledge.

Barcikowski, R. (1981). Statistical power with group mean as the unit of analysis. *Journal of Educational Statistics, 6*(3), 267–285.

Bock, R. D. (1989). *Multilevel analysis of educational data.* San Diego: Academic.

Bryk, A. S. & Raudenbush, S. W. (1992). *Hierarchical linear models: Applications and data analysis methods.* Newbury Park, CA: Sage.

Burstein, L. (1980). The analysis of multilevel data in educational research in evaluation. *Review of Research in Education, 8,* 158–233.

Chou, C. P. & Bentler, P. (1995). Estimates and tests in structural equation modeling. In R. Hoyle (Ed.), *Structural equation modeling: Concepts, issues, and applications* (pp. 37–55). Newbury Park, CA: Sage.

Cronbach, L. J. & Webb, N. (1975). Between and within class effects in a reported aptitude-by-treatment interaction: Reanalysis of a study by G. L. Anderson. *Journal of Educational Psychology, 6,* 717–724.

Curran, P. J. (2003). Have multilevel models been structural equation models all along? *Multivariate Behavioral Research, 38,* 529–569.

de Leeuw, J. & Kreft, I. (1986). Random coefficient models for multilevel analysis. *Journal of Educational Statistics, 11*(1), 57–85.

de Leeuw, J. & Kreft, I. G. (1995). Questioning multilevel models. *Journal of Educational Statistics, 20*(2), 171–189.

Dempster, A., Laird N., & Rubin, D. (1977). Maximum likelihood from incomplete data via the EM algorithm. *Journal of the Royal Statistical Society (Series B), 30,* 1–38.

Draper, D. (1995). Inference and hierarchical modeling in the social sciences. *Journal of Educational Statistics, 20*(2), 115–148.

Efron, B. & Morris, C. (1975). Data analysis using Stein's estimator and its generalizations. *Journal of the American Statistical Association, 74,* 311–319.

Enders, C. K. (2001). A primer on maximum likelihood algorithms available for use with missing data. *Structural Equation Modeling, 8*(1), 121–141.

Fisher, R. A. (1918). The correlation between relatives on the supposition of Mendelian inheritance. *Transactions of the Royal Society of Edinburgh, 52,* 399–433.

Fisher, R. A. (1922). On the mathematical foundations of theoretical statistics. *Philosophical Transactions of the Royal Society of London (Series A), 222,* 309–368.

Fisher, R. A. (1925). *Statistical methods for research workers.* London: Oliver & Boyd.

Fotiu, R. (1989). *A comparison of the EM and data augmentation algorithms on simulates small sample hierarchical data from research on education.* Unpublished doctoral dissertation, Michigan State University, East Lansing.

Goldstein, H. (1986). Multilevel mixed linear model analysis using iterative generalized least squares. *Biometrika, 73*(1), 43–56.

Goldstein, H. (1987). *Multilevel models in educational and social research.* London: Oxford University Press.

Goldstein, H. (1995). *Multilevel statistical models.* New York: Halsted.

Hartley, H. O. & Rao, J. N. (1967). Maximum likelihood estimation from the mixed analysis of variance model. *Biometrika, 54,* 93–108.

Harville, D. A. (1977). Maximum likelihood approaches to variance component estimation and to related problems. *Journal of the American Statistical Association, 72,* 320–340.

Heck, R. H., Thomas, S. L., & Tabata, L. N. (2010). *Multilevel and longitudinal modeling with IBM SPSS.* New York: Routledge.

Hofmann, D. & Gavin, M. (1998). Centering decisions in hierarchical models. Theoretical and methodological decisions for organizational science. *Journal of Management, 24,* 623–644.

Hox, J. J. (1995). *Applied multilevel analysis.* Amsterdam: T.T. Publikaties.

Hox, J. (2002). *Multilevel analysis: Techniques and Applications.* Mahwah, NJ: Lawrence Erlbaum.

Hox, J. J. (2010). *Multilevel analysis: Techniques and applications* (2nd ed.). New York: Routledge.

Hox, J. & Maas, C. (2001). The accuracy of multilevel structural equation modeling with pseudobalanced groups and small samples. *Structural Equation Modeling: A Multidisciplinary Journal, 8*(2), 157–174.

Hox, J. & Maas, C. (2002). The accuracy of multilevel structural equation modeling with pseudobalanced groups and small samples. *Structural Equation Modeling: A Multidisciplinary Journal, 8*, 157–174.

Hoyle, R. & Panter, A. (1995). Writing about structural equation models. In R. Hoyle (Ed), *Structural equation modeling: Concepts, issues, and applications* (pp. 158–176). Newbury Park, CA: Sage.

Jedidi, K. & Ansari, A. (2001). Bayesian structural equation models for multilevel data. In G. A. Marcoulides and R. E. Schumacker (Eds.), *New developments and techniques in structural equation modeling* (pp. 139–157). Mahwah, NJ: Lawrence Erlbaum.

Kaplan, D. & Elliott, P. R. (1997). A didactic example of multilevel structural equation modeling applicable to the study of organizations. *Structural Equation Modeling, 4*(1), 1–23.

Kish, L. (1957). Confidence limits for cluster samples. *American Sociological Review, 22*, 154–165.

Kreft, I. & de Leeuw, J. (1998). *Introducing multilevel modeling.* Newbury Park, CA: Sage.

Laird, N. M. & Ware, J. H. (1982). Random-effects models for longitudinal data. *Biometrics, 38*, 963–974.

Lawley, D. & Maxwell, A. (1963). *Factor analysis as a statistical method.* London: Butterworth.

Lindley, D. & Smith, A. (1972). Bayes estimates for the linear model. *Journal of the Royal Statistical Society, B34*, 1–41.

Little, R. & Rubin, D. B. (2002). *Statistical analysis with missing data* (2nd ed.). Hoboken, NJ: Wiley.

Loehlin, J. C. (1992). *Latent variable models: An introduction to factor, path, and structural analysis* (2nd ed.). Hillsdale, NJ: Lawrence Erlbaum Associates.

Longford, N. (1993). *Random coefficient models.* Oxford: Clarendon Press.

Marcoulides, G. A. & Heck, R. H. (1993). Organizational culture and performance: Proposing and testing a model. *Organization Science, 4*(2), 209–225.

Marcoulides, G. A. & Hershberger, S. (1997). *Multivariate statistical methods: A first course.* Mahwah, NJ: Lawrence Erlbaum.

Mehta, P. D. & Neale, M. C. (2005). People are variables too. Multilevel structural equations modeling. *Psychological Methods, 10*(3), 259–284.

Mehta, P. D. & West, S. G. (2000). Putting the individual back into individual growth curves. *Psychological Methods, 5*, 23–43.

Morris, C. (1995). Hierarchical models for educational data: An overview. *Journal of Educational Statistics, 20*(2), 190–200.

Muthén, B. O. (1984). A general structural equation model with dichotomous ordered categorical and continuous latent variable indicators. *Psychometrica, 49*, 115–132.

Muthén, B. O. (1989). Latent variable modeling in heterogenous populations. *Psychometrika, 54*, 557–585.

Muthén, B. O. (1991). Multilevel factor analysis of class and student achievement components. *Journal of Educational Measurement, 28*, 338–354.

Muthén, B.O. (1994). Multilevel covariance structure analysis. *Sociological Methods & Research, 22*(3), 376–398.

Muthén, B. & Asparouhov, T. (2011). Beyond multilevel regression modeling: Multilevel analysis in a general latent variable framework. In J. Hox & J.K. Roberts (Eds.), *Handbook of advanced multilevel analysis* (pp. 15–40). New York: Taylor and Francis.

Muthén, B., Asparouhov, T., Hunter, A., & Leuchter, A. (2011). Growth modeling with nonignorable dropout: Alternative analyses of the STARD antidepressant trial. *Psychological Methods, 16*, 17–33.

Muthén, B., Jo, B., & Brown, H. (2003). Comment on the Barnard, Frangakis, Hill, & Rubin article. Principal stratification approach to broken randomized experiments: A case study of school choice vouchers in New York City. *Journal of the American Statistical Association, 98*, 311–314.

Muthén, B.O. & Muthén, L. (1998–2006). *Mplus user's guide*. Los Angeles, CA: Authors.

Muthén, B.O. & Satorra, A. (1995). Complex sample data in structural equation modeling. *Sociological Methodology, 25*, 216–316.

Muthén, L.K. & Muthén, B.O. (1998–2012). *Mplus user's guide* (7th ed.). Los Angeles, CA: Authors.

Neter, J., Kutner, M.H., Nachtsheim, C., & Wasserman, W. (1996). *Applied linear regression models* (3rd ed.). Chicago, IL: Irwin.

Pawitan, Y. (2001). *In all likelihood: Statistical modeling and inference using likelihood*. Oxford: Clarendon Press.

Rabe-Hesketh, S., Skrondal, A., & Pickles, A. (2004). Generalized multilevel structural equation modeling. *Psychometrika, 69*(2), 167–190.

Raudenbush, S.W. (1988). Educational applications of hierarchical linear model: A review. *Journal of Educational Statistics, 13*(2), 85–116.

Raudenbush, S.W. (1995). Reexamining, reaffirming, and improving application of hierarchical models. *Journal of Educational Statistics, 20*(2), 210–220.

Raudenbush, S.W. & Bryk, A.S. (1986). A hierarchical model for studying school effects. *Sociology of Education, 59*, 1–17.

Raudenbush, S.W. & Bryk, A.S. (2002). *Hierarchical linear models* (2nd ed.). Newbury Park, CA: Sage.

Raudenbush, S.W., Bryk, A.S., Cheong, Y.F., & Congdon, R. (2004). *HLM6: Hierarchical linear and nonlinear modeling*. Lincolnwood, IL: Scientific Software International.

Rousseau, D.M. (1985). Issues of levels in organizational research: Multi-level and cross-level perspectives. *Research in Organizational Behavior, 7*, 1–37.

Rubin, H. (1950). Note on random coefficients. In T.C. Koopmans (Ed.), *Statistical inference in dynamic economic models* (pp. 419–421). New York: Wiley.

Schmidt, W.H. (1969). *Covariance structure analysis of the multivariate random effects model*. Unpublished doctoral dissertation, University of Chicago.

Selzer, M.H., Wong, W. H. M., & Bryk, A.S. (1996). Bayesian analysis in applications of hierarchical models: Issues and methods. *Journal of Educational Statistics, 21*, 131–167.

Shigemasu, K. (1976). Development and validation of a simplified m-group regression model. *Journal of Educational Statistics, 1*(2), 157–180.

Singer, J. & Willett, J. (2003). *Applied longitudinal data analysis: Modeling change and event occurrence*. New York: Oxford University Press.

Smith, A.F. (1973). A general Bayesian linear model. *Journal of the Royal Statistical Society (Series B), 35*, 61–75.

Spiegelhalter, D., Thomas, A., Best, N., & Gilks, W. (1994). *BUGS: Bayesian inference using Gibbs sampling, version 0.30*. Cambridge: MRC Biostatistics Unit.

Stiratell, R., Laird, N., & Ware, J. (1984). Random effects models for serial observations with binary response. *Biometrics, 40*, 961–971.

Strenio, J. L. (1981). *Empirical Bayes estimation for a hierarchical linear model*. Unpublished doctoral dissertation, Department of Statistics, Harvard University.

Tabachnick, B. G. (March 2008). *Multivariate statistics: An introduction and some applications*. Invited workshop presented to the American Psychology–Law Society. Jacksonville, FL.

Tate, R. L. & Wongbundhit, Y. 1983. Random versus nonrandom coefficient models for multilevel analysis. *Journal of Educational Statistics, 8*, 103–120.

Thomas, S. L. & Heck, R. H. (2001). Analysis of large-scale secondary data in higher education research: Potential perils associated with complex sampling designs. *Research in Higher Education, 42*(5), 517–550.

Wald, A. (1947). A note on regression analysis. *Annals of Mathematical Statistics, 18*, 586–589.

Walsh, J. E. (1947). Concerning the effect of the intraclass correlation on certain significance tests. *Annals of Mathematical Statistics, 18*, 88–96.

Wong, G. T. & Mason, W. M. (1985). The hierarchical logistic regression model for multilevel analysis. *Journal of the American Statistical Association, 80*(391), 513–524.

Wu, W., West, S. G., & Taylor, A. B. (2009). Evaluating model fit for growth curve models: Integration of fit indices from SEM and MLM frameworks. *Psychological Methods, 14*(3), 183–201.

3

MULTILEVEL REGRESSION
MODELS

Chapter Objectives

This chapter develops the basics of two-level multilevel regression modeling. We develop a series of models to explain variability in a random intercept and slope across level-2 units. We illustrate how to develop the successive models using Mplus input files and how to evaluate their suitability. We also consider how **centering** level-1 predictors can influence the interpretation of the model results.

Introduction

The material in the preceding chapters places the basic multilevel regression model in a larger family of models that we explore in this book—a family of models specifically designed to capitalize on hierarchical data structures. This chapter serves as a starting point for the development of a series of models included in this family. Most commonly, these models are conceived as two-level models, that is, with individuals nested within some type of groups (e.g., individuals working within product or service firms, students in classrooms or schools, patients within health clinics, voters within congressional districts). As we noted earlier, however, we can certainly extend our analyses to consider higher-order nesting of groups within groups.

Methodological progress across a number of different fields suggests that multilevel data structures can be studied from variety of different perspectives (Byrne, 2012; Mehta & Neale, 2005; Heck & Thomas, 2009; Muthén, 1991, 2002). The analysis of hierarchical data structures using structural equation modeling (SEM) involved resolving challenges in specifying between-group covariance matrices of varying sample sizes and providing appropriate ML estimation (Heck &

Thomas, 2009; Hox, 2002; McArdle & Hamagami, 1996; Muthén, 1991, 1994). In particular, we draw attention to recent work in model estimation using full information maximum likelihood (FIML) that has facilitated the use of the SEM framework to specify multilevel models with random slopes through the use of a raw data (or individual) likelihood function to estimate model parameters (e.g., see Muthén & Asparouhov, 2011; Mehta & Neale, 2005; Wu, West, & Taylor, 2009). This facility has opened up the analyses of both univariate and multivariate types of multilevel regression models where processes at lower levels of the data hierarchy can be examined in terms of their random variability across higher-order groups using SEM. With this added modeling facility, researchers can take advantage of some of the key features of SEM including estimating path models with mediated effects on two or more levels, models with observed and latent variables, and models that may focus on population mixtures (i.e., emergent subgroups of individuals with similar scores on the outcomes) at both the individual and group levels.

We begin here by providing an overview of the mathematical elements of the univariate multilevel regression model while illustrating the logic of the development of the model and interpretation of the results. As we noted earlier, the basic random coefficients, or multilevel regression approach, predates the appearance of the SEM approach by a number of years, owing to the relative simplicity of partitioning the variance associated with a single (or univariate) outcome, into its individual- and group-level portions, as opposed to the relatively more complex relationships embedded in structural equation models, which are inherently multivariate in nature (e.g., several variables defining a latent outcome, mediating variables between predictors and outcomes). In this latter case, more complex relationships embedded within a total population covariance matrix have to be partitioned into a within-group covariance matrix and a between-group covariance matrix. This basic difference in the univariate focus of multiple regression and the multivariate focus of SEM impacts the manner in which the models are usually specified—that is, multiple regression models are generally specified as a single equation with one or more predictors and an error term, while structural equation models are generally specified as a set of simultaneous equations contained within specific matrices (e.g., a factor-loading matrix to define constructs, an error covariance matrix for items defining factors, a factor covariance matrix, a matrix of structural relations between latent constructs, a matrix of structural relations between covariates and latent constructs).

After laying out some of these basics of the univariate multilevel regression model, we move on to generalizations that are increasingly common in behavioral sciences research by building a series of two-level models that set the stage for the development of a series of multivariate generalizations that are presented in subsequent chapters. This chapter provides a template for those that follow. Throughout the remainder of the book, each chapter begins with a conceptual overview, and then, through examples, we develop the relevant mathematical models, consider specific programming issues encountered when setting up the models with real data, and, finally, interpret the actual output generated and offer further possibilities for extension.

Overview of Multilevel Regression Models

Our guiding schema in Table 1.1 of Chapter 1 segments modeling choices into four discrete cells. Traditional single-level univariate models such as ordinary least squares (OLS) regression or ANOVA are limited in the ways in which data from multiple levels of analysis can be incorporated. Typically in these single-level models, data from subordinate levels of analysis are aggregated to higher levels or, alternatively, higher-level data are assigned as characteristics of the lower-level observations under study. As we developed in Chapter 2, each of these approaches can present statistical problems associated with either aggregation bias or noninde-pendence of observations. As importantly, both of these approaches for dealing with hierarchical data structures miss important conceptual opportunities to cap-ture potentially important cross-level interactions that enable the assessment of the effect of the organization on the individual or vice versa.

Multilevel regression is typically used in research situations where the con-cern is in explaining variation in a single outcome at two or more levels due to the direct effects of predictors included at different levels of a data hierarchy. The dependent variable is directly observed (as opposed to being a latent con-struct measured by several observed indicators), and the independent variables are hypothesized to affect the outcomes directly, as opposed to more complex for-mulations (e.g., path models), which may include both direct and indirect effects. Incorporating measurement error on outcomes or predictors, as well as examining possible mediating effects between a predictor and an outcome variable, features of the SEM framework, are not common to the typical univariate multilevel model. While these features can be addressed, they require more complex multilevel mod-els that represent extensions of this basic multilevel formulation.

The basic random effects, or univariate multilevel regression, approach for examining hierarchical data structures therefore predates the appearance of the SEM approach for examining multilevel data structures by a few years, owing to the relative simplicity of decomposing the variance associated with a single univariate outcome across a number of groups and individuals. In contrast, the SEM approach is broadly defined to investigate the specification and testing of a wide variety of models that can include latent variables with multiple observed indicators and more complex relationships between predictors and outcomes including direct and indirect effects. The approach is based on the examination of covariance structures requiring a set of matrix equations, and the software tradi-tionally required input statements that specified the model in terms of these several matrices. The multivariate formulation of SEM lent itself to large data sets with complete data at a single level of analysis.

One of the key early challenges in examining multilevel covariance structures was dealing with groups of differing sample sizes. Maximum likelihood estimation procedures for SEM at the time required balanced groups and relatively large samples for efficient estimation. This presented a considerable number of problems in working with typical multilevel data structures that might not have many individuals within groups (e.g., 20 or 30) but a relatively large number of groups (e.g., 100–200). Since summary covariance matrices are constructed from a single sample size, for multilevel modeling it would prove challenging to construct a separate covariance matrix for each group consisting of a different within-group sample size.

As we noted, however, this problem was resolved with the introduction of FIML to SEM, which facilitated the specification of a wider variety of multilevel models including those with random slopes. For estimating two-level models, for example, we can decompose the population covariance structure into separate within-group and between-group covariance matrices.[1] The decomposition of the sample data can be used to specify and test separate models for the within-group and between-group covariance structures. The application of FIML estimation to multilevel SEM, which relies on the raw data rather than just the summary covariance matrices, has facilitated estimating models when there are different numbers of individuals within each cluster by including them in a manner similar to including individuals with incomplete data in standard SEM analyses using ML estimation. The clusters are treated as the unit of analysis and the individuals within the clusters are treated as "variables," which allows the differing numbers of individuals within each cluster to be incorporated into the estimation procedure. As we noted, FIML estimation also allows random slopes to be incorporated into the analysis.

Building a Model to Explain Employee Morale

As we laid out in Chapter 2, there is a logical progression common to the development of all multilevel regression analyses. First, the researcher examines the variance in an outcome, Y, with special attention to the distribution of this variance within and between level-2 units. Second, attention is paid to development of a level-1 random-intercept model. Third, slopes of theoretical interest are examined to determine the amount of variation that exists across higher-level units. Finally, models are developed using higher-level predictors in an effort to explain between-unit variation in parameters discovered in previous stages. As we develop a series of multilevel models, it should become clear that at each stage of this progression there are a number of decisions that predetermine choices at subsequent stages.

Consider an example. What if a researcher were interested in employee morale across departments within a large firm? Think about the situation where the researcher has data on employees and the departments in which they are nested. In a traditional OLS regression analysis where one is interested in employee morale differences across departments, a common approach would be to simply aggregate all of the employee data to the department level and to make department-level comparisons from there. This obviously changes the focal outcome from actual employee morale within each department to average departmental performance—potentially creating a very different substantive focus than was intended. Moreover, this approach also drastically reduces employee variation on the outcome of interest and can lead to significant over- or underestimation of the associations of interest. This approach therefore can be both conceptually and statistically problematic.

The other strategy to enable an OLS regression analysis would be to assign departmental characteristics to employees, thereby arriving at single-level data structure to develop the model. Here the higher-level characteristics are brought down to the lower level to create a single level of analysis. Aside from the obvious conceptual compromises, this approach threatens a key assumption of the traditional regression model: independence of observations. In other words, since all departmental characteristics are the same for each member of the separate units, the values on these observations are dependent upon some shared characteristic—namely departmental membership. There may also be any number of individual characteristics that are in turn associated with department membership. The result of this strategy is often an underestimation of standard errors, which ultimately yields a higher probability of rejecting a null hypothesis than is probabilistically warranted.

The assumptions necessary for single-level regression models to yield unbiased linear estimates are most realistic when data have been collected through simple random sampling. This sampling approach is, however, rarely used in large-scale research in the social and behavioral sciences. There are many good reasons for this. One obvious reason is that primary units of analysis—be they people, animals, or microscopic organisms—typically exist within the context of larger organizational structures. That might be employees within organizations, students within classrooms, animals within specific habitats, and so forth. So, in addition to the efficient data collection strategies that often involve some form of cluster sampling, the conceptual interests of researchers in these areas are often focused on the relationships between variables on a number of different levels of analysis. This, in turn, requires complex sampling schemes that capture and preserve theoretically important information from each of the levels of conceptual or theoretical interest. Whatever the motivation, the fact is that, increasingly, data collected in social, health, and behavioral science research are hierarchically structured.

In contrast to a single-level regression analysis, consider the nature of a multilevel analysis—one that uses data, for example, on j organizations, with n employees nested within each organization. In this example, we have two distinct levels of data: organizational (Level 2) and individual (Level 1). Fully specified multilevel linear models require one continuously measured outcome variable at the lowest level of data and at least one independent variable at each level. From these data, one can use the multilevel modeling framework to specify a hierarchical system of regression equations that exploit the multilevel data structure.

Multilevel modeling techniques involve first estimating a level-1 model (the individual level in the current example) *within* each level-2 unit and then estimating a series of *between*-unit models using the within-unit estimates as dependent variables. At the individual level, we can specify a regression equation that can be estimated within each higher, level-2 unit. In other words, as in traditional regression, the researcher assumes that a single model is appropriate across all level-2 units in the sample. At this stage, the primary difference between traditional regression and multilevel regression is that, in the multilevel case, the researcher conceptualizes the overall data structure differently, acknowledging the existence of higher-level units in which lower-level units are nested.

Consider an example in which we will focus on the relationship between employee morale and professional satisfaction. We are interested in determining the ways in which morale varies, after controlling for a range of individual-level factors, and the degree to which this variation is related to overall department morale and a host of department characteristics. The data used here include information for the population of sales force employees at 15 multinational corporations. Included in the sample are 13,189 employees from 165 sales departments in these corporations. Questions guiding the analysis are as follows:

1. How does employee satisfaction with pay affect morale?
2. Does the level of departmental pay moderate the relationship between satisfaction and morale at Level 1?

Table 3.1 contains descriptive statistics for these files. The level-1 (individual) data contains the outcome variable, morale, measured on a scale of 0 to 40, with 40 indicating the highest level of morale (with a range of 11 to 40 shown in the table). There is an individual-level satisfaction measure (*Satpay*), which is measured on a 0–16 scale (with range from 0 to 16). There are two dummy variables capturing *gender* (female, coded 1) and *race/ethnicity* (white coded 1, other coded 0) and a weighting variable (*Lev1wt*). The level-2 variable predictor (*Pctbelow*) is

TABLE 3.1 Descriptive Statistics

	N	Minimum	Maximum	Mean	Std. Deviation
Departments					
Pctbelow	165	2.40	82.90	27.091	15.514
Individuals					
satpay	13189	0	16	8.882	3.415
morale	13189	11	40	26.306	6.192
female	13189	0	1	0.486	0.500
white	13189	0	1	0.446	0.497

continuous and captures the percentage of sales departments earning less, on average, than the focal department. There is also a level-2 sample weight (*Lev2wt*).

In Figure 3.1 (and Table 3.2) we provide a small subset of the data showing the variation in intercepts (where the lines cross the Y axis) and slopes.

TABLE 3.2 Sample of Predicted Random Intercepts and Slopes

	B morale	*Satpay Slope*
1	26.77	1.28
2	25.75	1.13
3	27.48	1.13
4	23.79	1.26
5	27.63	1.25
6	24.47	1.14
7	25.11	1.1
8	27.81	1.2
9	26.3	1.27
10	26.98	1.2
11	27.16	1.11
Total *N*	11	11

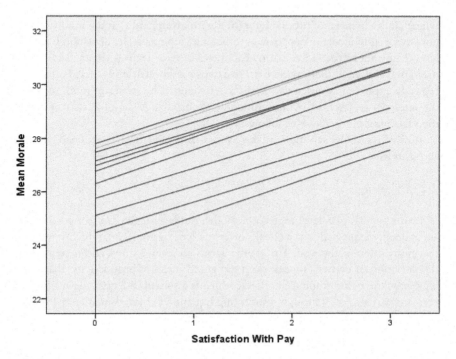

FIGURE 3.1 Random slopes.

As outlined in the first section of this chapter, there are three main steps involved in a hierarchical analysis. In the first step, the variance in the outcome is partitioned into its within-and between-unit components to provide a sense of the proportion of variance at each level and to provide an initial unadjusted estimate of the outcome. A second step involves developing and estimating a level-1 model and testing for any theorized random effects in level-1 parameters across level-2 units. The development and estimation of a level-2 model constitutes a third step. Level-2 models may be specified for a random level-1 intercept, as well as any randomly or nonrandomly varying level-1 parameter in the model.

Model 1: One-Way ANOVA Model

A first step before developing a multilevel regression model is to determine the variation in an outcome that lies within and between levels. This is accomplished through the specification of a **one-way ANOVA model** (alternatively referred to as the "no model" or "null model") in which no level-1 or level-2 variables are used. In this initial one-way ANOVA, or "no predictors" model, an individual's score (Y_{ij}) can be thought of as the sum of the individual cluster mean and an individual-specific deviation as follows:

$$Y_{ij} = \beta_{0j} + \varepsilon_{ij}, \tag{3.1}$$

where β_{0j} is the mean of productivity for the jth group, and ε_{ij} is the residual component for individual i in department j (that is, ε_{ij} represents the deviation from the level-2 unit mean for individual i). Each level-1 error term is assumed to have a mean of 0 and a constant variance σ^2. In a two-level model, level-1 fixed effects are typically expressed as unstandardized β coefficients. The subscript j indicates that the intercept represents the mean outcome for groups. At Level 2, we can model the variability in intercepts as follows:

Between groups, variation in the average intercept (β_{0j}) is assumed to vary across units:

$$\beta_{0j} = \gamma_{00} + u_{0j}. \tag{3.2}$$

In the typical two-level regression model, the level-2 fixed-effect coefficients are generally expressed as the Greek lowercase letter gamma (γ), which represents the mean value of the level-1 outcome across all level-2 units, and u_{0j} represents the deviation of cluster j's mean from the grand mean of productivity; that is, u_{0j} represents the random intercept effect, which is assumed to have a mean of 0 and constant variance σ^2. Through substituting Equation 3.2 into Equation 3.1 for β_{0j}, we arrive at a single equation, which can be written as

$$Y_{ij} = \gamma_{00} + u_{0j} + \varepsilon_{ij}, \tag{3.3}$$

where ε_{ij} is the level-1 residual variance and u_{0j} is the level-2 random effect, and γ_{00} is the grand mean. The null model therefore provides an estimated mean productivity score for all organizations. It also provides a partitioning of the variance between Level 1 (ε_{ij}) and Level 2 (u_{0j}). We will continue to use this notation in this chapter, in order to be consistent with commonly used notation in the two-level multilevel regression model. We note, however, that the Mplus notation is slightly different, owing that the typical SEM program makes use of several different matrices to specify level-2 means and within- and between-group fixed effects, residuals, and covariance parameters. We will develop this notation further beginning in Chapter 4.

Model 1 Statements

We next provide the **model syntax file** for the one-way ANOVA model. Two-level regression models can be easily specified using the Mplus syntax. Mplus also has a model generator. It is useful in specifying the preliminary steps in producing model statements (i.e., title, variables, format, single- or multilevel model). At present, however, it does not generate the model commands for the two-level models that we specify. Readers desiring further introduction to the syntax approach (or the Mplus language generator) can access the *Mplus 7 User's Guide* (Muthén & Muthén, 1998–2012), which is available in pdf format online at the authors' website (www.statmodel.com). The user's guide is very helpful in terms of the language used to specify the many different types of models that can be developed, the estimation options available, and the Mplus language statement required to specify models. We can specify the lines using capital letters or lowercase spelling (or a combination of both).

```
TITLE:       Model 1: Two-level (null) regression model;
DATA:        FILE IS: C:\ Mplus\ch3new.dat;
             Format is 5f8.0,3f8.2;
VARIABLE:    Names are deptid morale satpay female white pctbelow lev1wt
             lev2wt;
             Usevariables are deptid morale;
             Cluster is deptid;
             Between = ;
             Within = ;
ANALYSIS:    TYPE=Twolevel;
Model:       %Between%
             morale;
             %Within%
             morale;
OUTPUT:      Sampstat Tech1;
```

Each Mplus input file includes a TITLE command, a DATA command, a VARIABLE command, an ANALYSIS command (which includes estimation method and model specification), and an OUTPUT command. These appear at the far left of the typical input file as shown in the textbox. Commands must be one to a line and have a colon following the command. With the exception of the TITLE command (where inclusion of a semicolon at the end is optional), a semicolon is used to indicate that the statement has ended. Commands, options, and option settings can be shortened to four or more letters. The statements that comprise an input file can contain uppercase and lowercase letters; however, the statements cannot exceed more than 90 columns. Therefore, a statement may require more than one line to complete (e.g., such as defining the variables that appear in the data set). There are a few key words that indicate the specification of models (e.g., Is, Are, =, By, On). Comments can be placed anywhere within the input file but must be preceded with an exclamation mark (!), which signals the program to ignore the information that follows.

The TITLE command allows the user to identify the type of model being examined, its number in a series of models being developed, or other information that helps identify its key features. We labeled the first model as "Model1 null" to identify it as the first model in a series of models that will follow. The DATA statement provides information about where the file is located (File is) as well as how many columns each variable takes up in the data matrix. We note that with Windows 7 it is often best to create a file folder to hold Mplus input and data files outside of the Program Files folder where the Mplus program is typically installed. Input file examples in this book reference a folder named "Mplus" residing on the C: hard drive of the computer. Data need to be formatted as an ASCII file with the file extension of .dat or .txt. Data can formatted as fixed (i.e., referred to by the column length of each variable), or, if there are spaces between variables, it can be referred to as "free." Data in summary format (i.e., correlation or covariance matrix) require specification of the number of observations (Nobservations are).

The VARIABLE statement provides the labels for the variables (Names are) as well as which variables will be used in the current analysis (Usevariables are). In this case, we are only using the outcome variable (*Morale*) and the level-2 unit identifier (*Deptid*). We use this latter variable to provide the program with the level-2 clustering variable (Cluster = *Deptid*) and which variables are specified as individual-level variables and which are between-group variables. We do not have any predictors in this first model, but this will change in subsequent model building.

The ANALYSIS statement includes the type of model that is being specified—in this case, a two-level model with intercept only. Since there is only a random intercept, we can refer to the type of two-level model as follows (Type = Two-level). With unbalanced groups at Level 2, the default is ML estimation with standard errors that are robust to nonnormality (MLR). The between-groups portion of the model (%Between%) indicates that we are only asking for the variance components for *Morale*. Similarly, within groups (%Within%), the model specifies the variance in *Morale* that is within groups. Either level can be specified first.

Finally, the OUTPUT statement indicates that we are requesting sample statistics (Sampstat) and technical output (Tech1), which will provide the information about where each parameter is located within the matrix specification of Mplus. This is useful in understanding how many effects are to be estimated and where they will be found within the various matrices used to specify the two-level models in Mplus.

Model 1 Output

This initial "no predictors" model yields a number of important pieces of information. First, the null model provides an estimated mean morale score for all departments. Second, this model provides a partitioning of total variation in morale scores between Level 1 (ε_{ij}) and Level 2 (u_{0j}). Third, the null model provides a measure of dependence within each level-2 unit by way of the intraclass correlation, ρ. Fourth, a measure of the **reliability** of each department's mean morale score can be estimated. Finally, fifth, the model provides the means for a formal test of the hypothesis that all departments have the same mean morale scores.

Table 3.3 provides the variance decomposition for the outcome (or outcomes), which is provided in the initial Mplus ML estimated within and between group covariance matrices. From this output, we have all of the information necessary to determine the proportion of variance at each level of the outcome, Y. The variance components produced in this step can be used to create a measure of within level-2 unit dependence, which is determined by calculating the intraclass correlation ρ with knowledge of variance components σ_B^2 and σ_W^2 from Equation 3.4:

$$\rho = \frac{\sigma_B^2}{\left(\sigma_B^2 + \sigma_W^2\right)}. \tag{3.4}$$

Using the estimates in Table 3.2 and Equation 3.4, we can determine the within-department dependency, or intraclass correlation as follows:

$5.363/(5.363 + 33.302) = 5.363/38.665 = 0.139.$

In our data, the intraclass correlation is 0.139, or, in other words, roughly 13.9% of the total variance in morale scores is associated with departments as opposed to

TABLE 3.3 Estimated Variance Components Within and Between Departments

Parameter		Estimate	SE	Est./SE	Sig.
Within		33.302	0.595	55.995	0.000
Intercept [u_{0j}]	Variance	5.363	0.608	8.817	0.000

individuals. The intraclass correlation can also be considered as the correlation in outcomes for any two individuals in the same unit. Of course, the largest proportion of variance in morale scores is associated with individuals rather than departments.

Another important piece of information provided is the fixed-effect estimate of the grand mean of employees' morale scores. In Table 3.4 we have summarized the model's fixed effect intercept, which is estimated as 26.428 (SE = 0.189), as well as the ratio of the estimate to its standard error (Est./SE), which provides a test of the hypothesis that the mean is 0.0 ($p < 0.001$). Even though the test is statistically significant, the test regarding the intercept is generally of little interest, since we would expect the intercept describing individuals' average morale to be considerably larger than zero.

As we have established through the intraclass correlation, mean morale scores will vary from department to department. The reliability of the sample mean for any department as an estimate for its population mean can also be assessed with information gleaned from the variance components. Because sample sizes within each j are apt to differ, this reliability will vary across level-2 units. Reliability within any particular unit can be estimated with:

$$\lambda = \frac{\sigma_B^2}{\left[\sigma_B^2 + (\sigma_W^2/n_j)\right]}. \tag{3.5}$$

From the descriptive statistics generated in Table 3.1, we see that the within-level-2 unit n (n_j) ranges from 14 to 202. Using these within-group ns, we can calculate the range of reliabilities across the 165 departments in the sample. For example, using Equation 3.5, we can determine that the within-unit reliability for the department represented by 14 employees is:

$5.363/[(5.363 + (33.302/14)] = 0.693.$

This is contrasted with the department represented by 202 employees in which the within-unit reliability is much higher:

$5.363/[(5.363 + (33.302/202)] = 0.970.$

To summarize, the intraclass correlation provides a sense of the degree to which differences in outcome Y exist between level-2 units; that is, it helps answer the question of the existence or nonexistence of meaningful differences in outcomes between

TABLE 3.4 One-Way ANOVA or "Null Model"

Parameter	Estimate	S.E.	Est./SE	Sig.
Intercept	26.428	0.189	139.945	0.000

the level-2 units. These differences in outcomes determine the extent to which the data are hierarchically differentiated and, by extension, encourage or discourage the development of helpful level-2 models to explain the variance in Y. These estimated differences are only helpful if they are accepted as reliable indicators of real differences among departments' population means. Within-department reliability estimates provide the analyst a means by which this assumption can be checked.

The results from the one-way ANOVA model suggest that the development of a multilevel model is warranted. It is important to note also that we have a sufficient number of level-2 units to provide stability in estimation (see our discussion of power in Chapter 2).

Model 2: Level-1 Random-Intercept Model

With substantive theory as a guide, the analyst should now focus on developing a thoughtfully specified level-1 or **unconditional**[2] **model**. As with developing a model using traditional OLS regression, the analyst's primary concern is whether or not any predictor X_q should be included based on its contribution to explaining variance in the outcome. But unlike OLS, where the intercept and slope coefficients are fixed, multilevel regression requires the analyst to determine whether coefficients should be specified as fixed, random, or nonrandomly varying.

A good strategy for developing a level-1 model is to begin by testing the impacts of a minimal set of theoretically important predictors with fixed-slope coefficients, that is, by assuming the effect of each of these individual-level variables is homogeneous across departments. After specifying a random-intercept level-1 model, hypotheses concerning heterogeneity of individual slope coefficients can be tested. We again stress the importance of theory as a guide for the model development process. Without such a guide, these models can quickly become oversaturated and obscure information necessary for testing hypotheses related to research questions. For example, the absence of substantive theory may encourage the use of an overspecified, random-slopes-and-intercept model that the data are simply unable to support. Given the data requirements for estimating multilevel models, parsimony should be a key principle in model development.

At Level 1 in our example, we want to test for relationships between morale scores, satisfaction with pay, gender, and race. Our unconditional random-intercept level-1 model is:

$$Y_{ij} = \beta_{0j} + \beta_{1j} satpay_{ij} + \beta_{2j} female_{ij} + \beta_{3j} white_{ij} + \varepsilon_{ij},$$ (3.6)

where the implied level-2 model is:

$$\beta_{0j} = \gamma_{00} + u_{0j}.$$ (3.2, repeated)

$$\beta_{1j} - \beta_{3j} = \gamma_{10} - \gamma_{30}.$$ (3.7)

We note that Equation 3.7 implies that each slope coefficient for the within-group predictors is fixed rather than randomly varying at the group level. This is accomplished by not specifying a random variance for each predictor at Level 2 (i.e., $u_{1j} - u_{3j}$).

As the level-2 model above treats the intercept as an outcome, it is very important that the level-1 model yield an interpretable value for β_{0j}. The intercept in traditional OLS models is interpreted as the value of the outcome variable when all predictors ($X_{1 \ldots q}$) are set to zero (0). This interpretation is adequate when all Xs have a meaningful 0 point, as in the case of dummy variables or continuous measures that have scales bounding 0. Often, however, this condition does not hold, and, as a result, the intercepts are of little interpretative value to the analyst. Because multilevel models treat lower-level intercepts and slopes as outcomes, it is critical that these variables have realistic numerical meanings. For this reason, level-1 variables are often transformed through various forms of "centering," which yields meaningful 0 values for each variable and, hence, each intercept.

In cases where X values of 0 are not meaningful, such as satisfaction with pay (ranging from 0 to 16), the two of the most often used transformations are *grand-mean centering* and *group-mean centering*. Grand-mean centering ($X_{ij} - \bar{X}..$) of level-1 variables is as follows:

$$Y_{ij} = \beta_{0j} + \beta_{1j}\left(X_{ij} - \bar{X}..\right) + \varepsilon_{ij} , \tag{3.8}$$

which provides an intercept (β_{0j}) that is interpreted as an "adjusted" mean for group j:

$$\beta_{0j} = \mu_{Y_j} - \beta_{1j}(X._j - \bar{X}..) . \tag{3.9}$$

Grand-mean centering effectively equalizes level-2 units on each X_q at Level 1—that is, units are adjusted for the differences among individuals.

In contrast, group-mean centering of level-1 predictors ($X_{ij} - \bar{X}._j$) yields an intercept that is interpreted as an unadjusted mean for group j:

$$\beta_{0j} = \mu_{Y_j} , \tag{3.10}$$

which suggests that the variance for the intercepts is simply the variance in level-2 units. In this centering strategy, the intercept represents the outcome for a subject whose value on X_{ij} is equal to the mean of her or his respective level-2 unit. This has the effect of emphasizing differences between level-2 units resulting from the composition of the lower-level units they contain, since the intercepts are unadjusted for such differences within the units. We illustrate differences in centering strategies with respect to the models we build at the end of this chapter.

In the current example, we have chosen to center the level-1 variables on the grand mean of the sample. By doing this, we adjust β_{0j} for differences in departments' distributions of females, Caucasians, and level of satisfaction with pay. In other words, we can now say, if every department were the same in terms of the level-1 characteristics we have specified, the expected value for the mean morale score of any department would be β_{0j}. As we will show, this "equalization" of individual-level characteristics across departments substantially impacts the variance in department means. Of course, this would not be the case if we chose to center on department means rather than the grand mean.

Model 2 Statements

To estimate this model, we only need to make a few basic changes to our first model. We add the three within-group predictors to our Usevariables command line. We also note that they are "Within" predictors. We use a "Define" command to grand-mean center the three within-group predictors. To note that the predictors are grand-mean centered, we can either write "grandmean" in parentheses or shorten it to "grand":

Define: Center Satpay Female White (grandmean);

In the same way, we could write group-mean centering as "groupmean" or "group." We discuss centering strategies in more detail in the last section of this chapter. Finally, we specify the within-group regression model using the "on" command (i.e., short for "regressed on"). We can see that the outcome *Morale* is regressed on the three predictors (*satpay, female, white*).

```
TITLE:       Model 2: Level-1 random intercept model;
DATA:        FILE IS: C:\ Mplus\ch3new.dat;
             Format is 5f8.0,3f8.2;
VARIABLE:    Names are deptid morale satpay female white pctbelow lev1wt
             lev2wt;
             Usevariables are deptid morale satpay female white;
             Cluster is deptid;
             Between = ;
             Within = satpay female white;
Define:      Center satpay female white (grand);
ANALYSIS:    TYPE= Twolevel;
Model:       %Between%
             morale;
             %Within%
             morale on satpay female white;
OUTPUT:      SAMPSTAT TECH1;
```

TABLE 3.5 Level-1 Random-Intercept Model

Parameter	Estimate	S.E.	Est./SE	Sig.
Intercept	26.430	0.114	232.784	0.000
satpay	1.201	0.014	85.725	0.000
female	0.001	0.063	0.011	0.991
white	0.916	0.082	11.181	0.000

TABLE 3.6 Variance Components

Estimates of Covariance Parameters

Parameter		Estimate	S.E.	Est./SE	Sig.
Residual		17.544	0.288	60.852	.000
Intercept [u_{0j}]	Variance	1.851	0.231	8.029	.000

Model 2 Output

The relevant output from our level-1 random-intercept model appears in Table 3.5. From the fixed-effect output, we can see that the value for mean morale scores, adjusted for all level-1 characteristics in the model, is 26.430. This value is interpreted as the average of the mean adjusted-department morale—where each department's average has been adjusted for differences in the level-1 variables in the model. This can be compared to the unadjusted average from the null model of 26.428 reported in Table 3.4. Recall that we specified this model to allow this intercept to vary across departments. In Table 3.6, the ratio of the estimate to its standard error is significant, which indicates that, even after equalizing departments on the level-1 characteristics specified in our model, significant variation in these mean values still remains across departments. A more precise estimate of the variance remaining can be determined through the intraclass correlation. From Equation 3.5 we find that

$$1.851/(1.851 + 17.544) = 0.095,$$

indicating that the total variance between departments is diminished by about 32% relative to the intraclass correlation for the no-predictors model, when we control for the factors included in our model at Level 1. This is a direct function of the reduction in level-2 variance that renders departments more homogeneous in terms of the outcome. In other words, much of the variation in means across departments can be attributed to differences in pay satisfaction, gender, and race among employees in those departments. However, we also find that even after controlling for these differences, significant variation in means continues to exist across departments ($p < 0.001$).

In contrast with the intercept, which we specified as random, the slope coefficients in our level-1 model are fixed—that is, we are initially assuming that the effects of each variable are the same across departments. As in ordinary linear regression, the statistical significance of individual parameters is determined by a t-score resulting from dividing the parameter estimate by its standard error. In this case, we have reasonable faith in the standard error estimates because of the number of departments in the sample.

Among our level-1 predictors, females, on average, report the same level of morale as men ($\beta_{2j} = 0.001, p = 0.991$). Caucasian employees have morale scores 0.916 points higher than their nonwhite peers ($p < 0.05$). Finally, on average, a one-point increase in satisfaction with level of pay is associated with a 1.201 increase in employee morale scores ($p < 0.001$). This latter parameter is of special interest to us, and it, along with adjusted mean morale scores, becomes the focus of our next model.

Model 3: Specifying a Level-1 Random Slope

Our research question concerned a possible association between departmental pay levels and the morale of individual employees, net of a number of other individual level characteristics such as gender, race, and satisfaction. Implicit in this question is the assumption that morale varies from department to department. We observed in the level-1 model that was just estimated that, on average, the employee morale score was estimated to be roughly 26.4 points on a scale of 0 to 40. We also observed that mean morale scores, adjusted for gender, race, and satisfaction varied significantly from department to department. Given these observations, we now want to test the implicit proposition that satisfaction with pay, a measure tightly associated with morale, will also vary from department to department.

We next consider the results from this test. The level-1 model remains the same as before, but the level-2 model is now represented by two equations:

$$\beta_{0j} = \gamma_{00} + u_{0j} \tag{3.2, repeated}$$

$$\beta_{1j} = \gamma_{10} + u_1, \tag{3.11}$$

where β_{0j} represents the randomly varying intercept, while β_{1j} represents the randomly varying slope parameter for satisfaction with pay (*Satpay*).

Model 3 Statements

We also need only make a couple of changes in the input statements for Model 3. First, the analysis statement must be changed to accommodate this new type of model that is being specified—that is, a two-level model with random slope. If there is a random slope included, the model is referred to as follows (Type = Twolevel random). Second, within groups (%Within%), we must specify that *Morale* is regressed on *Female* and *White* as fixed effects (i.e., effects that do not vary at Level 2). Third, the random slope effect of *Morale* regressed on *Satpay* is indicated in Mplus language by the following line:

S | Morale on Satpay:

```
TITLE:       Model 3: Specifying a random slope;
DATA:        FILE IS: C:\ Mplus\ch3new.dat;
             Format is 5f8.0,3f8.2;
VARIABLE:    Names are deptid morale satpay female white pctbelow lev1wt
             lev2wt;
             Usevariables are deptid morale satpay female white;
             Cluster is deptid;
             Between = ;
             Within = satpay female white;
Define:      Center satpay female white (grand);
ANALYSIS:    Type = Twolevel random;
Model:       %Between%
             morale S;
             S with morale;
             %Within%
             morale on female white;
             S | morale on satpay;
OUTPUT:      SAMPSTAT TECH1;
```

Finally, at Level 2, we add the variance estimate for the random slope (S).

Model 3 Output

The output in Table 3.7 contains the relevant output from this specification. The fixed effects are similar to the previous model, so we turn our attention to the variance components. In Table 3.8, the hypothesis tests for the variance components indicate that significant variation still exists across departments both in terms of the intercept (average morale scores) ($Z = 8.082$, $p < 0.001$) and the slope for satisfaction with pay ($Z = 2.713$, $p = 0.014$). We can therefore reject the null hypothesis that the relationship between pay satisfaction and morale is constant

TABLE 3.7 Level-1 Random Intercept and Slope Model

Parameter	Estimate	S.E.	Est./SE	Sig.
Intercept	26.436	0.115	229.317	0.000
satpay	1.197	0.014	85.873	0.000
female	0.003	0.063	0.052	0.959
white	0.914	0.082	11.186	0.000

TABLE 3.8 Variance Components

		Estimates of Covariance Parameters			
Parameter		Estimate	S.E.	Est./SE	Sig.
Residual		17.455	0.292	59.829	0.000
Intercept + slope	Morale	1.861	0.230	8.082	0.000
	Covariance	0.006	0.019	0.340	0.734
	Satpay	0.008	0.003	2.713	0.007

across departments. We note the covariance between morale and pay satisfaction was not significant ($Z = 0.340, p > 0.10$).

Model 4: Explaining Variation in the Level-2 Intercept and Slope

Having established that variation in the intercept and slope parameters exists across departments, we now turn our attention to accounting for this variation. Is a department's overall pay level associated with its average morale level? We test this proposition by developing a level-2 intercept- and slopes-as-outcomes model. Again, the level-1 model remains the same as before:

$$Y_{ij} = \beta_{0j} + \beta_{1j}satpay_{ij} + \beta_{2j}female_{ij} + \beta_{3j}white_{ij} + \varepsilon_{ij}. \qquad \text{(3.6, repeated)}$$

The level-2 models are changed to include the level-2 characteristic of interest to us:

$$\beta_{0j} = \gamma_{00} + \gamma_{01}\text{pctbelow}_j + u_{0j}$$
$$\beta_{1j} = \gamma_{10} + \gamma_{11}\text{pctbelow}_j + u_{1j}, \qquad (3.12)$$

where *Pctbelow* represents the percentage of departments with average pay lower than department *j*.

Model 4 Statements

Again, we must make a couple of changes to the Mplus input file. First, we add the between-group variable (*pctbelow*) to the "Usevariables" command line. We also must specify that it is a between-group variable. Second, the between-groups portion of the model (%Between%) indicates that *Morale* is regressed on *pctbelow*, again defined by the key word "On" in Mplus language, and the random *Satpay-Morale* slope (S) is also regressed on *pctbelow*. The rest of the model can remain the same.

TITLE: Model 4: Explaining variation in the level-2 intercept and slope;
DATA: FILE IS: C:\ Mplus\ch3new.dat;
              Format is 5f8.0, 3f8.2;
VARIABLE: Names are deptid morale satpay female white pctbelow lev1wt
              lev2wt;
              Usevariables are deptid morale satpay female white pctbelow;
              Cluster is deptid;
              Between = pctbelow;
              Within = satpay female white;
Define: Center satpay female white pctbelow (grandmean);
ANALYSIS: Twolevel random;
Model: %Between%
              morale S on pctbelow;
              S with morale;
              %Within%
              morale on female white;
              S | Morale on satpay;
OUTPUT: SAMPSTAT TECH1;

Model 4 Output

The output from Model 4 appears in Table 3.9. Focusing first on the estimates for the equation modeling the intercept (β_{0j}), we see that level of departmental income has a small negative impact on average morale scores in each department. On average, a one-point increase in the percentage of departments with pay below department j is associated with a 0.026-point decrease in average morale scores, after controlling for salient employee-level characteristics. In short, employees in departments with higher overall pay report higher levels of morale, regardless of their satisfaction with their own pay level.

TABLE 3.9 Final Intercept- and Slopes-as-Outcomes Model

	Estimates of Fixed Effects			
Parameter	Estimate	S.E.	Est./SE	Sig.
Morale Intercept	26.362	0.113	233.072	0.000
pctbelow	−0.026	0.007	−3.574	0.000
female	0.005	0.063	0.074	0.941
white	0.910	0.082	11.064	0.000
Satpay Intercept	1.196	0.014	86.310	0.000
satpay *pctbelow	0.001	0.001	1.416	0.157

TABLE 3.10 Final Intercept- and Slopes-as-Outcomes Model

		Estimate	*S.E.*	*Est./SE*	*Sig.*
Parameter					
Residual		17.456	0.292	59.789	0.000
Intercept + slope	Morale	1.701	0.218	7.810	0.000
	Covariance	0.014	0.018	0.776	0.438
	Satpay	0.007	0.003	2.455	0.014

Estimates of Covariance Parameters

Examining the estimates for the equation modeling the level–1 satisfaction of pay effect, (β_{1j}), the results indicate that this effect is not influenced by the overall pay level of the department $(0.001, p = 0.157)$. Thus, in terms of morale, employees in better-paid departments tend to be just as sensitive to levels of satisfaction with their own pay as their counterparts in departments that are relatively less well paid. Again, this is after controlling for the individual characteristics of gender and race.

The hypothesis tests in Table 3.10 continue to indicate that significant variation in parameter estimates exists across departments, although as we might expect the variance components for the random intercept and for the random *Satpay* slope are now somewhat smaller. In cases where the analyst is able to specify powerful level-2 models, the Z statistics associated with these variance components are rendered nonsignificant. This would indicate there is little level-2 variance left to be accounted for by further analysis.

While the Z coefficients indicate that significant variability in the random parameters remains, it is useful to calculate the proportion of variance explained in each of the variance components of the model. This is accomplished by comparing the initial values of each of the components with those in the final model. By comparing the initial variance estimates (Table 3.3) with those reported above in Table 3.10, one can compute a proportional reduction of error measure similar to R^2 in regression. Within groups, the proportion of variance explained in mean morale scores across these models is $(33.302 - 17.456)/33.302 = 0.476$ (or 47.6%). Between groups, our final model accounted for nearly 70% of the initial between-department variance in morale scores $[(5.363 - 1.701)/5.363 = 0.683]$.

Centering Predictors

In this final section, we discuss centering the predictors in a little more detail. In multilevel models, it is important that the fixed effects can be readily interpreted in relation to the proposed goals of the research. Centering decisions concern how to rescale the explanatory variables so that the intercept can be defined most advantageously. Although there is no one correct decision in every instance, centering decisions should be made primarily on the basis of the conceptual questions under investigation (Hofmann & Gavin, 1998). Centering provides the expected value of an outcome Y when the covariate is equal to some designated value of theoretical interest (e.g., the unit mean, the overall sample mean).

Mean centering is most commonly used in multilevel studies (e.g., grand mean, group mean). There are, however, other options (e.g., the median, the within-group standard deviation of the within-group coefficient of variation) for centering variables (Plewis, 1989). We note that centering is also required in some situations in order to achieve a solution that converges (i.e., does not produce an error message). Where there are widely different means and variances across groups, it may be necessary to center the raw estimates in order to achieve model convergence (Hox, 2010).

As we have noted, alternative centering strategies can change the values of some parameters in a model. In Table 3.11, we illustrate the effects of different centering strategies where there is a random intercept only (Model 1) and where there is a random intercept and random slope (Model 2). We used the same data set from the extended example in this chapter with a continuous level-1 predictor (*Satpay*) to illustrate the effects of the centering strategies on model parameters. In this case, the natural metric for *Satpay* ranges from 0 to 16, with a mean of 8.882 and standard deviation of 3.415. Model 1 illustrates the effects of different centering strategies for a random intercept and *fixed* level-1 slope. As the table suggests, the natural metric estimate of *Satpay* and the grand-mean centered estimate (*GMSatpay*) are the same ($\gamma = 1.22$, $p < 0.01$); however, the location of the respective Y intercepts differs. The raw metric produces a Y intercept that represents satisfaction with salary for the lowest individual in the sample (which was coded Satpay = 0). For this individual, the expected morale level would be 15.60.

Grand-mean centering (i.e., where the grand mean is subtracted from individuals' levels of pay satisfaction) often facilitates the interpretation of a multilevel model, since it results in an intercept that can be interpreted as the expected value of Y when the predictor is at its grand mean value (0). The standard deviation, however, remains in the original metric. In this case, the original grand mean for *Satpay* (8.882) is rescaled to be zero, but the standard deviation remains 3.415. Where level-1 predictors are all grand-mean centered, the solution provides a level-2 intercept that has been adjusted for the level-1 predictors. One related advantage of grand-mean centering is that it helps the analyst interpret the variances for the intercept and slopes as the expected variance when all explanatory variables are equal to zero, that is, the expected variances for the "average" individual (Hox, 2010).

In contrast, standardizing a continuous predictor ($\bar{X} = 0$, $SD = 1$) has the same effect on the intercept as grand-mean centering, but it also changes the metric of the predictor by transforming the standard deviation from its original metric (in this case, 3.415) to be equal to 1.0. More specifically, when the continuous predictor is standardized (i.e., a z-score), it is in standard deviation units. Therefore, as in Model 1, the predictor's metric will be different from the grand-mean centered estimate ($\gamma = 1.22$); that is, the standardized estimate for *Zsatpay* is 4.16, suggesting that an increase in *Zsatpay* of $1 - SD$ would produce a 4.16 increase in morale.

In many cases, the uncentered or natural metric may be a logical choice, since for the natural metric the intercept is defined as the level of *Y* when *X* is zero (0.0). Some natural metric solutions, however, may have little practical importance in organizational studies (Kreft, de Leeuw, & Aiken, 1995). In the example in Table 3.11, there might be occasions where we prefer centering on the lowest individual in the sample. For example, if the lowest person in the sample had a Satpay score = 2, we could re-center that score to be equal to zero. Most often, it is convenient to center on the average level of the predictor in the sample. Importantly, we draw attention to the fact that for models with a random intercept only, solutions where the level-1 predictors are in their natural metrics, grand-mean

TABLE 3.11 The Effects of Different Centering Strategies

Variables	Satpay	ZSatpay	GMSatpay	GPSatpay	GPSatpay(1)
Model 1: Random Intercept					
Departments (N = 165)					
Intercept	15.60*	26.41*	26.41*	26.43*	10.01*
Mean satpay					1.85*
Individuals (N = 13,189)					
Fixed estimate	1.22*	4.16*	1.22*	1.21*	1.21*
Variance Components					
Level-2 variance	1.83*	1.83*	1.83*	5.65*	1.33*
Level-1 variance	17.73*	17.73*	17.73*	17.73*	17.73*
Parameters	4	4	4	4	5
-2 log likelihood	75705.30	75705.30	75705.30	75873.12	75660.82
Model 2: Random Slope					
Departments (N = 165)					
Intercept	15.64*	26.42*	26.42*	26.43*	9.88*
Mean satpay					1.86*
Random estimate	1.21*	4.14*	1.21*	1.20*	1.21*
Variance Components					
Level-2 slope	0.01*	0.10*	0.01*	0.01*	0.01*
Covariance	-0.07**	0.02	0.01	-0.03	0.02
Level-2 variance	2.42*	1.85*	1.85*	5.65*	1.33*
Level-1 variance	17.64*	17.64*	17.64*	17.63*	17.64*
Parameters	6	6	6	6	7
-2 log likelihood	75692.17	75692.17	75692.17	75857.34	75644.38

Note: Z = standardized; GM = grand-mean centered; GP = group-mean centered
*$p < 0.01$; **$p < 0.05$

centered, or standardized will produce equivalent models (i.e., in terms of deviance, or −2 log likelihood, and residual variances) as shown in Table 3.11 [for further discussion, see Hox (2010) or Raudenbush & Bryk, (2002)]. What this means is that the fit of the model is the same for raw metric, grand-mean, or standardized metrics when there is a random intercept.

Group-mean centering produces an intercept equal to the expected value of Y for an individual when x is equal to the group's mean. Unlike grand-mean centering, with group-mean centering, the unit means are *unadjusted* for differences among their members. Group-mean centering puts the attention more on relational advantages that some individuals may enjoy within their particular social group. It is important to emphasize that group-mean centered solutions are not the same as grand-mean or natural metric solutions. In contrast to the previous centering strategies, when we use group-mean centering of explanatory variables, the meaning of the model is changed (Hox, 2010). This is because group-mean centering separates the within-group and between-group portion of the predictor estimate; that is, the information concerning possible differences in the predictor across level-2 units is removed.

As Raudenbush and Bryk (2002) suggest, it is often desirable to group-mean center a predictor if the focus of the analysis is on producing an unbiased estimate of the within-group (level-1) effect, since group-mean centering results in a level-2 mean that is unadjusted for the level-1 predictor. If the analyst is interested in person-level variables (but where individuals are nested in groups), ignoring the nested structure of the data can lead to misleading results at Level 1 (Cronbach, 1976), since slope coefficients derived from the total covariance matrix (i.e., the covariance matrix based on the number of individuals in the study) will generally represent uninterpretable blends of their within-group and between-group estimates. Similarly, in this situation, the grand-mean centered estimates also represent a mix of the within-group slope and any difference in the slopes that might exist across groups (i.e., in the case where the slope varies randomly across groups), since the model with grand-mean centering actually involves both the individual estimates of X_{ij} and the level-2 mean of X as adjusted (Raudenbush & Bryk, 2002).

In Table 3.11, for the model with random intercept only (Model 1), we can observe that in the first model, the group-mean centered solution (*GPSatpay*) results in a similar intercept estimate (26.43), level-1 predictor ($\gamma = 1.21$), and level-1 variance (17.73) as the previous grand-mean model but different estimates of the level-2 intercept variance (5.65) and model −2 log likelihood (75873.12). We note that the level-2 intercept variance will typically be larger than in the previous solutions. This is because the level-2 intercepts in the group-centered solution are unadjusted, whereas the intercepts in the previous solutions are adjusted for the level-1 predictor. As Raudenbush and Bryk (2002) note, because mean *Satpay* is likely related to the intercept (and also the slope, as in Model 2), we might attempt to add a *Mean Satpay* variable to the level-2 model [as we do with *GPSatpay*(1) in the last column] in an effort to resolve the discrepancy in level-2 intercept variance between the previous centering solutions and the group-centered solution. Because group-mean centering results in a different type of model (i.e., by isolating the within-group portion of the estimate and removing the between-group differences in that portion of the estimate), however, one cannot simply add the mean for *Satpay* back at the group level (as in the last column of Table 3.11), since that results in adding more information that is not present in the raw scores (i.e., by adding one additional parameter to estimate). By adding another parameter, the model deviance will be smaller than the previous solutions for Model 1 (Raudenbush & Bryk, 2002). For example, in Table 3.11 we can observe for *GPSatpay*(1) that the −2LL estimate is the lowest of the previous four centering decisions (75660.82), reflecting the addition of the *Mean Satpay* parameter at Level 2.

Centering Predictors in Models With Random Slopes

Centering decisions can also be important in multilevel models where there are anticipated cross-level interactions, that is, where the analyst wishes to examine variability in slopes across groups by building a model with level-2 predictors to explain this variability. Grand-mean and group-mean centering approaches generally address different research questions, since grand mean centering puts the focus on level-2 relationships after adjustment for level-1 relationships. Moreover, the effects of level-2 predictors will be adjusted for differences between organizations in the mean of the *X* predictor (Raudenbush & Bryk, 2002). In contrast, group-mean centering is the better approach if the focus is on optimal estimation of level-1 effects that consider nesting, since group-mean centering removes confounding between-group effects in the level-1 predictors.

It is important to note that modeling random slopes at Level 2 introduces modeling cross-level interactions. Cross-level interactions refer to situations where level-2 variables are proposed to moderate the strength of level-1 relationships, such as the effect of individuals' satisfaction with salary (*Satpay*) on their morale. Cross-level interactions can actually be proposed as moderators of randomly varying level-1 slopes or as moderators of fixed within-group relationships. In this latter case, the slopes do vary from group to group, but rather than their variation being random, they vary as a function of the level-2 moderator (Raudenbush & Bryk, 2002). Cross-level interactions introduce another aspect to be considered—that is, the interpretation of the interaction. In regression models, the interpretation is typically the expected value of one predictor when the other one is equal to zero and vice versa (Hox, 2010). Therefore, we want to exercise some care in selecting a value for 0 that is meaningful and actually occurs in the data (Hox, 2010).

Given this, natural (or raw) metric solutions are often difficult to interpret, since the level of *Y* (i.e., the *Y* intercept) may fall outside of the range of individuals in the sample data when *X* is 0. In contrast, centering on the grand mean will produce an interaction coefficient interpreted as the effect of the first predictor on *Y* for individuals who are at the grand mean (0) on the other predictor. Grand-mean centering is one straightforward way to facilitate the interpretation of interactions. Group-mean centering is also appropriate where there are hypotheses involving interactions among level-1 variables, as in the case with cross-level interactions, since the level-2 variables proposed to moderate the level-1 relationship will be unaffected by adjustment within groups (as takes place in grand-mean centering).

In models where there is a randomly varying level-1 slope, different centering strategies will also produce different results. In Table 3.11, Model 2 indicates that the choice of centering will make a difference in estimating the level-2 intercept variance (when the standardized outcome *Zsatpay* is used), as well as the slope variance and covariance between the intercept and slope. As we noted previously, the variance of *Y* at Level 2 will typically be larger in group-mean models than in grand-mean or raw metric models, since the group means in the group-centered solution are unadjusted. The slope variance will also be different (i.e., generally larger in group-mean solutions), and we can observe that the covariance can be different across centering decisions when there is both a random intercept and slope. Because of our relatively large sample sizes, the estimation of the level-1 variance is almost the same in each instance. In such cases, centering generally does not make much difference (Raudenbush & Bryk, 2002). We again note in the last column of Model 2 that incorporating *mean Satpay* as a predictor in the between-department portion of the model does not solve the problem of the different estimates of slope variability produced by the different centering approaches. The extra parameter, however, again results in a better-fitting model.

In some situations, group-mean centering may be preferable to estimate slope heterogeneity properly (Raudenbush & Bryk, 2002). For example, when the level-1 sample size is small or moderate, or if the group mean of *X* varies across units, group-mean centering should be considered as a viable alternative if the focus of the analysis is to produce more robust estimates of unit-specific regression equations (Raudenbush & Bryk, 2002). Because grand-mean centered models produce an adjusted intercept for the level-1 predictors, in some cases (e.g., units that are very high or very low in mean *Satpay*), the adjusted means can be estimated with little accuracy. This happens because the adjusted mean for unit *j* represents the expected outcome for an individual in the department that is at the grand mean of *Satpay*, and if there are few individuals like this in a particular department, the department mean will be less reliably measured than for some other departments where a larger number of individuals have pay satisfaction levels that are at the grand mean in the sample (Raudenbush & Bryk, 2002). This can result in making the slope variability more homogeneous than it actually is and, therefore, can result in the underestimation of the slope variability at Level 2. As we noted, where sample sizes are large for any given level-2 unit, centering will not make much difference, as well as when the slope does not vary across level-2 units. We can see in this example that group-mean centering or grand-mean centering does not make too much difference in estimating the intercept for morale or the slope for *Satpay*. The centering decision, however, would make a difference in the size of the variance component at Level 2.

At the top of the data hierarchy (e.g., departments), the centering choices are not as critical as for predictors at lower levels (Raudenbush & Bryk, 2002). Usually it is convenient to center continuous variables at their grand means, as opposed to leaving them uncentered. We note that variables cannot be group centered at the highest level, since their "group" at that level is the level-2 sample of departments. Centering strategies are the same for dichotomous variables. Dummy-coded variables (0, 1) are often left in their natural metric, depending on the analyst's choice for the meaning of the reference group (coded 0) in the unit-level model. They can also be grand-mean or group centered. Dichotomous variables can also be effect coded (e.g., -1, $+1$), which results in a type of grand-mean centering.

Summary

We have shown, through the example used in this chapter, the ways in which the multilevel model is simply an extension of ordinary single-level regression. In the last chapter, we called attention to the numerous shortcomings of ordinary regression when faced with a hierarchical data structure (e.g., unit of analysis questions and dependence of observations within units). This chapter has demonstrated some of the advantages of working in a multilevel framework rather than the traditional single-level approach. Beyond the basic model we provide here, the mixed-modeling routines permit a range of other specification and tests (including residual analyses) that can be used to illustrate some of the more complex conceptual elements we introduced in this chapter.

We have provided the basics of two-level multilevel regression modeling through the development of a series of models to explain variability in a random intercept and slope across level-2 units. We illustrated model development by using the Mplus statistical software program. We paid considerable attention to the specification of Mplus input files and the interpretation of results. We also offered a fairly detailed consideration of how centering predictors can influence the interpretation of the model results.

Despite the clear advantages of multilevel mixed (or regression) models, limitations still remain. In the following chapters, we will extend the models we have worked with in Chapters 2 and 3 and consider structural equation modeling techniques that permit analysis of broader range of theoretical models and greater refinement of error specification. In the next chapter, we extend the basic two-level model to three levels and then also look at possible multivariate outcomes that can be specified within the mixed-model (or multilevel regression) framework. We cover some of the more complex specifications in subsequent chapters.

Notes

1. From a multilevel SEM perspective, the population covariance structure for individual i in cluster j would be

$$V(y_{ij}) = \Sigma_T = \Sigma_B + \Sigma_W. \tag{A3.1}$$

The within-group and between-group covariance structures can then be specified as the following:

$$\Sigma_W = \Lambda_W \Psi_W \Lambda'_W + \Theta_W$$
$$\Sigma_B = \Lambda_B \Psi_B \Lambda'_B + \Theta_B. \tag{A3.2}$$

The mean structure (specified at Level 2) is as follows:

$$\mu = \alpha_B + \Lambda_B \nu_B, \tag{A3.3}$$

where ν_B is a vector of latent factor means.
2. This level-1 model is often referred to as an unconditional model, that is, a level-1 model unconditional at Level 2.

References

Byrne, B. M. (2012). *Structural equation modeling with Mplus: Basic concepts, applications, and programming.* New York: Routledge Academic.

Cronbach, L. J. (1976). *Research in classrooms and schools: formulation of questions, designs and analysis.* Occasional Paper, Stanford Evaluation Consortium.

Heck, R. H. & Thomas, S. L. (2009). *An introduction to multilevel modeling techniques* (2nd ed.). New York: Routledge.

Hofmann, D. & Gavin, M. (1998). Centering decisions in hierarchical models. Theoretical and methodological decisions for organizational science. *Journal of Management, 24,* 623–644.

Hox, J. (2002). *Multilevel analysis: Techniques and applications.* Mahwah, NJ: Lawrence Erlbaum.

Hox, J. J. (2010). *Multilevel analysis: Techniques and applications* (2nd ed.). New York: Routledge.

Kreft, I. G., de Leeuw, J., & Aiken, L. (1995). The effects of different forms of centering in hierarchical linear models. *Multivariate Behavioral Research, 30,* 1–22.

McArdle, J. & Hamagami, F. (1996). Multilevel models from a multiple group structural equation perspective. In G. Marcoulides & R. Schumacker (Eds.), *Advanced structural equation modeling: Issues and techniques* (pp. 89–124). Mahwah, NJ: Lawrence Erlbaum.

Mehta, P. D. & Neale, M. C. (2005). People are variables too. Multilevel structural equations modeling. *Psychological Methods, 10*(3), 259–284.

Muthén, B. O. (1991). Multilevel factor analysis of class and student achievement components. *Journal of Educational Measurement, 28,* 338–354.

Muthén, B. O. (1994). Multilevel covariance structure analysis. *Sociological Methods & Research, 22*(3), 376–398.

Muthén, B. O. (2002). Beyond SEM: General latent variable modeling. *Behaviormetrika, 29,* 81–118.

Muthén, B. & Asparouhov, T. (2011). Beyond multilevel regression modeling: Multilevel analysis in a general latent variable framework. In J. Hox & J. K. Roberts (Eds.), *Handbook of advanced multilevel analysis* (pp. 15–40). New York: Taylor and Francis.

Muthén, L. K. & Muthén, B. O. (1998–2012). *Mplus user's guide* (7th ed.). Los Angeles, CA: Authors.

Plewis, I. (1989). Comment on "centering" predictors in multilevel analysis. *Multilevel Modeling Newsletter, 1*(3), 6, 11.

Raudenbush, S. W. & Bryk, A. S. (2002). *Hierarchical linear models* (2nd ed.). Newbury Park, CA: Sage.

Wu, W., West, S. G., & Taylor, A. B. (2009). Evaluating model fit for growth curve models: Integration of fit indices from SEM and MLM frameworks. *Psychological Methods, 14*(3), 183–201.

4

EXTENDING THE TWO-LEVEL REGRESSION MODEL

Chapter Objectives

This chapter extends the basic two-level univariate regression model to a three-level univariate model and several multivariate models. First, we develop a series of models to explain variability in a random intercept and slope across level-3 units. We illustrate how to develop the successive models using Mplus input files and how to evaluate their suitability. Second, we develop a multivariate model with two outcomes and extend this to a multilevel **path model** with mediating variable. In this latter type of model we illustrate how to use the matrix specification in Mplus for specifying multivariate multilevel models.

Introduction

The examples presented in the previous chapter demonstrated the basic multilevel regression model for examining hierarchical data structures. The basic two-level model can be readily extended to cross-sectional models involving several levels in a data hierarchy, regression discontinuity designs, and to multilevel longitudinal models involving individuals and groups. In this chapter we emphasize structural relations between observed variables both within and between groups and with single and multiple dependent variables. The chapter helps form a transition between the models in the previous chapter with direct effects only and univariate outcomes to a more complex type of model specification—one type being path models, which focus on direct and indirect effects between predictors and outcomes without defining a **measurement model** (e.g., observed items measuring underlying constructs). Path models allow researchers to investigate more complex theoretical models and, therefore, indirect effects. Indirect effects refer to the effect of a predictor X on an outcome Y through a third variable Z, which is between the two in a causal path (e.g., $X \rightarrow Z \rightarrow Y$). Such variables are often referred to as intervening or mediating variables. In this case, the indirect effect of X on Y depends on the strength of the direct relationship between X and Z and between Z and Y. Indirect effects can easily be overlooked within the typical multilevel regression study, which generally examines only the direct effects of a set of predictors on the outcome.

Models with more complex structural relations between variables can be used in addition to typical multilevel regression models formulated to investigate random intercepts and slopes across organizational units. As we noted previously, the facility of examining random slopes in SEM software is dependent on being able to represent data on individuals within clusters who may have different information (Mehta & Neale, 2005). To examine randomly varying slopes requires the facility to produce covariance matrices that are conditional on describing expected means and covariances for individuals based on the observed values of predictors within groups. This necessitated software being adapted to fit models that vary across individuals within a cluster, depending on their differing values on a covariate X_{ij}. As Mehta and Neale note, full information maximum likelihood (FIML) estimation allowed the covariance among individuals within a cluster to be modeled as a function of individuals' values on covariates. In theory, this means that there could potentially be different values of X_{ij} for every individual in the sample. This implies the dimension of the individual-level covariance matrix could vary across individuals, depending on the observed data.

Three-Level Univariate Model

Following typical notation for univariate multilevel regression models (Raudenbush & Bryk, 2002), we can define level-1 coefficients as the Greek letter pi (π), so that level-2 coefficients can be defined as β and level-3 coefficients as γ. For individual i in department j in organization k, the general level-1 model can then be defined as

$$Y_{ijk} = \pi_{0jk} + \sum_{p=1}^{P} \pi_{Pjk} a_{Pijk} + \varepsilon_{ijk}, \qquad (4.1)$$

where π_{0jk} is an intercept, a_{pijk} represent level-1 predictors ($p = 1, \ldots, P$), such as socioeconomic status, for individual i in level-2 unit j and level-3 unit k, and π_{pjk} are corresponding level-1 coefficients, and e_{ijk} is the residual variance. The level-1 variance of ε_{ijk} is assumed to be normally distributed with the mean equal to 0 and variance σ^2.

At Level 2, the general department model can be specified as

$$\pi_{pjk} = \beta_{p0k} + \sum_{q=1}^{Q_p} \beta_{pqk} X_{qjk} + r_{pjk}, \qquad (4.2)$$

where β_{p0k} is the intercept for organization k in modeling department effect, X_{qjk} are level-2 predictors ($q = 1, \ldots, Q_p$), such as organizational effectiveness, r_{pjk} are corresponding level-2 coefficients, and r_{pjk} represent level-2 random effects. Level-1 coefficients can be modeled at Level 2 as fixed at the same value for all level-2 units (i.e., $\pi_{pjk} = \beta_{p0k}$), which indicates that no predictors or random r_{pjk} component in Equation 4.2 are included in the model; as nonrandomly varying among level-2 units (i.e., Equation 4.2 without the random r_{pjk} component); or as randomly varying (Equation 4.2 with the random component r_{pjk} included). The level-2 random effects are collected in a covariance matrix whose dimensions depend on the number of random effects specified in the level-2 model.

Between organizations (Level 3), a general model can be defined as

$$\beta_{pqk} = \gamma_{pq0} + \sum_{s=1}^{S_{pq}} \gamma_{pqs} W_{sk} + u_{pqk}, \tag{4.3}$$

where γ_{pq0} is an intercept, W_{sk} are level-3 organizational predictors ($s = 1, \ldots, S_{pq}$) —for example, organizational size—γ_{pqk} are corresponding level-3 coefficients, and u_{pqk} represent level-3 random effects. The dimensions of the level-3 covariance matrix of random effects depend on the number of randomly varying effects in the model. Level-2 coefficients can be modeled at Level 3 as fixed ($\beta_{pqk} = \gamma_{pq0}$), as nonrandomly varying (i.e., Equation 4.3 without the random component u_{pqk}), or as randomly varying (as specified in Equation 4.3).

Initially, we can again examine the decomposition of variance in a univariate outcome associated with individuals, departments, and organizations. For a three-level model, the proportion of variability (intraclass correlation) in outcomes at Level 3 can be defined as

$$\rho = \sigma^2_{Level\,3} / (\sigma^2_{Level\,1} + \sigma^2_{Level\,2} + \sigma^2_{Level\,3}). \tag{4.4}$$

For Level 2, the intraclass correlation (ICC) would be

$$\rho = \sigma^2_{Level\,2} / (\sigma^2_{Level\,1} + \sigma^2_{Level\,2} + \sigma^2_{Level\,3}), \tag{4.5}$$

and for Level 1, the ICC would be

$$\rho = \sigma^2_{Level\,1} / (\sigma^2_{Level\,1} + \sigma^2_{Level\,2} + \sigma^2_{Level\,3}). \tag{4.6}$$

Developing a Three-Level Univariate Model

As a first example, consider a three-level model with a univariate outcome defined as math achievement. In this example, we primarily wish to examine whether classroom teaching effectiveness (i.e., a characteristic of teachers at Level 2) and aggregate teaching effectiveness (i.e., as a characteristic of schools at Level 3) affect student outcomes, after controlling for student socioeconomic background at each level. In addition, at the school level, we may be interested in examining whether the size of the slope coefficient describing the average impact of individual teacher effectiveness at Level 2 might vary randomly across schools; that is, does the effect of individual teaching effectiveness on math outcomes matter more in some school settings than others? If it does, we might develop a preliminary model to explain variation in individual teaching effectiveness across schools.

Research Questions

We investigate three research questions in this example. The first question is as follows: does having a more effective teacher confer an academic advantage to those students compared with their peers having a teacher of average effectiveness? The second research question then is the following: does individual teacher effectiveness vary across schools? We can address this question by examining the variance components for the slope at Level 3 of the model. If the slope does vary across schools, we can focus on building a model that explains variability in the random slope at the school level. This type of model concerns the presence of a cross-level interaction, that is, the potential effect a variable at a higher level of the data hierarchy may have on a relationship at a lower level. The third question focuses on whether teacher effectiveness at the classroom level is contingent on student composition. Addressing this question allows us to demonstrate how to investigate an **interaction** between two variables at the same level of the data hierarchy. This is also a common type of specification in a multilevel model.

Interactions can be interpreted as the amount of change in the slope of Y (achievement) with respect to X (teacher effectiveness) when Z (student classroom SES composition) changes by one unit. More specifically, we ask: does the dependence of a student's achievement score on the effectiveness of her teacher also depend on differing levels of socioeconomic status in the classroom? Keep in mind that interactions are not simply "additive," as are the main effects of variables in a model (i.e., the additional effect of teacher effectiveness in explaining achievement while holding SES composition constant) but, rather, they depend on the specific levels of the two variables from which they are produced (effectiveness and classroom SES). We can then test whether the interaction term added to the model produces a better fit than the main-effects-only model.

Data

For this example, we will use a random sample of 2,868 students nested in 250 classrooms within 60 elementary schools. The outcome is student scaled scores on a standardized math test. The sample data are found in the file ch4three.dat. The data have an identification code for Level 3 (*schcode*) and teacher (*teachid*) for Level 2 (*teachid*). Next is a math score, a measure of individual student socioeconomic status (coded 1 = low SES, 0 = else), a standardized ($M = 0$, $SD = 1$) assessment of each teacher's classroom teaching effectiveness (*teacheffect*), a classroom SES composition variable (*classlowses_mean*), and an aggregate (school-level) measure of student SES composition (*schlowses_mean*).

Model 1: Null (No Predictors) Model

Following the logic developed in the previous chapter, we start with a model with no predictors, so we can examine the decomposition of variance in the outcome associated with individuals, departments, and organizations. In this case, there is only a random intercept at each level. For individual i in class j in school k we have the following:

$$y_{ijk} = \pi_{0jk} + \varepsilon_{ijk}$$
$$\pi_{0jk} = \beta_{00k} + r_{0jk}$$
$$\beta_{00k} = \gamma_{000} + u_{00}. \tag{4.7}$$

Model 1 Statements

The input file is similar to the two-level file, except we define the model as three level (TYPE = threelevel) and add the cluster identifiers (CLUSTER = schcode teachid). We also must add the level-3 identifier (schcode) and the level-2 identifier (teachid) to the between part of the model. The output statement provides us with the sample descriptive statistics (sampstat). The output option TECH1 is used to request the arrays containing parameter specifications and starting values for all parameters to be estimated in the proposed model. This option is of use primarily when a traditional type of SEM specification is used. We develop this type of specification in the second part of this chapter. The output option TECH8 provides the optimization history of the model, which can be useful for determining how long the analysis takes to complete.

```
TITLE:      Model 1: Three-level (null) model;
DATA:       FILE IS C:\mplus\ch4three.dat;
            Format is 6f8.0,4f8.2;
VARIABLE:   Names are person teachid schcode math female lowses teffect
            lowses_m schses_m teff_m;
            Usevariables are teachid schcode math;
            CLUSTER = schcode teachid;
ANALYSIS:   TYPE = threelevel;
Model:

            %Between schcode%
```

```
                math;
                %Between teachid%
                math;
                %Within%
                math;
    OUTPUT:     sampstat tech1 tech8;
```

Model 1 Output

Table 4.1 presents the variance decomposition for the null (no predictors) model, and Table 4.2 presents the intercept estimate at Level 3 (mean = 598.616). From Table 4.1, we can estimate the total variance as 1830.463 by adding the three components together. The variance component associated with schools is 226.518; with classrooms it is 149.551; and within individuals it is 1454.394. From Equation 4.4, we can calculate the proportion of variance between schools as 0.124 [189.8867/(1454.394 + 149.551 + 226.518)] or 12.4%. Following Equation 4.5 the variance is 0.082 (8.2%) between classrooms, and from Equation 4.6, the student-level variance is 0.794 (79.4%). These proportions suggest there is adequate variability at each level to conduct a multilevel analysis.

We reiterate here that in multilevel modeling, explaining variance is more complex than in single-level regression models (Hox, 2010). First, there is the issue of dealing with unexplained variance at several levels. Second, if there are random slopes, the model becomes more complex, and explained variance (at each level) has no unique definition. As we noted in Chapter 3, one approach often used is to examine the change in residual variance that occurs by adding predictors within a sequence of models. The analyst begins with the intercept-only model as we have just presented. This serves as a baseline against which to evaluate subsequent reduction in the variance at each level as other variables are added to the model. The analyst should keep in mind, however, that when variables are added

TABLE 4.1 Estimated Variance Components for Model 1

Parameter		Estimate	SE	Est./SE	Sig.
Within		1454.394	78.160	18.608	0.000
Intercept (r_{0j})	Variance	149.551	52.453	2.851	0.004
Intercept (u_{0j})	Variance	226.518	65.121	3.478	0.001

TABLE 4.2 One-Way ANOVA or "Null Model"

Parameter	Estimate	S.E.	Est./SE	Sig.
Intercept	598.616	2.384	251.124	0.000

at Level 1, they can explain (i.e., reduce) variance at both Level 1 and at Level 2 (and perhaps even at Level 3). In contrast, variables added at higher levels of the model do not affect the variance present at lower levels. We therefore remind analysts to be cautious about placing too much emphasis on variance reduction approaches in accounting for outcome variance. Adding random slopes can also complicate accounting for variance at each level (Hox, 2010).

Model 2: Defining Predictors at Each Level

We first illustrate two primary centering strategies discussed in Chapter 3 in defining this example. As we discussed earlier, grand-mean centering (where the grand mean is subtracted from individuals' values on the variable) results in redefining the sample mean of the predictor to zero (0.0). Grand-mean centering the continuous predictors produces an equivalent model to leaving the predictors in their natural metrics, but it has the advantage of being able to interpret the resulting intercept in the model as the expected value of Y when they are at their mean values. This has the effect of adjusting the unit intercepts for differences in level-1 predictors within the units. In contrast, group-mean centering (where each group's mean is subtracted from individuals' values on the variable) results in unit intercepts that are unadjusted for differences within the units. More specifically, it produces an intercept equal to the expected value of Y for an individual when X is equal to the group's mean. We reiterate that group-mean centered solutions are not the same as grand-mean, standardized, or raw metric solutions.

In Mplus, grand-mean or group-mean centered variables can be computed using the Define command in the model input file. Categorical variables, such as dichotomous indicators, also present different options for centering, using *lowses* as an example. One option is to leave a dummy-coded (coded 0, 1) predictor in its natural metric. If *lowses* is entered in its natural metric, as is typical in multiple regression analyses, the reference group for the intercept will be the group coded 0 (i.e., did not participate in federal free/reduced lunch program) in school k, and the variance associated with the intercept will be interpreted as the variance in outcomes for that group of students between schools. If we grand-mean center a dummy-coded variable, it results in an intercept that may be defined as the mean outcome in school k, adjusted for the difference in the proportion of students participating in the federal free/reduced lunch program. This is an important distinction, for example, if we are concerned with making comparisons between schools after adjusting the outcomes for differences due to the various backgrounds of students with each school.

Grand-Mean Centering

In our second model, we will first grand-mean center our level-1 predictors, even though we could have just as easily chosen to leave them in their raw metrics.

At Level 1, we will propose that for individual i in class j in school k, student SES background (*lowses* coded 1; average/high SES coded 0) and gender (*female* coded 1, male coded 0) affect math achievement:

$$Y_{ijk} = \pi_{0jk} + \pi_{1jk} lowses_{ijk} + \pi_{2jk} female_{ijk} + \varepsilon_{ijk}. \tag{4.8}$$

At Level 2 (classrooms), we will add a measure of teacher effectiveness (*teffect*), with higher standardized scores indicating greater effectiveness, in producing student learning in the classroom and an aggregate measure of classroom SES composition (*lowses_m*):

$$\pi_{0jk} = \beta_{00k} + \beta_{01k} lowses\_m_{jk} + \beta_{02k} teffect_{jk} + r_{0jk},$$
$$\pi_{1jk} = \beta_{10k},$$
$$\pi_{2jk} = \beta_{20k}. \tag{4.9}$$

We will also grand-mean center these predictors in the intercept model. We will assume that student SES (*lowses*) and gender (*female*) are fixed at the same value for all level-2 units. Therefore, we do not include random variance components in Equation 4.9.

At Level 3 (schools), we will add aggregated measures of school SES (*schSES_m*) and teacher effectiveness (*teff_m*), which we also grand-mean centered, to explain variation in between-school math achievement:

$$\beta_{00k} = \gamma_{000} + \gamma_{001} schSES\_m_k + \gamma_{002} teff\_m_k + u_{00k},$$
$$\beta_{10k} = \gamma_{100},$$
$$\beta_{20k} = \gamma_{200},$$
$$\beta_{01k} = \gamma_{010},$$
$$\beta_{02k} = \gamma_{020}. \tag{4.10}$$

Equation 4.10 suggests that we will initially assume all level-1 and level-2 slopes are fixed, but the adjusted math intercepts vary across schools. The combined equation will then be the following:

$$\beta_{00k} = \gamma_{000} + \gamma_{100} lowses_{ijk} + \gamma_{200} female_{ijk} + \gamma_{010} lowses\_m_{jk} + \gamma_{020} teffect_{jk} +$$
$$\gamma_{001} schSES\_m_k + \gamma_{002} teff\_m_k + u_{00k} + r_{0jk} + \varepsilon_{ijk}. \tag{4.11}$$

This suggests 10 parameters to estimate (i.e., seven fixed effects, two random effects—the intercept residual variances at Level 2 and Level 3—and the level-1 residual). We note that the level-3 (school) intercepts in this model have been adjusted for individual SES and for class SES composition and teacher effectiveness at Level 2.

Model 2 Statements

We present the input statements for the model using grand-mean centering. The Define command is used to center the level-1 (*lowses, female*), level-2 (*teffect, lowses_m*), and level-3 (*teff_m, schses_m*) predictors as GRANDMEAN (which can be shortened to GRAND).

```
TITLE:     Model 2: Defining predictors at each level;
DATA:      FILE IS C:\mplus\ch4three.dat;
           Format is 6f8.0,4f8.2;
VARIABLE:  Names are person teachid schcode math female lowses teffect
           lowses_m schses_m teff_m;
           Usevariables are teachid schcode math female lowses teffect
           lowses_m teff_m schses_m;
           CLUSTER = schcode teachid;
           between = (teachid) teffect lowses_m (schcode) teff_m schses_m;
           within = female lowses;
define:    center lowses female teffect lowses_m teff_m schses_m
           (GRANDMEAN);
ANALYSIS:  TYPE = threelevel;
 Model:
           %Between schcode%
           math on schses_m teff_m;
           %Between teachid%
           math on lowses_m teffect;
           %Within%
           Math on lowses female;
OUTPUT:    sampstat tech1 tech8;
```

Model 2: Grand-Mean Centered Output

We present the fixed-effects output for Model 2 in Table 4.3. First, the output provides support for our first hypothesis that there is an academic advantage for students that is due to teacher effectiveness. At the classroom level, the table indicates that teacher effectiveness is statistically significant ($\gamma_{010} = 7.258, p < 0.001$). This suggests students in a classroom with a teacher whose effectiveness is 1 *SD* above the grand mean would score about 7.3 points higher than their peers in classrooms with teachers at the grand mean of effectiveness. We also note that the aggregate effect of teachers on outcomes compounds at the school level ($\gamma_{002} = 13.959, p < 0.001$). The interpretation of this school-level coefficient is straightforward: for two students having teachers of average effectiveness, attending

TABLE 4.3 Grand-Mean Centered Fixed-Effect Estimates

Parameter	Estimate	SE	Est./SE	Sig.
Intercept	598.644	1.283	466.724	0.000
SchSES_m	−22.071	9.856	−2.239	0.025
Teff_m	13.959	3.659	3.815	0.000
Lowses_m	−15.212	7.509	−2.026	0.043
Teffect	7.258	1.720	4.220	0.000
Lowses	−13.633	1.769	−7.708	0.000
Female	4.087	1.278	3.198	0.001

a school differing by 1 *SD* in collective teacher effectiveness is associated with an approximate 14-point increase on the standardized math test. This output, therefore, provides evidence to answer our first research question regarding potential academic advantages associated with teacher effectiveness.

The table also suggests the presence of effects associated with student SES at each level of the model; that is, there is an effect at the individual level ($\gamma_{100} = -13.633$, $p < 0.001$), which is also substantial at the classroom level ($\gamma_{020} = -15.212, p < 0.05$) and the school level ($\gamma_{001} = -22.071, p < 0.05$). This is often referred to as a *compositional* effect (which is defined as the difference in size between an organizational effect and an individual effect). With grand-mean centering, the compositional effect for school SES is estimated directly as the between-group fixed effect ($\gamma_{001} = -22.071$). At school level, the effect for SES can be interpreted as the expected difference in math outcomes between two students who have the same individual SES background (and are in classes with the same SES composition) but who attend schools differing by one unit (i.e., in this case, 1 *SD* in mean SES). Similarly, the composition effect at the classroom level ($\gamma_{020} = -15.212, p < 0.05$) is the difference in size between the individual SES and class-level SES effects. At the classroom level, the compositional effect for SES can be interpreted as the expected difference in math outcomes between two students who have the same individual SES but who are in classes differing by one unit (1 *SD*) in mean classroom SES.

We next provide the variance components for this model in Table 4.4. The covariance estimates suggest that the addition of predictors at each level reduces the proportion of variance associated with each level of the data hierarchy (see Table 4.1) substantially (i.e., from 1454.394 to 1419.509 at the student level; from 149.551 to 67.838 at the classroom level; and from 226.518 to

TABLE 4.4 Estimated Variance Components for Model 2 (Grand-Mean Centered)

Parameter		Estimate	SE	Est./SE	Sig.
Within		1419.509	74.976	18.933	0.000
Intercept (r_{0j})	Variance	67.838	24.662	2.751	0.006
Intercept (u_{0j})	Variance	25.044	11.147	2.247	0.025

25.044 at the school level). These reductions in variance at each level can be used to calculate an estimate of R^2 for that level [(M1 − M2)/M1]. For example, at the school level (Level 3) the reduction in variance would be calculated as (226.518 − 25.044)/226.518 and results in an R^2 coefficient of 0.89. At Level 2, the estimated coefficient would be 0.55.

Group-Mean Centering

We contrast these grand-mean results for Model 2 with results where we group-mean center the level-1 and level-2 predictors. Group-mean centering results in an intercept for each unit that is unadjusted for level-1 or level-2 predictors. In group-mean centered solutions, the effects of between-group predictors will also be unadjusted for within-group predictors. Because grand-mean centering produces group means that are adjusted for the predictors in the model, in some modeling situations the estimates for some units may not be very reliable. One situation is where there are small within-group sample sizes and considerable variability in slopes for particular covariates. For units with small sample sizes, the random slope may be estimated with little precision, which weakens the likelihood of detecting relationships between groups (Raudenbush & Bryk, 2002). This can make it difficult to disentangle parameter variance and error variance. In cases where the slope varies considerably across units for a predictor, and there is also variability across units in the levels of the predictors, resulting grand-mean centered estimates may be less credible than group-mean centered estimates (Raudenbush & Bryk, 2002). Cross-level interactions can also sometimes be a source of instability in a model's estimates. If this may be a potential problem, group-mean centering is a good centering choice, since this approach removes correlations between variables across levels (Kreft & deLeeuw, 1998). It is therefore important to give attention to decisions about model specification, especially when the focus is on the cross-level interactions.

Model 2 Statements

Given the previous grand-mean centered estimates in Table 4.4, if we instead used group-mean centering, for teacher effectiveness we would expect an aggregated level-3 teacher effectiveness coefficient of approximately 21.0 (i.e., 7.3 + 13.8 in Table 4.4). We can specify group-mean centering by replacing the input statement for Define as follows:

Define: CENTER lowses female (GROUPMEAN teachid);
CENTER teffect lowses_m (GROUPMEAN schcode);

This specification suggests that the level-1 background variables will be centered on their class means. At the class level, teacher effectiveness (teffect) and class composition (lowses_m) will be centered on their school means. This centering strategy results in level-2 and level-3 means that are unadjusted for within-group variables. We note that level-3 predictors can be either grand-mean centered or uncentered. Level-3 predictors cannot be "group" centered, as their mean is the sample grand mean.

Model 2: Group-Mean Centered Output

Table 4.5 presents the group-centered estimates for Model 2. The group-mean centered estimate for aggregated teacher effectiveness is consistent with our expected output translated from the grand-mean estimates. Comparison of Tables 4.5 and 4.3 suggests differences between the models related to the unstandardized coefficients for the level-3 aggregated teacher effectiveness ($\gamma_{002} = 20.366$) variable when it is group-mean centered versus when it is grand-mean centered ($\gamma_{002} = 13.959$). There are similar differences associated with the level-2 and level-3 unstandardized SES composition effects. It would be easy to misinterpret the meaning of these coefficients without a clear understanding of the difference between the two centering strategies. We also note that the level-3 estimates are still grand-mean centered. We reiterate this is because the estimates of the highest level in the data set cannot be centered on particular groups—that is, their "group" mean is the grand mean of the sample of schools.

The covariance estimates in Table 4.6 for the group-centered second model are slightly larger at Level 2 and Level 3 than the grand-mean centered covariance estimates in Table 4.4, since they are unadjusted for the covariates added at each level. It is important to note that predictors entered into the model can affect variance

TABLE 4.5 Group-Mean Centered Fixed-Effect Estimates

Parameter	Estimate	SE	Est./SE	Sig.
Intercept	616.829	2.881	214.127	0.000
SchSES_m	−44.250	6.307	−7.017	0.000
Teff_m	20.366	3.022	6.740	0.000
lowses_m	−19.944	6.485	−3.076	0.002
Teffect	8.264	1.639	5.043	0.000
Lowses	−13.632	1.755	−7.768	0.000
Female	4.324	1.386	3.121	0.002

TABLE 4.6 Estimated Variance Components for Model 2 (Group-Mean Centered)

Parameter		Estimate	SE	Est./SE	Sig.
Within		1417.586	74.856	18.937	0.000
Intercept (r_{0j})	Variance	71.063	25.247	2.815	0.005
Intercept (u_{00j})	Variance	25.779	12.577	2.050	0.040

accounted for at the level at which they are entered (e.g., Level 1 or Level 2), and they may also affect the variance accounted for at higher levels. For example, if grand-mean centering is used, adjustments for level-1 predictors may change the level and variability in the intercept across higher groupings. If group-mean centering is used, however, the level-1 predictors will not affect the level of the intercept or its variance across groups. In situations where accounting for variance is an important aim, the analyst may want to consider developing a level-1 model first and then adding level-2 and level-3 predictors as separate sets of variables, so that the variance accounted for at each subsequent level is only affected by predictors that are added at that level.

We also note that where there are multiple random effects (e.g., a random inter-cept and random slope), accounting for variance at successive levels may become more complicated if the slope and intercept are correlated. In this case, predictors entered into the slope equation, for example, may also affect variance estimates in the intercept equation (Raudenbush & Bryk, 2002). Centering on the group means tends to stabilize the model because it removes correlations (Paccagnella, 2006), so the resulting estimates may be more accurate. Group-mean centering may also be advantageous where the slope varies considerably for a particular pre-dictor, and there is also considerable variability in the levels of the predictors across the units (Raudenbush & Bryk, 2002).

Model 3: Does the Slope Vary Randomly Across Schools?

We next investigate whether the random teacher effect varies across schools. This will help us answer our second research question. The appropriate baseline slope model is the model with random slopes but no cross-level interactions (Hox, 2002). To indicate a random slope for the teacher effect at Level 3, we add a ran-dom coefficient (u_{02k}) to the relevant term in Equation 4.10, so it now is as follows:

$$\beta_{02k} = \gamma_{020} + u_{02k}. \tag{4.12}$$

In this model (Model 3), we will also need to change the covariance matrix from identity to diagonal at Level 3 in order to accommodate the additional ran-dom slope parameter in the model:

$$\begin{bmatrix} \sigma_I^2 & 0 \\ 0 & \sigma_S^2 \end{bmatrix}. \tag{4.13}$$

This implies the covariance between the level-3 intercept and level-3 random slope is 0. We could actually specify and test the covariance relationship by adding a line to the %Between schcode% portion of the model (S with math;). If we do this, it suggests the covariance matrix at Level 3 is unstructured, which would add one extra random parameter at Level 3:

$$\begin{bmatrix} \sigma_I^2 & \sigma_{IS} \\ \sigma_{IS} & \sigma_S^2 \end{bmatrix}. \tag{4.14}$$

When we actually did test this model preliminarily, we found the covariance was not significant so we left the level-3 random effects covariance matrix as diagonal. We will also leave the level-2 covariance matrix as identity, since there is only one random effect (the intercept) at that level. As Equation 4.10 indicated, there were 10 parameters to estimate in the previous model. After adding the random slope parameter at Level 3, through substitution, we arrive at the new combined equation, which adds the random slope parameter at Level 3:

$$\beta_{00k} = \gamma_{000} + \gamma_{100}lowses_{ijk} + \gamma_{200}female_{ijk} + \gamma_{010}lowses\_m_{jk} + \gamma_{020}teffect_{jk}$$
$$+ \gamma_{001}schSES\_m_k + \gamma_{002}teff\_m_k + u_{02k}teffect_k + u_{00k} + r_{0jk} + \varepsilon_{ijk}. \qquad 4.15$$

This makes a total of 11 parameters to estimate in Model 3. In addition to the seven fixed effects, there are now two random effects at Level 3 (i.e., intercept residual variance, teacher effectiveness slope residual variance), one random intercept residual variance at Level 2, and the level-1 residual variance.

Model 3 Statements

We must also make a few changes in the Mplus input file to accommodate the random slope in the model. First, in the ANALYSIS portion of the statements, we will add "random" to the Type command (TYPE = Threelevel random;) to indicate that the teacher effect parameter will be specified as randomly varying at Level 3. Second, at the classroom level we will specify that the slope for teacher effectiveness varies on the Model command line (S | math on teffect;). Finally, we will add the slope variance to the level-3 model (S;).

```
TITLE:       Model 3: Examining a randomly-varying slope;
DATA:        FILE IS C:\Mplus\ch4three.dat;
             Format is 6f8.0,4f8.2;
VARIABLE:    Names are person teachid schcode math female lowses teffect
             lowses_m schses_m teff_m;
             Usevariables are teachid schcode math female lowses teffect
             lowses_m teff_m schses_m;
             CLUSTER = schcode teachid;
             between = (teachid) teffect lowses_m (schcode) teff_m
             schses_m;
             within = female lowses;
define:      center lowses female teffect lowses_m teff_m schses_m
             (GRANDMEAN);
ANALYSIS:    TYPE = threelevel random;
Model:

             %Between schcode%
             math on schses_m teff_m;
```

```
                S;
                %Between teachid%
                math on lowses_m;
                S | math on teffect;
                %Within%
                Math on lowses female;
    OUTPUT:     sampstat tech1 tech8;
```

Model 3 Output

Table 4.7 provides the new variance components for Model 3 with random slope. There is initial evidence that the slope likely varies significantly across level-3 units (36.803, $p = 0.053$). This suggests building a slope model to examine this variability. We therefore can answer our second research question by noting that the size of individual teacher effects do seem to vary between schools.

Model 4: Developing a Model to Explain Variability in Slopes

Because classroom teacher effectiveness varies across schools, for our last model we turn our attention to building a parallel model to explain variability in the random slopes. In addition to the random slope, we will now add the same set of school predictors to the random teacher effectiveness slope:

$$\beta_{02k} = \gamma_{020} + \gamma_{021}schSES\_m_k + \gamma_{022}teff\_m_k + u_{02k}. \tag{4.16}$$

Substituting Equation 4.16 into the previous model, the combined equation will now be the following:

$$\begin{aligned}\beta_{00k} = &\gamma_{000} + \gamma_{100}lowses_{ijk} + \gamma_{200}female_{ijk} + \gamma_{010}lowses\_m_{jk}\\ &+ \gamma_{020}teffect_{jk} + \gamma_{021}schSES\_m_k + \gamma_{022}teff\_m_k + \gamma_{001}schSES\_m_k\\ &+ \gamma_{002}teff\_m_k + u_{02k}teffect_k + u_{00k} + r_{0jk} + \varepsilon_{ijk}.\end{aligned} \tag{4.17}$$

This model brings the total number of estimated parameters to 13 (i.e., nine fixed effects, three random variance parameters, and the level-1 residual).

TABLE 4.7 Estimated Variance Components for Model 3 (Grand-Mean Centered)

Parameter		Estimate	SE	Est./SE	Sig.
Within		1418.973	75.175	18.876	0.000
Intercept (r_{0j})	Variance	41.761	22.149	1.885	0.059
Intercept (u_{00j})	Variance	28.007	11.051	2.534	0.011
Slope (u_{02j})	Variance	36.803	19.024	1.935	0.053

Model 4 Statements

To examine slope variability across schools, in the %Between schcode% portion of the model, we will add an "on" command to reflect the regression of the random teacher effectiveness slope (S) on the two school predictors.

```
Model:
        %Between schcode%
        math on schses_m teff_m;
        S on schses_m teff_m;
        %Between teachid%
        math on lowses_m;
        S | math on teffect;
        %Within%
        Math on lowses female;
```

Model 4 Output

The fixed-effect results are shown in Table 4.8. They suggest that neither school-level predictor in the slope model explains variability in individual teacher effectiveness slopes across schools. This is not unexpected, since we might suspect this type of variability is more related to school processes (e.g., curriculum, academic expectations, strategies for meeting student needs). Table 4.9 presents the variance components. We can see there is still variability left to explain in intercepts at the school level. At this point, we will leave this model and turn our attention elsewhere.

TABLE 4.8 Grand-Mean Centered Fixed-Effect Estimates

Parameter	Estimate	SE	Est./SE	Sig.
Intercept	599.080	1.310	457.165	0.000
SchSES_m	−28.496	9.197	−3.099	0.002
Teff_m	13.879	3.274	4.239	0.000
Lowses_m	−12.226	7.213	−1.695	0.090
Teffect	6.573	1.730	3.798	0.000
SchSES_m*Teffect	6.450	5.283	1.221	0.222
Teff_m*Teffect	0.501	2.740	0.183	0.855
Lowses	−13.606	1.769	−7.689	0.000
Female	4.022	1.286	3.127	0.002

TABLE 4.9 Estimated Variance Components for Model 3 (Grand-Mean Centered)

Parameter		Estimate	SE	Est./SE	Sig.
Within		1419.166	75.328	18.840	0.000
Intercept (r_{0j})	Variance	41.852	21.916	1.910	0.056
Intercept (u_{00j})	Variance	26.514	11.355	2.335	0.019
Slope (u_{02j})	Variance	35.429	18.864	1.878	0.060

Defining Path Models

In the next section of the chapter, we introduce a second variation on the basic two-level modeling framework, that is, a model that has more than one dependent variable. In this case we will develop a two-level path model, with individuals defined at Level 1 and groups at Level 2. We could easily extend this type of path model to three levels. The multivariate multilevel model follows directly from the traditional single-level multivariate analysis of variance (MANOVA) model. The multivariate approach facilitates the development of more flexible models with multiple response variables, which can have different sets of explanatory variables at each level as well as mediating variables between the predictors and outcomes.

From an SEM perspective, we can consider the multilevel model with multivariate outcomes as a multilevel path model. An advantage of the multivariate approach using SEM is that it provides simultaneous estimation of the outcomes and adjustment for correlations between them. It also facilitates the use of different covariance structures at multiple levels. As Raykov and Marcoulides (2006) note, path models can be considered as resulting from a corresponding structural equation model that assumes explanatory relationships between its latent variables, independent variables that are measured with no error, and latent variables that are measured by single indicators with loadings fixed to 1.0. Outcomes can be continuous, categorical (discussed in Chapter 8), or combinations of these.

Path models allow researchers to investigate more complex theoretical models that include multiple dependent variables, intervening variables, and, therefore, indirect effects (i.e., combined effects through several paths). Indirect effects can be overlooked within the typical multilevel regression study, although it is possible to specify these types of models as multilevel regression models [see Raudenbush & Sampson (1999) and Raudenbush & Bryk (2002) for discussions of how to formulate similar models within a multilevel regression framework]. Models with more complex structural relations between predictors, intervening variables, and outcomes can be conceptualized in addition to typical models formulated to investigate random intercepts and slopes across organizational units that we have presented in the previous section of this chapter, as well as in Chapter 3.

The multilevel path model specification has a couple of limitations to consider relative to models that include latent factors. First, the unreliability of observed measures affects the variance decomposition of the variables across organizational levels into their within- and between-group components to some extent (Muthén, 1991). Observed scales used as substitute measures of latent factors therefore may introduce considerable unreliability into the model. Second, in a multilevel path model, measurement error in an outcome does not affect the estimation of the regression coefficients but will affect precision, statistical power, and the explanatory power of the covariates, whereas measurement error in the covariates will affect the accuracy of the regression coefficients (Kaplan, 1998; Raudenbush & Bryk, 2002). Where observed scales (e.g., composed of several survey items) are being used, therefore, it would be important to conduct a preliminary examination of the reliability of the items. When the focus is not specifically on measurement error, however, path models can be a useful approach to the multilevel modeling of organizational processes.

Single-Level Path Model

The basic single-level structural equation model has two submodels: the measurement model, which is used to define latent (underlying) constructs through a set of observed indicators, and the structural model, which is used to specify relationships between latent constructs or between a set of predictors and the latent constructs. Both models are typically defined using matrix specification because there may be multiple latent factors defined by observed indicators and then multiple sets of relationships between the constructs in a proposed model (e.g., direct and indirect effects). The basic measurement model can be specified as

$$y = \upsilon + \Lambda\eta + \varepsilon, \tag{4.18}$$

where for individual i, y is a vector of observed dependent variables; *upsilon* (υ) is a vector of measurement intercepts, which are usually set at zero; *lambda* (Λ) is a matrix of factor loadings for the observed variables; *eta* (η) refers to vector of latent variables; and *epsilon* (ε) is a vector of measurement errors for observed variables that is uncorrelated with other variables. The residuals are contained in the *theta* matrix (Θ). We develop multilevel measurement models in more detail in Chapter 5.

The second model consisting of the structural relationships can be defined in the Mplus framework as

$$\eta = \alpha + \mathbf{B}\eta + \Gamma x + \zeta, \tag{4.19}$$

where η is a vector of latent factors, α (*alpha*) is a vector of measurement intercepts, $\mathbf{B}$ (*beta*) is a matrix of regression coefficients relating the latent factors to each other, Γ (*gamma*) is a matrix of regression coefficients relating the covariates (x) to the latent factors, and ζ (*zeta*) is a vector of residuals (or errors in equations), which indicate that the latent factors are not perfectly predicted by the structural equations. The residuals for Equation 4.19 is contained in the *psi* (Ψ) matrix. Residuals are assumed to be normal and with zero means, with those associated with the dependent variables being uncorrelated with predictors. In addition, it is assumed that the matrix $I - B$ is invertible. In the case where all variables are observed, the **structural model** reduces to

$$y = \alpha + By + \Gamma x + \zeta. \tag{4.20}$$

Analysts sometimes refer to the systems of theoretical relations implied in the structural submodel as consisting of **exogenous and endogenous variables**. For example, in Equation 4.20 exogenous (x) variables are those whose variability is determined outside of the model, while endogenous (y) variables are those whose variability is determined by other variables in the model. This implies that within a proposed theoretical model, relationships can be defined between multiple endogenous variables (y) where some might serve as intervening variables between other endogenous variables or between exogenous (x) variables and endogenous variables.

These types of relationships are illustrated in Figure 4.1. The proposed model illustrated represents a multivariate multiple regression instead of a univariate multiple regression. The exogenous variables X_1 and X_2 have direct effects on the endogenous variable Y_1 and indirect effects on the endogenous variables Y_2 and Y_3. Notice that the indirect effects of x variables on Y_3 can compound through several paths. Y_1 has a direct effect on Y_3 and an indirect effect on Y_3 through Y_2. Y_2 has only a direct effect on Y_1. The proposed set of theoretical relations also suggests that some paths are fixed—that is, they are not estimated. The validity of this particular proposed model can be tested against an alternative model where a proposed fixed path is instead estimated.

Multilevel Path Model

In this example, consider a large random sample of employees ($N = 12,445$) nested within 160 product and service organizations. Employees are measured

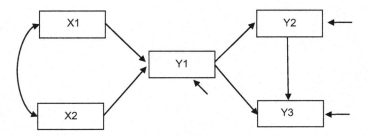

FIGURE 4.1 Proposed single–level path model.

on two outcomes, which are defined as their satisfaction with *benefits* (Y_{1ij}) and their satisfaction with workplace *conditions* (Y_{2ij}) in their organization. These two outcomes are measured on 10-point scales at the individual level. There are two demographic variables within organizations (*gender* and *ethnicity*). At the group level there are two organizational context variables and an intervening variable, which is a standardized measure of the productivity (*zproduct*) of the organization.

Separate models with latent and observed variables can be defined for individuals (Level 1) and organizations (Level 2). We can define vectors of observed outcomes for each individual i in cluster j $(Y_{1ij}, ..., Y_{Nij})'$ and for the between-cluster portion as $(\gamma_{1j}, ..., \gamma_{Nj})'$, for example, in the case where we had observed variables defining latent factors at both levels of the data hierarchy. We can also specify a vector of cluster means designated as eta $(\eta_{1j}, ..., \eta_{Nj})'$ and individual deviation from the cluster mean for each outcome designated as zeta $(\zeta_{1ij}, ..., \zeta_{Nij})'$. For the case with two outcomes, within groups, Equation 4.21 suggests each observed score for individual i in organization j can be summarized as the cluster mean and an individual-specific deviation from the mean:

$$Y_{1ij} = \eta_{1j} + \zeta_{1ij},$$
$$Y_{2ij} = \eta_{2j} + \zeta_{2ij}. \tag{4.21}$$

Each average outcome score can be expected to vary across clusters,

$$\eta_{1j} = \alpha_1 + \zeta_{1j},$$
$$\eta_{2j} = \alpha_2 + \zeta_{2j}, \tag{4.22}$$

where the intercepts are designated as α_1 and α_2, which are contained in a vector of grand means of the outcomes across clusters, and ζ_{1j} and ζ_{2j} are contained in a vector representing the deviations of cluster j's means from the grand means on the outcomes. Because the grand mean is a constant added to individuals' scores, when the cluster-level equation is substituted into the within–cluster model, each individual's score can be seen to vary as a result of cluster variability and individual variability within clusters:

$$Y_{1ij} = \alpha_1 + \zeta_{1j} + \zeta_{1ij}$$
$$Y_{2ij} = \alpha_2 + \zeta_{2j} + \zeta_{2ij}. \tag{4.23}$$

Moreover, for each outcome

$$\text{Var}(Y_{ij}) = \text{Var}(\zeta_j) + \text{Var}(\zeta_{ij}) = \sigma_b^2 + \sigma_w^2. \tag{4.24}$$

Each of the relationships proposed in the model can be specified with a particular matrix, which, in general, can be specified as either within groups or between groups. For example, observed variables proposed to define a vector of latent variables (η) can be specified in the lambda loading matrix, both within (Λ_W) and between groups (Λ_B). Similarly, errors observed in variables used to measure the latent variables can be specified in the theta matrix within (Θ_W) and between groups (Θ_B). Structural relationships between latent variables can be defined in the beta matrix within (B_W) and between groups (B_B), and residual variances in the equations (and covariances) are also contained in the psi matrix within (Ψ_W) and between (Ψ_B) groups. The alpha vector of factor means for multilevel models can only be defined at the group level.

In our current example, since there are no latent variables at Level 1, the within-organization path model can be specified using an "all Y" specification (i.e., where relationships between outcomes and predictors are defined within the beta matrix of structural relations) as follows:

$$Y_{Wij} = \eta_j + B_W Y_{Wij} + \zeta_{Wij}, \tag{4.25}$$

where Y_{Wij} is the within-group vector of observed variables (i.e., both outcomes and predictors), B_W is a matrix of regression coefficients relating within-group predictors (and intervening variables if there are any) to the outcomes, η_j is a vector of random intercepts, and ζ_{ij} represents errors in equations with groups, which are normally distributed with mean of 0 and some variance and are contained in covariance matrices Ψ_W.

Between groups we have the following:

$$\eta_j = \alpha_B + B_B Y_{Bj} + \zeta_{Bj}, \tag{4.26}$$

where η_j is the between-group random effects (which are considered as latent variables), B_B is a matrix of regression coefficients relating between-group predictors to the outcomes, and ζ_{Bj} represents errors in equations between groups, which are normally distributed with mean of 0 and some variance and are contained in covariance matrices Ψ_B.

Model 1: Two-Level Model With Multivariate Outcomes

Initially, we estimated the within- and between-group variance components for each outcome. For benefits, the within-group estimate was 2.161 and the between-group estimate was 0.263, for an intraclass correlation of 0.109 (i.e., 0.263/2.424). For conditions, the within-group estimate was 2.086 and the between-group estimate was 0.213, resulting in an intraclass correlation of 0.093 (0.213/2.299).

We will first specify a simple model with two correlated outcomes and with one predictor at within groups (*female*) and one predictor between groups (*org1*). Figure 4.2 presents the proposed theoretical model. The model specifies

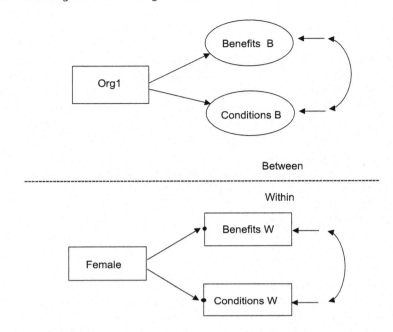

FIGURE 4.2 Proposed two-level model with multivariate outcomes.

direct effects for female on the two outcomes within organizations. Between organizations, we will specify that the first context variable is related to each outcome.

Within groups, we have the following specification in the Beta matrix. Since there are four variables (two outcomes and two predictors), the model specification will be 4 × 4. Note that there are no intercepts within groups. The order of the variables in the Beta matrix in Equation 4.27 is *benefits, conditions, female, and org1*. So we can see, for example, that there is path specified from the third variable (*female*) to the first (*benefits*) and a path specified from the third variable to the second variable (*conditions*):

$$
Y_{ij} = \begin{bmatrix} 0 & 0 & B_{1,3} & 0 \\ 0 & 0 & B_{2,3} & 0 \\ 0 & 0 & 0 & 0 \\ 0 & 0 & 0 & 0 \end{bmatrix} \begin{bmatrix} Y_{1ij} \\ Y_{2ij} \end{bmatrix} + \begin{bmatrix} \zeta_{1ij} \\ \zeta_{2ij} \end{bmatrix}.
\tag{4.27}
$$

Within groups, the residual variances for benefits and conditions are contained in Ψ_W. As Equation 4.28 suggests, there is a residual variance for benefits and for conditions, and a covariance between them.

$$\Psi_W = \begin{bmatrix} \Psi_{1,1} & & & \\ \Psi_{2,1} & \Psi_{2,2} & & \\ 0 & 0 & 0 & \\ 0 & 0 & 0 & 0 \end{bmatrix}. \tag{4.28}$$

Equations 4.27 and 4.28 indicate there are five parameters to estimate within groups. These include two structural parameters, two residual variances, and a covariance. Between groups, we can specify the level-2 model with the two latent outcomes as follows:

$$\begin{bmatrix} \eta_{1j} \\ \eta_{2j} \end{bmatrix} = \begin{bmatrix} \alpha_{1j} \\ \alpha_{2j} \end{bmatrix} + \begin{bmatrix} 0 & 0 & 0 & B_{1,4} \\ 0 & 0 & 0 & B_{2,4} \\ 0 & 0 & 0 & 0 \\ 0 & 0 & 0 & 0 \end{bmatrix} \begin{bmatrix} \eta_{1j} \\ \eta_{2j} \end{bmatrix} + \begin{bmatrix} \varsigma_{1j} \\ \varsigma_{2j} \end{bmatrix}. \tag{4.29}$$

In Equation 4.29, in the between-groups beta matrix, we can see that *org1* (the fourth variable in the matrix) is specified to explain differences in perceptions of *benefits* (the first variable) and *conditions* (the second variable). The between–group residuals are contained in Ψ_B.

$$\Psi_B = \begin{bmatrix} \Psi_{1,1} & & & \\ \Psi_{2,1} & \Psi_{2,2} & & \\ 0 & 0 & 0 & \\ 0 & 0 & 0 & 0 \end{bmatrix}. \tag{4.30}$$

Equations 4.29 and 4.30 suggest an additional seven parameters to estimate between organizations. There are the two cluster-level intercepts, two structural parameters, two group variances, and a covariance. The total number of estimated parameters is therefore 12.

Model 1 Statements

We next summarize the model statements. Since there is no random slope, we do not need a random command on the ANALYSIS line. We add "Standardized" to the OUTPUT commands so we can also present the standardized path coefficients in the model if desired. Mplus standardizes the estimates of within- and between-group covariates separately. This is useful in determining how much variance is explained at each level. Mplus provides three standardizations. These include StdYX, which uses the variances of the continuous latent variables as well as the variances of the background and outcome variables for standardization; StdY, which uses the variances of the continuous latent variables as well as the variances of the outcome variables for standardization (which should be used when dichotomous covariates are included in the model since a standard deviation change in a dichotomous variable is not meaningful); and Std, which uses the variances of the continuous latent variables for standardization (Muthén & Muthén, 1998–2012). Standardizations facilitate making comparisons about the strength of relationships between variables that are measured in different metrics. When the emphasis is on overall model fit, or where the outcome is in a metric that has inherent meaning for the interpretation between predictors and an outcome (e.g., dollars), it may be sufficient to report only the unstandardized solution.

TITLE:	Model 1: Two-level model with multivariate outcomes;
	FILE IS C:\mplus\ch4mv.dat;
	Format is 7f8.0,6f8.2;
VARIABLE:	Names are orgid female white satpay morale org1 org2
	benefit cond zresour zproduct lev1wt lev2wt;
	Usevariables are benefit cond female org1;
	within = female;
	between = org1;
	CLUSTER IS orgid;
ANALYSIS:	TYPE = twolevel;
	Estimator is mlr;
Model:	
	%Between%
	benefit cond on org1;
	benefit with cond;
	%Within%
	benefit cond on female;
	benefit with cond;
OUTPUT:	SAMPSTAT Standardized TECH1;

Model 1 Output

We can examine the relevant output for this model in Table 4.10. For benefits, the intercept was 4.519. We can see within groups female (0.697) affects benefits significantly ($p < 0.001$). For conditions, the intercept is 4.791, and female is once again is statistically significant (0.707, $p < 0.001$). Between groups, the

TABLE 4.10 Model 1 Unstandardized Estimates

Parameter	Estimate	SE	Est./SE	Sig.
Benefits Intercept	4.519	0.047	96.028	0.000
Org1	0.273	0.109	2.501	0.012
Female	0.697	0.027	25.517	0.000
Conditions Intercept	4.791	0.045	105.417	0.000
Org1	0.303	0.092	3.280	0.001
Female	0.707	0.029	24.135	0.000
Residual Variances				
Benefits (B)	0.248	0.035	7.092	0.000
Conditions (B)	0.198	0.029	6.852	0.000
Covariance (B)	0.205	0.030	6.829	0.000
Benefits (W)	2.040	0.039	52.121	0.000
Conditions (W)	1.961	0.040	49.190	0.000
Covariance (W)	1.356	0.036	38.111	0.000

TABLE 4.11 R-Square Estimates

Within Level				
Observed Variable	Estimate	S.E.	Est./S.E.	Two-Tailed P-Value
SATBEN	0.056	0.004	13.801	0.000
SATCOND	0.060	0.005	13.115	0.000
Between Level				
Observed Variable	Estimate	S.E.	Est./S.E.	Two-Tailed P-Value
SATBEN	0.051	0.040	1.272	0.203
SATCOND	0.076	0.047	1.618	0.106

organizational demographic also affects benefits $(0.273, p = 0.012)$ and conditions $(0.303, p = 0.001)$.

In Table 4.11 we can also examine the variance in benefits and conditions accounted for at each level by the single predictor included at each level. The results suggest each predictor only accounts for modest variance at each level.

We can also look at selected TECH1 output to see whether it matches with our specification in Equations 4.25–4.28. We can see five parameters are estimated within-groups (i.e., two structural relationships, two variances, and one covariance). In addition, seven are estimated between groups (i.e., two intercepts, three structural parameters, two variances, and one covariance).

PARAMETER SPECIFICAITON FOR WITHIN

BETA

	SATBEN	SATCOND	FEMALE	ORG1
SATBEN	0	0	1	0
SATCOND	0	0	2	0
FEMALE	0	0	0	0
ORG1	0	0	0	0

PSI

	SATBEN	SATCOND	FEMALE	ORG1
SATBEN	3			
SATCOND	4	5		
FEMALE	0	0	0	
ORG1	0	0	0	0

PARAMETER SPECIFICATION FOR BETWEEN

ALPHA

SATBEN	SATCOND	FEMALE	ORG1
6	7	0	0

BETA

	SATBEN	SATCOND	FEMALE	ORG1
SATBEN	0	0	0	8
SATCOND	0	0	0	9
FEMALE	0	0	0	0
ORG1	0	0	0	0

PSI

	SATBEN	SATCOND	FEMALE	ORG1
SATBEN	10			
SATCOND	11	12		
FEMALE	0	0	0	
ORG1	0	0	0	0

Model 2: Specifying a Mediating Variable Between Groups

We will next propose a model with an indirect effect between groups. We will add a second demographic variable within groups (*white* coded 1, else = 0). At the group level, we will add a second organizational context variable (*org2*) and an intervening variable, which is a standardized measure of the productivity (*zproduct*) of the organization. We will specify all relationships between variables. The proposed model has 22 parameters to estimate. The model is summarized in Figure 4.3.

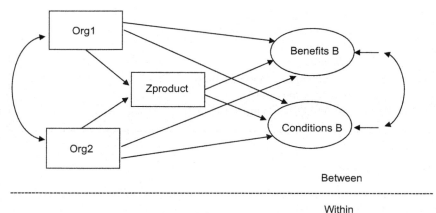

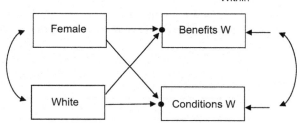

FIGURE 4.3 Full two–level multivariate model with mediated effects.

Model 2 Statements

We next provide the Mplus input file.

```
TITLE:      Model 2: Multivariate outcomes and mediating variable;
DATA:       FILE IS C:\mplus\ch4mv.dat;
            Format is 7f8.0,6f8.2;
VARIABLE:   Names are orgid female white satpay morale org1
            org2 benefit cond resour zproduct lev1wt lev2wt;
            Usevariables are benefit cond female white org1 org2 zproduct;
            within = female white;
            between = org1 org2 zproduct;
            CLUSTER IS orgid;
ANALYSIS:   TYPE = twolevel;
            Estimator is mlr;
Model:
            %Between%
            benefit cond on org1 org2;
```

```
        zproduct on org1 org2;
        benefit cond on zproduct;
        benefit with cond;
        %Within%
        benefit cond on female white;
        benefit with cond;
OUTPUT:  SAMPSTAT Standardized TECH1;
```

Model 2 Output

We provide the unstandardized estimates in Table 4.12. The table suggests that both level-1 predictors are significant on each outcome ($p < 0.001$). For *benefits*, the intercept is 4.413 and the estimates are 0.697 for *female* and 0.224 for *white*. For workplace *conditions*, the intercept is 4.678, and the estimates are 0.706 for

TABLE 4.12 Model 2 Unstandardized Estimates

Parameter	Estimate	SE	Est./SE	Sig.
Benefits Intercept	4.413	0.047	94.173	0.000
Org1	0.287	0.079	3.637	0.000
Org2	0.036	0.083	0.428	0.669
Zproduct	0.311	0.032	9.619	0.000
Female	0.697	0.027	25.656	0.000
White	0.224	0.029	7.776	0.000
Conditions Intercept	4.678	0.041	113.356	0.000
Org1	0.315	0.063	5.014	0.001
Org2	0.025	0.076	0.335	0.738
Zproduct	0.291	0.029	10.007	0.000
Female	0.706	0.029	24.345	0.000
White	0.247	0.028	8.742	0.000
Zproduct Intercept	0.119	0.104	1.145	0.252
Org1	−0.113	0.220	−0.509	0.611
Org2	−0.483	0.200	−2.415	0.016
Residual Variances				
Benefits (B)	0.133	0.020	6.637	0.000
Conditions (B)	0.093	0.015	6.248	0.000
Covariance (B)	0.095	0.016	6.082	0.000
Zproduct (B)	1.069	0.108	9.856	0.000
Benefits (W)	2.029	0.039	52.562	0.000
Conditions (W)	1.948	0.039	49.581	0.000
Covariance (W)	1.344	0.035	38.289	0.000

female and 0.247 for *white*. Between groups, as expected, *org1* is significant on *benefits* (0.287, $p < 0.001$) and *conditions* (0.315, $p < 0.001$). Similarly, *zproduct* affects *benefits* (0.311, $p < 0.001$) and workplace *conditions* (0.291, $p < 0.001$). We can see there are also some paths that are nonsignificant. More specifically, the paths from *org2* to *benefits* (0.036) and to *conditions* (0.025) are not statistically significant ($p > 0.05$). In addition, the path from *org1* to *zproduct* is not significant (-0.112, $p > 0.05$).

We can also examine the relevant TECH1 output for this model. We can see seven paths now estimated within groups, as a result of adding ethnicity to the model. Between groups, there are now 15 paths estimated for a total of 22 paths.

PARAMETER SPECIFICATION FOR WITHIN

BETA

	ZPRODUCT	BENEFIT	COND	FEMALE	WHITE
ZPRODUCT	0	0	0	0	0
BENEFIT	0	0	0	1	2
COND	0	0	0	3	4
FEMALE	0	0	0	0	0
WHITE	0	0	0	0	0
ORG1	0	0	0	0	0
ORG2	0	0	0	0	0

BETA

	ORG1	ORG2
ZPRODUCT	0	0
BENEFIT	0	0
COND	0	0
FEMALE	0	0
WHITE	0	0
ORG1	0	0
ORG2	0	0

PSI

	ZPRODUCT	BENEFIT	COND	FEMALE	WHITE
ZPRODUCT	0				
BENEFIT	0	5			
COND	0	6	7		
FEMALE	0	0	0	0	
WHITE	0	0	0	0	0
ORG1	0	0	0	0	0
ORG2	0	0	0	0	0

PSI

	ORG1	ORG2
ORG1	0	
ORG2	0	0

PARAMETERSPECIFICATIONFORBETWEEN

ALPHA

ZPRODUCT	BENEFIT	COND	FEMALE	WHITE
8	9	10	0	0

ALPHA

ORG1	ORG2
0	0

BETA

	ZPRODUCT	BENEFIT	COND	FEMALE	WHITE
ZPRODUCT	0	0	0	0	0
BENEFIT	13	0	0	0	0
COND	16	0	0	0	0
FEMALE	0	0	0	0	0
WHITE	0	0	0	0	0
ORG1	0	0	0	0	0
ORG2	0	0	0	0	0

BETA

	ORG1	ORG2
ZPRODUCT	11	12
BENEFIT	14	15
COND	17	18
FEMALE	0	0
WHITE	0	0
ORG1	0	0
ORG2	0	0

PSI

	ZPRODUCT	BENEFIT	COND	FEMALE	WHITE
ZPRODUCT	19				
BENEFIT	0	20			
COND	0	21	22		
FEMALE	0	0	0	0	
WHITE	0	0	0	0	0
ORG1	0	0	0	0	0
ORG2	0	0	0	0	0

PSI

	ORG1	ORG2
ORG1	0	
ORG2	0	0

Model 3: Revised Model Removing Nonsignificant Paths

We may decide to specify a revised model where we eliminate the nonsignificant paths. The revised model is specified in Figure 4.4. This model eliminates the three nonsignificant paths from the previous model. We could compare the fit of the first model with all paths estimated against the model where we removed the three nonsignificant paths. A nested model is one that can be derived from a more general model by removing parameters from the general model (Hox, 2002). In general, the fit of the two models can then be compared by examining the deviance statistic for each model. The difference in deviance between the two models has a chi-square distribution with degrees of freedom equal to the difference in number of parameters estimated in each model. The general model in this case has 22 parameters estimated while the nested model has three degrees of freedom,

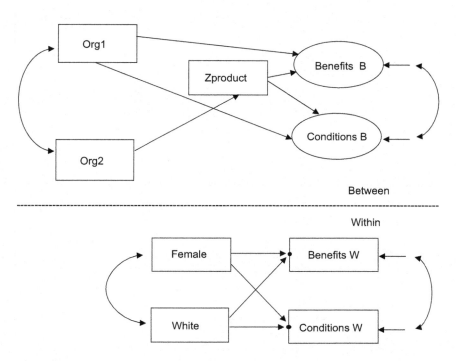

FIGURE 4.4 Revised two-level multivariate model with mediated effect.

since the three nonsignificant paths are eliminated from the model. In the case of a multilevel model using MLR for unbalanced group sizes, a scaling factor must be applied in order to obtain the correct test, since MLR uses the Muthén and Satorra (1995) rescaling of the chi-square statistic. The Mplus website (www.statmodel. com) provides information on how to conduct a chi-square difference test for nested models obtained with MLR estimation. We provide an example of how to conduct this type of test in Chapter 5.

Examining an Indirect Effect

In addition, in this model we will also test the significance of the indirect relationship between the organizational demographic (*org2*) on the two outcome variables through the intervening productivity (*zproduct*) variable.

Model 3 Statements

In order to test the indirect effect, we will add a Model Indirect statement to the input file as follows:

```
Model indirect:
        benefit ind zproduct org2;
        cond ind zproduct org2;
```

This model statement suggests that *org2* has an indirect effect on organizational-level perceptions of *benefits* and workplace *conditions*. We next provide the entire model statements.

```
TITLE:      Model 3: Revised multivariate model with mediating variable;
DATA:       FILE IS C:\mplus\ch4mv.dat;
            Format is 7f8.0,6f8.2;
VARIABLE:   Names are orgid female white satpay morale org1
            org2 benefit cond resour zproduct lev1wt lev2wt;
            Usevariables are benefit cond female white org1 org2 zproduct;
            within = female white;
            between = org1 org2 zproduct;
            CLUSTER IS orgid;
ANALYSIS:   TYPE = twolevel;
            Estimator is mlr;
```

```
Model:
        %Between%
        benefit cond on org1;
        zproduct on org2;
        benefit cond on zproduct;
        benefit with cond;
        %Within%
        benefit cond on female white;
        benefit with cond;
Model indirect:
        benefit ind zproduct org2;
        cond ind zproduct org2;
OUTPUT:    SAMPSTAT Standardized TECH1;
```

Model 3 Output

We provide the output in Table 4.13. The table suggests that both level-1 predictors are significant ($p < 0.001$). For benefits, the intercept is 4.422 and the estimates are 0.697 for *female* and 0.224 for *white*. For workplace conditions, the estimates are 0.706 for *female* and 0.247 for *white*. Between groups, as expected, the *org1* variable (0.278, $p < 0.001$) and *zproduct* (0.309, $p < 0.001$) both affect *benefits*. Similarly, *org1* (0.309) and *zproduct* (0.289) affect workplace *conditions*.

Regarding the test of the mediating effect, we also examined whether there was an indirect effect of *org2* on the outcomes (i.e., since the direct effects were not significant in the last model). It turns out that *org2* affects productivity (*zproduct*) directly ($-0.451, p < 0.05$). We also note that the indirect effect of *org2* on *benefits* (B $= -0.139$, SE $= 0.060$, Z $= -2,336, p = 0.019$) was significant, as was its indirect effect on *conditions* (B $= -0.131$, SE $= 0.056$, Z $= -2.322, p = 0.02$). This is referred to as full mediation, since the effect of the predictor variable is entirely through the mediator (*zproduct*).

Final R-Square Estimates

In Table 4.14, we can see that the model with intervening variable (*zproduct*) accounts for considerable more variance in the outcomes between groups (approximately 50% or more). The model, however, accounts for only modest (and nonsignificant) variance in the mediating predictor (i.e., 0.028, or 2.8%).

We note in passing that models that are not nested can be compared with Akaike's Information Criterion (AIC), which provides information about the best number of parameters to include in a model. The model with the number of parameters that produces the smaller AIC is considered the better of the two

TABLE 4.13 Final Revised Two-Level Multivariate Model Estimates

Parameter	Estimate	SE	Est./SE	Sig.
Benefits Intercept	4.422	0.039	112.301	0.000
Org1	0.278	0.075	3.691	0.012
Zproduct	0.309	0.031	10.111	0.000
Female	0.697	0.027	25.654	0.000
White	0.224	0.029	7.788	0.000
Conditions Intercept	4.684	0.035	132.643	0.000
Org1	0.309	0.060	5.158	0.001
Zproduct	0.289	0.027	10.560	0.000
Female	0.707	0.029	24.354	0.000
White	0.248	0.028	8.766	0.000
Zproduct Intercept	0.087	0.093	0.939	0.348
Org2	−0.451	0.195	−2.319	0.020
Indirect Effects				
Org2–Benefit	−0.139	0.060	−2.336	0.019
Org2–Conditions	−0.131	0.056	−2.322	0.020
Residual Variances				
Benefits (B)	0.133	0.020	6.576	0.000
Conditions (B)	0.093	0.015	6.160	0.000
Covariance (B)	0.095	0.016	5.988	0.000
Zproduct (B)	1.071	0.109	9.840	0.000
Benefits (W)	2.029	0.039	52.560	0.000
Conditions (W)	1.948	0.039	49.581	0.000
Covariance (W)	1.344	0.035	38.286	0.000

TABLE 4.14 Final *R*-Square Estimates

Within Level Observed Variable	Estimate	S.E.	Est./S.E.	Two-Tailed p-Value
BENEFIT	0.062	0.004	13.985	0.000
COND	0.067	0.005	13.964	0.000
Between Level Observed Variable	Estimate	S.E.	Est./S.E.	Two-Tailed p-Value
ZPRODUCT	0.028	0.024	1.156	0.248
BENEFIT	0.479	0.057	8.450	0.000
COND	0.549	0.054	10.222	0.000

models being compared. As a rough comparison, if we looked at the AIC for the full model (22 parameters) it was 81,087.657. The second model with 19 parameters was smaller at 81,082.143, which would make the second model a more parsimonious representation of the data. Of course, there could be other possible representations that might be even better.

Summary

In this chapter, we extended the basic two-level univariate regression model by presenting an example of a three-level univariate model as well as two examples of multivariate path models. We also introduced the Mplus matrix specification for multivariate models. This makes it very easy to specify separate models with direct and indirect effects at two or three levels. In the next chapter, we introduce the concept of working with latent variables within and between groups, focusing in particular on incorporating measurement error in defining constructs through their observed indicators.

References

Hox, J. (2002). *Multilevel analysis: Techniques and applications.* Mahwah, NJ: Lawrence Erlbaum.

Hox, J. J. (2010). *Multilevel analysis: Techniques and applications* (2nd ed.). New York: Routledge.

Kaplan, D. (1998). Methods for multilevel data analysis. In G. A. Marcoulides (Ed.), *Modern methods for business research* (pp. 337–358). Mahwah, NJ: Lawrence Erlbaum.

Kreft, I. & de Leeuw, J. (1998). *Introducing multilevel modeling.* Newbury Park, CA: Sage.

Mehta, P. D. & Neale, M. C. (2005). People are variables too. Multilevel structural equations modeling. *Psychological Methods, 10*(3), 259–284.

Muthén, B. O. (1991). Multilevel factor analysis of class and student achievement components. *Journal of Educational Measurement, 28*, 338–354.

Muthén, B. O. & Satorra, A. (1995). Complex sample data in structural equation modeling. In P. Marsden (Ed.), *Sociological Methodology, 1995*, 216–316.

Muthén, L. K. & Muthén, B. O. (1998–2012). *Mplus user's guide* (7th ed.). Los Angeles, CA: Authors.

Paccagnella, O. (2006). Centering or not centering in multilevel models? The role of the group mean and the assessment of group effects. *Evaluation Review, 30*(1), 66–85.

Raudenbush, S. W. & Bryk, A. S. (2002). *Hierarchical linear models* (2nd ed.). Newbury Park, CA: Sage.

Raudenbush, S. W. & Sampson, R. J. (1999). "Ecometrics": Toward a science of assessing ecological settings with applications to the systematic social observation of neighborhoods. *Sociological Methodology, 29*, 1–41.

Raykov, T. & Marcoulides, G. A. (2006). *A first course in structural equation modeling.* Mahwah, NJ: Lawrence Erlbaum Associates.

5

DEFINING MULTILEVEL LATENT VARIABLES

Chapter Objectives

In this chapter, we consider further some of the ways in which structural equation modeling (SEM) methods can be integrated with multilevel regression to investigate a wide variety of models containing hierarchical data structures, focusing in particular on incorporating measurement error in defining constructs through their observed indicators. We first develop a single-level model with two latent factors. We then extend this model to consider the nesting of individuals within departments. Finally, we extend this model to consider the nesting of departments within organizations. This overview of models with latent variables foreshadows our further development of these issues and models in subsequent chapters.

Introduction

The examples presented in the previous two chapters demonstrated the basic multilevel regression model for examining hierarchical data structures. The approach highlights the decomposition of variance in a dependent variable into its within- and between-group components (e.g., intercepts, slopes) within a single model. Unexplained variability in these components can be thought of as representing the effects of unknown or unmeasured (or latent) variables that, because they are not directly observed, must be inferred from the observed cases sampled to represent the population (Muthén, 2002; Raudenbush & Bryk, 2002; Snijders & Bosker, 1999). Associations among latent parameters can be obscured both by missing data from individuals in the sample as well as errors in the measurement of the observed indicators (Raudenbush & Bryk, 2002). As we have shown, it is possible to set up and run many types of univariate and multivariate models, including those with intervening variables, using Mplus.

In this chapter, we consider further some of the ways that SEM methods can be integrated with multilevel regression to investigate a wide variety of models containing hierarchical data structures, focusing in particular on incorporating measurement error in defining constructs through their observed indicators. The incorporation of measurement errors allows us to correct for unreliability within our multilevel models, thereby providing more accurate estimates of the structural relationships between variables. As we described in Chapter 1, multilevel regression modeling and SEM have evolved from different fields. Multilevel regression modeling has been primarily concerned with the partitioning of variance in a univariate outcome into its within- and between-group components and the explanation of that variance with sets of within- and between-group predictors. As we have noted, the SEM framework is broadly defined to accommodate the specification and testing of a wide variety of theoretical models that include latent variables (e.g., continuous, categorical), measurement error, multiple indicators, simultaneity, and complex structural relationships including reciprocal causation. One primary aim of the SEM approach was to provide more accurate estimates of structural relations between variables by including measurement error. The method combined advantages of factor analysis in defining constructs with the simultaneous linear equations approach. In actuality, SEM subsumes most linear modeling methods as special cases (Curran, 2003; Jöreskog & Sörbom, 1993; Rigdon, 1998). Latent variables can be used to represent a number of different statistical concepts including random coefficients, sources of variation in multilevel analyses, missing data, growth trajectories, finite mixtures, and latent classes (Muthén, 2002).

The SEM approach has also been referred to as *covariance structure* analysis, which comes from the practice of using a mathematical model to describe the covariance matrix of a set of observed variables from a smaller set of underlying factors, but it can be extended to include the analysis of other types of structures (e.g., means, random coefficients). The mathematical model is generally represented as a set of **matrix** operations used to solve a system of linear equations, and the software (e.g., LISREL) traditionally required input statements that specified the model in terms of the Greek names of these matrices used to store information about the relationships implied in the proposed model. More recently, some software programs have eased the use of the Greek names to identify the matrices and instead allow analysts to specify the models as path diagrams or, in the case of Mplus, by using simple statements such as "by" (measured by) to define the latent factors through their observed indicators and "on" (regressed on) to specify structural relations between the latent factors or between the latent factors and observed covariates. Users can also refer to the matrix and vector specification in Mplus by including a specific output request.

Although the SEM approach and corresponding software have been widely accepted in the analysis of single-level multivariate data, the techniques have only recently been more widely applied to the analysis of multilevel data structures. In part, this is because the SEM literature has traditionally focused on different types of research questions, and in part it is due to a lack of appropriate software and the associated difficulty in estimating multilevel data correctly with SEM techniques that were designed for single-level multivariate analyses. Since the publication of our first edition in 2000, however, considerable advances in SEM software have made it easier to apply SEM-based modeling techniques to the analysis of hierarchical data structures. Methodological work on multilevel SEM is continuing on a number of issues presently. Some of these include evaluating estimation methods under a variety of conditions including missing data, identifying potential biases in model parameters under various sampling conditions, examining the properties of fit indices in multilevel data structures, applying sample weights, and determining statistical power.

There are a number of specific features of SEM that lend themselves to investigating a wide range of multilevel, multivariate models. SEM facilitates the specification of latent variable models that address the effects of clustering and include measurement errors both within and between groups. The first SEM submodel, referred to as the measurement model, is used to define a small number of underlying (or latent) constructs through measuring their observed indicators. The measurement model corrects the constructs for errors in their observed measures and is therefore important in establishing the reliability and validity of variables used in an organizational analysis. Correcting for measurement error facilitates more accurate estimation of the model's structural parameters. For multilevel modeling, this latter point is especially important because most previous multilevel regression research on organizations assumes that predictors at all levels of a data hierarchy are measured without error. Incorporating the benefits of factor analysis (i.e., defining constructs through their observed indicators) and path analysis (including direct, indirect, and total effects), as well as cross-level interactions, can provide more complete tests of multilevel conceptual frameworks (Muthén, 1994; Raudenbush & Bryk, 2002).

Latent Variables

Many social processes are conceived as structural processes operating among unobserved constructs. Factor analysis is a useful general approach for investigating the relationships between constructs and their observed indicators because it provides a mathematical model that links the observations, or manifestations, of the underlying processes to the theories and constructs through which we interpret and understand them (Ecob & Cuttance, 1987). In social and behavioral science research, analysts and students are often interested in examining how various constructs such as job satisfaction, morale, or leadership may affect behavior such as employee productivity or turnover. Because constructs such as leadership are abstract, however, they cannot be readily observed in their abstract form. Instead, they must be defined first through a set of observed measures, which we hypothesize to measure the unobserved constructs.

The Measurement Model

The technique used to define measurement models is referred to in the SEM literature as *confirmatory* factor analysis (CFA). It is referred to as CFA because of the emphasis on proposing a set of theoretical relationships before actually testing the model against the data to determine whether it "confirms" the existence of the proposed factor model. The goal of the CFA analysis is to reproduce the original observed matrix of covariances by clustering subsets of the observed variables with a smaller number of latent factors. The analysis proceeds by assessing whether a sample covariance or correlation matrix is consistent with a hypothetical matrix implied by the specification of a theoretical model (Rigdon, 1998). A series of restrictions is placed on a covariance matrix, and then the proposed model is tested against the data to determine how well the proposed restrictions fit the data. Exploratory factor analysis items must load on all factors. Factors must be either orthogonal or correlated, and covariances between residuals are not permitted. In CFA the analyst has flexibility in proposing the specific factor model. For example, observed items may be restricted to define only particular latent factors, covariances may be specified between some or all factors, and covariances between specific error terms can be permitted. This flexibility allows the analyst to define a wide variety of potential models for individuals and groups, forcing more refined thinking about the presumed relationships. The other SEM submodel, the structural model, readily affords the researcher flexibility in defining models with direct effects, indirect effects, reciprocal effects, and multiple outcomes.

Through CFA, the researcher can assess the reliability and validity of the measurements through the careful specification of constructs and their indicators prior to their actual testing with data. This is often a step that is given little attention in the preliminary stages of investigating theoretical models. It is important to consider how well key variables in a study are measured because the lack of measurement quality in defining constructs can be an important limitation to the credibility of results stemming from the test of a particular theoretical model. **Construct validation** takes place when a researcher believes an instrument reflects a particular construct, to which certain meanings are attached. The proposed interpretation generates specific hypotheses that may be tested about the relations among the constructs, which are a means of confirming or disconfirming the claim (Cronbach & Meehl, 1955).

As we noted in the last chapter, SEM analyses are generally referred to by a defining a set of **vectors** and matrices (see Raykov & Marcoulides, 2006 for further discussion) using Greek letters and corresponding symbols. We provide both the names of the Greek letters and corresponding symbols the first time we use them. We use these interchangeably throughout our discussion to help facilitate interpretation of the Mplus output. Specifying the measurement model involves defining the observed indicators (continuous variables, categorical variables) in terms of latent factors. A smaller set of latent factors is hypothesized to be responsible for the specific pattern of variances and covariances present among a set observed variables in a sample covariance matrix. This matrix is decomposed by a model that assumes that unobserved variables (e.g., dimensions of leadership) are generating the pattern, or structure, among the observed variables. Each of the observed variables is conceptualized as a linear function of one or more factors (Long, 1983). There are two types of factors in the model: common factors that may affect more than one observed variable and unique, or residual factors, that may affect only one observed variable. Restrictions on the factor loadings and factor covariance matrix are needed to identify the model.

The basic measurement model can be represented in matrix form as

$$y_i = v + \Lambda\eta_i + \varepsilon_i, \tag{5.1}$$

where for individual i, y is a $p \times 1$ vector of observed dependent variables, v is a p-dimensional parameter vector of measurement intercepts (contained in the *nu* vector in the TECH1 Mplus output), *eta* (η) is an m-dimensional vector of latent variables, *lambda* (Λ) is a $p \times m$ matrix of factor loadings, and *epsilon* (ε_i) is a $p \times 1$ vector of measurement errors that are uncorrelated with the factors, but possible correlations may exist among the error terms. The errors are contained in the *theta* (Θ) matrix. The model-implied mean vector is the following:

$$\mu = v + \Lambda\alpha, \tag{5.2}$$

where *alpha* (α) is an m-dimensional vector of factor means. The covariance structure is

$$V(y) = \Lambda\Psi\Lambda' + \Theta, \tag{5.3}$$

where *psi* (Ψ) is an $m \times m$ matrix of factor variances and covariances, and Θ is a $p \times p$ covariance matrix of residuals assumed to be normally distributed with mean of zero and some variance. As Equation 5.1 suggests, the observed variables are linked to the underlying factors through the factor loading matrix (Λ).

To illustrate, we might propose that a vector of six items ($y_1 - y_6$) define two latent factors, with three items measuring each factor. Each item also has a separate error term ($\varepsilon_1 - \varepsilon_6$). In matrix form, the proposed model can be referred to ($y = \Lambda_y \eta + \varepsilon$) as shown in Figure 5.1. This type of matrix specification for observed items loading on factors is an important building block for the multilevel CFA models that follow in this chapter and the SEM analyses presented in subsequent chapters. The measurement model facilitates the specification of the model definition equations (Raykov & Marcoulides, 2006), or the relationships between the observed and latent variables that define a proposed model. In this case there

$$
\begin{bmatrix} y_1 \\ y_2 \\ y_3 \\ y_4 \\ y_5 \\ y_6 \end{bmatrix} = \begin{bmatrix} 1 & 0 \\ \lambda_{21} & 0 \\ \lambda_{31} & 0 \\ 0 & 1 \\ 0 & \lambda_{52} \\ 0 & \lambda_{62} \end{bmatrix} \begin{bmatrix} \eta_1 \\ \eta_2 \end{bmatrix} + \begin{bmatrix} e_1 \\ e_2 \\ e_3 \\ e_4 \\ e_5 \\ e_6 \end{bmatrix}
$$

FIGURE 5.1 Proposed two-factor CFA model.

are six equations, or one for each observed y variable. For example, the equation for y_2 would be

$$
y_2 = \lambda_2 \eta_1 + \varepsilon_2, \tag{5.4}
$$

where λ_{21} in Figure 5.1 indicates that y_2 loads on the first factor (η_1). Specific parameters may be fixed to a constant (often to 0 or 1) or freely estimated as indicated by its presence in the lambda matrix (λ_{21}). Two parameters may be constrained to be equal to each other, but they are not fixed to a particular value ahead of time. In Figure 5.1 several parameters are fixed at 0 to indicate that they do not belong with either factor 1 or 2. One observed variable on each factor is fixed to 1.0 to provide a metric to measure the factor (since latent factors have no scale of measurement). In Mplus, by default, the first observed variable named on the "measured by" line is fixed to 1.0.

The theta matrix of item residuals in measuring the factors is usually assumed to be diagonal (with off-diagonal elements fixed to 0.0) as in Equation 5.5, but in the CFA approach, off-diagonal elements fixed to zero can also be changed so that they are estimated:

$$
\Theta = \begin{bmatrix} \varepsilon_{1,1} & & & & & \\ 0 & \varepsilon_{2,2} & & & & \\ 0 & 0 & \varepsilon_{3,3} & & & \\ 0 & 0 & 0 & \varepsilon_{4,4} & & \\ 0 & 0 & 0 & 0 & \varepsilon_{5,5} & \\ 0 & 0 & 0 & 0 & 0 & \varepsilon_{6,6} \end{bmatrix}. \tag{5.5}
$$

The factor variances and covariances are contained in the psi matrix. For two proposed factors, the factor variance-covariance matrix Ψ will look like the following:

$$
\Psi = \begin{bmatrix} \sigma_{1,1}^2 & \\ \sigma_{2,1} & \sigma_{2,2}^2 \end{bmatrix}. \tag{5.6}
$$

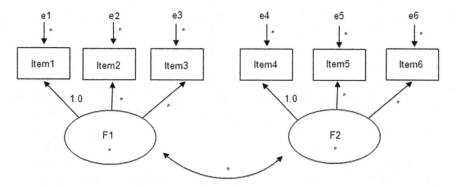

FIGURE 5.2 Proposed two-factor model.

This suggests that the factor variances are on the diagonals, and the covariance is off the diagonal. Since the matrix is symmetrical, we need only refer to the lower (or upper) triangle.

We illustrate the model in visual form in Figure 5.2. We can see that the first item defining each factor (i.e., item1 and item4) have been fixed at 1.0 to provide a metric for measuring the factor. In Figure 5.2 we can count up 13 parameters to be estimated (i.e., four factor loadings, three factor variances and covariances, and six error terms). There are an additional six item intercepts being estimated for a total of 19 parameters. The item intercepts are typically not shown in SEM diagrams.

The basic measurement model in Equation 5.1 can be extended to consider covariates that affect the y variables directly, as in the following:

$$y_i = \upsilon + \Lambda\eta_i + Kx_i + \varepsilon_i, \tag{5.7}$$

where x_i is a $q \times 1$ vector of independent (background) variables and K is a corresponding $p \times q$ matrix of regression slopes. Usually only a few of the rows in K would be nonzero, where such a nonzero value would correspond to a y variable that was directly affected by one more x variables (Muthén, 1998–2004). Alternatively, it is also possible to simplify the specification of the measurement model in Equation 5.4 by placing any x_i covariate relationships with particular y_i observed variables within the Beta matrix of regression coefficients (as in Equation 5.8).

Structural Model

The second part of the model (consisting of the structural relationships) can be defined in the Mplus framework as

$$\eta_i = \alpha + B\eta_i + \Gamma x_i + \zeta_i, \tag{5.8}$$

where η is a vector of latent factors, α is a vector of measurement intercepts, Beta (β) is a nonsingular matrix of regression coefficients for regressions among the latent factors; x_i is a set of covariates; Gamma (Γ) is a matrix of regression coefficients relating the covariates (x) to the latent factors; and Zeta (ζ) is a vector of residuals (or errors in equations), with zero means, and uncorrelated with the other latent variables, covariates, and ε_i. The covariance matrix of ζ is denoted Ψ. In Equation 5.5, for example, we might define a relationship where the two factors (η_1 and η_2) could be regressed on an observed variable such as gender. In practice, it is efficient to place relationships between observed x_i covariates and latent variables within the Beta matrix of structural coefficients. We might instead propose that the second factor (η_2) is regressed on the first factor (η_1) with the coefficient expressing this relationship defined as β. The structural part of the equation would then be defined as

$$\eta_2 = \beta_{21}\eta_1 + \zeta_2. \tag{5.9}$$

As the structural part of the model suggests, variance in latent factors can be explained through a series of structural equations linking various covariates and latent factors to each other, and in the case of a multilevel model, variance in factors can be decomposed across levels of the data hierarchy and explained by structural equations at each level. We refer to these types of structural models more specifically in Chapter 6. Latent growth curve models can be defined similarly through several repeated measures (e.g., such as $y_1 - y_4$) that load on latent level and shape factors (discussed in Chapter 7). Moreover, mixture models add categorical latent variables to the analysis, which can be related to other continuous latent factors, categorical latent factors, or observed items (as developed in Chapter 8).

Proposing a CFA Model

In this proposed two-factor model in Figure 5.1, each observed variable has been restricted to load on only one common factor with the loadings on the other factors specified as fixed to zero (0). We note that in the examples that follow the items are continuous variables that are normally distributed. We illustrate CFA models with ordinal indicators in Chapter 8. We will assume the two latent factors (F1 and F2) define different aspects of individuals' work lives (e.g., work satisfaction, social relationships). We will also assume that the first three items will measure F1 and the second three items will measure F2. Of course, we could decide to have one item load on both factors if our theory suggested that relationship. Because these restrictions are imposed, the model becomes confirmatory, in that various **model fit indices** will be used to evaluate how well this particular model fits the data, as opposed to some other that we might propose. Besides having a unique factor for each observed variable, through using matrix specification the researcher may also choose whether or not particular residuals are specified to covary (e.g., ε_5 and ε_6). Similarly, we can decide whether the factors should covary. We could even specify the size of the relationship between two parameters (loadings, error covariances, factor covariances) or define specific items to load equally on each factor. Thus, there is great flexibility afforded by this approach for investigating underlying structures.

The TECH1 output provided in Mplus is useful for seeing how the proposed model is specified. In this case, the vector of individual item intercepts is specified in Nu. There is one estimated parameter for each item intercept (parameters 1–6). The factor loadings are specified in the Lambda matrix. For F1, we can see that item1 is not estimated (0), since it is specified to be fixed at 1.0 automatically by the program in order to provide a metric for defining the factor. Therefore, it does not count as an estimated parameter (i.e., it has a 0). Item2 and item3 are estimated (shown as parameters 7 and 8). Items 1–3 are not specified to define F2, so they are fixed to 0. On F2, item4 is fixed to 1 to define a metric for that factor, so it is not freely estimated (0). Item5 and item6 are estimated as parameters 9 and 10 in the model. The errors associated with the factor loadings are defined in the Theta matrix. There is one error term estimated for each item (as parameters 11–16). We note that the covariances between errors are typically fixed at 0. Sometimes, however, it may be the case that one or more item errors are assumed to be correlated. In that case, a specific item covariance can be freely estimated. The Alpha vector contains the latent factor means, which we have restricted to be 0. The Beta matrix can be used to specify relationships between factors. In this initial model the possible causal relationships between factors are not estimated (i.e., fixed to 0). Finally, the latent factor variances and the covariance between them are contained in the Psi matrix as parameters 17–19. We note that the numbering of individual parameters in a proposed model can change depending on what parameters are estimated versus fixed to 0.

TECHNICAL 1 OUTPUT

PARAMETER SPECIFICATION

NU

ITEM1	ITEM2	ITEM3	ITEM4	ITEM5	ITEM6
1	2	3	4	5	6

LAMBDA

	F1	F2
ITEM1	0	0
ITEM2	7	0
ITEM3	8	0
ITEM4	0	0
ITEM5	0	9
ITEM6	0	10

THETA	ITEM1	ITEM2	ITEM3	ITEM4	ITEM5	ITEM6
ITEM1	11					
ITEM2	0	12				
ITEM3	0	0	13			
ITEM4	0	0	0	14		
ITEM5	0	0	0	0	15	
ITEM6	0	0	0	0	0	16

ALPHA	F1	F2
	0	0

BETA	F1	F2
F1	0	0
F2	0	0

PSI	F1	F2
F1	17	
F2	18	19

If we were to regress the two latent factors F1 and F2 on a predictor such as female (as implied in Equation 5.7), we can see in the TECH1 output that these two structural relations (actually specified in the Beta matrix) would become the 17th and 18th parameters estimated in the model, respectively, with the factor variances and covariances then becoming the final estimated parameters in the model (19–21).

TECHNICAL 1 OUTPUT

PARAMETER SPECIFICATION

BETA	F1	F2	FEMALE
F1	0	0	17
F2	0	0	18
FEMALE	0	0	0

PSI	F1	F2	FEMALE
F1	19		
F2	20	21	
FEMALE	0	0	0

As the matrix specification in Figure 5.1 and visual representation in Figure 5.2 suggest, in the CFA approach theoretical constraints postulated on the basis of theory and previous empirical findings are imposed on the set of relationships in a proposed model before the model is tested with actual data. To define the proposed model adequately, the researcher should already know the number of constructs, the specific construct with which each of the observed variables is to be associated, the particular pattern of correlations between constructs, the relationships among the unique factors (i.e., residuals) and observed variables, and possibly even the relationships among the set of unique factors (Long, 1983). Several statistical and practical tests can be used to determine whether the data confirm the set of relationships implied in the hypothesized model. If the model is consistent with the data (i.e., it reproduces the observed variation present in the data), the researcher has preliminary evidence of its construct validity. Depending on the degree of model misfit, the researcher may need to locate the one or more parameters that may be responsible for the model misfit. In other cases, the model may need to be reconceptualized.

Model Identification

In testing a proposed CFA model against data, it is important to make sure that the model has been identified properly, even though the output will issue warnings about models that are not properly identified. **Model identification** is a complicated issue that has been widely discussed in the SEM literature (e.g., Bollen, 1989; Bollen & Long, 1993; Jöreskog & Sörbom, 1989; Marcoulides & Hershberger, 1997). Identification has to do with the adequacy of information necessary for parameter estimation. We need to have sufficient information to solve for unknown values in the model-implied equations. If a model is not identified (referred to as being under-identified), it is possible to find an infinite number of values for the parameters, each set of which would be consistent with the covariance equation (Long, 1983). Model estimation assumes that the model has been identified; that is, either there is just enough information to solve each parameter (referred to as a just-identified model) or there is more than enough information (referred to as an overidentified model).

In a general sense, the problem of identification is dealt with by restricting the number of parameters estimated from the total number of parameters that could be estimated. Thus, overidentified models (i.e., with more than enough available variances and covariances than needed to obtain a unique solution) are desired because they will have positive degrees of freedom (df). For this reason, only overidentified models may be tested for their fit against the data. Several important pieces of information provided in the Mplus output can help with thinking about model identification. Initially, we want to ensure that the model estimation terminates normally. If it does, the following statement is issued:

THE MODEL ESTIMATION TERMINATED NORMALLY.

Regarding model identification, we can look are the number of parameters that are to be estimated in the model, which is summarized right after the model estimation statement. Finally, we can examine the number of degrees of freedom that exist, which is summarized in the chi-square test as part of the model fit information. A just-identified model, which has as many parameters estimated as is possible given the number of variables in the observed covariance matrix, will have no degrees of freedom available. By definition, this model fits the data perfectly. An underidentified model, which has does not have enough available information to solve the implied equations, will have negative degrees of freedom.

Here is a simple illustration regarding how we can figure out the total number of variance and covariance parameters estimated using our first single-level example. First, we make use of the fact that in a covariance matrix there is $p(p + 1)/2$ variances and covariances, where p refers to the number of variables in the matrix. If we have three variables in the covariance matrix, there will be $3(4)/2$, or 6 variance-covariance parameters—the three variances in the diagonals and the three covariance parameters either above or below the diagonal of the matrix. A secondary piece of information is that in SEM, we also may estimate k intercepts (i.e., one for each observed variable in the covariance matrix). This comes from the fact that most SEM software programs use a so-called augmented covariance-mean matrix, where the variable means are added as the last line of the matrix. In traditional covariance matrix structure analysis, however, only the information regarding the number of variances and covariances in the covariance matrix would typically be used. In our small example, therefore, we would have a total of nine possible parameters to estimate (6 variances/covariances + 3 intercepts = 9). We note that Mplus automatically assumes the possible estimation of the variance-covariance components and the observed variable intercepts in calculating the total number of parameters estimated in a model, so that if the analyst fixes the three intercepts to 0, there will be three degrees of freedom gained in the model test.

Let's now specify a simple theoretical model; we will propose the following:

1. $A \rightarrow B$
2. $B \rightarrow C$
3. $A \rightarrow C$

This formulation uses up our six available variance-covariance parameters, since we will estimate two residual variances for the dependent variables (one for B and one for C), one variance (A), and we have three equations from the three covariances present in the matrix. We also estimate the three intercepts, we will have used up the available nine of nine possible parameters. In Table 5.1, we obtain the following information regarding the chi-square coefficient.

This is what we refer to as a *just-identified* model, since there are no degrees of freedom and nine parameters estimated. If we eliminate the direct path between A and C (i.e., by fixing it to 0), however, we will obtain one degree of freedom, as shown in Table 5.2. This is an example of an *overidentified* model, since there

TABLE 5.1 Selected Model Fit Information

Number of Free Parameters	9
Chi-Square Value	0.000
Degrees of Freedom	0
P-Value	0.000

TABLE 5.2 Selected Model Fit Information

Number of Free Parameters	8
Chi-Square Value	100.435
Degrees of Freedom	1
P-Value	0.000

TABLE 5.3 Selected Model Fit Information

Number of Free Parameters =	10
Chi-Square Value =	0.000
Degrees of Freedom	−1
P-Value	0.000

are only eight parameters estimated from the nine possible parameters. We can note that there is an accompanying chi-square coefficient (100.435) and positive degrees of freedom (i.e., 1 *df*).

If instead, we use our just-identified model (with nine parameters) and try to estimate an additional path ($C \rightarrow A$), we will have proposed too many equations for the available information about the covariances between the observed variables, and we have a resulting *underidentified* model. We also receive the following warning:

THE DEGREES OF FREEDOM FOR THIS MODEL ARE NEGATIVE. THE MODEL IS NOT IDENTIFIED. NO CHI-SQUARE TEST IS AVAILABLE. CHECK YOUR MODEL.

In addition, the model fit information in Table 5.3 indicates an impossible situation.

Model Fit Indices

After ensuring that a proposed model is just identified or overidentified, we can examine how well it fits the data. To examine a proposed model's fit to the data, the analyst can select from several commonly used indices from the more than 30 model fit indices available [see Marcoulides & Hershberger (1997) for a complete explanation of fit indices]. Not all of the fit indices define model fit in the same way [see Byrne (2012) for further discussion of Mplus fit indices]. The likelihood ratio test defines fit in terms of the discrepancy between the observed covariance matrix S and model-implied (or restricted) covariance matrix $\Sigma(\theta)$. Assuming multivariate normality, the likelihood ratio test follows a chi-square distribution and is often referred to a chi-square test, which uses the sample size and the value of the discrepancy function ($\chi^2 = N - 1(F_{min})$ with degrees of freedom equal to the number of unique elements in S minus the number of parameters (q) estimated. The null hypothesis (H_0) basically tests that $\Sigma - \Sigma(\theta) = 0$, and the chi-square test simultaneously tests the extent to which the model residuals in $\Sigma - \Sigma(\theta) = 0$ are 0 (Bollen, 1989). In other words, the null hypothesis the tests whether the implied factor loadings, factor variances and covariances, and residuals in the proposed model are a valid representation of the observed data. It is important to note, however, that it may not be the only valid representation of the data, as other models might also fit as well or better in the case where the fit of the model is not perfect. The probability value (p) associated with the chi-square statistic represents the likelihood of obtaining a χ^2 value that exceeds the value when H_0 is true (Byrne, 2012). Higher p values are therefore preferred.

The root-mean-square error of approximation (RMSEA) also measures the discrepancy between hypothesized model and the sample data. RMSEA combines information about the discrepancy between the observed and model-implied covariance matrices with a parsimony criterion for the degrees of freedom (i.e., more parsimonious models are preferred). The index approximates a noncentral χ^2 distribution, which implies that it does not require a true null hypothesis; that is, it accounts for the likelihood that the proposed model is somewhat imperfect (Byrne, 2012). More specifically, RMSEA measures the amount of model discrepancy per degree of freedom, which provides a test of "close fit" rather than the "absolute" fit of the chi-square test (Marcoulides & Hershberger, 1997). Values of 0.06 or lower represent good fit to the data (Hu & Bentler, 1999), while values of 0.07–0.08 are often viewed as representing reasonable errors of approximation in the population (Browne & Cudeck, 1993).

Residual-based indices [e.g., standardized root-mean-square residual (SRMR)] evaluate model fit in terms of the average size of the residuals. The SRMR represents the average size of the residuals in fitting the implied model covariance matrix $\Sigma(\theta)$ to the sample covariance matrix S, with values of 0.05 or smaller often taken as evidence of a good model fit.

Akaike's information criterion (AIC) and the Bayesian information criterion (BIC) indices are useful in comparing a series of models, with the number of parameters that produces the lowest AIC or BIC considered the best. Moreover, AIC and BIC do not require models to be nested (i.e., where one model results from another by restricting one or more paths to zero). AIC and BIC take into consideration both the fit of the model as well as its complexity as defined by the number of parameters estimated (with BIC assigning a slightly greater penalty than AIC in this regard). AIC tends to be more commonly used. In Mplus, AIC is defined as -2(log likelihood) $+ 2q$, where the log likelihood is the H_0 value in the output and q refers to the number of parameters estimated.

Other indices [e.g., comparative fit index (CFI) and Tucker-Lewis index (TLI)] define fit in "relative" terms, that is, as compared to a baseline independence (null) or "ill-fitting" model (i.e., a model where the variances are unrestricted and the covariances among observed variables are set to zero). Mplus also includes the estimated intercepts (means) of the observed variables in the independence model. The general equation is as follows:

$$CFI = \left| \frac{(\chi_b^2 - df_b) - (\chi_m^2 - df_m)}{(\chi_b^2 - df_b)} \right|. \tag{5.10}$$

Researchers can consider the conditions of the independence model and whether it is appropriate for the particular model being investigated (Wu et al., 2009). As Marcoulides and Hershberger (1997) note, however, there is no necessity to compare CFI or other relative fit indices to the default baseline model. Any pair of **nested models** can be compared (e.g., a specific hypothesized baseline model and a nested alternative model). For example, for examining latent growth curve models (see Chapter 8), Wu et al. suggest making an adjustment to the independence baseline model (e.g., estimating an intercept-only baseline model consisting of the mean of the intercept and the residual variances of the observed variables comprising the repeated measures). Another possible more restrictive model would be an intercept and single constant residual variance (Wu et al., 2009). In comparison to CFI, TLI is considered a nonnormed index since it can exceed the range of 0.0–1.0 used in defining CFI. TLI also includes a penalty for model complexity regarding included parameters that do not contribute as much to model fit as more essential parameters. Its value will therefore typically be lower than CFI.

In general terms, fit indices are influenced by sample size in either direct or indirect ways. For example, in the chi-square test statistic sample size enters directly into the calculation, which can increase Type I error rates (i.e., tendency to reject a good-fitting model as the sample size increases). In contrast, in small samples increased error rates may result from the asymptotic distribution not being well approximated (Bollen, 1989). RMSEA (which is discrepancy per degree of freedom fit index that provides a "close test" of fit), relative fit indices (e.g., CFA), and information indices (AIC, BIC) are generally thought to be less affected by sample size than absolute fit indices such as the chi-square statistic (Mehta & Neale, 2005; Wu et al., 2009). Most SEM fit indices were designed for use with single-level data and relatively large sample sizes required for ML estimation; consequently, there is less known about how these indices may operate optimally with two- or three-level data in terms of the influence of within-cluster and cluster-level sample sizes, distributional properties of variables, and model misspecification (Mehta & Neale, 2005; Wu et al., 2009). Information-type indices (AIC, BIC) are useful in multilevel SEM with random slopes since the covariance-based fit indices are not clear because they are particularly affected by sample size (Mehta & Neale, 2005). Liu, Rovine, and Molenaar (2012), for example, found AIC and BIC were generally able to identify the true error structure in growth curve models where sample sizes were not too small.

Although the chi-square index is probably the most commonly used statistical index of model fit, it does have the undesirable property of being affected by sample size. We reiterate that the null hypothesis concerning the fit of the model tested actually only refers to the overidentifying constraints; that is, the chi-square value represents the lack of fit due to the overidentifying constraints in the model, as opposed to the whole model (Hoyle & Panter, 1995). The χ^2 coefficient, which would be 0 for a perfect-fitting model, is rather large in our proposed model ($\chi^2 = 495.186, 8df, p < 0.001$) summarized in Table 5.1, which indicates there is considerable error in the model. We should keep in mind, however, that with a sample of nearly 3,000 individuals, we might reject a model that is actually a good empirical representation of the data, if we relied only on the χ^2 coefficient.

Other "rule of thumb" criteria for SEM, such as CFI = 0.95, RMSEA = 0.06, and SRMR = 0.08 (e.g., Hu & Bentler, 1998, 1999), are commonly used; however, they are based more on practical experience and simulations using covariance structure models without mean structures (Wu et al., 2009). They are also differentially affected by issues related to model misspecification, distribution of variables, and sample size (Wu et al., 2009). With ML estimation, CFI performs consistently across a variety of modeling conditions including relatively small sample sizes ($50 < n < 250$) and moderate departures from normality (see Hoyle & Panter, 1995; Hu & Bentler, 1998). CFI and RMSEA have been found to be more sensitive to misspecifications in factor loadings than misspecification in factor covariance (Hu & Bentler, 1998), while SRMR showed the opposite effect. It should be noted, however, that later work has also shown that the severity of model misspecification should also be considered (Fan & Sivo, 2005).

Model 1: Examining a Single-Level CFA Model

Consider a simple situation where we wish to define two factors for a random sample of individuals ($N = 2{,}720$). We will use this data set to investigate some different factor models in this chapter. We assume six continuous items measure two latent factors as specified in Figure 5.2. For p variables, in this case six observed items, there can be a total of 42/2 parameters (or 21) variance-covariance parameters that can be estimated ($[p(p + 1)/2]$), plus k intercept parameters (6). This will result in a total of 27 possible parameters. The proposed model in Figure 5.2 actually only implies 19 parameters to estimate (i.e., four factor loadings, six error terms, three factor variances and covariances, and six intercepts), which will leave 8 degrees of freedom in the chi-square test, as shown in Table 5.1. In the model statements, we note TYPE = general (since it is a single-level model) and the estimator is maximum likelihood (the default).

```
TITLE:      Model 1: Single-level CFA model;
DATA:       FILE IS C:\mplus\3LCFA.dat;
            Format is 11f8.0,7f8.2;
VARIABLE:   Names are orgcode deptid item1 item2 item3 item4 item5 item6
            age female deptsize dept_m orgsize empstab orgdemos
            orgqual orgprod1 orgprod2;
            Usevariables are item1 item2 item3 item4 item5 item6;
ANALYSIS:   TYPE = general;
            Estimator is ML;
Model:
            F1 by item1 item2 item3;
            F2 by item4 item5 item6;
OUTPUT:     sampstat standardized tech1;
```

Model 1 Output

The selected output presented in Table 5.4 provides confirmation that we did indeed estimate 19 parameters. By general standards, this model can be evaluated as acceptable (e.g., CFI = 0.967, SRMR = 0.037). We will illustrate how CFI is estimated. We can see the baseline chi-square test statistic for the model is 14,996.901 (with 15 degrees of freedom). The model chi-square test statistic is 495.186 for 8 degrees of freedom. Applying Equation 5.10, we can estimate the CFI as 0.967 (14494.715/14981.901 = 0.967).

We can construct the default baseline model as well (with 15 degrees of freedom) and test its fit to the data. By fixing all the item factor loadings to 0, fixing the factor variances to 1.0, and assuming no covariance structure between factors (i.e., all of which assumes there is no covariance structure among observed variables in the covariance matrix), we can obtain the same baseline "ill-fitting" model (i.e., which estimates six item intercepts and six item error terms). The output from this baseline model as we specified it is presented in Table 5.5. This provides one illustration of how the baseline model output is constructed in the Mplus output (see Table 5.4), as well as how various baseline models could be constructed for comparative purposes.

TABLE 5.4 Selected Model Fit Information

Number of Free Parameters = 19
Chi-Square Test of Model Fit = 495.186, degrees of freedom = 8, $p = 0.000$
Chi-Square Test for Baseline Model = 14996.901, degrees of freedom =15, $p = 0.000$
Comparative Fit Index (CFI) = 0.967
Standardized Root Mean Square Residual (SRMR) = 0.037

TABLE 5.5 Mplus Output for Baseline Model Estimated

Chi-Square Test of Model Fit	
Value	14996.901
Degrees of Freedom	15
P-Value	0.0000

We will assume for now that the model is "good enough" to examine how well the items serve as measures of the latent constructs by examining the factor loadings and factor variances and covariances. In Table 5.6 we present the parameter estimates for this first model. We can see there are 19 estimated parameters (i.e., remembering the first item of each factor being set to 1.0 by default). The model shows preliminarily that the items measure the factors well, since each has a significant factor loading. We note that the item chosen to provide a metric for each factor does not have a statistical test associated with it (shown by 999 in the Mplus output).

Since the unstandardized estimates are sometimes harder to interpret, we next present the standardized estimates of the factor loadings in Table 5.7. We can note a couple of things. First, the items load well on the factors (generally about 0.89 or above), except perhaps for item6 (loading = 0.685). If we square the factor loading ($0.684 \times 0.684 = 0.468$) and subtract this from 1.0, we will obtain the residual in the table below for item6 (i.e., $1.0 - 0.468 = 0.532$). This suggests that an item that was perfectly measured would load 1.0 on the factor and would correspondingly have no error, since if we squared the loading and subtracted it from 1.0 we would obtain the residual of 0.0 (i.e., $1.0 - 1.0 = 0.0$). Second, we can also see that in the standardized solution the factor variances are set to 1.0 and so the covariance (0.872) can be interpreted as the correlation between the two factors. We can conclude that there is considerable overlap between the two constructs.

One important distinction between *exploratory* factor analysis (an approach with which the reader may already be familiar) and CFA is that in the confirmatory approach, the researcher first specifies a *particular* pattern of observed variable loadings (Λ) on the factors (η_i) guided by theory. This results in many elements in the lambda matrix being *fixed* to 0.0 (i.e., not estimated), which facilitates being able to examine the proposed model's fit to the data. In contrast, in the exploratory factor method, every observed variable is *free* to be identified with, or *load*, on every factor (which also necessitates fixing particular parameters so the process will obtain a solution).

Restricting paths to 0.0 in CFA is what provides the "test" of a particular hypothesized model to the data and in most cases is needed to identify a unique solution to the set of equations. If the restricted relationships *do not* fit the data, there will be a large discrepancy between the hypothesized model with the pattern

TABLE 5.6 Unstandardized Model Results

		Estimate	S.E.	Est./S.E.	Two-Tailed P-Value
F1	BY				
ITEM1		1.000	0.000	999.000	999.000
ITEM2		1.762	0.024	72.993	0.000
ITEM3		2.132	0.028	76.121	0.000
F2	BY				
ITEM4		1.000	0.000	999.000	999.000
ITEM5		1.378	0.019	72.062	0.000
ITEM6		0.750	0.018	42.191	0.000
F2	WITH				
F1		45.271	1.458	31.044	0.000
Intercepts					
ITEM1		19.075	0.125	152.888	0.000
ITEM2		32.061	0.214	149.930	0.000
ITEM3		30.797	0.257	119.733	0.000
ITEM4		30.641	0.184	166.197	0.000
ITEM5		38.207	0.266	143.433	0.000
ITEM6		36.795	0.188	195.916	0.000
Variances					
F1		33.786	1.143	29.561	0.000
F2		79.819	2.556	31.233	0.000
Residual Variances					
ITEM1		8.555	0.309	27.668	0.000
ITEM2		19.544	0.814	24.024	0.000
ITEM3		26.440	1.128	23.439	0.000
ITEM4		12.635	0.693	18.228	0.000
ITEM5		41.474	1.588	26.111	0.000
ITEM6		51.052	1.512	33.755	0.000

of restricted paths and the actual data. In this case, the researcher would have to reconceptualize at least some aspect of the hypothesized model (e.g., perhaps by relaxing one of the fixed factor loadings so the item could load on two factors simultaneously). If the discrepancy between the hypothesized model and the data is small, the researcher has established some initial evidence confirming the proposed model's construct validity.

A second distinction between the two factor analysis approaches is that in the exploratory approach, factors must either be correlated or uncorrelated. In contrast, the CFA approach allows considerable flexibility in determining which factors are proposed to correlate and which might not. A third important distinction

TABLE 5.7 Standardized Model Results

		Estimate	S.E.	Est./S.E.	Two-Tailed P-Value
F1	BY				
ITEM1		0.893	0.005	189.104	0.000
ITEM2		0.918	0.004	226.833	0.000
ITEM3		0.924	0.004	240.074	0.000
F2	BY				
ITEM4		0.929	0.004	212.236	0.000
ITEM5		0.886	0.005	168.253	0.000
ITEM6		0.684	0.011	61.024	0.000
F2	WITH				
F1		0.872	0.007	131.179	0.000
Intercepts					
ITEM1		2.931	0.044	66.429	0.000
ITEM2		2.875	0.043	66.181	0.000
ITEM3		2.296	0.037	62.797	0.000
ITEM4		3.187	0.047	67.415	0.000
ITEM5		2.750	0.042	65.592	0.000
ITEM6		3.757	0.054	69.026	0.000
Variances					
F1		1.000	0.000	999.000	999.000
F2		1.000	0.000	999.000	999.000
Residual Variances					
ITEM1		0.202	0.008	23.942	0.000
ITEM2		0.157	0.007	21.143	0.000
ITEM3		0.147	0.007	20.675	0.000
ITEM4		0.137	0.008	16.798	0.000
ITEM5		0.215	0.009	23.026	0.000
ITEM6		0.532	0.015	34.702	0.000

between the two approaches is that in CFA the theta matrix of residuals (Θ) is not restricted to being diagonal (i.e., where error variance for each observed variable is represented on the diagonals and the off-diagonals elements are fixed to 0.0). This greater flexibility permits the specification of covariances between error terms by estimating one or more off-diagonal elements within the matrix. It is important to note, however, that these differences in specifying proposed models make model identification (i.e., determining whether a unique solution exists) in CFA more difficult because as a result of this increased flexibility, there are many more possible parameters that can be estimated. We note that Mplus has a well-developed routine for exploratory factor analysis (EFA). Interested readers can consult the

Mplus 7 User's Guide for information on how to specify single-level and multilevel EFA models. These models are useful when there is only minimal knowledge about the relationships between observed variables and possible underlying factors in the data.

Model 2: Freeing an Error Covariance

To illustrate this, in the second model, we will free an error term in Θ between item6 and item3 (by adding the statement ITEM6 with ITEM3). If we do this, there will now be one more path to estimate (for a total of 20). We can confirm this in the model fit information in Table 5.8.

Model 2 Output

We can see in the above information that making this one change resulted in a considerable improvement in our model (i.e., the χ^2 coefficient dropped by nearly 148 for 1 degree of freedom, and both the CFI and SRMR improved as well). Although we usually do not recommend making model changes regarding error terms unless there is some sort of a theoretical rationale for doing so (since simply freeing error terms can tend to capitalize on chance to improve the model), in this case we will accept this change, since in actuality item3 and item6 are similar types of items (referring to perceptions) while the other four indicators refer to skills.

We note in passing that models incorporating measurement errors in defining outcomes can also be specified within a multilevel regression framework (Raudenbush & Bryk, 2002). In this type of formulation, the level-1 model is considered as the measurement model where the constructs are defined in terms of their observed items or indicators. This formulation results in a "true score" outcome that has been corrected for measurement error. The level-2 model then becomes the model that investigates differences in the latent outcome between individuals. It is also possible to add a group structure, such as individuals nested within organizations, at Level 3. In this formulation, the latent variables themselves can vary at two levels (Raudenbush & Bryk, 2002). Measurement error is also incorporated into the study of individual change as latent growth and initial (or end) status parameters in the SEM latent variable framework or as true-score parameters in the multilevel regression framework.

TABLE 5.8 Selected Model Fit Information for Revised Model

Number of Free Parameters = 20
Chi-Square Test of Model Fit = 347.461, degrees of freedom = 7, $p = 0.000$
Comparative Fit Index (CFI) = 0.977
Standardized Root Mean Square Residual (SRMR) = 0.032

Extending the Generalizability of a Model

In practice, the researcher may not have only one measurement model (or set of restrictions) in mind, but rather a series of competing models. Testing the adequacy of each proposed model in sequence is known as an alternative-models approach (see Hoyle & Panter, 1995 for further discussion). Through these comparisons, the researcher can determine whether alternative models fit just as well (called an equivalent model) or better or worse than the primary model (see Rigdon, 1998). Construct validation is therefore an ongoing process of defining and checking to see whether the defined construct is useful within a larger system of theoretical relations among the constructs. Because of the emphasis on theory in using this approach, it is important to begin with clear definitions about constructs, using previous research and theoretical models as guides in their definition. In operationalizing constructs, however, it is important to keep in mind that the observed indicators are not the construct itself but only a set of possible manifestations of it.

Once a model's preliminary construct validity has been established, researchers often investigate whether the same model fits across other groups, samples, or settings. This process is referred to as testing a model's invariance or generalizability and is a second way of investigating its construct validity (examining covariance matrices across groups is actually one of the building blocks for defining multilevel models with SEM). In Chapter 1, we developed the idea that variability in a univariate outcome such as a math score within individuals and between groups (e.g., males and females) could also be considered from a multivariate perspective using MANOVA, where a sample sum of squares and cross-products (SSCP) matrix consisting of several outcomes (e.g., reading, math, language) could be decomposed into a within-groups SSCP matrix and a between-groups SSCP matrix, and the group effect examined by calculating the ratio of the within-groups determinant to the total sample (i.e., within-group + between-group) determinant. For example, a researcher might investigate whether the same factor structure can be confirmed in a new sample of subjects or in different subgroups (e.g., males and females, product and service organizations).

In SEM, such tests of model invariance across groups can be conducted by imposing constraints on particular parameters of interest across a number of groups and determining how well this model fits each of the covariance matrices of the groups or samples being compared. In this way, hypotheses can be tested about the invariance of the factor structure (e.g., same number of factors, same factor variances and covariances), whether the same pattern of factor loadings exists, and whether there are invariant measurement errors across the groups examined. In the past, factor analyses typically ignored the multilevel character of the data. In part, this was because creating the proper within- and between-group covariance matrices, especially for unbalanced sampling designs, was problematic because of limitations associated with SEM software programs.

Testing the generalizability of a model helps extend the usefulness of a theory by confirming and, if necessary, modifying a set of proposed relationships in a variety of different settings and groups. Of course, examining a model's construct validity across a number of different samples can be directly applied to multilevel research. In the multilevel application, we extend the basic premise of fitting the model across several groups to a larger number of organizations. In fact, in the multilevel situation, we can test the measurement properties of a construct (i.e., how well it is defined by its indicators) and its generalizability across groups simultaneously.

Multilevel Measurement Models

In single-level CFA, the relationships among the observed variables are characterized by the covariances among these variables contained in a sample covariance matrix. The observations are assumed to be independently and identically distributed. Of course, where individuals are clustered in organizations, this will no longer be the case. The general statistical model for multilevel SEM is complicated and, as a practical matter, was difficult to implement in software programs because of the complexities in computing separate covariance matrices for units of varying sample sizes (Hox, 1995; McArdle & Hamagami, 1996). This is because SEM techniques have traditionally depended on large sample sizes for efficient estimation. As noted previously, however, the introduction of FIML (and Bayesian estimation methods) in recent years has greatly expanded the facility of SEM to examine a wider set of research problems with data consisting of various hierarchical structures, sample sizes, variable distributions, and completeness.

The basic measurement model presented in Equation 5.1 can be readily adapted for multilevel analysis. The two-level factor model refers to a total covariance matrix and is therefore a model for one population with observations at two levels of aggregation. The total score for each individual is decomposed into a within-group component (the individual deviation from the group mean) and a between-group component (the disaggregated group means). Muthén (1989, 1990, 1991, 1994) provided one way to simplify the analysis of multilevel data using conventional SEM software by assuming there is one population of individuals who are clustered into groups.

This decomposition is used to compute separate within-groups and between-groups covariance matrices, which are orthogonal (uncorrelated) and additive. If we decompose the population data, the population covariance structure for this model for individual i in cluster j would be:

$$V(y_{ij}) = \Sigma_T = \Sigma_B + \Sigma_W. \tag{5.11}$$

Consistent with the single-level specification of the covariance structure specified in Equation 5.3, the between-groups covariance structure model can be represented in matrix notation as

$$\Sigma_{\mathrm{B}} = \Lambda_{\mathrm{B}}\Psi_{\mathrm{B}}\Lambda_{\mathrm{B}}' + \Theta_{\mathrm{B}}, \tag{5.12}$$

and the within-group covariance matrix representing within-unit variation can be represented as

$$\Sigma_{\mathrm{W}} = \Lambda_{\mathrm{W}}\Psi_{\mathrm{W}}\Lambda_{\mathrm{W}}' + \Theta_{\mathrm{W}}. \tag{5.13}$$

The factor means are represented at the cluster level as

$$\mu_j = \Lambda_j \alpha. \tag{5.14}$$

One important difference between the SEM formulation and the typical multilevel regression formulation is that the former defines the model at the level of the cluster (i.e., group) rather than for the entire sample vector. As a result, the corresponding likelihoods are computed at the cluster and entire sample levels, respectively (Mehta & Neale, 2005). The likelihood of a vector of observations for y_j is

$$-2\log L_j = K_j + \log\left|\Sigma_j\right| + (y_i - \mu_j)'\Sigma_j^{-1}(y_j - \mu_j), \tag{5.15}$$

where $K_j = N_j * \log(2\pi)$. Because the clusters are assumed to be randomly sampled, however, the log likelihood for the entire sample can be obtained by summing the individual cluster likelihoods across the n clusters (Mehta & Neale, 2005). The multilevel latent variable specification typically uses what is referred to as a *general-specific* factor model; that is the cluster-level model corresponds to the general part, while the individual-level model corresponds to the specific part of the model (Gustafsson, 2002; Mehta & Neale, 2005). A hierarchical factor model can also be specified, but it requires further restrictions including invariant factor loadings across levels and zero variances of observed indicators at the cluster level [see Mehta & Neale (2005) for further discussion of the specification hierarchical factor models].

Multilevel CFA (ML-CFA) models encourage researchers to use more refined analyses of construct validity and measurement invariance by examining relationships among factor structures, factor loadings, and errors at different organizational levels. For example, we can examine the amount of measurement error in the observed variables used to define latent factors both within and between groups. The unreliability of these measures affects the decomposition of variance, which can affect the intraclass correlations (Muthén, 1991). The within-level variation includes individual-level measurement error variance, which tends to inflate the contribution of within-level variation to the calculation of the intraclass correlations. Multilevel CFA therefore gives results that correspond to those that would be obtained from perfectly reliable measures (Muthén, 1994). When we look at an error-free variance ratio for the intraclass correlation of a latent factor, we are gaining a more precise estimate of the within- and between-level contributions of the observed indicators in defining the factor.

To represent the hierarchical nature of the data in a multilevel SEM analysis, the subscript j or c is typically used to represent the cluster (group) component ($j = 1, 2, \ldots, n$) and i represents the individual component ($i = 1, 2, \ldots, N$). We will use j to designate the cluster since this is consistent with notation in Chapter 4 (note that in Chapter 8 we use c to designate classes of individuals within organizations). As an example, consider a number of items that are proposed to measure an underlying organizational factor. Following Muthén's (1991, 1994) discussion of multilevel covariance structure analysis, the multilevel measurement model can be expressed as

$$y_{ij} = v_j + \Lambda\eta_{ij} + \varepsilon_{ij}, \tag{5.16}$$

where y_{ij} is a vector of observed variables, v_j is a $p \times 1$ vector of measurement intercepts, Λ is a $p \times m$ matrix of factor loadings, η_{ij} is an m-dimensional of latent factors, and ε_{ij} is a p-dimensional vector of residuals that are independently and identically distributed with unknown variances. The vector of measurement intercepts (v) is set to 0 for the individual-level model, since each individual's score results from an individual-specific deviation from the group mean. We note that the intercepts for the observed items are considered as random parameters that vary across clusters. Unlike conventional single-level analyses, where independence of observations is assumed over all N observations, in multilevel SEM, independence is only assumed over the j clusters (Muthén, 1991, 1994).

The model implies that the observed scores of all individuals within the cluster load onto a common set of cluster-level latent variables (η). Following Equation 5.2, the latent factor means can be specified as randomly varying across organizations (Muthén, 1991, 1994) as

$$\eta_{ij} = \alpha + \eta_{Bj} + \eta_{Wij}, \tag{5.17}$$

where α is the overall expectation (grand mean) for η_{ij}, η_{Bj} is a random factor component capturing organizational effects, and η_{wij} is a random factor component varying over individuals within their organizations. This suggests that there are two sources of variability in the individual's score. The between-group portion of the model addresses across-group variation rather than across-individual variation (Muthen, 1991); that is, the between-group component contains the group contribution to the individual's score. The advantage of this approach is that group-centered deviation scores (for the pooled within-group covariance matrix) are uncorrelated with the disaggregated group means used for the between-groups matrix (Hox, 1995). The between-factor component (η_{Bj}) and the within-factor component (η_{wij}) are therefore independent, as in conventional random effects ANOVA. Conditional on individual i being in organization j, the mean of factor

η_{ij} is $\alpha + \eta_{Bj}$, where η_{Bj} varies randomly across organizations (Muthén, 1994). It is therefore possible to specify organizational differences in two parameters—that is, α (the intercept) and the variance of η_{Bj} (which we denote as Ψ_B).

A more general formulation of the multilevel CFA model containing the between-cluster and the within-cluster components can then be specified as:

$$y_{ij} = v_B + \Lambda_B \eta_{Bj} + \varepsilon_B + \Lambda_{Wij} \eta_{Wij} + \varepsilon_{Wij}. \tag{5.18}$$

The y indicators of the latent factors within groups are assumed to vary across clusters. In the between-groups part of the model, the random intercepts are continuous latent variables that vary across clusters. They are shown in Mplus figures as having closed circles at the end of the arrows pointing from the latent factors to them to illustrate that they represent random intercepts (Muthén & Muthén, 1998-2012). Correspondingly, items will load on factors through their respective loading matrices (Λ_B, Λ_w) between and within groups. The latent factors are identified at each level by fixing an observed variable at each level to 1.0 (to provide a metric to define the factor). Other factor loadings, factor variances, and residual variances are shown as having within- and between-groups components that are allowed to be freely estimated at each level. A vector of measurement intercepts is defined for the observed indicators at the cluster level (v_B). Of course, other more restricted models can be tested for invariance subsequently (e.g., factor loadings, factor variances, residuals). The basic CFA factor model can also be extended by adding a regression component to capture the effects of covariates at the individual level (e.g., gender) on y_{ij} or group level (e.g., organizational size) that affect the latent variables, as implied in Equations 5.2 and 5.3 for single-level models.

Multilevel Factor Variance Components

The previous discussion suggests that the model parameters implied in a single-level analysis (e.g., factor variances and covariances, error variances and covariances), can be decomposed into within- and between-groups covariance matrices as in Equations 5.12 and 5.13. If we wish to examine the variance components of the latent factor, which we described in ψ, we can break the total factor variance down into a between-organization variance component and a within-organization variance component:

$$V(\eta_{ij}) = \psi_T = \psi_B + \psi_W. \tag{5.19}$$

Because the observed scores are not independent for individuals in the same organization, we can estimate the proportion of the factor variance that is between organizations (ψ_B) relative to the total factor variance (ψ_T). This corresponds to an adjustment made for the individual measurement properties of the observed variables comprising each factor (e.g., differing intraclass correlations). The latent variable counterpart of an intraclass correlation for observed variables can therefore be expressed as

$$\psi_B / (\psi_B + \psi_W). \tag{5.20}$$

The previous CFA formulation describes the latent factor as having between- and within-groups components, with the between-group component typically serving as the general part and the within-group component serving as the specific part of the model. Keep in mind, however, that in the absence of a common scale of measurement being established across levels, the magnitude of the variances of a factor at each level are not directly comparable (Mehta & Neale, 2005). It is often useful to establish a common scale of measurement across levels, so that factor variances across levels can be directly compared. Holding each item loading to be invariant with its counterpart across levels (i.e., item 1 within groups with item 1 between groups, item 2 with item 2, and so forth) is one way to equate the scales of the factor across levels so that the factor variances at each level can be directly compared (Mehta & Neale, 2005). The adequacy of this more restrictive factor model can be tested by comparing the difference in fit between a more general, or unconstrained, model (i.e., with separate factor loadings at each level) and a nested, or constrained, model (i.e., where the factor loading of each observed variable is restricted to be the same within and between groups). We discuss this formulation further with an example later in the chapter.

Another measurement model that can be used for examining clustered data is the hierarchical factor model (Bauer, 2003; Curran, 2003; Harnqvist, Gustafsson, Muthén, & Nelson, 1994; Mehta & Neale, 2005). This formulation involves testing the assumption of invariant factor loadings across levels, as in the general-specific model and, additionally, the assumption zero variability of the observed indicators at the cluster level (Mehta & Neale, 2005). If these two prerequisites hold, this latter formulation results in a hierarchical factor model, where latent variables at the individual level (similar to first-order factors) are used to define the latent factor at the higher level (Mehta & Neale, 2005).

Estimating ML-CFA Models

Model estimation involves finding parameter values (i.e., factor loadings, factor variances and covariances, unique factors) such that the predicted covariance matrix is as close as possible to the observed covariances contained in the sample matrix [see Long (1983) for further discussion of this issue]. A function that measures how close a given reproduced covariance matrix is to the sample covariance matrix is referred to as a *fitting* function (Long, 1983). Several fitting functions are available for estimating the parameters of the model, each with slightly different assumptions. The evaluation of difference between the observed and reproduced covariance matrices depends on which of several methods of estimating the model's parameters is used.

As we have noted previously, maximum likelihood (ML) estimation is the most frequently used method to obtain parameter estimates. ML proceeds by maximizing the likelihood function; that is, the ML method attempts to find the most likely population parameter estimates that produced the observed covariance matrix, assuming that the observed covariance matrix is from a multivariate normal population (see Lawley & Maxwell, 1963). If one considers the sample matrix (S) to represent the population matrix (Σ), then the difference between the reproduced sample matrix and the sample matrix should be very small if the model is consistent with the data. First, initial parameter estimates (or starting values) are obtained for parameters in the model. After initial estimates are obtained, in ML the predicted matrix is readjusted after each iteration by assigning greater weight to variables that are more strongly associated with the factor until eventually an optimal solution is reached, that is, when there is little difference between the structure implied by the proposed model and the reproduced sample covariance matrix. Sometimes this process may require a considerable number of iterations, and under some circumstances (e.g., samples under 100 individuals), the program will fail to converge on a solution.

We reiterate that earlier applications of SEM to nested data structures were limited by the availability of proper estimation methods. Conventional SEM was limited to complete data (missing data were eliminated) and large sample sizes (Bassiri, 1988; Fotiu, 1989; Mehta & Neale, 2005; Muthén, 1989). Common approaches to missing data also do not work well with SEM methods. Listwise deletion can take a toll on sample size and introduce additional biases, and pairwise deletion is inconsistent with some SEM estimation techniques (Rigdon, 1998). Estimating nested data with ML estimation required balanced group sizes. Muthén (1990) offered a way around these limitations when he demonstrated that the pooled within-groups sample matrix S_{PW} is an unbiased ML estimator of the within-groups population matrix (Σ_W), within sample size $N\text{--}G$. Therefore, the population within-groups structure can be estimated directly by testing a model for the pooled within-groups sample covariance matrix. His solution to ML estimation of unbalanced group-level data was to compute a single S^*_B matrix and compute a scaling factor s in a manner similar to the average of the group sizes. Muthén (1991, 1994) proposed quasi-likelihood estimator (referred to as MUML in Mplus) that provided estimation of unbalanced multilevel data structures using the multiple group analysis feature available on SEM software.

More recently, however, the availability of full-information maximum likelihood (FIML) estimation has increased the flexibility of applying SEM methods to multilevel models. FIML estimation was introduced as a way of handling missing data (e.g., Arbuckle, 1996). As we have noted, because conventional SEM focuses on sample covariance and mean structures, individuals with missing data provide a challenge in finding optimal estimates of model parameters. In particular, the availability of estimation based on individual likelihood has made it possible to investigate more complex models that accommodate unbalanced data structures, since in this estimation approach likelihood is computed using individual data vectors (Mehta & Neale, 2005). The ML fit function for a sample of individuals is obtained by summing an individual log-likelihood function over all the individuals, which allows missing data without listwise deletion and facilitates the computation of model implied mean and covariance matrices for each unique individual response pattern (Mehta & Neale, 2005). Variables that are missing are eliminated from the individual's mean and covariance matrix, so that the dimension of the covariance matrix differs across individuals depending on the number of observations present for that individual (Mehta & Neale, 2005).

FIML therefore offers greater computational efficiency and provides increased options for estimating models. In Mplus, FIML (available as MLR and MLF) facilitates the analysis of both continuous and categorical outcomes within unbalanced sample sizes, random intercepts and slopes, and missing data. MLR has robust standard errors and a chi-square test statistic (when applicable) that are robust to nonnormality and non-independence of observations, while MLF estimation has standard errors approximated by first-order derivatives and a conventional chi-square test statistic (Muthén & Muthén, 1998–2006). The implementation of FIML in Mplus also decreases the need to use MUML for estimating multilevel models (Yuan & Hayashi, 2005). The Bayesian approach for estimating models also has some conceptual advantages over traditional ML methods, allowing the incorporation of prior information about model parameters and the estimation of individual-specific parameters and the uncertainty in such estimates (Jedidi & Ansari, 2001). It can be especially useful where sample sizes are small. As of Mplus Version 7, this approach is available for multilevel and other models.

As we have suggested, missing data can be a problem in SEM applications, depending upon the extent to which the data are missing and whether or not the data are missing at random. Where SEM traditionally required complete data, a number of alternative strategies [e.g., bootstrapping (Arbuckle, 1996)] have been developed for dealing with various missing data situations [see also Stoolmiller, Duncan, and Patterson (1995)]. For example, plausible values for missing data can also be imputed using the EM (expectation maximization) algorithm, which reduces bias due to missing data (Peugh & Enders, 2004). EM is a common method for obtaining ML estimates with incomplete data. In this approach, the model parameters are viewed as missing values to be estimated. Obtaining estimates involves an iterative, two-step process where missing values are first imputed, and then a covariance matrix and mean vector are estimated. The process repeats until the difference between covariance matrices from adjacent iterations differs by a trivial amount [see Peugh & Enders (2004) for further discussion].

The process can be repeated to create a number of imputed data sets, where each simulates a random draw from the distribution of plausible values for the missing data (Peugh & Enders, 2004). One of the advantages of this approach is that other variables can also be used to supply information about missing data, but they need not be included into the actual model estimation.

Mplus provides a number of options for examining missing data. Mplus provides FIML estimation under missing completely at random (MCAR) or missing at random (MAR) conditions. Starting with Mplus Version 5 (Type = Missing) is the default. For listwise deletion of cases, LISTWISE=ON is typed in the DATA command. In this case, observations without complete data are eliminated from the analysis (Muthén & Muthén, 1998–2012). It is often useful to determine the amount of missing data as a first step as well as the number of missing data patterns. Multiple data sets can be developed using multiple imputation, with parameter estimates generated from a large set of Monte Carlo simulations. We discuss missing data further in Chapter 10.

Model 3: Defining a Two-Level CFA Model

We will now define the previous single-level factor model for two levels. Consider that we have the same 2,720 individuals who are nested in 373 level-2 units, which in this case are departments. The intraclass correlations (which summarize the amount of variance between departments) are 31.8% for item1, 26.2% for item2, 24.8% for item3, 31.0% for item4, 26.9% for item5, and 21.7% for item6. These coefficients suggest there is considerable variability in the items that exists at the group level.

In order to define a two-level model, in the Mplus input statements we need to specify a cluster variable (Cluster is deptid) and in the Analysis statement, we define the model as two level (Type = twolevel;). We use %Within% to define the within-group part of the model. We define first factor (F1) for individuals by using a "By" statement, which shows that F1 is measured by item1, item2, and item3. As noted previously, the metric of the underlying factor is automatically defined by the program by fixing the first factor loading 1.0 (shown in Figure 5.3). The other indicators are freely estimated (as indicated by asterisks in Figure 5.3). We could include an asterisk and a starting value if desired (e.g., item2*1.5). The variance of the first factor is freely estimated by the program by default (also shown by an asterisk in Figure 5.3). The three residuals for the observed indicators (noted as arrows in the figure) are also freely estimated (also shown by the asterisks in Figure 5.3). We could, however, fix an item variance to zero if desired (e.g., item1@0;). We will define a second factor (F2) in the same manner. It is measured by item4, item5, and item6, and the loading for item4 fixed at 1.0. By default, the residuals are not correlated. Within groups, however, we will also free the covariance between item6 and item3, as in our first model (item6 with item3). The model statement file appears as follows:

```
TITLE:      Model 3: CFA model;
DATA:       FILE IS C:\mplus\3LCFA.dat;
            Format is 11f8.0,7f8.2;
VARIABLE:   Names are orgcode deptid item1 item2 item3 item4 item5 item6
            age female deptsize dept_m orgsize empstab orgdemos orgqual
            orgprod1 orgprod2;
            Use variables are deptid item1 item2 item3 item4 item5 item6;
            cluster is deptid;
ANALYSIS:   TYPE = twolevel;
            Estimator is MLR;
Model:
            %between%
            DF1 by item1 item2 item3;
            DF2 by item4 item5 item6;
            item1@0 item4@0;
            %within%
            F1 by item1 item2 item3;
            F2 by item4 item5 item6;
            item6 with item3;
OUTPUT:     sampstat standardized tech1;
```

We use %Between%" to refer to the between-groups portion of the model. Once again, the "By" statement specifies that the first factor is measured by item1, item2, and item3, while the second factor is measured by item4, item5, and item6. We use DF1 and DF2 to refer to the group-level factors separately from the individual-level factors. In the between-group portion of the model, residual variances are often very small, which reflects high reliability. On some occasions, they can be fixed to 0.0 to avoid estimation problems when they approach zero, or they can be estimated. Between groups, we ended up fixing the error terms of the two items whose factor loadings were fixed to 1.0 to 0.0 (i.e., item1@0, item4@0). This was necessary to achieve model convergence. We estimated the other error terms (as shown in the figure).

The proposed model is summarized in Figure 5.3. In Mplus diagrams, the filled circles at the end of the arrows from the within-group factors (F1) to the represent random intercepts for the observed items that vary across clusters. Observed variables for each individual are assumed to have a unique, person-specific, within-cluster source of variance (Mehta & Neale, 2005). The between-group factors have to be defined differently from the within-group factors in the Mplus model statements. The metric of the factors is also set by fixing the first indicator loading for each factor (i.e., item1, item4) to 1.0. In the two-level diagram, the random

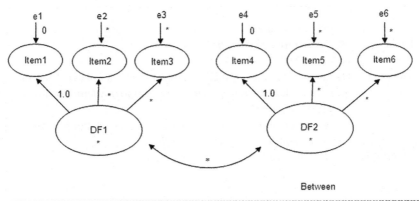

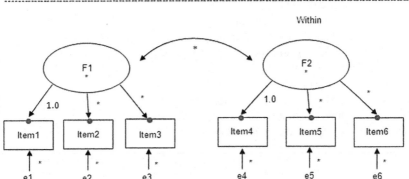

FIGURE 5.3 Proposed two-level factor model.

intercepts of the observed variables defined in the within-individual portion of the model are referred to in the between-group part of the model as circles instead of rectangles because they are considered as continuous latent variables that vary across clusters (Muthén & Muthén, 1998–2006). They are the indicators of the between-group latent factors (DF1 and DF2). We chose to estimate the intercepts for the indicators comprising each factor and we fixed the means of the factors to 0.0.

Within groups, we estimated all the error terms and also the error covariance between item6 and item3 (which was nonsignificant at Level 2). We note in passing that there are a number of different ways to specify the within-group and between-group factors, and the various ways may change the meaning of the model. For example, if the residual variances are all fixed to 0.0 and the factor loading is specified to be equal on the within and between parts of the model, it implies a model where the individual-level latent factor has a random intercept that varies across the clusters (Mehta & Neale, 2005; Muthén & Muthén, 1998–2006). Users can request the model specification information for the proposed model by putting TECH1 on the output line of the Mplus model specification statements.

We can use the variance-covariance formula [$p(p + 1)/2$]) to determine the number of variance-covariance parameters estimated when we add a group level to our model. We simply double the number of variance-covariance parameters ($21 + 21$) and add the k intercept parameters (which are now estimated at Level 2). So the total will be 48 possible parameters. Remembering that we added one error parameter in our individual-level model, we will estimate four factor loadings, three factor variances/covariances, and seven error terms for a total of 14 parameters. At the department level, we found that we had to fix the error terms for item1 and item4, which are used to define the metric for each factor. We also found that we did not need to estimate the covariance between item6 and item3. Therefore, we will estimate four factor loadings, three factor variances and covariances, and four error terms for a total of 11 parameters. We also estimate the six item intercepts at this level for a total of 17 parameters. This makes 31 total estimated parameters (i.e., 14 at the individual level + 17 at the group level). We can confirm this in the selected model output. Since we have a total of 48 parameters that could be estimated ($21 + 21 + 6 = 48$), we have 17 degrees of freedom (see Table 5.5), so we easily have an *overidentified* model.

We note that the single-level baseline model used in estimating the CFI had 12 estimated parameters (i.e., six error terms and six item intercepts) and 15 degrees of freedom for a single-level model. The corresponding two-level baseline model therefore has 18 estimated parameters (i.e., six error terms within groups, six error terms between groups, and six item intercepts) and 30 degrees of freedom.

As we noted earlier, in proposing a model, we actually hope to *fail to reject* the null hypothesis; that is, we wish to accept that the model tested with data does not significantly differ from an *ideal* model. It is important to keep in mind, however, that failure to reject a particular model does not mean that it is the only *correct* model. Other models could also be tested that might fail to be rejected. For this reason, we actually look at quite a bit of information to give us hints about the suitability of a particular model. Part of the art of modeling is to look at a variety of information about a model including its fit, possible modifications that could be made, the sensibility of its parameter estimates, and its residuals. It is often useful to assess the model's preliminary fit first before focusing too much attention on the actual parameter estimates. We can assess the accuracy of the theoretical model in accounting for the variances and covariances present in the data through examining a number of goodness-of-fit tests provided. Remember that with an overidentified model (i.e., more than enough variances and covariances to solve the set of equations), we will have a positive number of degrees of freedom in the model.

TABLE 5.9 Selected Model Fit Information for Revised Model

Number of Free Parameters	31
H_0 Value	−53617.912
H_0 Scaling Correction Factor for MLR	4.2595
H_1 Value	−53369.557
H_1 Scaling Correction Factor for MLR	3.0385
Akaike (AIC)	107297.824
Bayesian (BIC)	107480.984
Chi-Square Test of Model Fit	611.444
Degrees of Freedom $= 17, p$	0.000
Comparative Fit Index (CFI)	0.861
Chi-Square Test of Baseline Model	4297.578
Degrees of Freedom $= 30, p$	0.000
RMSEA	0.113
SRMR (Within)	0.044
SRMR (Between)	0.038

Examining the Fit Indices

We will first examine the fit indices to see the extent to which the proposed model is consistent with the data. We can see in Table 5.9 that this initial two-level model does not provide a strong fit to the data. More specifically, the chi-square value is 611.444 for 17 degrees of freedom and the CFI is only 0.861. For multilevel SEM, the more important sample size is the number of level-2 units, given that in the multilevel situation, the CFA models are fit to the cluster-level covariance matrix and the within-cluster covariance matrix. The within-groups covariance matrix is generally based on a substantially larger number of cases than the between-groups covariance matrix. Because of this, the model will often fit better within groups than between groups. This can pose a challenge in trying to evaluate the overall fit of a proposed multilevel model.

We can again estimate the baseline model directly to illustrate how the value in the output is obtained. For the two-level setting, in this case the obtained baseline chi-square (which models the means as well as the between- and within-level variances of the dependent variables) is 4297.578 for 30 degrees of freedom. If we fix the six item loadings to 0 on a single factor at each level and set its variance to 1.0 at each level, we will obtain a model that estimates the 12 theta error parameters within and between groups along with the six intercepts (for 18 parameters). This will provide a model with 30 degrees of freedom. The resulting chi-square coefficient using MLR estimation is consistent with the Mplus output coefficient (i.e., 4298.439 against 4297.578).

As we noted earlier in this chapter, another index that is useful in assessing the fit within groups versus between groups is the standardized root-mean-square residual (SRMR). In our initial two-level model, we can see the between-groups portion actually fits a bit better (SRMR = 0.038) than within groups (SRMR = 0.044), but this is not generally the case (given the differences in sample size). We note in passing that because missing data can affect both the number of observations per individuals and individuals per cluster, this can raise questions about the appropriate sample size used for computing various fit indices (Mehta & Neale, 2005). In our example, this is not a problem, as all of our level-2 units are included. We also note that some fit indices may be affected by whether the number of individuals or clusters is used in calculating the index. For these reasons, we emphasize that it is also important to examine several statistical and practical indices in determining whether or not to reject a particular model.

A few of the typical model fit indices are useful in comparing models. For example, from the likelihood function in Table 5.5, we can calculate the deviance statistic (by multiplying by −2), which is defined as −2LL (log likelihood), where the log is the natural logarithm and likelihood is the value of the likelihood function at convergence. In general, models with lower deviance fit better than models with higher deviance (Hox, 2002). Akaike's Information Criterion (AIC), which is derived from the deviance statistic and includes a penalty function based on the number of estimated parameters in the model, and the Bayesian Information Index (BIC) can also be used to compare the fit of various models. For unbalanced group sizes that require MLR estimation, a more general model can be compared to a nested model (i.e., with more restricted parameters) by applying correction factors to the two model likelihoods (summarized in Table 5.5).

Even with an acceptable model fit, however, we also need to examine the parameters that have been estimated to determine the model's suitability (e.g., substantive factor loadings, relatively low errors of measurement). On the other hand, without an adequate model fit, it may be necessary to reconceptualize the model. Quite often, some part of the proposed model does not fit the data well. As opposed to blindly searching for the piece of the proposed model that does not fit the data (i.e., by simply looking at the model modification indices for the parameter changes that will provide the largest improvement in fit), we recommend using a theoretically based strategy for making model modifications. Once the fit of the model is determined to be adequate, it is important to assess the size of the parameter estimates.

Examining the Model Parameters

Table 5.10 presents the unstandardized parameter estimates for Model 3. This first set of estimates is for an unrestricted model, that is, where factor loadings of the model are allowed to vary across levels and the residual variances for the between-level factor indicators were estimated. The squared multiple correlations provide information about how well the individual tests define the latent achievement factor within and between groups. In general, the tests seem to measure the achievement factor adequately at both levels, with R-square estimates ranging

TABLE 5.10 Model 3 With Unrestricted Factor Loadings: Unstandardized Estimates

Measure	Factor Loading	Variance	R^2
		Unrestricted Model 1	
Within Groups			
F1		23.636	
Item1	1.000	7.542	0.758
Item2	1.772	20.853	0.781
Item3	2.237	15.819	0.882
F2		55.199	
Item4	1.000	11.393	0.829
Item5	1.403	35.996	0.751
Item6	0.730	49.369	0.374
Between Groups			
F1		13.364	
Item1	1.000	0.000	1.000
Item2	1.591	0.763	0.978
Item3	1.601	11.484	0.749
F2		29.915	
Item4	1.000	0.000	1.000
Item5	1.254	5.184	0.901
Item6	0.781	3.177	0.852

from 0.374 (item6) to 0.882 (item3) within groups (indicating relatively more error) and from 0.745 (item3) to 0.978 between groups (keeping in mind two error terms were set to 0.0, so the resulting R-square estimates will be 1.0).

Model 4: Applying Equality Constraints on Factor Loadings

If we would like to examine the factor variance that is attributable to groups versus individuals more closely, we need to make a couple of changes in the specification of the within- and between-group factor loadings. Invariant factor loadings make the common variance attributed to the latent factor directly comparable across levels (Mehta & Neale, 2005). We next summarize the changes in Mplus input statements needed to restrict the factor loadings to be invariant across levels. We need to change the definition of the item loadings within and between groups.

Formatting the Mplus input statements slightly differently allows the analyst to restrict the loadings to be equal by adding numbers to each line regarding the indicators of the factors in the within- and between-groups models. Since the first item defining each factor is already restricted to 1.0 by default, we do not have to use a number to define them as equal within and between groups. Therefore, we can use 1 to restrict item2 loadings to be equal [item2 (1)], and 2 can be used to restrict item3 loadings to be equal [item3 (2);]. Similarly, we use 3 to restrict item5 loadings to be equal [item5 (3)] and 4 to restrict item6 loadings to be equal [item6 (4);]. We note that we can only include one item per line when we fix the loadings to be equal and we put a semi-colon after the last item measuring each factor. These changes will result in four parameters being removed from the general model, since the factor loading for item2, item3, item5, and item6 will be restricted to be invariant across the within- and between-groups models.

```
Model:
         %between%
         DF1 by item1
            item2(1)
            item3(2);
         DF2 by item4
            item5(3)
            item6(4);
         item1@0 item4@0;
         %within%
         F1 by item1
            item2(1)
            item3(2);
         F2 by item4
            item5(3)
            item6(4);
         item6 with item3;
```

Model 4 Output

Compared with the more general model estimated previously, this model as summarized in Table 5.11 will now have 27 estimated parameters. We can see that this model fits better, for example, with the CFI up considerably to 0.956. The chi-square coefficient is also considerably smaller (208.577, for 21 degrees of freedom). The RMSEA is 0.057 against 0.113 for the previous model.

The coefficients in Table 5.12 are from the more restricted (or nested) model, where the factor loadings were constrained to be the same within and between groups. We will discuss this model in more detail subsequently. We can see in the table that these estimates are actually quite similar to the first set of single-level estimates summarized in Table 5.6. The resulting factor variance within groups for F1 was 25.392 and for F2 it was 55.715, while the corresponding factor variances between groups were 27.049 for DF1 and 9.913 for DF2. Hence, from

TABLE 5.11 Selected Model Fit Information for Revised Model

Number of Free Parameters	27
H_0 Value	−53639.639
H_0 Scaling Correction Factor for MLR	3.3875
H_1 Value	−53369.557
H_1 Scaling Correction Factor for MLR	3.0385
Akaike (AIC)	107333.278
Bayesian (BIC)	107492.805
Chi-Square Test of Model Fit	208.577
Degrees of Freedom = 21, p	0.000
Comparative Fit Index (CFI)	0.956
RMSEA	0.057
SRMR (Within)	0.041
SRMR (Between)	0.041

TABLE 5.12 Model 4 With Invariant Cross-Level Factor Loadings: Unstandardized Estimates

Measure	Factor Loading	Variance	R^2
Within Groups			
F1		25.392	
Item1	1.000	7.715	0.767
Item2	1.724	20.472	0.787
Item3	2.137	16.709	0.874
F2		55.715	
Item4	1.000	11.246	0.832
Item5	1.367	36.969	0.738
Item6	0.740	49.222	0.383
Between Groups			
F1		9.913	
Item1	1.000	0.000	1.000
Item2	1.724	0.710	0.976
Item3	2.137	12.561	0.783
F2		27.049	
Item4	1.000	0.000	1.000
Item5	1.367	4.872	0.912
Item6	0.740	3.376	0.815

Equation 5.20 we can estimate the latent variable counterpart for the ICC is 9.913/(9.913 + 25.392) or 9.913/35.305, which is 0.281. This indicates that about 28.1% of the variance in Factor 1 lies between departments. For Factor 2, the variance that lies between groups is 32.7% (27.049/82.779). This result suggests that measurement errors associated with the observed items can affect the individual-level variance contributing to the intraclass correlations for the observed variables (Muthén, 1991). The multilevel CFA formulation corrects for the different unreliability associated with measuring each of the items.

We reiterate that the previous multilevel CFA models that we investigated used the general-specific factor model as a template. As Mehta and Neale (2005) note, there are at least two additional questions we can ask of this multilevel CFA model. First, if we have random intercepts of observed variables defined, can there be a random intercept for the individual-level achievement factor? Second, what meaning do we attach to the achievement factor at the individual level, and does the group-level factor have the same meaning? Conceptually, the invariance of factor loadings equates the scales of the common factor across levels. Table 5.12, however, suggests that the individual-level indicators continue to have variability at the group level (i.e., except item1 and item4, which were fixed to 0.).

In contrast, we could instead specify a hierarchical factor model, in which one or more latent variables at the individual-level (i.e., first-order factors) define a latent factor at the higher level. The invariance of factor loadings across levels in the general-specific model and zero variability for the observed indi-cators between groups are necessary prerequisites for specifying this type of more restrictive hierarchical factor model (Bauer, 2003; Curran, 2003; Mehta & Neale, 2005).

Standardized Estimates

The parameter estimates presented in Table 5.10 and 5.12 were unstandardized. Standardized estimates can be useful for comparing the factor loadings and resid-ual variances for variables that are measured in different metrics (Hox, 2010). The procedures for standardizing parameter estimates in SEM, and therefore their meanings, vary across software programs, depending on whether the solution is standardized to a metric within each group or to a metric that is common across all groups (Jöreskog & Sörbom, 1989). Mplus standardizes estimates of within- and between-groups observed variables and factors separately. This is useful in determining how much variance is explained at each level.

We again point out that the Mplus output provides three different standard-ized estimates (Muthén & Muthén, 1998–2012). The first standardized solution is referred to as STDYX. This uses the uses the variances of the continuous latent variables as well as the variances of the background and outcome variables for standardization. This standardization is similar to a standardized beta as in the linear regression of y on x (i.e., which can be interpreted as the as the change in y expressed in standard deviation units for a standard deviation change in x). The second standardization is referred to as STDY, which uses the variances of the continuous latent variables as well as the variances of the outcome variables for standardization. This standardization is appropriate to use with dichotomous predictors, as it can be interpreted as the standard deviation change in Y for a change in the covariate from 0 to 1. The third is referred to as STD. This standardization uses the variances of the continuous latent variables for standardization.

In testing multilevel models and reporting parameter estimates, therefore, it is important to be clear about how the sample was obtained, what particular methods were used to obtain the parameter estimates, how they were standardized, and the criteria by which the overall model and the individual estimates were evaluated (Hoyle & Panter, 1995). Where the emphasis is on overall model fit, it may be sufficient to report only the unstandardized solution. Remember, however, that standardizations facilitate making comparisons about the strength of relationships between variables that are measured in different metrics.

Comparing Model 3 and Model 4

Ideally, when we make model changes, we should emphasize strategies that compare the alternative models, rather than merely making a series of changes in our proposed model through examining the model modification indices. We emphasize that model modifications should be made sparingly and with regard to theory and statistical power. For example, with smaller numbers of organizational-level units, it would be unlikely that arbitrary modifications would replicate in other samples (MacCallum, Roznowski, & Necowitz, 1992). The researcher may have particular alternative models in mind. For example, researchers sometimes wish to compare the fit of two or more nested models. A nested model is one that can be derived from a more general model by removing parameters from the general model (Hox, 2010). They can then be compared by examining the deviance statistic for each model. The difference in deviance between the two models has a chi-square distribution with degrees of freedom equal to the difference in number of parameters estimated in each model. A formal statistical test can be conducted to determine whether the more general model fits significantly better than the restricted model. Models that are not nested can be compared with Akaike's information index (AIC), which provides information about the best number of parameters to include in a model. The model with the number of parameters that produces the smallest AIC is considered the best model.

To illustrate the technique for nested models, we will evaluate which of our two models (with unrestricted versus restricted factor loadings) fits the data better. We will evaluate whether restricting the four factor loadings to be invariant within and between groups resulted in an improved fit of the model to the data. We can test the difference in fit between a more general model (with freely estimated factor loadings) and a more restricted (or nested) model with the factor loadings to be the same for each pair of items. The Mplus website (www.statmodel.com) provides information on how to conduct a chi-square difference test for nested models obtained with MLR estimation (which is necessary with unbalanced group sample sizes) using the log likelihood. Because MLR uses the Muthén-Satorra (1995) rescaling of the chi-square statistic, the typical chi-square difference test cannot be used for difference testing of nested models. For the MLR estimation, the model fit information portion of the Mplus output provides a caution that chi-square difference testing must be done using a scaling correction factor that is printed in the model fit portion of the output.

To conduct the test, first, we need to estimate the general and nested models using MLR. The comparison model in Table 5.9 with freely estimated factor loadings has 31 parameters estimated, while the nested model has 27 parameters estimated (in Table 5.11). The output provides log likelihood values L_0 and L_1 for the H_0 and H_1 models, respectively, as well as the necessary scaling correction factors (referred to as c_0 and c_1) for the H_0 and H_1 models, respectively. The log likelihood obtained for the first (comparison) model was $-53{,}617.912$, with scaling factor $(c_0) = 4.2568$ and 31 estimated parameters $(p_0 = 31)$. For the nested model, the L_1 was $-53{,}369.557$, with scaling factor $(c_1) = 3.0385$ for 27 estimated parameters $(p_1 = 27)$.

Second, we compute the difference test scaling correction, where p_0 is the number of parameters in the nested model and p_1 is the number of parameters in the comparison model. This is computed as:

$$cd = (p_0 \times c_0 - p_1 \times c_1)/(p_0 - p_1). \tag{5.21}$$

In the example, we can calculate the correction as equal to 12.480:

$$(31 \times 4.2568 - 27 \times 3.0385)/(31 - 27) = 12.480325.$$

Finally, we compute the chi-square difference test (TRd) as

$$TRd = -2 \times (L_0 - L_1)/cd. \tag{5.22}$$

This results in a coefficient of 39.801 estimated as follows:

$$-2 \times [(-53{,}617.912) - (-53{,}369.557)]/12.480 = 39.801.$$

Based on this calculation, the difference in chi square between the more general model and the model with invariant factor loadings for 4 degrees of freedom is beyond the required level (i.e., a chi-square coefficient of 9.488 or greater would be required for 4 degrees of freedom at $p = 0.05$). This suggests that restricting the factor loadings results in a significant improvement in the model's fit to the data.

TABLE 5.13 Intraclass Correlations for Items Comprising the Two Factors and Average Cluster Sizes

Level	Item 1	Item 2	Item 3	Item 4	Item 5	Item 6	Avg. Cluster Size
Organization	0.147	0.185	0.205	0.200	0.202	0.104	18.378
Department	0.151	0.052	0.034	0.087	0.046	0.100	7.292

Extending the CFA Model to Three Levels

We will next extend our two-level factor model to consider organizations as well. We have 148 organizations at Level 3. We can extend the two-level covariance structure specified in Equations 5.12 and 5.13 to include a third level, with the mean structure now at the organizational level rather than the departmental level. Conditional on individual i being in department j in organization k, the mean of factor η_{ijk} is $\alpha + \eta_{Bk}$, where η_{Bk} varies randomly across organizations (Muthén, 1994). The between-factor department component (η_{Bjk}), the between-factor organization component (η_{Bk}), and the within-factor component (η_{Wijk}) are therefore independent components.

In Table 5.13, we can see that the variance components for Level 2 are different when we add the third level. First, we can see there is only about 1–2% variance in items 1–3 comprising DF1 and about 3–5% variance for DF2. Second, the table suggests most of the variability in items is at the organizational level (ranging from 10–20%), while there is less variability in items present at the departmental level (ranging from a little over 3% to 15%).

Model 5: Invariant Loadings at Levels 1 and 2

Our initial three-level model maintains the invariant loadings for the individual and department levels (now Levels 1 and 2), but we will estimate the factor loadings separately for the organizational level. We again need to make a few changes. For the Analysis statement, we must change the Type command to indicate three levels (Type = threelevel). We also must add the additional third level by changing %BETWEEN% at the department level to %BETWEEN deptid% and adding %BETWEEN orgcode% to represent the organizational level. We show these changes in the relevant part of the input statements. We also fixed item1 and item4 to 0.0 at Level 3.

```
                    CLUSTER = orgcode deptid;
ANALYSIS:           TYPE = threelevel;
                    Estimator is MLR;
```

Model:

```
%Between orgcode%
OF1 by item1 item2 item3;
OF2 by item4 item5 item6;
item1@0 item4@0;
%between deptid%
DF1 by item1
item2(1)
item3(2);
DF2 by item4
item5(3)
item6(4);
item1@0 item4@0;
%within%
F1 by item1
item2(1)
item3(2);
F2 by item4
item5(3)
item6(4);
item6 with item3;
```

Since we had 27 parameters estimated in the last model, if we add four estimated factor loadings, four error terms (fixing two error terms again), and three factor variances, we should have a total of 38 parameters estimated. We note that the six item intercepts will now be estimated at the organizational level, but this will not change the number of parameters estimated. We can confirm this in the output.

Model 5 Fit Indices

Overall, we can see in Table 5.14 that the three-level model with 38 parameters estimated fits reasonably well (e.g., CFI $= 0.960$, RMSEA $= 0.043$). Most of the

TABLE 5.14 Selected Model Fit Information for Initial Three-Level Model

Number of Free Parameters	38
AIC	107034.935
Chi-Square Test of Model Fit	184.607
Degrees of Freedom $= 31, p$	0.000
Comparative Fit Index (CFI)	0.960
RMSEA	0.043
SRMR (Within)	0.040
SRMR (Between Departments)	0.231
SRMR (Between Organizations)	0.023

model misfit seems to be at the departmental level (i.e., SRMR = 0.231). We may be able to improve the fit, however, by imposing equality constraints on the factor loadings at the organizational level.

Model 6: Including Equality Constraints at Level 3

Next we will specify the factor loadings at the organizational level to be constrained. When we restrict the factor loadings, we will now estimate 34 parameters instead of 38. We will include these changes to the input file.

```
%Between orgcode%
OF1 by item1
item2 (1)
item3 (2);
OF2 by item4
item5 (3)
item6 (4);
item1@0 item4@0;
```

Model 6 Fit Indices

The resulting model fit information is contained in Table 5.15. The CFI is slightly lower at 0.958. The SRMR is 0.040 (within), 0.223 (departments), and 0.021 (organizations). Both indices indicate a slightly better fit. RMSEA is only 0.042, which is somewhat lower than the other model (RMSEA = 0.043).

TABLE 5.15 Selected Fit Information for Three-Level Model With Invariant Cross-Level Factor Loadings

Number of Free Parameters	34
AIC	107031.374
Chi-Square Test of Model Fit	199.380
Degrees of Freedom = 35, p	0.000
Comparative Fit Index (CFI)	0.958
RMSEA	0.042
SRMR (Within)	0.040
SRMR (Between Departments)	0.223
SRMR (Between Organizations)	0.021

Model 7: Restricting Errors to Zero at Level 2

We may be able to improve the fit at the departmental level (Level 2) by fixing the level-2 errors to 0. We can change the model statement regarding the errors in the %BETWEEN deptid% portion of the model. We replace the statement item1@0 item4@0 with the following statement:

```
item1–item6@0;
```

Model 7 Fit Indices

Making these changes will result in 30 parameters to estimate (since two error terms were already fixed to 0.0). We present the fit indices in Table 5.16. The results are not clear, however, since the CFI deteriorated some (CFI = 0.940). The RMSEA is also a bit higher at 0.058. We note, however, that the SRMR is considerably improved at the department level (SRMR = 0.013).

Comparing Models 6 and 7

Finally, we might wish to make a formal model test to examine whether our final model with factor constraints and fixed errors at Level 2 represents a significant improvement from our three-level factor model with equality constraints on the factor loadings. Following Equations 5.21 and 5.22, we find that the chi-square difference test (TRd) is 29.237 (for 4 df). This exceeds the required coefficient of 9.488 at $p = 0.05$. This suggests that Model 7 with error terms restricted to 0 at Level 2 represents an improved model over Model 6.

TABLE 5.16 Selected Model Fit Information for Three-Level Model With Invariant Cross-Level Factor Loadings: Department-Level Error Terms Fixed to 0

Number of Free Parameters	30
AIC	107054.268
Chi-Square Test of Model Fit	392.566
Degrees of Freedom = 39, p	0.000
Comparative Fit Index (CFI)	0.931
RMSEA	0.058
SRMR (Within)	0.043
SRMR (Between Departments)	0.013
SRMR (Between Organizations)	0.028

TABLE 5.17 Three-Level Model With Invariant Cross-Level Factor Loadings and Department-Level Error Terms Fixed to 0.0: Unstandardized Estimates

Measure	Factor Loading	Variance	R^2
Within Departments			
F1		25.858	
Item1	1.000	7.951	0.765
Item2	1.733	19.822	0.797
Item3	2.120	17.876	0.867
F2		56.434	
Item4	1.000	11.535	0.830
Item5	1.364	38.960	0.729
Item6	0.748	50.964	0.383
Between Departments			
DF1		0.596	
Item1	1.000	0.000	1.000
Item2	1.733	0.000	1.000
Item3	2.120	0.000	1.000
DF2		3.487	
Item4	1.000	0.000	1.000
Item5	1.364	0.000	1.000
Item6	0.748	0.000	1.000
Between Organizations			
F1		7.225	
Item1	1.000	0.000	1.000
Item2	1.733	0.725	0.968
Item3	2.120	10.191	0.761
F2		18.885	
Item4	1.000	0.000	1.000
Item5	1.364	2.362	0.937
Item6	0.748	1.557	0.872

Model 7 Parameter Estimates

We present our final set of model estimates in Table 5.17. From the factor variances, we can estimate the intraclass correlations for each factor at the organizational and department levels. For Factor 1, we note the variances are 25.858, 0.596, and 7.225 for Levels 1, 2, and 3, respectively. For Factor 2, they are 56.434, 3.487, and 18.885. Following Equation 5.19, we can now break the total factor variance down into a between-organization variance component, a between-departments variance component, and a within-departments variance component:

$$V(\eta_{ij}) = \psi_T = \psi_{BO} + \psi_{BD} + \psi_{WD} \tag{5.23}$$

The latent variable intraclass correlation for latent variables can therefore be expressed as follows:

$$\psi_{BO}/(\psi_{BO} + \psi_{BD} + \psi_{WD}) \tag{5.24}$$

We can similarly estimate the department-level variance component by placing ψ_{BD} in the numerator of Equation 5.24 instead of ψ_{BO}. We can therefore calculate the between-organization factor ICC for F1 as 0.215 and 0.240 for Factor 2. The corresponding department ICCs are 0.018 for Factor 1 and 0.044 for Factor 2.

We also note that the final correlations between factors (not tabled) were 0.83 at Level 1, 0.76 at Level 2, and 0.98 at Level 3. We point this out because the correlation between factors at the organizational level is almost 1.0; it would be possible to also investigate a model with one factor at the organizational level. Since our emphasis was on demonstrating how a two-factor model might be built, we will accept this as the final model. When we estimated such a model with only one factor at the organizational level (and 30 parameters estimated), we found that the AIC was 107,117.554, which was larger than our previous model (107,054.268). In addition, relative to the previous model, the overall RMSEA was larger (0.060), and the SRMR coefficients were considerably larger at the departmental (0.091) and organizational (0.078) levels.

Summary

When actually estimating multilevel CFA models, it is likely that some problems may occur. The between-group structure may be more difficult to estimate (e.g., due to a smaller sample size, or perhaps the necessity of defining a more simplified factor structure). Missing data can also be a problem. It can be challenging for the full multilevel model to generate a solution, sometimes because of the differences in sample sizes in the within- and between-groups portions of the model. The analyst may need to define model starting values to help the program iterate to a solution. In these situations, it can help to build the model in stages. One strategy is to define and add the factors one at a time within the multilevel model. It is sometimes difficult to determine exactly where the problem lies, so remember that patience is a virtue when working toward a solution!

References

Arbuckle, J. (1996). Full information estimation in the presence of incomplete data. In G. A. Marcoulides & R. Schumacker (Eds.), *Advanced structural equation modeling: Issues and techniques* (pp. 243–278). Mahwah, NJ: Lawrence Erlbaum Associates.

Bassiri, D. (1988). *Large and small sample properties of maximum likelihood estimates for the hierarchical model.* Unpublished doctoral dissertation, Michigan State University.

Bauer, D. J. (2003). Estimating multilevel linear models as structural models. *Journal of Educational and Behavioral Statistics, 28,* 135–167.

Bollen, K. (1989). *Structural equations with latent variables.* New York: Wiley.

Bollen, K. & Long, J. (1993). *Testing structural equation models.* Newbury Park, CA: Sage.

Browne, M. W. & Cudeck, R. (1993). Alternative ways of assessing model fit. In K. A. Bollen & J. S. Long (Eds.), *Testing structural equation models* (pp. 136–162). Newbury Park, CA: Sage.

Byrne, B. M. (2012). *Structural equation modeling with Mplus: Basic concepts, applications, and programming.* New York: Routledge Academic.

Cronbach, L. J. & Meehl, P. (1955). Construct validity in psychological tests. *Psychological Bulletin, 52,* 281–302.

Curran, P. J. (2003). Have multilevel models been structural equation models all along? *Multivariate Behavioral Research, 38,* 529–569.

Ecob, R. & Cuttance, P. (1987). An overview of structural equation modeling. In P. Cuttance & R. Ecob (Eds.), *Structural modeling by example* (pp. 9–23). Cambridge: Cambridge University Press.

Fan, X. & Sivo, S. A. (2005). Sensitivity of fit indices to misspecified structural or measurement model components: Rationale for two-index strategy revised. *Structural Equation Modeling, 12,* 343–367.

Fotiu, R. (1989). *A comparison of the EM and data augmentation algorithms on simulates small sample hierarchical data from research on education.* Unpublished doctoral dissertation, Michigan State University, East Lansing.

Gustafsson, J. E. (2002). Measurement from a hierarchical point of view. In H. I. Braun, D. N. Jackson, & D. E. Wiley (Eds.), *The role of constructs in psychological and educational measurement* (pp. 73–95). Mahwah, NJ: Lawrence Erlbaum Associates.

Harnqvist, K., Gustafsson, J. E., Muthén, B., & Nelson, G. (1994). Hierarchical models of ability at class and individual levels. *Intelligence, 18,* 165–118.

Hox, J. J. (1995). *Applied multilevel analysis.* Amsterdam: T.T. Publikaties.

Hox, J. (2002). *Multilevel analysis: Techniques and applications.* Mahwah, NJ: Lawrence Erlbaum.

Hox, J. J. (2010). *Multilevel analysis: Techniques and applications* (2nd ed.). New York: Routledge.

Hoyle, R. & Panter, A. (1995). Writing about structural equation models. In R. Hoyle (Ed.), *Structural equation modeling: Concepts, issues, and applications* (pp. 158–176). Newbury Park, CA: Sage.

Hu, L.-T. & Bentler, P. M. (1998). Fit indices in covariance structure modeling: Sensitivity to underparameterized model misspecification. *Psychological Methods, 3,* 424–453.

Hu, L.-T. & Bentler, P. M. (1999). Cutoff criteria for fit indices in covariance structure analysis. *Structural Equation Modeling, 6,* 1–55.

Jedidi, K. & Ansari, A. (2001). Bayesian structural equation models for multilevel data. In G. A. Marcoulides & R. E. Schumacker (Eds.), *New developments and techniques in structural equation modeling* (pp. 139–157). Mahwah, NJ: Lawrence Erlbaum.

Jöreskog, K. G. & Sörbom, D. (1989). *LISREL 7: User's reference guide.* Chicago: Scientific Software.

Jöreskog, K. G. & Sörbom, D. (1993). *LISREL 8: User's reference guide.* Chicago: Scientific Software.

Lawley, D. & Maxwell, A. (1963). *Factor analysis as a statistical method.* London: Butterworth.

Liu, S., Rovine, M. J., & Molennar, P. C. M. (2012). Selecting a linear mixed model for longitudinal data: Repeated measures analysis of variance, covariance pattern model, and growth curve approaches. *Psychological Methods, 17*(1), 15–30.

Long, J. S. (1983). *Confirmatory factor analysis.* (Sage Series on Quantitative Applications in the Social Sciences, No. 13), Newbury Park, CA: Sage.

MacCallum, R. C., Roznowski, M., & Necowitz, L. B. (1992). Model modifications in covariance structure analysis. The problem of capitalization on chance. *Psychological Bulletin, 111,* 490–504.

Marcoulides, G. A. & Hershberger, S. (1997). *Multivariate statistical methods: A first course.* Mahwah, NJ: Lawrence Erlbaum.

McArdle, J. & Hamagami, F. (1996). Multilevel models from a multiple group structural equation perspective. In G. Marcoulides & R. Schumacker (Eds.), *Advanced structural equation modeling: Issues and techniques* (pp. 89–124). Mahwah, NJ: Lawrence Erlbaum.

Mehta, P. D. & Neale, M. C. (2005). People are variables too. Multilevel structural equations modeling. *Psychological Methods, 10*(3), 259–284.

Muthén, B. O. (1989). Latent variable modeling in heterogenous populations. *Psychometrika, 54,* 557–585.

Muthén, B. O. (June 1990). *Mean and covariance structure analysis of hierarchical data.* Paper presented at the Psychometric Society meeting in Princeton, New Jersey.

Muthén, B. O. (1991). Multilevel factor analysis of class and student achievement components. *Journal of Educational Measurement, 28,* 338–354.

Muthén, B. O. (1994). Multilevel covariance structure analysis. *Sociological Methods & Research, 22*(3), 376–398.

Muthén, B. O. (1998–2004). *Mplus technical appendices.* Los Angeles, CA: Muthén & Muthén.

Muthén, B. O. (2002). Beyond SEM: General latent variable modeling. *Behaviormetrika, 29,* 81–118.

Muthén, B. O. & Muthén, L. (1998–2006). *Mplus user's guide.* Los Angeles, CA: Authors.

Muthén, B. O. & Satorra, A. (1995). Complex sample data in structural equation modeling. *Sociological Methodology, 25,* 216–316.

Muthén, L. K. & Muthén, B. O. (1998–2012). *Mplus user's guide* (7th ed.). Los Angeles, CA: Muthén & Muthén.

Peugh, J. A. & Enders, C. K. (2004). Missing data in educational research: A review of reporting practices and suggestions for improvement. *Review of Educational Research, 74*(4), 525–556.

Raudenbush, S. W. & Bryk, A. S. (2002). *Hierarchical linear models* (2nd ed.). Newbury Park, CA: Sage.

Raykov, T. & Marcoulides, G. A. (2006). *A first course in structural equation modeling.* Mahwah, NJ: Lawrence Erlbaum Associates.

Rigdon, E. (1998). Structural equation models. In G. A. Marcoulides (Ed.), *Modern methods for business research* (pp. 251–294). Mahwah, NJ: Lawrence Erlbaum Associates.

Snijders, T. & Bosker, R. (1999). *Multilevel analysis: An introduction to basic and advanced multilevel modeling.* Newbury Park, CA: Sage.

Stoolmiller, M., Duncan, T., & Patterson, G. (1995). Predictors of change in antisocial behavior during elementary schools for boys. In R. Hoyle (Ed.), *Structural equation modeling: Concepts, issues, and applications* (pp. 236–253). Newbury Park, CA: Sage.

Wu, W., West, S. G., & Taylor, A. B. (2009). Evaluating model fit for growth curve models: Integration of fit indices from SEM and MLM frameworks. *Psychological Methods, 14*(3), 183–201.

Yuan, K. H. & Hayashi, K. (2005). On Muthen's maximum likelihood for two-level covariance structure models. *Psychometrika, 70,* 147–167.

6

MULTILEVEL STRUCTURAL EQUATION MODELS

Chapter Objectives

In this chapter we examine structural relations between latent variables within and between groups. The models can include combinations of observed predictors and latent variables, mean structures, and random slopes, as well as direct, indirect, and reciprocal effects. The examination of factor structures at the individual and group levels emphasizes the usefulness of the SEM approach to account for sources of error in the measurement of constructs at multiple levels of a data hierarchy, which improves the accuracy of the model's estimated structural parameters. We develop a series of models that illustrate some of the possible relationships that can be investigated where latent variables are the major focus of the analyses.

Introduction

The focus of the last chapter was on establishing the reliability of measurement of constructs in the presence of clustered data. Accounting for measurement error at the individual level is a key way of improving the comparison of differences in constructs across organizations. This allows the analyst to decompose the variance in the factors into their individual- and group-level variance components. Viewed from the perspective of locating sources of error, the SEM approach is similar to the variance decomposition approach underlying generalizability theory; that is, it is used to locate multiple sources of error to improve the quality of measurement. This type of variance decomposition of constructs can encourage a more refined analysis of structural differences between groups in a data hierarchy. SEM makes possible the specification of models with latent variables at two and three levels, as well as models that have latent variables as independent and mediating variables within or between groups. The SEM latent variable approach is also opening up new opportunities for investigating complex relationships in multilevel settings involving repeated measures, categorical outcomes, and mixture models where some latent variables are continuous and others are categorical (see Muthén, 2001, 2002, 2008; Muthén & Asparouhov, 2009).

In the first part of the chapter, we extend our basic latent two-level latent variable model developed in the last chapter to examine relationships between covariates with random slopes. The second part of the chapter extends the use of latent constructs at two levels in the investigation of structural parameters between latent variables. We extend the examination of "error free" structural parameters, particularly between groups, which is a type of model that is well suited to SEM. Our goal is to illustrate how the SEM approach is ideal for modeling multivariate outcomes and for examining separate sets of structural relationships within and between groups involving direct effects, indirect effects, and **reciprocal effects** between variables.

Multilevel Models With Latent Variables and Covariates

It is useful to return to the idea of multilevel SEM as decomposing variance between and within groups and then specifying and testing a model for each level of the hierarchical data structure. The various multilevel models we will describe in this chapter can be estimated in the same way as we outlined in Chapter 5— by decomposing a population covariance matrix into separate within-group and between-group covariance matrices. As we noted in Chapter 5, SEM proceeds by assessing whether a sample covariance matrix is consistent with a hypothetical covariance matrix as implied by the specification of a theoretical model (Rigdon, 1998). The basic statistical theory underlying SEM is based on examining the variances and covariances among the observed variables. Observed variables hypothesized to define latent constructs are characterized by the covariances between the variables in a sample covariance matrix. This matrix is decomposed by a model that assumes that the unobserved variables are generating the pattern or structure observed among the observed variables. As long as the proposed theoretical model is mathematically identified (i.e., having sufficient information to solve for unknown values in the model-implied equations) and sample sizes are adequate at each level, the proposed theoretical model can be estimated by imposing restrictions on the respective covariance matrices and examining the fit of this model against the data.

A first type of multilevel confirmatory factor analysis (CFA) model incorporates observed covariates into the analysis. We can develop the proposed multilevel model with latent variables in several steps to illustrate how the factor model at two levels is brought together with separate structural models at each level. The analysis builds on the two-factor example developed in the last chapter. Within groups, we have a random sample of individuals ($N = 2,720$) who are measured on six items that define two latent factors. In this case we will nest the individuals within the 148 organizations at Level 2. For this example, we will specify a covariate within groups and one between groups.

In general, the two-level modeling framework considers a vector of p observed variables that can contain cluster-specific, group-level variables z_j ($j = 1, 2, \ldots, J$) and within-group variables (y_{ij} and x_{ij}) for individual i in cluster j, where

$$v_{ij} = \begin{pmatrix} z_j \\ y_{ij} \\ x_{ij} \end{pmatrix} = v_j^* + v_{ij}^* = \begin{pmatrix} v_j^* \\ v_{y_j}^* \\ v_{x_j}^* \end{pmatrix} + \begin{pmatrix} 0 \\ v_{y_{ij}}^* \\ v_{x_{ij}}^* \end{pmatrix}. \tag{6.1}$$

The asterisked components are independent between- and within-group components of their respective variable vectors (Muthén & Satorra, 1995). The between-group covariance matrix (Σ_B) contains the between-group observed covariates (z_j), group-level variation in intercepts (y_j), and possible between-group variation in the within-group covariates (x_j). The within-group covariance matrix (Σ_W) contains the individual-level observed y_{ij} variables, the within-group observed covariates (x_{ij}), and zeros (0) for the group-level variables.

In the Mplus modeling framework, variation in dependent outcomes, such as our proposed latent factors, could be explained by several sources. These sources include between-group predictors (z_j) like organizational context variables, which are conceived of as affecting only the between-group variability in the outcomes, or individual-level predictors (x_{ij}), such as gender, that in some models could be considered as being fixed within groups—that is, having no between-group variation, or within-group covariates that may be decomposed into their own within- and between-group components (x_{ij} and x_j). An example of this latter formulation might be a variable such as employee motivation that can be conceived as having a within-group (or individual) component as well as a between-group (or organizational) component. More specifically, we might think of individual motivation affecting each individual's outcomes, while collective motivation might affect group outcomes. In some cases, the researcher might also wish to consider certain background variables such as gender as having a between-group component as well. In this latter case, this would be interpreted as the effect of the proportion of males or females in the organization (depending on coding) on an outcome.

Model 1: Two-Level CFA With Observed Predictors

We note that observed predictors that are specified as within-groups only can be mentioned in the VARIABLE statement in the Mplus input file as WITHIN. Observed predictors that are between-groups only can be mentioned as BETWEEN. Observed variables that are not mentioned on the WITHIN or the BETWEEN statements are measured on the individual level and can be modeled on both the within- and between-group levels. In this first example, we have one predictor defined within groups (*female*) and one contextual covariate (*orgdemos*) defined between groups.

TITLE: Model 1: Two-level CFA with observed predictors;

DATA: FILE IS C:\mplus\3LCFA.dat;

     Format is 11f8.0,7f8.2;

VARIABLE: Names are orgcode deptid item1 item2 item3 item4 item5 item6

     age female deptsize dept_m orgsize empstab orgdemos orgqual

     orgprod1 orgprod2;

     Usevariables are orgcode item1 item2 item3 item4 item5 item6

     female orgdemos;

     Cluster = orgcode;

     Within = female;

     Between = orgdemos;

Once again, in defining our basic within-group and between-group models, we provide both the name of the Greek letters and corresponding symbols the first time we use them. We use these interchangeably throughout our discussion to help facilitate interpretation of the Mplus output. Within groups, the basic measurement model is specified in a manner similar to our previous CFA model in Chapter 5:

$$v_{ij}^* = \Lambda_W \eta_{Wij} + \varepsilon_{Wij}, \tag{6.2}$$

where in this case v_{ij}^* is a p-dimensional vector of observed y_{ij} and x_{ij} variables (with group z_j predictors fixed to 0); eta (η_{wij}) is an m-dimensional vector of latent factors; lambda (Λ_w) is a $p \times m$ matrix, which is used to define the within-group factor loadings; and epsilon (ε_{wij}) is a p-dimensional vector of measurement errors associated with observed items contained in the theta covariance matrix(Θ_w). We will again free the error covariance between item6 and item3 within groups.

The corresponding within-groups structural part of the model is then specified as

$$\eta_{Wij} = B_W \eta_{Wij} + \zeta_{Wij}, \tag{6.3}$$

where Beta (B_W) is a corresponding m-dimensional matrix of regression coefficients for latent variables and covariates and zeta (ζ_{Wij}) represents errors in equations, which are contained in psi (Ψ_w). In this case, we will add female (coded 1) as an explanatory variable within groups. In this type of model, the structural relationships between gender and the two latent factors are specified in the beta matrix.

Between organizations, the measurement model is defined as

$$y_j^* = \nu_B + \Lambda_B \eta_{Bj} + \varepsilon_{Bj},\tag{6.4}$$

where y_j^* is a p-dimensional vector of cluster-level observed variables, ν_β is a p-dimensional vector of observed item intercepts (contained in Nu in the Mplus output), Λ_B is a $p \times m$ dimensional matrix containing the between–group factor loadings of the items on the latent factors, $\eta_{\beta j}$ is an m-dimensional vector of latent factors, and ε_{Bj} is a p-dimensional vector of residuals for items defining latent factors contained in Θ_B. The structural part of the model is defined as

$$\eta_{Bj} = \alpha_j + B_B \eta_{Bj} + \zeta_{Bj},\tag{6.5}$$

where α_j is an m-dimensional vector of latent factor means, B_B is an m-dimensional of corresponding regression coefficients relating latent variables to each other and observed predictors, and ζ_{Bj} is a vector of errors in equations contained in Ψ_B. As noted, we will again define two latent factors between groups and regress the two factors on an organizational-level covariate (i.e., a weighted indicator of organizational context).

The general mean and covariance structure model for two-level data (Muthén, 1998–2004) can then be expressed as follows (where I is an identity matrix):

$$\mu = \nu_B + \Lambda_B (I - B_B)^{-1} \alpha_B,\tag{6.6}$$

$$\Sigma_B = \Lambda_B (I - B_B)^{-1} \Psi_B (I - B_B)^{\prime -1} \Lambda_B' + \Theta_B,\tag{6.7}$$

$$\Sigma_W = \Lambda_W (I - B_W)^{-1} \Psi_W (I - B_W)^{\prime -1} \Lambda_W' + \Theta_W.\tag{6.8}$$

The initial two-level model is summarized in Figure 6.1. We note that we will again specify each item loading to be equal between and within groups, although this is a not necessary step for all multilevel models with latent variables. The model suggests 33 parameters are estimated (i.e., 16 within groups and 17 between groups).

Model 1 Statements

We next provide the model input statements for Model 1. We note that the Data statement information is the same from Chapter 5. Between groups, the first three items define the first organizational factor, while the second three items define the second organizational factor. Within groups, the first three items define the first individual factor, and the second three items define the second factor. At each level the factors are regressed on a predictor.

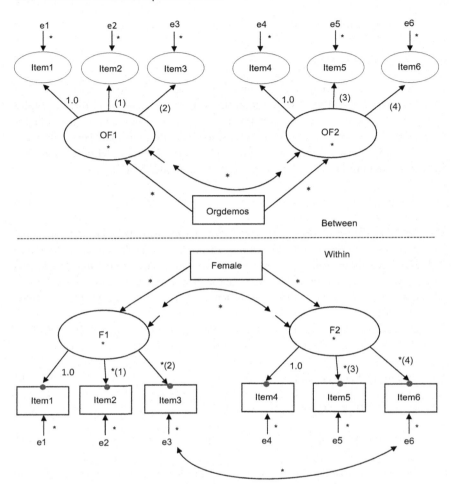

FIGURE 6.1 Proposed two-level CFA with background predictors.

```
ANALYSIS:    TYPE = Twolevel;
             Estimator is MLR;
Model:
             %Between%
             OF1 by item1
             item2(1)
             item3(2);
             OF2 by item4
             item5(3)
             item6(4);
```

```
            OF1 OF2 on orgdemos;
            %within%
            F1 by item1
            item2(1)
            item3(2);
            F2 by item4
            item5(3)
            item6(4);
            item6 with item3;
            F1 F2 on female;
OUTPUT:     sampstat standardized modindices tech1;
```

Once again, it is instructive to examine the TECH1 output to confirm how the model is specified in terms of the matrix specification and the number of parameters estimated. Within groups, this includes four factor loadings in the Lambda matrix (i.e., on the within-group factors F1 and F2), remembering that item1 and item4 are not estimated since they are fixed to 1.0 to provide a metric for the factor. There are also seven error terms to be estimated in the Theta matrix (i.e., one for each item and also covariance between item6 and item3), two structural paths regarding the regression of the latent factors F1 and F2 on *female* in the Beta matrix, and three factor variances and covariances in the Psi matrix. This is a total of 16 estimated parameters.

Between groups, there are six item intercepts estimated, which are contained in the Nu vector. There are three factor variances and covariances estimated in Psi, six error terms for the between-group errors in measuring the latent factors estimated in Theta (since the covariance between item6 and item3 is not estimated between groups), and two structural paths regarding the regression of the two latent factors OF1 and OF2 on the organizational demographic variable (*orgdemos*). This is a total of 17 parameters between groups. The factor loadings in the Lambda matrix are fixed to the same value as the estimates within groups (so they are shown as estimates 1, 2, 3, and 4) but load on the between-group factors OF1 and OF2. As the TECH1 output in Tables 6.1 and 6.2 suggests, there are 33 parameters estimated. Because the latent factor means are not of particular interest in this example, we fix them to zero (in the between-group Alpha vector) and estimate the between-group item intercepts (as shown in the between-group Nu vector).

Model 1 Output

Table 6.1 presents the intraclass correlations for the six items in the study. They range from 0.130 to 0.220, which suggests that there is considerable variability

TECHNICAL 1 OUTPUT

PARAMETER SPECIFICATION FOR WITHIN

LAMBDA

	F1	F2	OF1	OF2	FEMALE	ORGDEMOS
ITEM1	0	0	0	0	0	0
ITEM2	1	0	0	0	0	0
ITEM3	2	0	0	0	0	0
ITEM4	0	0	0	0	0	0
ITEM5	0	3	0	0	0	0
ITEM6	0	4	0	0	0	0
FEMALE	0	0	0	0	0	0
ORGDEMOS	0	0	0	0	0	0

THETA

	ITEM1	ITEM2	ITEM3	ITEM4	ITEM5	ITEM6	FEMALE	ORGDEMOS
ITEM1	5							
ITEM2	0	6						
ITEM3	0	0	7					
ITEM4	0	0	0	8				
ITEM5	0	0	0	0	9			
ITEM6	0	0	10	0	0	11		
FEMALE	0	0	0	0	0	0	0	
ORGDEMOS	0	0	0	0	0	0	0	0

BETA

	F1	F2	OF1	OF2	FEMALE	ORGDEMOS
F1	0	0	0	0	12	0
F2	0	0	0	0	13	0
OF1	0	0	0	0	0	0
OF2	0	0	0	0	0	0
FEMALE	0	0	0	0	0	0
ORGDEMOS	0	0	0	0	0	0

PSI

	F1	F2	OF1	OF2	FEMALE	ORGDEMOS
F1	14					
F2	15	16				
OF1	0	0	0			
OF2	0	0	0	0		
FEMALE	0	0	0	0	0	
ORGDEMOS	0	0	0	0	0	0

PARAMETER SPECIFICATION FOR BETWEEN

NU

	ITEM1	ITEM2	ITEM3	ITEM4	ITEM5	ITEM6	FEMALE	ORGDEMOS
	17	18	19	20	21	22	0	0

LAMBDA

	F1	F2	OF1	OF2	FEMALE	ORGDEMOS
ITEM1	0	0	0	0	0	0
ITEM2	0	0	1	0	0	0
ITEM3	0	0	2	0	0	0
ITEM4	0	0	0	0	0	0
ITEM5	0	0	0	3	0	0
ITEM6	0	0	0	4	0	0
FEMALE	0	0	0	0	0	0
ORGDEMOS	0	0	0	0	0	0

THETA

	ITEM1	ITEM2	ITEM3	ITEM4	ITEM5	ITEM6
ITEM1	23					
ITEM2	0	24				
ITEM3	0	0	25			
ITEM4	0	0	0	26		
ITEM5	0	0	0	0	27	

	F1	F2	OF1	OF2	FEMALE	ORGDEMOS		
ITEM6	0	0	0	0	0	28	0	0
FEMALE	0	0	0	0	0	0	0	
ORGDEMOS	0	0	0	0	0	0		

BETA

	F1	F2	OF1	OF2	FEMALE	ORGDEMOS
F1	0	0	0	0	0	0
F2	0	0	0	0	0	0
OF1	0	0	0	0	0	29
OF2	0	0	0	0	0	30
FEMALE	0	0	0	0	0	0
ORGDEMOS	0	0	0	0	0	0

PSI

	F1	F2	OF1	OF2	FEMALE	ORGDEMOS
F1	0					
F2	0	0				
OF1	0	0	31			
OF2	0	0	32	33		
FEMALE	0	0	0	0	0	
ORGDEMOS	0	0	0	0	0	0

ALPHA

	F1	F2	OF1	OF2	FEMALE	ORGDEMOS
	0	0	0	0	0	0

TABLE 6.1 Item Interclass Correlation Coefficients

Items	ICC
Item1	0.178
Item2	0.195
Item3	0.212
Item4	0.220
Item5	0.213
Item6	0.130

across groups. Of course, these intraclass correlations would change if we added the department level in between the individual and organizational levels; however, for illustrating these modeling techniques we will assume two levels of the data hierarchy.

Next we provide the fit indices for this proposed model in Table 6.2. We can first confirm that the model did indeed estimate 33 parameters. Most often, we examine the overall fit of the hypothesized model to the sample data first, using several fit criteria. We then attempt to isolate the sources of model misfit by examining the model's individual parameters and perhaps its modification indices. If we start with the chi-square coefficient for Model 1, we immediately notice it is larger than we would like (468.301 for 27 df). As readers may recall, our constrained three-level model in Chapter 5 with 34 estimated parameters had a chi-square coefficient of 199.380 for 35 df). However, for purposes of demonstration, we will assume we are working with a two-level structure and our first model represents a type of baseline model against which we will build some subsequent models. Other supporting evidence includes the CFI (0.908), RMSEA (0.078), and SRMR, which is 0.049 within groups and 0.023 between groups. The chi-square, CFI, and RMSEA coefficients all suggest that we could certainly find better fitting models than Model 1. On the other hand, the SRMR estimates are within acceptable boundaries (see Chapter 5 for further discussion of these indices).

What this suggests is that fit indices, which describe model misfit in various ways, often lack clarity in evaluating an isolated model's suitability (Saris, Satorra, & van der Veld, 2009). Although the fit indices are useful in arriving at a preliminary view of a model's suitability, in most instances, we may be interested in building a series of models that may help us arrive at a more informed evaluation of a final model's suitability in describing the sample data. In this type of model-building sequence, we may be able to eliminate specific models as not being as adequate as others we have tested. Ultimately, however, the plausibility of any proposed model's fit to the sample data is a matter of judgment, which should take into consideration theoretical, statistical, and practical considerations (Byrne, 2012).

TABLE 6.2 Model 1 Fit Indices

MODEL FIT INFORMATION	
Number of Free Parameters	33
Log Likelihood	
H_0 Value	−53432.688
H_0 Scaling Correction Factor for MLR	3.8660
H_1 Value	−53146.492
H_1 Scaling Correction Factor for MLR	2.6763
Information Criteria	
Akaike (AIC)	106931.376
Bayesian (BIC)	107126.352
Sample-Size Adjusted BIC $(n^* = (n + 2)/24)$	107021.501
Chi-Square Test of Model Fit	
Value	468.301*
Degrees of Freedom	27
P-Value	0.0000
Scaling Correction Factor for MLR	1.2223
RMSEA (Root Mean Square Error of Approximation)	
Estimate	0.078
CFI/TLI	
CFI	0.908
TLI	0.858
SRMR (Standardized Root Mean Square Residual)	
Value for Within	0.049
Value for Between	0.023

A quick glance at the model modification indices suggests most of the current model's misfit is associated with within-groups item error covariances. We summarize the within-group item error covariances in Table 6.3. For example, if we were to free the covariance between item1 and item2, the corresponding modification index suggests an expected reduction in chi square of 110.106, which would indicate a resulting chi-square coefficient of about 358.195 (468.301 − 110.106). If we subsequently make this change to the model statements (item1 WITH item2), we actually obtain a chi-square coefficient of 355.081. Similarly, the CFI increases to 0.932 and RMSEA decreases to a more acceptable value of 0.068 (fit indices not tabled). Freeing such error covariance parameters, however, can seldom be justified on theoretical grounds, even if it does improve the model's overall fit to the data.

TABLE 6.3 Modification Indices for Model 1 Within-Group Error Covariances

ITEM2	WITH ITEM1	110.106	−5.422	−5.422	−0.437
ITEM3	WITH ITEM1	126.090	7.087	7.087	0.601
ITEM4	WITH ITEM2	26.900	2.795	2.795	0.185
ITEM4	WITH ITEM3	39.094	−3.612	−3.612	−0.251
ITEM5	WITH ITEM1	13.706	−1.853	−1.853	−0.107
ITEM5	WITH ITEM4	95.793	19.114	19.114	0.902
ITEM6	WITH ITEM1	14.706	2.050	2.050	0.103
ITEM6	WITH ITEM2	19.580	3.983	3.983	0.125
ITEM6	WITH ITEM4	31.284	−4.753	−4.753	−0.196

We will therefore accept our Model 1 as "good enough" for now to proceed. Unless our intention is to test a series of well-known theoretical relationships ahead of time (e.g., such as testing a fully mediated versus partially mediated theoretical relationship), when building a series of models in a more exploratory fashion, as in this example, it is often the case that some of our subsequent models may end up fitting the data a bit better than our initial model. Hence, it is often useful to think of the first model as a type of preliminary model against which others can be examined.

In Table 6.4, we next provide the within-group and between-group parameter estimates. The individual parameters also provide information about overall fit of the proposed model, for example, by considering how well the items measure the proposed factors. First, we can see that the unstandardized item loadings for item1 and item4 are fixed to 1.0 to provide a metric for defining each latent factor and the other items are again specified as freely estimated within groups, and their corresponding between-group values constrained to be the same. Second, we can also see that each standardized item loading (STDYX) is relatively strong (i.e., ranging from 0.626 to 0.932 within groups and from 0.881 to 0.996 between groups) and statistically significant (i.e., with p values below 0.001). The standardized estimates are somewhat higher in the between-group model, as we might expect, since the item errors are usually small between groups, after correction for the within-group item unreliability. Third, we can see the structural relationships between the predictors and latent variables are also statistically significant. More specifically, within groups we can see that female affects F1 and F2 positively (0.863 and 0.968, respectively, with $p < 0.001$). This suggests females have more positive views of work-life processes compared with males. Within groups, gender only accounts for about 1% of the variance in F1 and about 0.5% in F2. Between groups, we can see that organizational demographics affects OF1 and OF2 negatively (−2.584 and −4.131, respectively, with $p < 0.001$). Organizational demographics accounts for about 66% of the group-level variance in OF1 and about 63% of the group-level variance in OF2.

TABLE 6.4 Mplus Estimates for Two-Level CFA With Covariates

		Estimate	S.E.	Est./S.E.	p	STDYX
Within Level						
F1	BY					
ITEM1		1.000	0.000	999.000	999.000	0.878
ITEM2		1.740	0.052	33.615	0.000	0.894
ITEM3		2.122	0.095	22.330	0.000	0.932
F2	BY					
ITEM4		1.000	0.000	999.000	999.000	0.914
ITEM5		1.366	0.036	38.221	0.000	0.859
ITEM6		0.749	0.027	27.619	0.000	0.626
F1	ON					
FEMALE		0.863	0.199	4.328	0.000	0.169*
F2	ON					
FEMALE		0.968	0.336	2.880	0.004	0.127*
F2	WITH					
F1		32.056	2.846	11.264	0.000	0.824
ITEM6	WITH					
ITEM3		9.755	0.990	9.859	0.000	0.323
Residual Variances						
ITEM1		7.766	1.186	6.547	0.000	0.229
ITEM2		19.810	1.619	12.235	0.000	0.200
ITEM3		17.914	2.387	7.505	0.000	0.132
ITEM4		11.526	1.028	11.213	0.000	0.165
ITEM5		38.929	2.358	16.513	0.000	0.263
ITEM6		50.980	1.955	26.076	0.000	0.609
F1		25.993	2.489	10.445	0.000	0.993
F2		58.244	3.395	17.155	0.000	0.996
Between Level						
OF1	BY					
ITEM1		1.000	0.000	999.000	999.000	0.968
ITEM2		1.740	0.052	33.615	0.000	0.995
ITEM3		2.122	0.095	22.330	0.000	0.881
OF2	BY					
ITEM4		1.000	0.000	999.000	999.000	0.996
ITEM5		1.366	0.036	38.221	0.000	0.972
ITEM6		0.749	0.027	27.619	0.000	0.940
OF1	ON					
ORGDEMOS		−2.584	0.191	−13.517	0.000	−0.815
OF2	ON					
ORGDEMOS		−4.131	0.323	−12.790	0.000	−0.791

TABLE 6.4 (Continued)

		Estimate	S.E.	Est./S.E.	p	STDYX
OF2	WITH					
OF1		3.920	0.715	5.480	0.000	0.919
Intercepts						
ITEM1		18.735	0.215	87.261	0.000	6.716
ITEM2		31.422	0.365	86.191	0.000	6.653
ITEM3		29.949	0.458	65.418	0.000	4.603
ITEM4		30.231	0.349	86.670	0.000	6.766
ITEM5		37.620	0.500	75.211	0.000	6.016
ITEM6		36.488	0.301	121.154	0.000	10.295
Residual Variances						
ITEM1		0.488	0.155	3.136	0.002	0.063
ITEM2		0.224	0.352	0.635	0.525	0.010
ITEM3		9.480	8.796	1.078	0.281	0.224
ITEM4		0.166	0.209	0.797	0.426	0.008
ITEM5		2.157	0.611	3.528	0.000	0.055
ITEM6		1.466	0.536	2.735	0.006	0.117
OF1		2.451	0.456	5.378	0.000	0.336
OF2		7.417	1.370	5.414	0.000	0.375

*The SDY (standardized y only) standardization is reported for female since it is dichotomous (Muthén & Muthén, 1998–2004).

Model 2: Specifying a Random Level-1 Slope

A second type of relationship of interest is whether or not an individual-level slope varies across groups. We investigated this type of relationship earlier in Chapter 2. We typically begin with the variances of the within-group slopes fixed at zero in the between-groups part of the model. Subsequently, we can test whether one or more of within-group slopes might vary in size across the organizational units. Such relationships are usually based on a theoretical interest. We caution that when the analyst has a large number of level-1 predictors in the model, it would seldom be an optimal strategy to treat them all as randomly varying at the organizational level of the model without giving some consideration to the possible theoretical basis for these decisions.

In Model 2, we will test whether the within-group slope relationship describing the regression of F2 on female varies randomly between organizations. We might have a theoretical interest in examining whether there are organizational settings that are more or less equitable in terms of gender perceptions about organizational work processes as defined by latent factors F1 and F2. If the variance parameter for the slope is significant between groups, we can consider building a model to explain the observed variability in the size of the effect. If the slope variance is not statistically significant, however, we would typically fix its variability again to zero between groups.

Model 2 Statements

Investigating this type of random-slope model necessitates making a couple of changes in our model input statements. First, we must change the ANALYSIS: Type statement to include random slopes (Type = Twolevel Random). Second, we need to add a random slope command in the within-group portion of the model statements (S2 | F2 on female). We will designate the slope as S2 to indicate it is the slope of female on the second factor (F2). Third, we need to add the slope variance (S2) between groups. Including a random slope will add an estimated mean parameter (i.e., the average of the slope parameter between groups) and a variance parameter to the between-group portion of the model, which will therefore remove one fixed regression slope parameter within groups. We next illustrate the changes in the Mplus input file.

```
ANALYSIS:   TYPE = Twolevel random;
            Estimator is MLR;
Model:      %Between%
            OF1 by item1
            item2(1)
            item3(2);
            OF2 by item4
            item5(3)
            item6(4);
            OF1 OF2 on orgdemos;
            S2;
            %Within%
            F1 by item1
            item2(1)
            item3(2);
            F2 by item4
            item5(3)
            item6(4);
            item6 with item3;
            F1 on female;
            S2|F2 on female;
OUTPUT:     Sampstat Tech1;
```

Model 2 Output

When we actually estimated this model, however, we found the size of the female-F2 slope parameter (S2) was significant between groups (not tabled); however, the variance for this relationship (S2) was not statistically significant. It turns out that in either case, the slope variance for gender does not vary across groups (results not tabled). We also note in passing that when there is a random slope in the ANALYSIS command (TYPE = Twolevel random), we have a reduced set of fit indices that is available (i.e., log likelihood, AIC, and BIC), as summarized in Table 6.5. Through quick comparison of AIC and BIC indices, we can see that Model 2 (with 34 parameters) does not fit the data as well as Model 1 based on the larger AIC (106932.854 versus 106931.376, respectively) and BIC (107133.739 versus 107126.352, respectively).

Model 3: Specifying Female as Having Within- and Between-Group Components

Another type of model relationship we will illustrate is where a within-group predictor may be specified as having a within-group and a between-group component. In Model 3, we will propose that gender might have within- and between-group components that affect OF1. Conceptually, this type of variable specification suggests that in addition to the effect of gender on individuals' perceptions within organizations, at the group level, the proportion of females in the organization has an effect on group perceptions of OF1. Investigating this type of relationship necessitates making a couple of changes to the Mplus input file.

Model 3 Statements

First, we do not specify female as being a "within-group" predictor exclusively. If the within-group variable is not specified in the VARIABLE statement as being

TABLE 6.5 Model 2 Fit Indices

MODEL FIT INFORMATION	
Number of Free Parameters	34
Log Likelihood	
H_0 Value	−53432.427
H_0 Scaling Correction Factor for MLR	3.7811
Information Criteria	
Akaike (AIC)	106932.854
Bayesian (BIC)	107133.739
Sample-Size Adjusted BIC	107025.711
$(n^* = (n + 2)/24)$	

a "Within" predictor, it can appear on both levels in the model, which assumes it is decomposed into two uncorrelated (i.e., group-mean centered) latent variables (see Muthén & Muthén, 1998–2012, for further discussion of latent covariates). Therefore, we also do not list female as a "Between" predictor. This specification suggests that the observed variable is considered as a latent variable instead of an observed variable on the between level.

```
TITLE:      Model :3 Two-level model (female defined at both levels);
DATA:       FILE IS C:\Mplus\3LCFA.dat;
            Format is 11f8.0,7f8.2;
VARIABLE:   Names are orgcode deptid item1 item2 item3 item4 item5 item6
            age female deptsize dept_m orgsize empstab orgdemos orgqual
            orgprod1 orgprod2;
            Usevariables are orgcode item1 item2 item3 item4 item5 item6
            female orgdemos;
            Cluster = orgcode;
            Within = ;
            Between = orgdemos;
```

Second, in the model statements we can specify the female-outcome relationship at each level (i.e., F1 on female and OF1 on female). We note that in this model we will keep the random variance for the female-F2 slope (S2) in the %WITHIN% model, even though it was found to not be significant previously. This helps illustrate how this type of two-level demographic variable could be specified along with a within–group random slope. We also set the between–group variances of item1 and item4 to zero for this model (which often facilitates model estimation).

```
ANALYSIS:   TYPE = twolevel random;
            Estimator is MLR;
Model:
            %between%
            OF1 by item1
            item2(1)
            item3(2);
            OF2 by item4
            item5(3)
            item6(4);
            item1@0 item4@0;
            S2;
```

```
              OF1 OF2 on orgdemos;
              OF1 on female;
              %within%
              F1 by item1
              item2(1)
              item3(2);
              F2 by item4
              item5(3)
              item6(4);
              item6 with item3;
              S2|F2 on female;
              F1 on female;
OUTPUT:       sampstat tech1;
```

Model 3 Output

We examine the relevant between-group estimates in Table 6.6. First, we can see that the mean of S2 is statistically significant at the group level (0.931, $p < 0.01$); however, variance is not significant between groups (0.655, $p = 0.304$), as we noted previously for Model 2. Second, we can see that the proportion of females in the organization does not affect perceptions of OF1 (–0.922, $p = 0.992$). In particular, the standard error for this parameter is large (91.574), which indicates that it is not well estimated. This provides evidence that our hypothesis advanced that the proportion of females in the organization affects OF1 cannot be rejected.

In Table 6.7 we present the fit indices for Model 3. Again, for quick comparison, for Model 3 (with 33 estimated parameters), we can see the AIC is considerably larger than for Model 2, with 34 estimated parameters (AIC = 110,897.614 versus 106,932.854, respectively). So far, our model building results suggest that Model 2 (with a randomly varying slope) and Model 3 (with a demographic variable defined both within and between groups) do not represent plausible models compared with the first model, since the key theoretical relationship specified in each model was not supported when tested against the data. As these initial model tests suggest, at some point we typically will decide that our within-groups model is relatively well specified and turn our attention to the between-groups portion of the model.

Model 4: Adding a Latent Factor Between Groups

We next specify how we can add a latent independent factor between groups. In this case, between organizations we will define an organizational process factor, which is measured by six observed scales. It is proposed to affect both OF1 and OF2. Notice that in this formulation, as summarized in Figure 6.2, the between-group observed variables measuring organizational processes are indicated as

TABLE 6.6 Model 3 Between-Group Unstandardized Estimates

			Estimate	S.E.	Est./S.E.	p
Between Level						
OF1		BY				
	ITEM1		1.000	0.000	999.000	999.000
	ITEM2		1.734	0.050	34.518	0.000
	ITEM3		2.120	0.095	22.410	0.000
OF2		BY				
	ITEM4		1.000	0.000	999.000	999.000
	ITEM5		1.365	0.035	38.644	0.000
	ITEM6		0.747	0.027	27.451	0.000
OF1		ON				
	ORGDEMOS		−2.528	0.466	−5.429	0.000
	FEMALE		−0.922	91.574	−0.010	0.992
OF2		ON				
	ORGDEMOS		−4.158	0.327	−12.731	0.000
OF2		WITH				
	OF1		3.989	0.740	5.390	0.000
Means						
	S2		0.931	0.344	2.710	0.007
Intercepts						
	ITEM1		19.613	45.926	0.427	0.669
	ITEM2		32.988	79.646	0.414	0.679
	ITEM3		31.845	97.307	0.327	0.743
	ITEM4		30.244	0.350	86.418	0.000
	ITEM5		37.636	0.502	75.005	0.000
	ITEM6		36.498	0.303	120.547	0.000
Variances						
	S2		0.655	0.637	1.027	0.304
Residual Variances						
	ITEM1		0.000	0.000	999.000	999.000
	ITEM2		0.712	0.343	2.074	0.038
	ITEM3		10.128	9.342	1.084	0.278
	ITEM4		0.000	0.000	999.000	999.000
	ITEM5		2.293	0.584	3.929	0.000
	ITEM6		1.564	0.511	3.058	0.002
	OF1		2.576	0.483	5.338	0.000
	OF2		7.515	1.341	5.604	0.000

TABLE 6.7 Model 3 Fit Indices

MODEL FIT INFORMATION	
Number of Free Parameters	33
Log Likelihood	
H_0 Value	-55415.807
H_0 Scaling Correction Factor for MLR	3.9377
Information Criteria	
Akaike (AIC)	110897.614
Bayesian (BIC)	111092.591
Sample-Size Adjusted BIC ($n^* = (n + 2)/24$)	110987.739

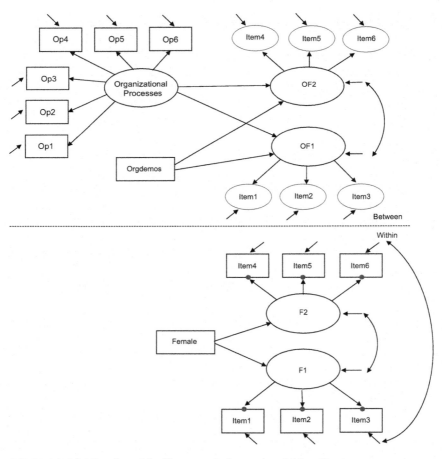

FIGURE 6.2 Multilevel model of latent and observed variables affecting outcomes.

rectangles. Variables measured only on the between–groups level are referred to in the "Between" list of variables in the Mplus VARIABLE statement. We note in passing that an individual-level covariate defined at the group level (e.g., *female* in Model 3) would be defined as an oval in a corresponding figure at the group level and as a rectangle at the individual level).

Model 4 Statements

First, between groups we define the organizational process factor (*Orgpro*) as measured by six observed indicators (i.e., *op1* through *op6*). Second, we will simplify our model statements by removing the constraints on the observed items measuring the two latent dependent variables within and between groups. We note that the constrained item specification is more useful when the focus is on comparing the factor variances within and between groups directly (as in a CFA-type model). In this case, our concern is more on modeling structural relationships within and between groups. We next provide the complete model input statements for Model 4.

```
TITLE:      Model 4: Adding a latent variable between groups;
DATA:       FILE IS C:\mplus\Ch6SEMfull.dat;
            Format is 11f8.0,13f8.2;
VARIABLE:   Names are orgcode deptid item1 item2 item3 item4
            item5 item6 age female deptsize dept_m orgsize empstab
            orgdemos orgqual orgprod1 orgprod2 op1 op2 op3 op4op5 op6;
            Usevariables are orgcode item1 item2 item3 item4
            item5 item6 female orgdemos op1 op2 op3 op4 op5 op6;
            Cluster is orgcode;
            Within = female;
            Between = orgdemos op1 op2 op3 op4 op5 op6;
ANALYSIS:   TYPE = twolevel;
            Estimator is MLR;
Model:
            %Between%
            Orgpro by op1 op2 op3 op4 op5 op6;
            OF1 by item1 item2 item3;
            OF2 by Item4 item5 item6;
            OF1 OF2 on orgdemos orgpro;
            %Within%
            F1 by item1 item2 item3;
            F2 by item4 item5 item6;
            item6 with item3;
            F1 F2 on female;
OUTPUT:     sampstat standardized tech1;
```

Model 4 Output

We provide the model fit indices in Table 6.8. For the proposed model, the chi square is 709.645 with 72 *df* ($p = 0.000$). However, the CFI (0.926) and RMSEA (0.057) and standardized SRMR within groups (0.049) are reasonable values for an adequate-fitting model. We do note that the SRMR between groups (0.107) is a bit too high. Once again, while we could continue to seek better-fitting models, we will assume this model is adequate for demonstration purposes and proceed to examine the parameter estimates.

The parameter estimates are included in Table 6.9. Regarding the model to explain the two latent factors (OF1 and OF2), we can note that organizational process affects OF2 significantly ($1.767, p < 0.01$). There is preliminary evidence that it also affects OF1 ($0.576, p < 0.06$). We note in passing that the table also indicates that organizational demographics affect both OF1 ($-2.415, p < 0.001$) and OF2 ($-3.907, p < 0.001$).

Model 5: Testing an Indirect Effect

Another relationship of interest may be whether there exists an indirect effect between a predictor (such as organizational demographics) and the outcome

TABLE 6.8 Model 4 Selected Model Fit Indices

MODEL FIT INFORMATION	
Number of Free Parameters	57
Log Likelihood	
H_0 Value	−54072.360
H_0 Scaling Correction Factor for MLR	2.8270
H_1 Value	−53708.697
H_1 Scaling Correction Factor for MLR	1.8212
Information Criteria	
Akaike (AIC)	108258.721
Bayesian (BIC)	108595.499
Sample-Size Adjusted BIC	108414.392
($n^* = (n + 2)/24$)	
Chi-Square Test of Model Fit	
Value	709.645*
Degrees of Freedom	72
P-Value	0.000
Scaling Correction Factor for MLR	1.025
RMSEA (Root Mean Square Error of Approximation)	
Estimate	0.057
CFI/TLI	
CFI	0.926
TLI	0.898
SRMR (Standardized Root Mean Square Residual)	
Value for Within	0.049
Value for Between	0.107

TABLE 6.9 Model 4 Unstandardized Estimates

		Estimate	S.E.	Est./S.E.	Two-Tailed P-Value
Within Level					
F1	BY				
ITEM1		1.000	0.000	999.000	999.000
ITEM2		1.718	0.053	32.114	0.000
ITEM3		2.115	0.098	21.588	0.000
F2	BY				
ITEM4		1.000	0.000	999.000	999.000
ITEM5		1.357	0.045	30.366	0.000
ITEM6		0.747	0.031	24.364	0.000
F1	ON				
FEMALE		0.867	0.201	4.301	0.000
F2	ON				
FEMALE		0.963	0.340	2.834	0.005
F2	WITH				
F1		32.248	2.981	10.817	0.000
ITEM6	WITH				
ITEM3		9.742	0.990	9.837	0.000
Residual Variances					
ITEM1		7.725	1.171	6.596	0.000
ITEM2		19.981	1.631	12.250	0.000
ITEM3		17.773	2.408	7.381	0.000
ITEM4		11.441	1.068	10.710	0.000
ITEM5		39.110	2.469	15.837	0.000
ITEM6		51.015	1.954	26.108	0.000
F1		26.248	2.594	10.118	0.000
F2		58.472	3.625	16.131	0.000
Between Level					
ORGPRO	BY				
OP1		1.000	0.000	999.000	999.000
OP2		1.452	0.222	6.534	0.000
OP3		1.536	0.215	7.140	0.000
OP4		1.440	0.245	5.865	0.000
OP5		1.208	0.132	9.137	0.000
OP6		1.331	0.157	8.497	0.000
OF1	BY				
ITEM1		1.000	0.000	999.000	999.000
ITEM2		1.855	0.061	30.437	0.000
ITEM3		2.077	0.084	24.748	0.000

TABLE 6.9 (Continued)

		Estimate	S.E.	Est./S.E.	Two–Tailed P–Value
OF2	BY				
ITEM4		1.000	0.000	999.000	999.000
ITEM5		1.406	0.043	32.492	0.000
ITEM6		0.756	0.051	14.895	0.000
OF1	ON				
ORGPRO		0.576	0.305	1.891	0.059
OF2	ON				
ORGPRO		1.767	0.577	3.063	0.002
OF1	ON				
ORGDEMOS		−2.415	0.182	−13.272	0.000
OF2	ON				
ORGDEMOS		−3.907	0.308	−12.693	0.000
OF2	WITH				
OF1		3.463	0.628	5.510	0.000
Intercepts					
OP1		−0.022	0.081	−0.276	0.783
OP2		−0.078	0.079	−0.984	0.325
OP3		−0.034	0.082	−0.418	0.676
OP4		−0.015	0.080	−0.188	0.851
OP5		−0.049	0.078	−0.628	0.530
OP6		−0.007	0.077	−0.090	0.929
ITEM1		18.735	0.216	86.894	0.000
ITEM2		31.433	0.364	86.332	0.000
ITEM3		29.956	0.458	65.352	0.000
ITEM4		30.242	0.354	85.545	0.000
ITEM5		37.643	0.506	74.374	0.000
ITEM6		36.499	0.303	120.318	0.000
Variances					
ORGPRO		0.412	0.094	4.364	0.000
Residual Variances					
OP1		0.569	0.069	8.197	0.000
OP2		0.065	0.012	5.589	0.000
OP3		0.033	0.009	3.668	0.000
OP4		0.086	0.014	6.376	0.000
OP5		0.288	0.045	6.444	0.000
OP6		0.145	0.025	5.899	0.000

TABLE 6.9 (Continued)

	Estimate	S.E.	Est./S.E.	Two-Tailed P-Value
ITEM1	0.501	0.152	3.299	0.001
ITEM2	0.013	0.342	0.037	0.971
ITEM3	9.595	8.835	1.086	0.277
ITEM4	0.258	0.224	1.151	0.250
ITEM5	2.018	0.596	3.389	0.001
ITEM6	1.327	0.523	2.540	0.011
OF1	2.239	0.402	5.569	0.000
OF2	6.286	1.294	4.858	0.000

through a mediator (i.e., in this case, organizational processes). The hypothesis proposed is that organizational demographics influence F2 both directly and indirectly through its influence on the organization's processes.

Model 5 Statements

We have to make a couple of changes in the model statements. First, between groups, we specify the regression of organizational processes on organizational demographics (orgpro on orgdemos;). Second, a model with an indirect effect can be specified by adding the following lines to the model statement after the within-groups model is specified.
Model indirect:
OF2 ind orgpro orgdemos;
This model statement indicates that organizational demographics (orgdemos) exerts an indirect effect on F2 through organizational processes (orgpro). We provide the model statements next, focusing on the model portion of the input statements.

```
Model:
        %Between%
        orgpro by op1 op2 op3 op4 op5 op6;
        OF1 by item1 item2 item3;
        OF2 by item4 item5 item6;
        OF1 OF2 on orgpro orgdemos;
        orgpro on orgdemos;
        %Within%
        F1 by item1 item2 item3;
        F2 by item4 item5 item6;
        item6 with item3;
        F1 F2 on female;
```

> Model indirect:
>   OF2 ind orgpro orgdemos;
> OUTPUT: sampstat standardized tech1;

Model 5 Output

We summarize the relevant fit indices in Table 6.10. We note that adding the direct effect between organizational demographics and organizational processes improves the fit of the model between groups (i.e., SRMR between = 0.054).

In Table 6.11 the relevant between-group direct and indirect parameter estimates are summarized. There are three relevant effects in examining whether a partial mediation effect holds. First, the regression of OF2 on organizational demographics is significant (-3.903, $p < 0.001$). Second, the unstandardized direct effect of the regression of organizational processes on organizational demographics is also statistically significant (-0.136, $p = 0.022$). Third, the unstandardized indirect effect is -0.241 ($p = 0.066$). Therefore, we would likely conclude that there is not a statistically significant indirect effect between the organizational demographics and OF2.

TABLE 6.10 Model 5 Fit Indices

MODEL FIT INFORMATION	
Number of Free Parameters	58
Log Likelihood	
H_0 Value	−54069.934
H_0 Scaling Correction Factor for MLR	2.7973
H_1 Value	−53708.697
H_1 Scaling Correction Factor for MLR	1.8212
Information Criteria	
Akaike (AIC)	108255.867
Bayesian (BIC)	108598.554
Sample-Size Adjusted BIC	108414.269
$(n^* = (n + 2)/24)$	
Chi-Square Test of Model Fit	
Value	705.647*
Degrees of Freedom	71
P-Value	0.0000
Scaling Correction Factor for MLR	1.0238
RMSEA (Root Mean Square Error of Approximation)	
Estimate	0.057
CFI/TLI	
CFI	0.926
TLI	0.897
SRMR (Standardized Root Mean Square Residual)	
Value for Within	0.049
Value for Between	0.054

TABLE 6.11 Model 5 Between-Groups Direct and Indirect Effect Estimates

MODEL RESULTS

	Estimate	*S.E.*	*Est./S.E.*	*Two-Tailed P-Value*
BETWEEN				
Direct Effects				
OF2 ON				
ORGDEMOS	−3.903	0.308	−12.673	0.000
ORGPRO ON				
ORGDEMOS	−0.136	0.060	−2.291	0.022
Indirect Effect				
ORGDEMOS to OF2				
Sum of indirect	−0.241	0.131	−1.839	0.066

TABLE 6.12 Model 5 Between-Groups *R*-Square

Latent Variable	*Estimate*	*S.E.*	*Est./S.E.*	*Two-Tailed P-Value*
ORGPRO	0.033	0.029	1.123	0.261
OF1	0.675	0.060	11.255	0.000
OF2	0.686	0.061	11.168	0.000

In terms of *r*-square estimates between groups, in Table 6.12, we can see that organizational processes and demographics account for about 68% and 69% of the variance in OF1 and OF2, respectively. Demographics account for about 3% of the variance in organizational processes.

Model 6: Adding a Relationship Between the Latent Outcomes

Model 6 Statements

In Model 6, we demonstrate how we might define the between–group regression of OF2 on OF1 (OF2 on OF1;) in the between-groups portion of the model statement.

```
Model:
        %Between%
        orgpro by op1 op2 op3 op4 op5 op6;
        OF1 by item1 item2 item3;
        OF2 by item4 item5 item6;
        OF1 on orgdemos orgpro;
```

```
OF2 on orgdemos orgpro;
OF2 on OF1;
orgpro on orgdemos;
```

Model 6 Output

In the TECH1 output, we note the resulting change in the beta matrix from specifying the regression OF2 on OF1 (as parameter estimate 54).

PARAMETER SPECIFICATIONS FOR BETWEEN

BETA

	F1	F2	ORGPRO	OF1	OF2
F1	0	0	0	0	0
F2	0	0	0	0	0
ORGPRO	0	0	0	0	0
OF1	0	0	51	0	0
OF2	0	0	53	54	0
FEMALE	0	0	0	0	0
ORGDEMOS	0	0	0	0	0

BETA

	ORGDEMOS	FEMALE
F1	0	0
F2	0	0
ORGPRO	0	50
OF1	0	52
OF2	0	55
FEMALE	0	0
ORGDEMOS	0	0

We provide the fit indices in Table 6.13. We can see that the model fits relatively the same as the previous model.

We will concentrate on the between–group structural relationships in Model 6,
which are presented in Table 6.14. First, the regression of OF2 on OF1 is statistically
significant ($1.548, p < 0.001$). Second, we observe that organizational processes
do not directly affect OF1 ($0.577, p > 0.05$) but do affect OF2 ($0.876, p < 0.01$).
Third, we can see that once the relationship between organizational demographics
and OF1 is accounted for ($-2.413, p < 0.001$), organizational demographics do

TABLE 6.13 Model 6 Fit Indices

Number of Free Parameters	58
Log Likelihood	
H_0 Value	−54069.935
H_0 Scaling Correction Factor for MLR	2.7974
H_1 Value	−53708.697
H_1 Scaling Correction Factor for MLR	1.8212
Information Criteria	
Akaike (AIC)	108255.870
Bayesian (BIC)	108598.557
Sample-Size Adjusted BIC	108414.272
$(n^* = (n + 2)/24)$	
Chi-Square Test of Model Fit	
Value	705.753*
Degrees of Freedom	71
P-Value	0.0000
Scaling Correction Factor for MLR	1.0237
RMSEA (Root Mean Square Error of Approximation)	
Estimate	0.057
CFI/TLI	
CFI	0.926
TLI	0.897
SRMR (Standardized Root Mean Square Residual)	
Value for Within	0.049
Value for Between	0.054

not affect OF2 ($-0.168, p > 0.05$). We might investigate whether organizational demographics exerts an indirect effect on OF2. When we did subsequently test that proposed relationship, however, we found the indirect effect to be nonsignificant ($-0.119, p > 0.05$). We leave this to readers to test if they wish. We also note in passing that the regression of OF2 on OF1 increases the between-group variance accounted for in OF2 to about 95% (not tabled).

Model 7: Specifying a Reciprocal Relationship Between Outcomes

Finally, we can propose a model where OF1 is also regressed on OF2 (OF1 on OF2;). Reciprocal-effect models offer an alternative means of unpacking the issue of causal ordering. Such models propose that relationships among variables in a proposed model could have reciprocal or bi-directional effects. The model implies that two (or more) variables may be both a cause and an effect of each other. We summarize this type of mutual causation with double arrows between major constructs. Thus, a reciprocal-influence model can provide evidence to answer questions about whether the proposed relationship between two variables is mutually reinforcing rather than solely unidirectional.

TABLE 6.14 Model 7 Between-Group Structural Relationships

Observed Variable		Estimate	S.E.	Est./S.E.	Two-Tailed P-Value	STDYX
OF1	ON					
	OF2	0.393	0.203	1.940	0.052	0.556
OF2	ON					
	ORGPRO	0.862	0.375	2.301	0.021	0.120
	OF1	1.342	0.404	3.323	0.001	0.948
OF1	ON					
	ORGDEMOS	−1.417	0.288	−4.924	0.000	−0.371
OF2	WITH					
	OF1	−0.487	0.270	−1.802	0.071	−0.487
ORGPRO	WITH					
	ORGDEMOS	−0.099	0.043	−2.301	0.021	−0.181

Note: STDYX refers to standardized estimates.

Of course, longitudinal data provides a clear temporal element where mutual influence can be observed over time. Within a cross-sectional design, mutual influence implies that two or more variables that are measured at the same time may be both a cause and effect of each other (Kline, 2005; Marsh & Craven, 2006). If one proposes the existence of a reciprocal effect between two variables, this implies more than a simple cause-and-effect ($A \rightarrow B$) relationship from the independent variable (A) to the dependent variable (B). It also implies the converse; that is, B affects A ($B \rightarrow A$). This type of reciprocal effect is indicated with bidirectional arrows ($A \rightleftarrows B$), suggesting that A and B mutually affect each other.

For cross-sectional data, we can think of a reciprocal relationship as requiring the assumption of equilibrium. More specifically, one must assume that the relationship specified in a reciprocal relationship between variables A and B (or among variables in a feedback loop) has already manifested its effects, and therefore, the system is essentially in a balanced state (Kline, 2005). This means that its estimation does not depend on the particular time in which the data were collected (Kline, 2005). As Klein notes, we must also assume stationarity of the causal structure—that is, it does not change over time. Since this cannot be supported with cross-sectional data, it is a proposition that must be argued.

Reciprocal relationships cannot be estimated in analyses using multiple regression, since multiple regression implies only one dependent variable, but they pose no special difficulties for structural models estimated with iterative model-fitting techniques. The presence of a reciprocal effect in a structural model makes it nonrecursive. In terms of diagrammatic representation (as in Figure 6.3), it is important to note that reciprocal influence indicated by a bidirectional arrow is not the same as a two-headed arrow ($A \leftrightarrow B$). This latter relationship simply indicates a covariance (or correlation) between the two variables. To specify a reciprocal-influence model using SEM, it is important to make sure that we have met model identification rules. These include the following conditions:

- Each latent variable is assigned a scale of measurement.
- The number of free parameters estimated must be less than or equal to the number of nonredundant elements in the observed covariance matrix.
- Every latent variable with unrestricted variance must emit at least two direct paths to observed indicators or other latent variables when these latter variables have unrestricted error variances (see Bollen & Davis, 2009).

We summarize the key aspects of this relationship in Figure 6.3. Interpreting reciprocal effects in cross-sectional research designs is more difficult than might appear at first glance. We must assume that some of the described phenomena clearly precede the others in terms of their occurrence in time. In this case, we will assume that organizational demographics and the organizational process factor precede individuals' resulting perceptions of work-life processes. As shown in the figure, the errors in equations involved in a reciprocal relationship (i.e., represented as short single-headed arrows) are typically specified as correlated. Correlated residual variances are consistent with the logic of reciprocity, since if

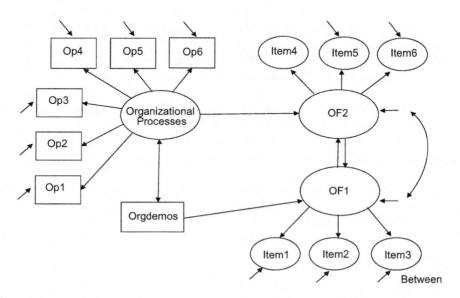

FIGURE 6.3 Model 7: Between-level model defining a reciprocal-effect relationship.

we assume that A and B mutually influence each other, we may reasonably expect that they have common omitted causes (Anderson & Williams, 1992; Kline, 2005). In addition, some of the error in predicting one outcome is assumed to be due to other variables in the model and vice versa (i.e., they don't have the exact set of same predictors).

More specifically, as Kline (2005) indicates, this requirement (referred to as the rank condition) means that each variable in a feedback loop has a unique pattern of direct effects on it from variables that are outside the loop. Variance in the pattern of direct effects provides a means of ensuring that the free parameters (e.g., regression coefficients, standard errors, residual variances) of each variable involved in a feedback loop can be uniquely estimated. If all of the direct effects influencing both OF1 and OF2 were from the same set of predictors, then the whole nonrecursive model would fail the rank condition (Kline, 2005). In addition, the order condition requires that for models with feedback loops the number of variables excluded from the mathematical equation for each variable in a feedback loop exceeds the total number of endogenous variables in the whole model minus 1 (Kline, 2005). In this case, OF1 and OF2 are the endogenous variables in that model (i.e., their variance is determined by other exogenous variables in the model).

We note for the model in Figure 6.3 that each latent variable is scaled, and the degrees of freedom associated with the model are greater than zero. In addition, there are two endogenous variables (OF1 and OF2) in a feedback loop. Therefore, each of these variables must have a minimum of one ($2 - 1 = 1$) other variable excluded from each of their equations, which we can verify from Figure 6.3. More specifically, organizational demographics (*orgdemos*) is excluded from the equation for OF2, and organizational process (*orgpro*) is excluded from the equation for OF1. Because there is one variable excluded from the equation of each endogenous variable in Figure 6.3, the order condition is satisfied. The rank condition is satisfied since each has a unique set of predictors. For defining factor metrics for OF1 and OF2, in this model we fixed the factor variances to 1.0 and estimated the six item loadings (shown in the model statements with an asterisk for the first item defining OF1 and OF2 between groups).

It can be challenging from a technical standpoint to obtain a solution that converges, even if the model is properly identified. They may require start values that are very close to the actual estimated values. For models that converge, the analyst should check the model estimates carefully to make sure that they make sense (i.e., standardized factor loadings below 1.0, positive error variances, standard errors that are reasonable).

Model 7 Statements

We next summarize the key relationships in the between-groups portion of the model statement.

Model:
%between%
orgpro by op1 op2 op3 op4 op5 op6;
OF1 by item1* item2 item3;
OF2 by item4* item5 item6;
OF1 on orgdemos;
OF2 on orgpro;
OF2 on OF1;
OF1 on OF2;
OF1@1 OF2@1;
OF2 with OF1;
 orgpro with orgdemos;

We summarize the relevant proposed relationships in the Beta matrix in the TECH1 output. We can see the added parameter of OF1 regressed on OF2 as parameter 52.

PARAMETER SPECIFICATION FOR BETWEEN

BETA

	F1	F2	ORGPRO	OF1	OF2
F1	0	0	0	0	0
F2	0	0	0	0	0
ORGPRO	0	0	0	0	0
OF1	0	0	0	0	52
OF2	0	0	54	55	0
FEMALE	0	0	0	0	0
ORGDEMOS	0	0	0	0	0

BETA

	ORGDEMOS	FEMALE
F1	0	0
F2	0	0
ORGPRO	0	0
OF1	53	0
OF2	0	0
FEMALE	0	0
ORGDEMOS	0	0

Model 7 Output

In Table 6.14 we summarize the key structural relationships in the between-groups portion of the model. The interpretation of the proposed relationships is that organizational demographics directly influences OF1 (-1.417, $p < 0.001$). In addition, organizational process influences OF2 positively and significantly (0.862, $p < 0.05$). Finally, OF1 influences OF2 (1.342, $p = 0.001$) and there is preliminary evidence that OF2 simultaneously influences OF1 (0.393, $p = 0.052$). For demonstration purposes, we suggest this latter relationship provides initial support the notion of mutual influence.

For this final model we note the r-square coefficients in Table 6.15. The model r-square estimates suggest the between-level model accounts for considerable variance in the two outcome factors (i.e., 91%, and 95%).

TABLE 6.15 Model 7 R-Square Coefficients

Observed Variable	Estimate	S.E.	Est./S.E.	Two-Tailed P-Value
Within Level				
Observed				
ITEM1	0.774	0.013	59.616	0.000
ITEM2	0.796	0.020	39.524	0.000
ITEM3	0.869	0.014	60.533	0.000
ITEM4	0.837	0.017	49.907	0.000
ITEM5	0.734	0.016	44.679	0.000
ITEM6	0.391	0.026	15.193	0.000
Latent				
F1	0.007	0.003	2.239	0.025
F2	0.004	0.003	1.405	0.160
Between Level				
Observed				
OP1	0.420	0.064	6.566	0.000
OP2	0.930	0.018	51.032	0.000
OP3	0.967	0.012	80.836	0.000
OP4	0.908	0.021	42.654	0.000
OP5	0.677	0.055	12.387	0.000
OP6	0.835	0.036	23.215	0.000
ITEM1	0.932	0.021	45.143	0.000
ITEM2	0.999	0.014	69.101	0.000
ITEM3	0.756	0.177	4.267	0.000
ITEM4	0.987	0.012	85.762	0.000
ITEM5	0.951	0.015	64.705	0.000
ITEM6	0.896	0.038	23.582	0.000
Latent				
OF1	0.906	0.050	18.189	0.000
OF2	0.953	0.027	35.422	0.000

TABLE 6.16 Model 7 Final Fit Indices

MODEL FIT INFORMATION	
Number of Free Parameters	60
Log likelihood	
H_0 Value	−54256.200
H_0 Scaling Correction Factor for MLR	2.7344
H_1 Value	−53894.962
H_1 Scaling Correction Factor for MLR	1.8071
Information Criteria	
Akaike (AIC)	108632.399
Bayesian (BIC)	108986.903
Sample-Size Adjusted BIC	108796.264
$\quad (n^* = (n + 2)/24)$	
Chi-Square Test of Model Fit	
Value	705.926*
Degrees of Freedom	71
P-Value	0.0000
Scaling Correction Factor for MLR	1.0234
RMSEA (Root Mean Square Error Of Approximation)	
Estimate	0.057
CFI/TLI	
CFI	0.926
TLI	0.897
SRMR (Standardized Root Mean Square Residual)	
Value for Within	0.049
Value for Between	0.054

Finally, we provide the model fit indices for Model 7 in Table 6.16. The indices suggest the reciprocal influence model provides a reasonable fit to the data.

Summary

The flexibility of the SEM approach makes it an ideal modeling strategy for researchers to use in examining two-level cross-sectional or longitudinal models where measurement error is important to include. The examples included in this chapter provide an introduction to various ways in which SEM can be used for conducting multilevel modeling—yielding greater conceptual clarity in defining relationships among variables and greater precision of the estimates where there are clustering features present. Their appropriate use, however, depends on guidance from strong theory to explicate relationships and the collection of quality data. As the techniques continue to become more readily available, their use in a variety of research fields should expand rapidly.

References

Anderson, S. E., & Williams, L. J. (1992). Assumptions about unmeasured variables with studies of reciprocal relationships. The case of employee attitudes. *Journal of Applied Psychology, 77,* 638–650.

Bollen, K. A. & Davis, W. R. (2009). Two rules of identification for structural equation models. *Structural Equation Modeling, 16,* 523–536.

Byrne, B. M. (2012). *Structural equation modeling with Mplus: Basic concepts, applications, and programming.* New York: Routledge Academic.

Kline, R. B. (2005). *Principles and practice of structural equation modeling* (2nd ed.). New York: Guilford Press.

Marsh, H. W. & Craven, R. G. (2006). Reciprocal effects of self-concept and performance from a multidimensional perspective: Beyond seductive pleasure and unidimensional perspectives. *Perspectives on Psychological Science, 1,* 133–163.

Muthén, B. O. (1998–2004). *Mplus technical indices.* Los Angeles, CA: Muthén & Muthén.

Muthén, B. O. (2001). Latent variable mixture modeling. In G. A. Marcoulides & R. E. Schumacker (Eds.), *New developments and techniques in structural equation modeling* (pp. 1–33). Mahwah, NJ: Lawrence Erlbaum Associates.

Muthén, B. O. (2002). Beyond SEM: General latent variable modeling. *Behaviormetrika, 29,* 81–118.

Muthén, B. O. (2008). Latent variable hybrids: Overview of old and new models. In G. R. Hancock & K. M. Samuelson (Eds.), *Advances in latent variable mixture models* (pp. 1–24). Charlotte, NC: Information Age Publishing.

Muthén, B. & Asparouhov, T. (2009). Growth mixture modeling: Analysis with non-Gaussian random effects. In G. Fitzmaurice, M. Davidian, G. Verbeke, & G. Molenberghs (Eds.), *Longitudinal data analysis* (pp. 143–165). Boca Raton: Chapman & Hall/ CRC Press.

Muthén, B. O. & Satorra, A. (1995). Complex sample data in structural equation modeling. *Sociological Methodology, 25,* 216–316.

Rigdon, E. (1998). Structural equation models. In G. A. Marcoulides (Ed.), *Modern methods for business research* (pp. 251–294). Mahwah, NJ: Lawrence Erlbaum Associates.

Saris, W. E., Satorra, A., & van der Veld, W. M. (2009). Testing structural equation models or detection of misspecifications? *Structural Equation Modeling, 16,* 561–582.

7

METHODS FOR EXAMINING INDIVIDUAL AND ORGANIZATIONAL CHANGE

Chapter Objectives

In this chapter, we present an introduction to multilevel regression and SEM methods that can be used to examine changes in individuals and organizations over time. The multilevel regression approach makes use of repeated observations for each individual defined at Level 1 with differences between individuals specified at Level 2. This requires multiple subject lines for the repeated measures to define the individual's growth over time in a basic two-level model. In contrast, the SEM approach treats the repeated measures in a manner similar to observed items defining latent intercept and slope factors. Group-level variables (e.g., departments, organizations) can be defined above the individual growth models in either approach. Despite their basic differences in specifying individual and organizational change, both approaches generally yield similar results across a wide variety of longitudinal modeling situations.

Introduction

In many organizational studies the outcome and process variables are only measured on one occasion. A limitation of cross-sectional data, however, is that they are not well suited to investigations of processes that are assumed to be dynamic. This is because it is difficult to establish the proper time ordering necessary to address causal relationships in cross-sectional analyses. It therefore becomes more difficult to rule out alternative explanations. Analyses based on cross-sectional data may only lead to partial understandings of processes at best, and misleading interpretations at worst (Davies, 1994).

Time is a key factor in understanding how organizational processes unfold, as well as how their impacts may be observed. Process itself is dynamic and time ordered. Limitations of data and method have in the past restricted the quantitative analysis of organizational processes. Increasingly, however, both the concepts and methods are becoming available that can provide more rigorous and thorough examinations of longitudinal data. Although there has been considerable development of longitudinal data analysis techniques for use with various types of research designs (e.g., experimental, time series, nonexperimental), there is still a need to make the techniques more accessible to organizational researchers.

In this chapter we present an introduction to methods that can be used to examine changes in individuals and organizations over time. The chapter represents an extension of the multilevel methods introduced in the previous chapters. First, we briefly outline several ways of collecting and analyzing longitudinal data. While there are a number of ways to examine longitudinal data, we next introduce two broad approaches for examining changes within individuals and groups. The first approach focuses on estimating growth or change from the perspective of random-coefficients (multilevel) modeling, which can be easily defined using the Mplus software. The second approach focuses on the use of latent variables, which are common in structural equation modeling (SEM), for examining individual and organizational change. A number of examples are also provided to help the reader think about different ways that longitudinal data analysis can broaden the conceptual possibilities for designing studies to answer research questions about individual and organizational change processes.

Readers should keep in mind that there are different ways to analyze longitudinal data. Among considerations in selecting software to analyze change are the types of designs supported, data input options (e.g., number of hierarchical levels supported), diagnostics, ability to incorporate sample weights, and technical support (Singer & Willett, 2003). Both the multilevel modeling (MLM) and SEM approaches are developed here. We will show in this chapter that dealing with the MLM approach is quite straightforward. We then move from the straightforward MLM approach to studying growth or change from an SEM perspective, often referred to as either latent change analysis (LCA) or **latent curve analysis** (LCA).

We find the SEM perspective to be of great value when thinking about change in the multilevel context. That said, there is a certain amount of inherent complexity in specifying such models using SEM that has, in our view, served to limit the multilevel examination of growth primarily to the MLM approach—where the specification of a random intercept equation and a random slope equation greatly (and at times problematically) simplify this complexity. The relatively straightforward nature of the MLM approach to modeling change comes at the expense of ignoring issues associated establishing measurement invariance across time or groups, variance decomposition of mediating processes in the process (and at times, even separate growth processes), and the nature of error structures within and across groups being examined. Venturing into the realm of the SEM approach to modeling growth therefore requires much more theoretical guidance. This is necessary if only to help the analyst understand what the results of these models mean. We believe, however, that being forced to think more carefully about the parameters being estimated results in a much better appreciation of the meaning of the model and its nuances. In the sections that follow, we develop several basic types of individual change models for a variety of purposes and designs. Through these models we hope to highlight some of the trade-offs between ease of specification and meaningfulness of results.

Analyzing Longitudinal Data

One of the obvious benefits of longitudinal data collection is the increased ability to disentangle causal relationships. Cross-sectional data are unable to resolve the ambiguity in correlations or other measures of association. The development of proper methods to examine change, however, has challenged researchers for many years. In the past there have been inadequacies in the conceptualization, measurement, and design of change studies (Raudenbush & Bryk, 2002).

Repeated-Measures ANOVA

Traditionally, repeated measures analysis of variance (ANOVA) has been used to examine changes in individuals across time in experimental and quasi-experimental designs. Hypothesis tests can be conducted to determine whether the means of the variables measured at different time points are equal or to determine the shape of the growth, or change, trend (e.g., linear, quadratic, exponential). Researchers have identified a number of limitations with repeated measures ANOVA, however (Hox, 2010; Raudenbush & Bryk, 2002; Raykov & Marcoulides, 2006). These shortcomings include the inability to examine random variation in growth rates, in measurement error, problematic assumptions such as the normality of the data across between-subject factors, and the equality of the covariance matrices across measurements. For example, if we are investigating changes over time in male and female salaries within a profession related to education and experience, we may observe differences in the normality of the salary data (e.g., women may have been denied equal entry to the profession, or their participation may have been restricted to certain areas of practice). Initial inequities between males and females might influence subsequent measurements of their salaries (e.g., if one group's salary becomes more varied over time in ways that are not related to education and experience). Other limitations include handling the unequal spacing of measurements, incorporating missing data without using listwise deletion, defining variables as both independent and dependent variables in the model, including time-varying and time-invariant covariates, and extending the model to consider macro-level variation, for example, due to organizations or communities (Duncan, Duncan, & Strycker, 2006; Raudenbush & Bryk, 2002).

Growth Modeling and Other Approaches

Duncan and his colleagues (2006) demonstrate that repeated measures ANOVA, random-coefficients approaches such as multilevel regression modeling, and latent growth curve modeling all address individual change in terms of initial levels and changes in these levels over time. More recently accessible approaches such as latent growth curve modeling have produced greater flexibility in how the change trend is modeled and how other variables may affect it across time. For example, unlike in repeated measures ANOVA, where differences in growth appear as an interaction between groups and repeated measurement occasions, in random-coefficients growth modeling, the change in successive measurements can be directly modeled. This formulation results in each individual having a separate growth curve or trajectory and facilitates comparisons of individuals' trajectories according to group membership (e.g., clusters, latent classes) in terms of their level, shape of the trajectories, and variability. Emergent modeling options also open up possibilities for examining more complex relationships in the data where both independent and dependent variables may be changing over time, where changes in individuals and groups are examined simultaneously, and where separate growth trends can be compared before and after a treatment is introduced (i.e., piecewise growth functions).

Newer approaches offer greater flexibility in testing hypotheses concerning the developmental trends (Raykov & Marcoulides, 2006). Similar to other types of multilevel analyses, change models may be proposed and tested against the data, and their adequacy assessed through various fit indices, analyses of residuals, and comparisons between simpler or more complex models. The types of models used to examine longitudinal data vary widely, not only in the types of research and data problems they address, but also in the terminology used to describe their specific features. To some extent, the various modeling approaches are also tied to specific disciplines that may favor particular ways of examining changes over time for the types of research questions that are considered important.

Besides the random-coefficients and SEM approaches for modeling changes over time introduced in this chapter, alternative approaches exist for analyzing various types of longitudinal data. These include event history analysis (used to examine the timing of events within an observational period), Markov latent class models (often used in hazard models to examine changes in individuals' states over time, such as how choices at previous points in time affect subsequent choices), and Box-Jenkins (ARIMA) methods (used to examine the extent to which an outcome can be explained by a predictor over and above its own past values). Further discussion of these methods can be found in Dale and Davies (1994) and Hershberger, Molenaar, and Corneal (1996). Interested readers can examine particular approaches more closely, depending on their research concerns and the structure of their data. We note, however, that the differences among the methods can be substantial for certain aspects of modeling longitudinal changes. The common element is that each approach in this class of models deals with the high correlations between successive measurements in modeling changes over time.

Random-Coefficients Growth Modeling

In growth (or change) models, successive measurements are nested within individuals. The approach therefore provides a convenient means of examining heterogeneity in individuals' growth trajectories (Bryk & Raudenbush, 1992; Muthén, 2002). Figure 7.1 presents a summary of possible three-level, random-coefficients growth modeling available in Mplus. Similar to other multilevel models, the figure suggests a number of within-level and cross-level effects that may influence individual change. Typically, we assume that a number of individuals have been sampled and measured on several occasions on one or more variables. Because multilevel modeling does not require balanced data, it is not a problem

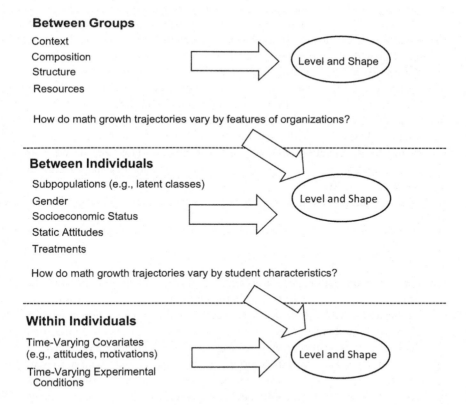

FIGURE 7.1 Defining variables in a multilevel growth trajectory model.

if all measurements are not available on all participants (Hox, 2010). This can be beneficial if there are subjects who drop out over the course of a longitudinal study. Because we often have considerable information about individuals before they drop out of a longitudinal study, it is likely there will be less bias in estimating the model's parameters if we can retain individuals with partially complete data. This multilevel specification of individual growth can be extended to include situations where the timing and spacing of the measurements differ across individuals. In random-coefficients growth modeling, within- and between-individual changes are typically represented through a two-level univariate model where repeated measures are nested within individuals (see also Hox, 2010; Raudenbush & Bryk, 2002; Singer & Willett, 2003). A third level can be added to model changes between organizational units (e.g., departments, organizations).

Defining the Level-1 Model

The level-1 part of the model represents the change each member of the population is expected to experience during the time period under study (Singer & Willett, 2003). Each person's successive measurements can be represented by an individual growth trajectory (or growth curve) and random error. We assume that the observed status at time t for individual i is a function of a systematic growth trajectory plus random error. This general level-1 equation represents our hypothesis about the shape of each individual's true trajectory of change over time (Singer & Willett, 2003). **Polynomial curves** are often used for describing individual growth because they can be estimated using standard linear modeling procedures, and they are very flexible (Hox, 2010). We note, however, that there are other ways of specifying the trajectory (e.g., see Heck, Thomas, & Tabata, 2013).

At Level 1, the systematic growth for each individual i at time t can be represented as

$$y_{ti} = \pi_{0i} + \pi_{1i}T_{ti} + \pi_{2i}X_{ti} + \varepsilon_{ti}, \tag{7.1}$$

where π_{0i} is the intercept parameter (which is defined as the level of the individual's "true" status at some relevant point in the series of measurement occasions), T_{ti} is a time-related variable of interest (e.g., which could be the occasion at which y is measured or an individual's age in months or years), with individual i measured on t occasions, X_{ti} is a time-varying covariate, and ε_{ti} represents random error in measuring individual i at time t. Although a basic linear model with a constant growth rate π_{1i} over T_{ti} is often assumed, we note that often higher-order polynomial functions (e.g., quadratic, cubic) are used to represent more complex change over time (e.g., acceleration over time, deceleration over time, or acceleration followed by deceleration followed by acceleration).

The level-1 model specified in Equation 7.1 requires at least one more wave of data than the number of growth parameters in the model (Singer & Willett, 2003). So, for example, if there are three measurement occasions, the model will support a random intercept (π_{0i}) and a random linear effect (π_{1i}) for T. With four occasions, the model will support a random intercept, and random linear, and quadratic effects for T; and with five occasions, there can be random intercept and random linear, quadratic, and cubic effects for T. These are minimum data requirements. As Singer and Willet argue, more waves of data increase the precision of estimating higher-order polynomials.

Equation 7.1 also indicates that one or more time-varying covariates (X_{ti}) can be added to the level-1 model as needed. Time-varying covariates (i.e., predictors that also change over repeated measurement occasions) provide a way of accounting for temporal variation that may increase or decrease the value of an outcome predicted by the individual growth trajectory (Raudenbush & Bryk, 2002). For example, we might consider a situation where a predictor such as student SAT scores upon entrance to the institution, which is measured considerably before each cohort's graduation rate each year, might affect graduation rates at time t. Alternatively, if we had only one measure of SAT scores (or used an aggregate measure) we could then enter this covariate at the between–institution level (i.e., Level 2). One of the advantages of specifying a time-varying covariate at Level 1 is that the effect of SAT level on graduation rate can then be modeled as a random parameter at Level 2. We note that as the number of random effects specified in the model increase (i.e., growth parameters and time-varying covariates), it can be more difficult to fit the model at higher levels of the data hierarchy. For example, if all level-1 growth parameters are specified as random, there are time-varying random covariates, and the level-1 variances and covariances are to be estimated, it may be necessary to restrict some parameters to zero in order to ensure that all of them can be properly estimated (Raudenbush & Bryk, 2002).

The growth trajectory parameter in Equation 7.1 is the most important parameter because it represents the rate at which individual i changes over time. The general level-1 model facilitates the representation of higher polynomial regression coefficients in addition to linear growth ($\pi_{1i}T_{ti}$), including quadratic ($\pi_{2i}T_{ti}^2$) and cubic ($\pi_{3i}T_{ti}^3$) growth parameters (assuming there are sufficient repeated measurements). In terms of interpretation, however, if one considers that the linear trajectory model represents *constant* rate of change over time and the quadratic trajectory model represents *change* in the rate of change over time, it becomes increasingly more difficult to interpret models of higher polynomial degrees (Raykov & Marcoulides, 2006). Other types of nonlinear functions sometimes used to examine individual change are logistic and exponential functions. The specification of the general level-1 model implicitly assumes that all the change trajectories have a common algebraic form, but not every individual has the same trajectory (Singer & Willett, 2003). Each person, therefore, draws her or his parameter values (i.e., intercept, slope) from an unknown (underlying) bivariate distribution of intercepts and slopes.

Most commonly, at Level 1, a simple error structure is assumed for (ε_{it}), represented as

$$\varepsilon_{it} \sim N(0, \sigma_\varepsilon^2), \tag{7.2}$$

which suggests that the errors are independent and normally distributed (N), with a mean of zero and constant variance over time (Raudenbush & Bryk, 2002). The residual variance parameter (σ_ε^2) represents the variation in residuals around each individual's true change trajectory (Singer & Willett, 2003). In Mplus, the level-1 error structure is contained in the within-group Psi (Ψ_W) matrix. Restrictions about the residuals can be relaxed, however. Other error structures can also be considered, such as autocorrelation among errors for each person or error that is dependent on the individual's measurement occasions. More complex error structures can be useful where there are many time points per subject. We often begin with a more simplified error structure at Level 1, but it is prudent to investigate the possibility that other level-1 covariance structures may fit the data better before settling on a final latent curve model.

Defining the Level-2 Model

At Level 2, a set of between-individual static X predictors (e.g., gender, socioeconomic status, health status, an experimental treatment) can be added to explain variation in individuals' intercepts (often defined as initial status) and growth rates (Raudenbush & Bryk, 2002). Specifically, for each of the $P + 1$ individual growth parameters,

$$\pi_{pi} = \beta_{p0} + \sum_{q=1}^{Q_p} \beta_{qp} X_{qi} + r_{pi}, \tag{7.3}$$

where X_{qi} might include individual background characteristics; β_{pq} represents the effect of X_q on the pth growth parameter; and r_{pi} is a matrix of random effects. At Level 2, the set of $P + 1$ random effects for individual i is a full covariance matrix, Ψ_B, dimensioned $(P + 1) \times (P + 1)$, which is assumed to be multivariate normally distributed, with means of zero, and some variances and covariances between level-2 residuals. For example, a polynomial of degree 2 (T_{ii}^2) can have a 3×3 covariance matrix of random effects at Level 2. The complete set of residual variances and covariances (i.e., Level 1 and Level 2) is often referred to as the model's variance components (Singer & Willett, 2003).

Extending the Model to Examine Changes Between Organizations

The individual growth model can be further broken into its within- and between-groups parts. At Level 3, for example, we can model differences in growth across organizations using the general modeling framework to examine variation in the level-2 random intercept and slope parameters.

Defining the Level-3 Model

The subscript j is added to the model to indicate the inclusion of the group level at Level 3. Following Raudenbush and Bryk (2002), the model defining level-3 variables that explain random β_{pqj} parameters can be written as

$$\beta_{pqj} = \gamma_{pq0} + \sum_{s=1}^{Q_{pq}} \gamma_{pqs} Z_{sj} + u_{pqj}, \tag{7.4}$$

where γ_{pq0} is the intercept for the organizational-level model, Z_{sj} are organizational predictors, γ_{pqs} are structural parameters for the level-3 predictors, and u_{pqj} represent the organizational-level random effects. The residuals from the level-3 equations are assumed to be normally distributed, have means of zero, and some unknown variance and covariance between all pairs of elements (Raudenbush & Bryk, 2002). In Mplus, the residual variances and covariances are also collected in the Psi matrix ($\Psi_{\beta3}$) specified at Level 3. The dimensionality of the matrix depends on the number of random level-2 coefficients in the model.

Examining Changes in Institutions' Graduation Rates

We next provide an extended example of a two-level growth model to illustrate how a model is formed, tested against the data, and the results interpreted. Readers may be familiar with situations where the researcher might examine individuals' academic growth over time. In such cases, the unit of analysis is the individual. In the following example, we will consider an application of random-coefficients growth modeling to examine possible increases in institutional graduation rates of student athletes after the implementation of an NCAA policy enacted to raise academic standards of entering freshman student athletes. The assumption under consideration is that raising the academic standards for student athletes should lead to an increase in graduation rates over the period of the study.

In this small random sample of the complete data, the graduation rates of incoming freshman athletes from 20 public and private institutions were compiled over a 4-year period. In Table 7.1, the first wave of data represents the student-athlete graduation rate at the sample institutions immediately before the

TABLE 7.1 Observed Graduation Means for Sample Public and Private Institutions

	Overall		Public		Private	
Year	Mean	SD	Mean	SD	Mean	SD
1	46.35	16.33	42.27	18.60	51.33	16.33
2	49.85	15.34	44.27	19.97	56.67	15.34
3	54.05	13.02	47.91	18.51	61.56	13.02
4	58.80	8.06	45.82	18.32	74.67	8.06

policy was introduced. Waves 2 through 4 represent the graduation rates of student athletes admitted in the first 3 years after the policy was implemented. The overall pre-policy mean graduation rate is 46.35 ($SD = 16.33$), and the years 2 through 4 means show that the graduation rates increased steadily after the policy was introduced. By the end of the 4-year period, institutions in this small subset of the data raised their graduation rates considerably (Mean = 58.80, $SD = 8.06$).

The individual trajectories of the random sample of 20 institutions are represented in Figure 7.2. It appears that the majority of the individual trajectories increase slightly over time, although a few are negative. The first concern in the

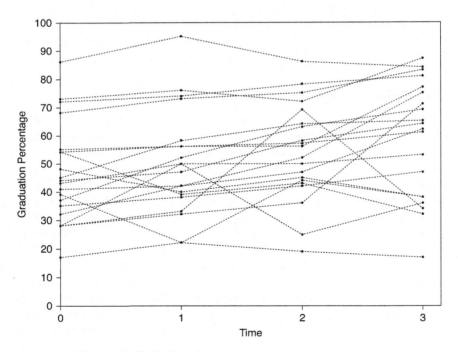

FIGURE 7.2 Observed individual graduation percentages.

analysis is whether there is any statistically significant change in graduation levels that took place after the policy was implemented. For example, it might be that there was no increase in graduation rates over the series of measurements after the policy was introduced. This would provide preliminary evidence that the policy did not achieve its stated goal of raising graduation rates among student athletes. Second, we might want to examine possible differences in changing graduation rates over time between public and private institutions and according to the prestige of their football programs. We note in passing that the limitation of our simple time series design is that we only have one measure before the implementation of the policy, so we cannot test whether or not graduation trends were increasing, decreasing, or stable before the introduction of the policy. A stronger time-series design would have several pre- and post-policy graduation rate measures to establish a possible difference in graduation rate trends before and after the policy was introduced. We address this type of **piecewise growth model** subsequently in this chapter.

In many situations where we examine change over time, it is convenient to propose that a linear growth trajectory will describe the data adequately. When the time periods are reasonably short and there are not too many observations per individual, the linear growth model can often provide a good approximation for more complex models that cannot be fully modeled because of the sparse number of observations (Raudenbush & Bryk, 2002).

Model 1: Within-Individuals (Level-1) Model

Often in defining growth models, analysts may first define a null (or no predictors) model at Level 1, which simply estimates the grand mean across the measurement occasions of the outcome. This initial model does not include a growth rate parameter at Level 1 (as is specified in Equation 7.7). The null model provides one way to think about initial variance decomposition within and between individuals in a growth model. We can also define an "unconditional" growth model as Model 1, which has no level-2 predictors but can include the time-related growth parameter specified at Level 1. An unconditional model to describe individual growth at Level 1 can be expressed as the following:

$$y_{it} = \pi_{0i} + \pi_1 growthrate_{it} + \varepsilon_{it}, \tag{7.5}$$

where π_{0i} is defined as the initial status intercept, and π_{1i} is the expected linear growth rate for individual i during a fixed unit of time (i.e., in this case, 1 year). The residuals (ε_{it}), which represent random error in measuring institution i's graduation rates at occasion t, are assumed to be independent, normally distributed, with mean of zero and common variance $(0, \sigma_\varepsilon^2)$. Each individual institution therefore has its own growth trajectory (developed from the intercept and slope), with likely variability present in the random coefficients across the set of institutions. We note in passing that time-varying covariates (e.g., yearly academic support expenditures for athletes) could also be added to the level-1 model.

Between-Individuals (Level-2) Model

Between individuals, at Level 2 the initial status and slope (growth) coefficients for the individual-level model can be specified as follows:

$$\pi_{0i} = \beta_{00} + r_{0i} \tag{7.6}$$

$$\pi_{0i} = \beta_{10} + r_{1i}. \tag{7.7}$$

Equations 7.6 and 7.7 suggest that each random coefficient (π_{0i} and π_{1i}) has its own intercept (β_{00} and β_{10}, respectively), which describes the average across the set of institutions and a random coefficient (r_{0i} and r_{1i}, respectively). It is the addition of the residual variance term (r) that makes the coefficient randomly varying, as opposed to fixed, for the sample. This formulation suggests that there is variability in the estimates of respective intercept and growth slope across the random sample of institutions. We note that the random-effects covariance matrix at Level 2 is an unstructured, symmetric matrix (with means of zero) and variances and covariances defined as follows:

$$\begin{bmatrix} \sigma_I^2 & \\ \sigma_{I,S} & \sigma_S^2 \end{bmatrix}, \tag{7.8}$$

where the intercept (I) and slope (S) variances are in the diagonals and the covariance ($\sigma_{I,S}$) is the off-diagonal element. We note that the off-diagonal element above the diagonals is redundant in this type of random-coefficients matrix, so we do not include it in Equation 7.8. The dimension of this covariance matrix depends on the number of random effects at Level 2. Since there is a random intercept and one random slope, the dimensionality of the matrix is 2×2. In some situations, we might restrict the covariance to zero (e.g., if the estimate is nonsignificant). This simple, unconditional model provides useful evidence in determining the specification of the level-1 model and in developing baseline statistics for evaluating subsequent models.

Coding the Time Variable

It is important to note that the meaning of the intercept parameter (π_{0i}) depends on the scaling of the time variable. In this example, the time metric is yearly intervals (coded as 0, 1, 2, 3). Most often, researchers code the first measurement occasion as 0, so that the intercept parameter can be interpreted as the true initial status graduation rate of football student athletes in institution i at time point $T_{ti} = 0$. Defining the intercept as initial status serves as a baseline for interpreting the subsequent change that takes place over time for each individual institution in the sample. In this case, this represents the last cross-section of graduation data for freshman football players before the implementation of the policy. Because the intervals are equally spaced at yearly intervals (i.e., 0–3), the growth slope then represents the true yearly rate of change in institution i's graduation rate. If a quadratic term were added to the model over the 4-year period, it would be scaled in a similar manner by squaring the linear intervals (i.e., 0, 1, 4, 9). The quadratic component represents any increase or decrease in the rate of change for each time interval. We note that if the time-related variable (T) is not measurement occasions but, rather, a variable such as age, setting the first observation to 0 likely will not be desirable, since this would imply the interpretation of Y_i when the individual's age $= 0$. We might, for example, center age on a theoretically relevant point in time, such as the individual's age at the first measurement occasion.

One disadvantage of using polynomial functions to define growth trajectories, however, is that there are strong correlations between the components defining the function (e.g., linear, quadratic, cubic). If the intervals are equally (or nearly equally) spaced, as in our example, and there is little or no missing data, one approach for dealing with the multicollinearity is to transform the polynomials to be orthogonal, or uncorrelated (Hox, 2010). The linear, quadratic and cubic components can be recoded to be orthogonal using a table of orthogonal contrasts.[1] The new contrasts can be saved in the database and used in defining the individual growth trajectory. Interpreting the meaning of the polynomial contrasts can become challenging, however. In such situations, the use of graphs for the average trajectory and for subsets of individuals can facilitate the interpretation of the higher-order polynomial trajectory. Of course, in situations where higher-order polynomials are not needed (e.g., they are nonsignificant in the analysis), it would not be necessary to use orthogonal transformations.

Because the repeated observations are nested within individuals, both the number of observations and the timing of the observations may vary randomly across individuals (Raudenbush & Bryk, 2002). It is also possible to change the centering point to other time points in the sequence (e.g., the last time point), depending on the goals of the research. Centering on the last time point in a series of measurement occasions, for example, would result in an intercept parameter that describes the levels of institutions' graduation rates at the end of the time-series and a linear growth factor that describes the expected (lower) rate of growth for each previous yearly occasion (e.g., $T_{ti} = -3, -2, -1, 0$).

The choice of the appropriate modeling approach and coding of time should be based on the ease with which model parameter estimates can be interpreted,

TABLE 7.2 Level-1 Data Structure for Graduation Percentages

ID	TIME	GPERCENT
1	0	17
1	1	22
1	2	19
1	3	17
2	0	54
2	1	39
2	2	43
2	3	32
3	0	28
3	1	32
3	2	36
3	3	71
4	0	45
4	1	58
4	2	64
4	3	65
5	0	37
5	1	52
5	2	63
5	3	69
6	0	44
6	1	47
6	2	58
6	3	64

always keeping in mind the substantive questions of the research study (Raykov & Marcoulides, 2006). For readers previously familiar with the multilevel regression approach, the time intervals (coded 0–3) are actually entered in the level-1 data set as a variable (*Time*), and each time point corresponds to a specific graduation percentage for each institution, as shown in Table 7.2. This necessitates four data lines per institution in the level-1 data set, as opposed to data sets with which the reader may be more familiar that consist of only one data line per institution. For example, for institution ID #1, the graduation percentage corresponding to time point 0 (the first year) is 17%, and for time point 3 (the last year), it is also 17%. The data are linked to successive levels with unique identifiers.

Model 1 Statements

We next summarize the model statements for our initial growth model. We note that since the data are balanced, we will use ML estimation in this example.

TITLE:	
	Model 1: Within-individuals model;DATA:
	File is C:\mplus\ch7ex1.dat;
	Format is 3f8.0, f4.0,2f8.0;
VARIABLE:	Names are id private prestige index1 graduate growrate;
	Usevariables are id graduate growrate;
	cluster = id;
	within= growrate;
	between = ;
ANALYSIS:	Type = twolevel random;
	Estimator is ML;
Model:	%between%
	graduate;
	S;
	graduate with S;
	%within%
	S | graduate on growrate;
OUTPUT:	sampstat TECH1;

TECH1 Specification Output

It is instructive in this initial model to show how the typical multilevel model is specified using SEM matrix specification. The parameters estimated in this first model (from Equations 7.5–7.8) can be obtained by including TECH1 in the Model statements. We next provide relevant TECH1 output. Within individuals (Level 1), the output indicates that the estimated residual variance for initial graduation status is contained in the within-groups Psi matrix as parameter 1. This is the only within-groups output in this model. At Level 2, the estimated means for the random growth rate slope and initial status intercept are contained in Alpha (parameters 2 and 3). The estimated variances for the random effects are contained in the between-groups Psi matrix (as parameters 4 and 6), and the covariance between them is specified as parameter 5. The TECH1 output therefore confirms there are six parameters to be estimated.

PARAMETER SPECIFICATION FOR WITHIN
PSI

	S	GRADUATE	GROWRATE
S	0		
GRADUATE	0	1	
GROWRATE	0	0	0

PARAMETER SPEPCIFICATION FOR BETWEEN
ALPHA

	S	GRADUATE	GROWRATE
	2	3	0

PSI

	S	GRADUATE	GROWRATE
S	4		
GRADUATE	5	6	
GROWRATE	0	0	0

Model 1 Output

The fit indices are presented in Table 7.3. The fit indices confirm six estimated parameters. In the case where this first model is the baseline model, we can note the log–likelihood coefficient (−313.843) and the other indices (e.g., AIC, BIC) for comparison against subsequent models.

The parameter estimates for Model 1 are summarized Table 7.4. For the model for initial status (π_{0i}), the coefficient is 46.030, which represents the initial status graduation rate. For the growth rate model (π_{1i}), the coefficient is 4.155. This suggests that after the initial graduation percentage of about 46%, graduation rates on average increased by almost 4.2% per year. Significant z-tests (i.e., the ratio of the coefficient to its standard error) indicate that both parameters are necessary for describing the growth trajectory. As we noted previously, it would also be possible to examine a null model consisting only of the repeated measurements of y_{it} without the growth rate parameter. This model can be used to partition the variance in the graduation grand-mean estimate into its within-individual and between-individual components, regardless of time [see Singer & Willett (2003) for further discussion]. These components can be used to calculate an intraclass correlation (ICC). Mplus estimates the ICC from the initial between-group and within–group covariance matrices [i.e., in the case, 237.709/(237.709 + 112.841) = 0.678), not

TABLE 7.3 Model Fit Indices

MODEL FIT INFORMATION	
Number of Free Parameters	6
Log Likelihood	
H_0 Value	−313.843
Information Criteria	
Akaike (AIC)	639.686
Bayesian (BIC)	653.978
Sample-Size Adjusted BIC	635.058
($n^* = (n + 2)/24$)	

TABLE 7.4 Unconditional Model of Linear Growth

	Coefficient	Standard Error	Est./SE	P-Value
Fixed Effects				
Mean initial status, β_{00}	46.030	3.913	11.763	0.000
Mean growth rate, β_{10}	4.155	1.146	3.625	0.000
Random Effects				
Initial status, u_{0i}	264.215	97.158	2.719	0.007
Growth rate, u_{1i}	14.264	8.679	1.644	0.100
Covariance	−15.041	21.655	−0.695	0.487
Level-1, ε_{ti}	60.023	13.463	4.458	0.000

Note: ICC = 0.699

tabled]. With the growth rate included at Level 1, the Mplus output for the ICC is slightly different at 0.699 (see Table 7.4), which suggests that almost 70% of the variance in graduation percentages lies between institutions in the sample.

Next, it is important to consider the nature of the deviations of the individual growth trajectories from the mean growth trajectory. The estimates of the initial status (π_{0i}) and slope (π_{1i}) variances in Table 7.4 are 264.215 and 14.264, respectively. The simplest test of homogeneity, that there is no true variation in individual growth parameters, involves the use of a z-test statistic (i.e., the ratio of the estimate to its standard error). For initial status variance, between individuals the z-test coefficient is 2.719 ($p < 0.01$). This leads to rejecting the null hypothesis that there is no variation among the institutions' initial graduation percentages. For growth rates, the z-test coefficient is 1.644, $p = 0.10$). In this case, given the small sample size (and the large ICC of almost 0.70), we might reject the null hypothesis of no significant variation in institutions' growth rates. We also note in passing that since variance parameters cannot be negative, we could opt to use a one-tailed test of significance by dividing the two-tailed significance level by 2 [see Hox (2010) for further discussion].

The random-coefficients growth model also provides an estimate of the correlation between initial status and growth. For a linear growth model, it is the correlation between π_{0i} and π_{1i}. It is important to note that the magnitude of the correlation between the intercept and growth parameter depends on the specific time point selected for the intercept and the scaling of the time variable (a_{ti}). It is therefore necessary to give some attention to the definition and scaling of time-related parameters because this affects the meaning one attaches to the coefficients [for other discussions, see Hox (2010), Raykov & Marcoulides (2006), and Singer & Willett (2003)]. In this case, the level-2 random covariance parameter was −15.041. This suggests that institutions that had lower initial graduation rates gained at a somewhat greater rate and vice versa; however, the relationship was not statistically significant ($p = 0.487$). We could fix the covariance parameter to zero subsequently if we wished. We reiterate that if we were interested in ending graduation rates, we could define the intercept parameter as end status. This will result in a different correlation between the intercept and growth rate.

Model 2: Explaining Differences in Random Growth Parameters Between Institutions

In the second model, we will again allow both the intercept and slope parameters to vary randomly across institutions (as in Equations 7.6 and 7.7). The variation in each may likely be partially explained by between-institutional characteristics. We will consider two predictors that may account for systematic variation in the intercept and slope parameters between institutions. The first is institutional prestige (i.e., defined as each school's on-field performance record consisting of wins, championships, and Top 25 finishes compiled over several years). Prestige was constructed as a factor score (Mean $= 0$, $SD = 1$) and then dummy coded, with scores above 0.5 of a standard deviation being defined as high prestige (coded 1). The other variable is institutional type, which is dummy coded ($0 =$ public and $1 =$ private).

The two level-2 submodels are now defined as:

$$\pi_{0i} = \beta_{00} + \beta_{01} private_i + \beta_{02} prestige_i + r_{0i} \tag{7.9}$$

$$\pi_{1i} = \beta_{10} + \beta_{11} private_i + \beta_{12} prestige_i + r_{1i}. \tag{7.10}$$

The β parameters in the level-2 model represent the model's *fixed effects*. These parameters capture systematic differences in trajectories between individuals according to values of the predictors. The level-2 variance components (defined in the psi matrix) have variances as $\Psi_{1,1}$ (for the intercept) and $\Psi_{2,2}$ (for the growth rate) and covariance defined as $\Psi_{2,1}$.

Model 2 Statements

We need to make a couple of changes in the VARIABLE and Model statements in order to accommodate Model 2. We add the two variables (i.e., *private* and *prestige*) as between-group predictors. Between groups, they are proposed to explain changes in initial status (*graduate*) and growth (S).

```
VARIABLE:   Names are id private prestige index1 graduate growrate;
            Usevariables are id graduate growrate private prestige;
            cluster = id;
            within= growrate;
            between = private prestige;
```

```
define:      center private prestige(grand);
ANALYSIS:    Type = twolevel random;
             Estimator is ML;
Model:       %between%
             graduate on private prestige;
             S on private prestige;
             graduate with S;
             %within%
             S | graduate on growrate;
OUTPUT:      sampstat tech1;
```

TECH1 Output

In the specification of parameters for Model 2, we can see in the relevant TECH1 output that the four between–institution structural parameters (i.e., two for each random effect) are contained in the between–groups Beta matrix. Overall, therefore, there will now be 10 total parameters estimated.

TECHNICAL 1 OUTPUT

PARAMETER SPECIFICATION FOR WITHIN

PSI

	S	GRADUATE	GROWRATE	PRIVATE	PRESTIGE
S	0				
GRADUATE	0	1			
GROWRATE	0	0	0		
PRIVATE	0	0	0	0	
PRESTIGE	0	0	0	0	0

PARAMETER SPECIFICATION FOR BETWEEN

ALPHA

	S	GRADUATE	GROWRATE	PRIVATE	PRESTIGE
	2	3	0	0	0

BETA

	S	GRADUATE	GROWRATE	PRIVATE	PRESTIGE
S	0	0	0	4	5
GRADUATE	0	0	0	6	7
GROWRATE	0	0	0	0	0
PRIVATE	0	0	0	0	0
PRESTIGE	0	0	0	0	0

PSI	S	GRADUATE	GROWRATE	PRIVATE	PRESTIGE
S	8				
GRADUATE	9	10			
GROWRATE	0	0	0		
PRIVATE	0	0	0	0	
PRESTIGE	0	0	0	0	0

Model 2 Output

As Table 7.5 indicates, the true initial status graduation level for public institutions is 46.028. The unstandardized coefficients suggest that private schools start with graduation rates about 6.5% higher than public schools ($\beta_{01} = 6.529$). On average, at initial status, high-prestige schools graduate about 1.3% more student athletes than more typical schools ($\beta_{02} = 1.313$). Both z-ratios (i.e., the ratio of the parameter to its standard error), however, are not statistically significant in this small data set. For the growth rate model, the average gain per year in percentage of freshman football players graduating in public institutions is 4.156%. The graduation rates for private institutions increase significantly at 6.059 (z-test $= 3.100, p < 0.01$) per year faster than the graduation rates for public institutions. This change can be confirmed in Table 7.1 by examining the actual observed scores for public and

TABLE 7.5 Linear Model of Graduation Growth Examining the Effects of Prestige and Institutional Type

	Coefficient	Standard Error	Est./SE	P-Value
Fixed Effects				
Model for initial status, π_{0i}				
Intercept, β_{00}	46.028	3.837	11.995	0.000
Private, β_{01}	6.529	8.052	0.811	0.417
High prestige, β_{02}	1.313	8.177	0.161	0.872
Model for growth rate, π_{1i}				
Intercept, β_{10}	4.156	0.931	4.463	0.000
Private, β_{11}	6.059	1.954	3.100	0.002
High prestige, β_{12}	−0.003	1.985	−0.001	0.999
Random Effects				
Initial status, r_{0i}	252.587	93.582	2.699	0.007
Growth rate, r_{1i}	5.374	6.101	0.881	0.378
Covariance	−25.698	19.146	−1.342	0.180
Level-1, e_{ti}	59.854	13.388	4.471	0.000

private institutions in this example. Prestige, however, is not significantly related to institutional growth (z-test $= -0.003, p > 0.10$).

We can also determine how much variance in the random coefficients is accounted for by the predictors. The proportion of variance explained is the ratio of the difference between the total parameter variance estimated from the unconditional model and the residual parameter variance from the fitted model relative to the total parameter variance. For intercepts, the amount of variance accounted for by the predictors is not substantial; that is, the variance component drops from about 264.2 to about 252.6 between the two models [$(264.2 - 252.6)/264.2 = 11.6/264.2 = 4.4\%$]. For the growth rate ($r_{1i}$), the addition of institutional type and prestige reduces the residual variance considerably [$(14.3 - 5.4)/14.3 = 8.9/14.3 = 62.2\%$]. In this example, therefore, the predictors account for 62.2% of the variance in graduation growth rates.

Other Types of Random-Coefficients Models

Other types of growth trajectories can also be formulated (e.g., quadratic) to model various nonlinear relationships. In principle, a polynomial of any degree could be fit, providing the time series is sufficiently long [see Raudenbush & Bryk (2002) for further discussion], but higher-degree polynomial functions are more difficult to interpret. It is also possible to add time-varying covariates to the level-1 model, for example, differing levels of resources over time might affect growth. Researchers can also develop piecewise growth models, where the growth trajectories are split into separate linear components, each with its own model. This type of modeling would be useful in comparing growth rates during two different periods, such as several measurements taken before and the time after a policy is introduced [e.g., see Heck & Takahashi (2006) for one illustration].

These other types of models are all forms of the broader class of multilevel random-coefficients models we have presented in the first part of this chapter.

Examining Individual Change With SEM

The SEM approach offers a contrasting framework to use in analyzing various kinds of longitudinal data. In the SEM framework, the distinction between Level 1 (within individuals) and Level 2 (between individuals) in the random-coefficients approach is not made because the outcomes are considered as multivariate data in a T-dimensional vector $(y_1, y_2, \ldots, y_T)'$. Because of this difference in conceptualizing the data structure, in SEM the repeated measures over time can be expressed as a type of single-level CFA (or measurement model), where the intercept and growth latent factors are measured by the multiple indicators of y_t. The structural part of the SEM analysis can then be used to investigate the effects of covariates or other latent variables on the latent change factors. Once the overall latent curve model has been defined through relating the observed variables to the latent factors that represent the change process, it can be further divided into its within- and between-groups parts, similar to other multilevel SEM models we have presented. This allows the analyst to define separate sets of variables that explain levels of outcomes and change rates at the individual and organizational levels.

Until recently, FIML estimation for multilevel latent curve models was limited by the complexity of specifying multilevel models with existing SEM software and the computational demands in trying to estimate the models. This was because ML estimation with SEM required large sample sizes for optimal estimation of information summarized in covariance matrices. Early attempts approached the multilevel problem as a type of multiple-group analysis (i.e., comparing a model's fit across several covariance matrices), where one might need 150–200 individuals per group for efficient estimation of model parameters in each group. Muthén (1994, 1998–2004) reformulated the multilevel problem as a type of two-group SEM (i.e., with group and individual covariance matrices) and proposed a limited information estimator (MUML in Mplus) that made model estimation easier within the SEM framework.

Willett and Sayer (1996) and Meredith and Tisak (1990) demonstrated how models examining individual change could be examined using SEM. The availability of full information maximum likelihood (FIML) estimation for missing data has enhanced the usefulness of SEM methods (e.g., alleviating the need for listwise deletion, allowing unequal intervals between measurement occasions) for examining individual change (Duncan et al., 2006; McArdle & Anderson, 1990; Mehta & Neal, 2005). As Mehta and Neal note, FIML has allowed fitting SEM to individual data vectors by making available estimation methods that are based on individual likelihood, which could accommodate unbalanced data structures (e.g., different numbers of individuals within clusters).

Because the SEM approach makes direct use of latent variables, it has been referred to in the literature as latent growth curve analysis, latent change analysis, or simply as latent growth models. We use the term latent curve analysis (LCA) because it emphasizes that the models are applicable to all cases in which one is interested in studying change (either growth or decline), including those with a more complex pattern of change such as growth followed by decline or vice versa [e.g., see also Duncan, Duncan, Strycker, Li, & Alport (1999); Raykov & Marcoulides (2006)].

Intercept and Slope (IS) and Level and Shape (LS) Models

In the LCA approach, individual growth is captured as latent variables that are measured by the repeated observations of y. Part of the individual growth may be summarized as a level (or intercept) factor, which makes use of the relative standing of a particular individual with respect to his or her peers, and the growth trend may be summarized as one or more factors that describe its shape (e.g., a linear, quadratic, or various nonlinear trajectories) per some unit of time. Two specific ways of addressing individual growth include the **Intercept and Slope**

(IS) model (e.g., as in the previous random-coefficients example) and the **Level-and-Shape (LS) model** (McArdle, 1988). The primary assumption of the IS model is that change occurs in a specific type of trajectory (e.g., linear, quadratic, or cubic trajectories). For example, from an SEM perspective, linear growth over several years can be represented by a two-factor model—more specifically, with one factor describing the intercept, often defined as initial status, and another factor defining the linear slope, or growth rate per year. A third factor can be added to capture a possible quadratic component in the data (i.e., change in the rate of change), a fourth representing a cubic component, and so on. In practice, however, it is often difficult to fit a model with a strict definition of trajectory to the data (Raykov & Marcoulides, 2006). More specifically, one often starts with the assumption that the change is of a certain type, requiring a certain set of slope factors (e.g., linear or linear and quadratic) and proceeds to set up the model to test the existence of a particular type of trajectory against the data. Although this strategy may often work, in some cases, less may be known about the actual shape of the trajectory. Where there is little theoretical guidance regarding the actual shape of the trajectory, the researcher may need to explore different functions that define the actual shape (e.g., polynomial, logistic). Sometimes looking at a number of individuals' trajectories can aid in this process.

The LS model has not attracted as much attention as the IS model, despite the fact that it has a number of advantages over the IS model (Raykov & Marcoulides, 2006). The LS model is less restrictive in terms of describing the shape of the change trajectory. It is often a preferable modeling approach to utilize, therefore, because it would be expected to fit the data better, since the LS model does not impose a specific type of change trajectory upon the pattern of change ahead of testing the model (Raykov & Marcoulides, 2006). In actuality, the IS model can be considered as a special case of the LS model when the coding of time is fixed according to the interval in which the repeated measurements were obtained, as when yearly measurements are obtained (e.g., 0, 1, 2, 3). For illustrative purposes, in the graduation example presented previously, we will fit both IS and LS models and provide insight concerning choices researchers have in modeling growth or developmental data using LCA.

In order to examine individual growth over time with SEM techniques, it is necessary to change the way the data are organized for the last analysis, where the repeated measures nested within individuals required four lines per individual. As we have noted, SEM depends on the analysis of covariance structures. As the reader may recall, covariance matrices summarize information about variables (i.e., variances are contained in the diagonal elements of the matrix, and covariances between variables are contained in the off-diagonal elements). For examining growth or change, variable means are needed to determine what the pattern of growth looks like over time. To facilitate the analysis of growth using SEM, therefore, the means of the observed variables are added to the covariance matrix. This matrix is produced automatically in Mplus when the raw data are used.

Defining the Latent Curve Model

Consider the previous example where we were interested in examining changes in the graduation rates of freshman student athletes over 4 years ($y_1 - y_4$) in a random sample of 20 Division 1A institutions. The model is summarized in Figure 7.3. In conducting a latent curve analysis, the researcher's first concern is typically to establish the level of initial status (or end status) and the rate of change. Fitting the two-factor latent curve model is accomplished first by fixing the intercept factor loadings to 1.0. Because the repeated measures are considered as factor loadings, there are several choices regarding how to parameterize the growth rate factor. In this case, we can define a linear model by using 0, 1, 2, 3 to represent fixed successive linear measurements. Since the first factor loading is fixed at zero, we show it as a dotted line in Figure 7.3. Alternatively, researchers may not indicate the loading from the factor to the observed indicator in their path diagrams since it is fixed to zero.

The Measurement Model

The two-level growth model developed earlier in the chapter can be expressed in SEM terms by using the general measurement and structural models (Muthén, 2002). The measurement model appears as

$$y_{it} = \nu_t + \Lambda\eta_i + Kx_i + \varepsilon_{it}, \tag{7.10}$$

where y_{it} is a vector of graduation outcomes at time $(y_{i1}, y_{i2}, \ldots, y_{iT})'$ for individual i (i.e., in this case an institution, because institutions are the unit of analysis), ν_t is a vector of measurement intercepts set to 0 at the individual level, is a $p \times m$ design matrix representing the change process, η_i is an m-dimensional vector of latent variables $(\eta_0, \eta_1)'$, K is a $p \times q$ parameter matrix of regression slopes relating

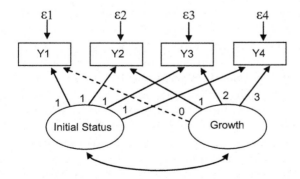

FIGURE 7.3 Proposed growth model examining changes in institutional graduation rates.

x_i $(x_{1i}, x_{2i}, \ldots, x_{pi})'$ to the latent factors, and ε_{it} represents time-specific errors contained in Θ. The factor loadings for the latent factors (i.e., in this case, η_{0i} and η_{1i}) are contained in the factor-loading matrix, as in the following:

$$\Lambda_t = \begin{bmatrix} 1 & 0 \\ 1 & 1 \\ 1 & 2 \\ 1 & 3 \end{bmatrix}. \tag{7.11}$$

Fixing the loadings of the four measurement occasions on the first factor (η_{0i}) to a value of one (1.0) ensures that it is interpreted as a true (i.e., error-free) initial status factor, that is, representing a baseline point of the underlying developmental process under investigation. Because the repeated measures are parameters (i.e., factor loadings) in a latent curve model (i.e., instead of data points in a multilevel model), the researcher can hypothesize that they follow particular shapes or patterns. The slope factor (η_{1i}) can be defined as linear with successive time points of 0, 1, 2, 3. This scaling indicates the slope coefficient will represent successive yearly intervals, starting with initial status as time score 0 (i.e., the loading from the growth rate factor to y_1 is shown as a dotted line in Figure 7.3). All parameters are fixed, therefore, in the Λ_t matrix in this type of specification (which in some cases may be an undesirable restriction).[2] If the linear model does not fit the data well, a quadratic factor could also be added to the factor-loading matrix (i.e., which requires an intercept factor, a linear slope factor, and a quadratic slope factor with loadings 0, 1, 4, 9 as a third column). The psi covariance matrix (Ψ) contains latent factor variances and covariances.[3]

In this case for the model proposed there would be nine parameters to estimate [three in Ψ, four in Θ, and two intercepts (i.e., initial status, slope)]. As we noted, defining the shape of the change ahead of testing has been referred to as an intercept and slope (IS) approach (Raykov & Marcoulides, 2006). By fixing the factor loadings to a particular pattern ($t = 0, 1, 2, 3$), the hypothesized growth shape may then be tested against the actual data and its fit determined by examining various SEM fit indices.

Alternatively, we may actually know little about the shape of the individual trajectories. Various types of nonlinear growth can also be captured within the basic two-factor LCA formulation by using different patterns of free (estimated) and fixed factor loadings within the basic level and shape (LS) formulation. In Mplus model statements, the asterisk (*) option is used to designate a free parameter, such as a factor loading. For the LS formulation, we fix the first time score to zero and the last time score to 1.0, while allowing the middle time scores to be freely estimated (0, *, *, 1). This can allow for valleys and peaks within the overall growth interval being measured (e.g., 0, –0.5. 1.2, 1). The factor-loading matrix would be the following:

$$\Lambda_t = \begin{bmatrix} 1 & 0 \\ 1 & * \\ 1 & * \\ 1 & 1 \end{bmatrix}.$$ (7.12)

We could also capture other types of nonlinear growth, using combinations of free and fixed factor loadings within the factor-loading matrix. For example, we could allow the last time score, or the last two time scores, to be freely estimated [(0, 1, 2, *) or (0, 1, *, *)]. In addition to describing possible peaks or valleys, this type of formulation would allow for the estimation of various trajectories where the change might accelerate (e.g., 0, 1, 3, 6) or decelerate (e.g., 0, 1, 1.5, 1.75) over time.

As these models suggest, the basic two-factor LCA formulation is quite flexible in allowing the researcher to consider both the levels of the growth or decline over time as well as the shape of the trend, which summarizes the growth rate over a specified time interval. The analyst can observe whether the change is positive or negative, whether the individual institutions are converging over time, and whether there is heterogeneity in the level and rate of change across the individuals in the sample (Willett & Sayer, 1996).

The Structural Model

After the measurement model is used to relate the successive observed measures to the initial status and growth rate factors (similar to factor analysis), the second SEM model (i.e., the structural model) is used to relate one or more time-invariant covariates to the random effects (i.e., initial status and growth trend factors). The general structural model for individual i is then

$$\eta_i = \mu + B\eta_i + \Gamma x_i + \zeta_i,$$ (7.13)

where μ is vector of measurement intercepts, B is an $m \times m$ parameter matrix of slopes for the regressions among the latent variables, Γ is an $m \times q$ slope parameter matrix relating x covariates to latent variables, and ζ_i is a vector of residuals with covariance matrix Ψ. Consistent with the growth modeling approach, η_i contains intercept (η_{0i}) and slope (η_{1i}) factors whose variability can be explained by one or more covariates:

$$\eta_{0i} = \alpha_0 + \gamma_0 x_i + \zeta_{0i},$$ (7.14)

$$\eta_{1i} = \alpha_1 + \gamma_1 x_i + \zeta_{1i},$$ (7.15)

where α_0 and α_1 are measurement intercepts and γ_0 and γ_1 are structural parameters describing the regressions of latent variables on a covariate.[4] Each component has its own residual (ζ_{0i} and ζ_{1i}), which permits the quality of measurement associated with each individual's growth trajectory to differ from those of other individuals.

It is important to keep in mind that the random-coefficients and the latent curve approaches describe individual development in a slightly different manner. First, as we noted the SEM formulation treats the individual's change trajectory as single-level, multivariate data. The approach accounts for the correlation across time by the same random effects influencing each of the variables in the outcome vector (Muthén & Asparouhov, 2003). In contrast, the random-coefficients approach used in the previous example treats the trajectories as univariate data and accounts for correlation across time by having two levels in the model. A second difference is the manner in which the time scores (i.e., the scaling of the observations) are considered. For random-coefficients growth modeling, the time scores are data; that is, they are pieces of information entered in the level-1 (within-individual) data set to represent what the individual's level of outcomes were at each particular point in time. For LCA, however, the time scores are considered as model parameters; therefore, they are defined as factor loadings on the growth factors. The individual scores at each time interval are therefore not represented as data points within the data set. Finally, latent curve modeling typically proceeds from an analysis of means and covariance structures. In contrast, random-coefficients (multilevel) growth modeling creates a separate growth trajectory with intercept and slope for each individual. Random-coefficients multilevel models are typically not described in terms of means and covariance structures (Raudenbush, 2001).

Model 1: Specifying the IS Model

In the next section, we will define the basic latent curve model using both the IS and LS specifications. We will use the intercept and slope (IS) specification as Model 1. In this model, fixing the intercept loadings at 1.0 and the defining slope factor with time scores 0, 1, 2, 3 ensures that the intercept factor is an initial status factor. The resulting slope factor will specify the change in graduation rates between each successive interval. In this example, the growth is positive, which suggests that the graduation rates are expected to rise after the policy is implemented. Alternatively, if we fixed the intercept loadings to 1.0 and placed the 0 time score at the end of the sequence (e.g., $-3, -2, -1, 0$), the intercept factor would be defined as an end status factor (i.e., using the negative intervals preserves the slope as positive between intervals). If we centered on the last interval (0) and instead defined the previous yearly intervals as positive (i.e., 3, 2, 1, 0), the resultant slope would be negative. This would suggest that each successive interval before the end is smaller by the amount of the slope coefficient.

Model 1: IS Model Statements

We provide the modeling statements for the linear IS model next. We can use the letter i to define the intercept and s to define the slope. We can also fix the repeated-measure intercepts to 0 also specify the estimation of the initial status factor intercept (I) and slope (S) by adding the following line:

[grad1-grad4@0 i s];

We also note that we can plot the estimated growth over the four repeated measures using a Plot command and defining the series we wish to plot.

```
TITLE:       Model 1: Specifying the IS model;
DATA:        File is C:\mplus\ch7grad1.txt;
VARIABLE:    Names are id grad1 grad2 grad3 grad4 private prestige;
             Usevariables are grad1 grad2 grad3 grad4;
ANALYSIS:    Type = general;
             Estimator is ML;
Model:
             i by grad1@1 grad2@1 grad3@1 grad4@1;
             s by grad1@0 grad2@1 grad3@2 grad4@3;
             [grad1-grad4@0 i s];
Plot:        Type is plot3;
             Series is grad1-grad4(*);
OUTPUT:      Sampstat standardized tech1;
```

As a result of using a linear time score pattern, the mean of the growth rate factor describes the growth taking place between yearly intervals. By specifying the change trajectory in increments of years, as was done in the IS model, the correlation between the intercept and slope factors reflects the relationship between the initial point (set at the year before the policy was implemented) and the slope of the specifically *a priori* proposed linear trajectory (Raykov & Marcoulides, 2006). This may or may not be the appropriate model to describe the change process being examined. If the particular proposed linear model does not fit the data well, as a next step, the analyst usually attempts to use a higher-order polynomial trajectory model to fit to the data (e.g., quadratic, cubic, or higher, depending on the available number of assessments). Unfortunately, such models are generally extremely difficult to interpret and cannot always adequately reflect the trajectories actually encountered in the data (Raykov & Marcoulides, 2006).

Model 2: Specifying the LS Model

In contrast, if we knew less about the actual shape of the growth over the 4-year interval, we might use a level and shape (LS) approach. We can look at change more flexibly by specifying some of the time scores in the series of measurements by freeing those loadings on the shape factor [i.e., freely estimated factor loadings can be shown in Mplus with an asterisk (*)]. Importantly, this flexibility encourages the analyst to consider a number of different trajectory shapes without defining separate quadratic or cubic factors. For example, we could fix the first measurement to 0 and the last measurement to 1, while allowing the other two middle occasions be freely estimated (i.e., 0, *, *, 1). This type of model would result in a growth rate factor describing the overall change that took place during the 4 years of data collection (as opposed to the yearly change), while allowing more flexibility in the graduation levels to rise or fall during the middle measurements (i.e., by freeing those factor loadings). By setting the parameter for the first time score to be equal to 0, the parameter of the final time to be equal to 1, and to allow the second and third loadings to be estimated (as opposed to fixed to a particular value), the freed loadings now reflect the cumulative proportion of total change between two time points relative to the total change occurring from the first to the last time point (regardless of the trajectory shape, even if it is nonlinear) and the correlation between the level and shape factors simply reflects their degree of overlap (Raykov & Marcoulides, 2006).

Model 2: LS Model Statements

To define the model in this manner, we would simply change the Model portion of the input file to reflect the new coding (and we can replace *i* with *l* to denote "level") as follows:

```
Model:
        l by grad1@1 grad2@1 grad3@1 grad4@1;
        s by grad1@0 grad2* grad* grad4@1;
        [grad1-grad4@0 l s];
```

As we noted previously, using the LS specification, it is possible to investigate other types of nonlinear growth by specifying some of the time scores as being freely estimated (e.g., 0, 1, 2, *). This will allow the program to compute an estimate of the last time score. For example, the final time score might be estimated as 4.5. This would mean that the growth between the third and fourth intervals is accelerating and does not conform to a linear trend (which would be fixed at 3.0 for a linear model). If the last time score actually confirms a linear model, it would be estimated as approximately 3.0.

Model Identification

As readers will recall, the SEM approach to model fitting involves specifying a proposed set of relationships and then testing those relationships against the data. Models that are consistent with the data will produce stronger evidence of fit (as assessed through various fit indices). Estimation of the proposed SEM model assumes that it has been properly identified. If a model were not identified (i.e., underidentified), it would be possible to find an infinite number of values for its parameters, and each set would be consistent with the covariance equation. It is therefore necessary to have just enough information to solve each parameter (just-identified) or more than enough information (overidentified).

In general, the problem of estimation is dealt with by restricting the number of parameters actually estimated from the total number of parameters in the model that could be estimated. This should result in a positive number of degrees of freedom in the model (i.e., a just-identified model would result in no degrees of freedom and therefore lead to perfect fit for the model). In a covariance structure analysis, the restriction is that the number of parameters estimated must be less than or equal to $p(p + 1)/2$, where p is the number of observed variables in the model. Thus, there is one covariance equation for each of the independent elements of the $p \times p$ covariance matrix. In the case where there are four indicators this would result in 10 nonredundant elements in the covariance matrix. In a mean structure analysis of $t = 4$ repeated measures, there are altogether $q = [p(p + 1)/2] + t$ pieces of information that must be fit. The number of parameters in the model is estimated in the following manner: $[4(5)/2] + 4 = 14$ data points.

The model in Figure 7.3 has nine parameters to be estimated (i.e., four residual variances, two latent factor variances, one covariance between the factors, and two latent factor means). In this example, all of the factor loadings are fixed to assigned values. In order to obtain the number of degrees of freedom in the model, it is necessary to subtract the number of model parameters estimated from q. So, there are $14 - 9$, or 5 degrees of freedom in this model.

Model 1 IS Output

The model fit indices for the IS model are presented in Table 7.6. The various fit indices all suggested that the model fit the data well [e.g., $\chi^2 (5, N = 20) = 1.850$, $p = 0.87$]. The nonsignificant chi-square coefficient suggests that the model should not be rejected on statistical grounds alone. Of course, we caution that

TABLE 7.6 Model 1 Fit Indices

Number of Free Parameters	9
Chi-Square Test of Model Fit	
Value	1.850
Degrees of Freedom	5
P-Value	0.8695
Information Criteria	
Akaike (AIC)	641.537
Bayesian (BIC)	650.498
Sample-Size Adjusted BIC	622.754
$(n* = (n + 2)/24)$	

TABLE 7.7 Model 1 Estimates for Intercept and Slope LCA

		Estimate	S.E.	Est./S.E.	Two-Tailed P-Value
Intercept (Initial Status)					
	GRAD1	1.000	0.000	999.000	999.000
	GRAD2	1.000	0.000	999.000	999.000
	GRAD3	1.000	0.000	999.000	999.000
	GRAD4	1.000	0.000	999.000	999.000
Growth Slope					
	GRAD1	0.000	0.000	999.000	999.000
	GRAD2	1.000	0.000	999.000	999.000
	GRAD3	2.000	0.000	999.000	999.000
	GRAD4	3.000	0.000	999.000	999.000
Factor Means					
	Intercept	46.211	3.897	11.859	0.000
	Slope	4.036	1.136	3.551	0.000
Variance/Covariance					
	Intercept	286.669	96.716	2.964	0.003
	Slope	16.179	10.605	1.526	0.127
	Cov	−22.986	23.316	−0.986	0.324
Residual Variances					
	GRAD1	18.675	30.894	0.604	0.546
	GRAD2	41.128	20.156	2.040	0.041
	GRAD3	78.240	33.255	2.353	0.019
	GRAD4	92.544	54.682	1.692	0.091

in testing models the failure to reject a particular model does not eliminate the possibility that there could be other models that would result in similar or stronger model fit criteria (e.g., smaller chi-square coefficient, higher CFI, etc.) as the model under consideration.

In Table 7.7, we present the parameter estimates for the IS model. The initial status level is estimated as 46.211, and the slope is estimated as 4.036. The initial status mean is consistent with the original observed mean summarized in Table 7.1 (i.e., Mean = 46.35). The slope estimate indicates the average graduation rate increases about 4% per year after the initial measurement occasion. The covariance between the initial status factor and the growth trend factor is negative (−22.986, $p > 0.05$), with correlation of −0.34 (not tabled), suggesting that institutions with lower initial graduation rates tend to increase their graduation levels more over time than institutions with higher initial status graduation rates (and vice versa). In contrast, if we had defined the initial status factor as an end status factor, the resulting covariance between the intercept and slope factors would be positive (9.56, $p > 0.05$, $r = 0.23$, not tabled).

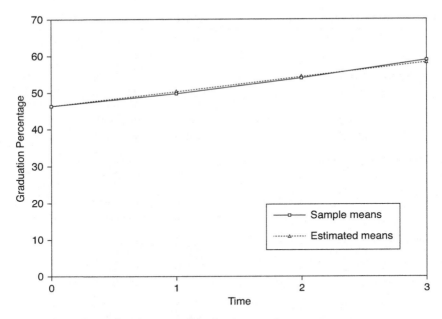

FIGURE 7.4 Observed and estimated graduation trends.

We can also compare the model-estimated means and observed means in Figure 7.4. The figure shows that in this example the linear trajectory seems to represent the observed sample data quite well.

Model 2 LS Output

The LS approach will provide slightly different estimates as a result of not fixing the two middle loadings on the growth factor. If we estimate the factor loadings at time 2 and time 3 (0, *, *, 1), we would expect the mean growth rate over the length of the study to be about 12.0, that is, about roughly four points between waves 2 through 4 of the time series. When the model is parameterized in this fashion, it will now have three degrees of freedom as tested (i.e., $5 - 2 = 3$) because two growth factor loadings are freely estimated. We do not summarize the estimates, but resulting mean growth rate turns out to be 12.418, with the initial status mean as 43.253. This yields an estimated last measurement of about 58.671 ($46.253 + 12.418$), which is a bit less than the last observed mean of 58.80 in Table 7.1. As this implies, setting the growth metric in different ways adjusts the resulting growth coefficients correspondingly (including the covariance between the level and shape factors) but *usually* does not affect the overall interpretation of the data. It is a good idea, however, to be aware of these types of alternative parameterizations of the basic model to define the individual change trajectories, since the LCA approach readily offers this flexibility.

Comparing the Fit of the IS and LS Models

We can compare the fit of the initial IS and LS models to the data (as well as other changes we might also consider). Keep in mind that our illustrations are primarily to demonstrate the potential of the techniques for examining a series of alternative models, more than actually testing important substantive differences between the models in these simple examples. In Table 7.8, in addition to the log likelihood (which we will make use of subsequently), we present four commonly used fit indices to evaluate the fit of a series of model specification changes (see Chapter 5 for more detailed discussion of the specific indices). If we compare the fit of the LS model (Model 2) to the IS model (Model 1), we can see the chi-square coefficient is not significant for either model ($p > 0.05$), and the CFI is the same in both model (CFI = 1.00). In contrast, we can see the SRMR is somewhat larger for the LS model (SRMR = 0.108) than the IS model (SRMR = 0.100). Additionally, the AIC for the LS model is larger at 645.474 than the AIC for the IS model (641.537). Based on these results across the selected indices, we would likely conclude that the IS model is slightly better fitting than the LS model and is more parsimonious since it has one less parameter estimated.

Next we compare two more possible changes. In Model 3, we fix the covariance between the intercept and slope factors from the IS model (Model 1) to 0.0. Therefore, it has one more degree of freedom than Model 1. This change results in a higher SRMR (0.185) than noted for Model 1 and Model 2. Finally, for Model 4, we assert that the growth rate for Model 1 peaks at the third year and then falls back to the level of the second year for the last interval (i.e., 0, 1, 2, 1) and, therefore, we fix the last estimate for the growth slope at 1.0 (grad4@1). This will have the same number of parameters estimated as Model 1, but we note that

TABLE 7.8 Comparing Alternative Models With Mplus Fit Indices

	χ^2	df	p	CFI	SRMR	Log Likelihood	AIC
Model 1 (a, 0-3 = fixed)	1.850	5	0.87	1.00	0.100	−311.768	641.537
Model 2 (a, 1,2 = free)	1.787	6	0.62	1.00	0.108	−311.737	645.474
Model 3 ($\sigma_{is} = 0$)	3.042	6	0.80	1.00	0.185	−312.364	640.729
Model 4 (a, 3@1)	11.351	5	0.05	0.90	0.202	−316.519	651.038

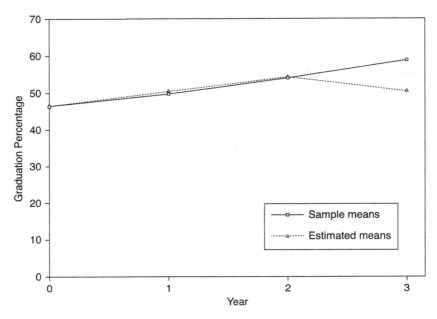

FIGURE 7.5 Fixing *grad4* measurement loading to 1.0.

in Table 7.8, the X^2 coefficient is much larger (11.351) than the other models. Similarly, the other fit indices identify it as the worst-fitting model of four models presented in the table.

We can also see where the error comes from if we look at the estimated and observed values of the data in Figure 7.5. We see the large discrepancy in estimated and observed values for the last year of the study. This illustrates that the estimated values and observed values should agree substantially for a well-fitting model.

Nested Models

As discussed in Chapter 5, a more thorough test for comparing models can be conducted when the first model is nested within an alternative model. A model is nested within another model if it can be derived directly by fixing one or more parameters in the alternative model to zero or some other constant (Marcoulides & Hershberger, 1997). The nested model will have greater degrees of freedom than the comparison model. For example, in Table 7.8, Model 2 is nested within Model 1, since it can be derived from Model 1 by freeing the two growth factor loadings (for a total of 3 degrees of freedom). We can obtain Model 3 from Model 1 by imposing an additional constraint on the covariance between the two factors (*i* with s@0), so we gain a degree of freedom. We note, however, that Model 1 and Model 4 are not nested since they have the same number of estimated parameters.

Let's say we wish to compare the fit of Model 4 against Model 2. One way to compare them is to make use of the model log likelihoods. Model deviance can be defined for each model as −2 multiplied by the log likelihood (−2LL). The difference in deviance between the two models is distributed as chi square with degrees of freedom equal to the difference in the number of parameters between the models. For Model 2, the −2LL is −2(−311.737) or 623.474, and for Model 4, it will be −2(−316.519) or 633.038. The difference then between the two models is 9.564, which for 2 degrees of difference, is significant at $p < 0.05$. We can use a chi-square table to determine that a chi-square coefficient of 5.99 is required for 2 degrees of freedom at $p = 0.05$. We note that if we take the two chi-square estimates for the model (11.351 − 1.787), we obtain the same estimate. In this case, we would reject the implied hypothesis that Model 4 fits the data as well as Model 2 and conclude that it is worse fitting than Model 2.

We might also wish to test Model 3 against Model 1. We assume the null hypothesis that the covariance between the intercept and slope factors (σ_{ls}) is zero and test this against the data. When this parameter is restricted to zero, we gain a degree of freedom for Model 3 (i.e., 6 degrees of freedom rather than 5). In this case, using the difference in −2LL between Model 3 and Model 1 (624.728 − 623.536) or the difference in model chi-square coefficients (3.042 − 1.850), the result is nonsignificant (i.e., $\chi^2 = 1.192$, 1 df, $p > 0.05$). The required chi-square coefficient for 1 degree of freedom is 3.84 at $p = 0.05$. The nonsignificant test for 1 degree of freedom therefore implies that Model 3 (with covariance between the factors restricted to zero) fits the data as well as Model 1. Therefore, we would accept Model 1 as being a better model than Model 3, since it is more parsimonious (i.e., it has one more degree of freedom).

Model 3: Adding Covariates to the IS Model

After investigating a series of preliminary models, we will assume that the intercept and slope (IS) formulation defines institutional change in graduation rates over the course of the data collection. As Model 3 in the series of latent curve models we are building, we next may wish to add covariates that may explain differences in individual institutions' graduation trajectories. In this example, we will add institutional prestige (i.e., win-loss records, bowl appearances) and institutional type as fixed predictors, as we did in the earlier random-coefficients formulation of this model. Alternatively, it would also be possible to add a time-varying covariate (i.e., as a separate growth process that might be correlated with graduation change over time). For example, we could conceptualize a variable like resource levels (or perhaps coaching turnover) as having temporal variation that has resulting effects on athletes' graduation rates. If desired, using a model comparison approach, covariates can be added separately or in sets and their influence evaluated using likelihood ratio tests.

Model 3 Statements

We provide the model input statements next for the IS model with covariates. We use the basic Model 1 specification for this analysis, as we noted the model fit the data better with the intercept and slope covariance freely estimated.

```
TITLE:       Model 3: Adding covariates to the IS model;
DATA:        File is C:\mplus\ch7grad1.txt;
VARIABLE:    Names are id grad1 grad2 grad3 grad4 private prestige;
             Usevariables are grad1 grad2 grad3 grad4 private prestige;
define:      center prestige private (grandmean);
ANALYSIS:    Type = general;
             Estimator is ML;
Model:
             i by grad1@1 grad2@1 grad3@1 grad4@1;
             s by grad1@0 grad2@1 grad3@2 grad4@3;
             [grad1-grad4@0 i s];
             i s on private prestige;
OUTPUT:      Sampstat Standardized Tech1;
```

Model 3 Output

The results for the covariate model are summarized in Table 7.9. The intercept factor mean is 46.097 and the slope factor mean is 4.159. The coefficients for institutional type (7.233, $p > 0.05$) and prestige (1.153, $p > 0.05$) indicate no statistically significant differences in initial status graduation rates with respect to the covariates. Over time, however, private schools increase at a statistically significant rate of about 6.5% per year more than public schools ($p < 0.01$), while institutional prestige was unrelated to change ($-0.432, p > 0.05$). Overall, the two covariates accounted for about 5% of the variation in the initial status factor and about 51% of the variance in the slope factor (not tabled).

Table 7.10 presents the relevant model fit criteria. We can confirm that there were 13 free parameters. The chi-square coefficient (with 9 degrees of freedom) was 9.695 ($p > 0.05$), which implies that the model is consistent with the data. Similarly, the CFI (0.991) and RMSEA (0.061, $p > 0.05$) indices indicate a strong fit of the model to the data.

Extending the Latent Curve Model

This basic two-factor latent curve model can be extended in a number of ways. For example, as we noted, if an intercept and slope (IS) model is used, a quadratic

TABLE 7.9 Model 2 LCA Estimates

	Estimate	S.E.	Est./S.E.	P-Value
Factor Intercepts				
I	46.097	3.830	12.036	0.000
Slope	4.159	0.931	4.465	0.000
I ON				
PRIVATE	7.233	8.085	0.895	0.371
PRESTIGE	1.153	8.242	0.140	0.889
S ON				
PRIVATE	6.479	2.076	3.121	0.002
PRESTIGE	−0.432	2.048	−0.211	0.833
Covariance				
S With I	−32.503	19.354	−1.679	0.093
Residual Variances				
GRAD1	31.261	35.133	0.890	0.374
GRAD2	39.230	20.865	1.880	0.060
GRAD3	99.621	38.258	2.604	0.009
GRAD4	38.715	37.953	1.020	0.308
Intercept	268.562	92.831	2.893	0.004
Slope	9.823	8.227	1.194	0.232

TABLE 7.10 Model Fit Criteria

Number of Free Parameters	13	
Log Likelihood		
H_0 Value	−304.361	
H_1 Value	−299.513	
Information Criteria		
Akaike (AIC)	634.721	
Bayesian (BIC)	647.666	
Sample-Size Adjusted BIC	607.590	
$(n^* = (n + 2)/24)$		
Chi-Square Test of Model Fit		
Value	9.695	
Degrees of Freedom	9	
P-Value	0.3758	
RMSEA (Root Mean Square Error of Approximation)		
Estimate	0.062	
90 Percent C.I.	0.000	0.264
Probability RMSEA $<= 0.05$	0.416	
CFI/TLI		
CFI	0.991	
TLI	0.986	
SRMR (Standardized Root Mean Square Residual)		
Value	0.118	

factor could be added to capture curvilinear types of growth [see Duncan et al. (2006) for further discussion]. The quadratic growth factor requires three random effects: an intercept (initial status) factor (i), a linear growth factor (s), and a quadratic growth factor (q). As in the previous example, if the linear time scores were 0, 1, 2, 3 (for the 4 years), the time scores for the quadratic growth factor would be the squared values of the linear time scores (0, 1, 4, 9), which are automatically estimated in Mplus version 7 when the analyst designates the quadratic growth factor (q) in the model input statement.

Latent curve analysis can also include multiple-group analyses, where groups may be defined by a categorical time-invariant variable. This allows for identifying group differences in the means of random effects or examining the possibility of different variance-covariance parameters across groups, as well as possible differences across groups in a_t, for example, when the time-related measurements are treated as model parameters as in SEM formulations [see Muthén & Muthén (1998–2012) for further discussion]. More complex models, such as piecewise growth models (i.e., separate growth trends) growth models that include incremental or decremental growth trends for one group versus another, and parallel growth models are also relatively easy to formulate and test. We provide one example of a piecewise growth model in the last section of the chapter.

Multilevel Latent Curve Analysis

The basic latent curve model formulated as a single-level (multivariate) model can also be extended to include situations where we wish to include group-level variables (e.g., organizational variables) in modeling change. In the following example, the specific analysis involves decomposing student growth represented in the level and shape factors into their within- and between-school components and examining the effects of individual background factors and school processes (e.g., tracking, differential curricula, class size) on the growth factors. Time-specific residuals associated with measurement occasions (ε_{it}) are also decomposed into within- and between-group components, with the latter term typically fixed at zero in random-coefficients modeling (Muthén & Asparouhov, 2003). Hence, the two-level growth model in the SEM framework is compatible with the three-level, random-coefficients model presented earlier in the chapter (Duncan et al., 2006; Muthén & Muthén, 2005).[5]

Examining Variables That Influence Student Growth in Math

Consider a study that focuses on the educational value that the quality of the school's processes adds to student growth. In many cases, comparisons are made between schools on the basis of outcome levels without taking into consideration schools' growth over time. In cross-sectional studies of school outcomes, for example, the contribution of the school is often underestimated in the process of adjusting schools' achievement scores for the backgrounds of their students. Because the quality of school processes is believed to be cumulative and to apply to all students, growth in student achievement is likely a more appropriate criterion for judging whether differences in the perceptions of staff, parents, and students about the quality of school processes explain differences in student growth. In this example, the focus is on determining the impact of measures of school quality on student learning, after controlling for student background within schools and community socioeconomic status between schools.

Data and Variables

The data consist of 7,029 students randomly selected from a sample of 49 middle schools. Students were measured on a standardized achievement test in math over three occasions (grades 6, 7, 8). The math outcomes were reported as scale scores. Scale scores are generally the most appropriate metric for investigating student growth if the scores have been vertically equated to permit year-to-year assessments of individual change [e.g., see Goldschmidt, Kilchan, & Martinez (2004); Seltzer, Frank, & Bryk (1994)].

For the within-school model, student background variables include gender (1 = female) and socioeconomic status (1 = participation in free/reduced school lunch, else = 0). The between-school model includes school quality and school SES variables. School quality is defined as a composite variable consisting of several survey items assessing the quality of school leadership, expectations for students, classroom instructional practices, evaluation of student progress, school climate, and home/school relations. It is standardized (mean = 0, SD = 1) such that higher scores indicate stronger perceptions about the quality of several key school processes. The school-level control is a standardized measure (mean = 0, SD = 1) of student socioeconomic composition (CSES), which was compiled from information about student and community SES and coded such that higher scores indicate higher community SES.

Defining the Proposed Model

The proposed model is summarized in Figure 7.6. The latent factors are shown as ovals. Within groups, the repeated observed scores (e.g., math test scores on three occasions) and predictors (e.g., student background) are shown as rectangles. Two-headed arrows indicate correlations between variables, while single-headed arrows indicate structural relationships and errors.

Model Statements

We provide the model input statements next. In this example, we use a level and shape (LS) model to formulate the growth (with loadings defined as 0, *, 1),

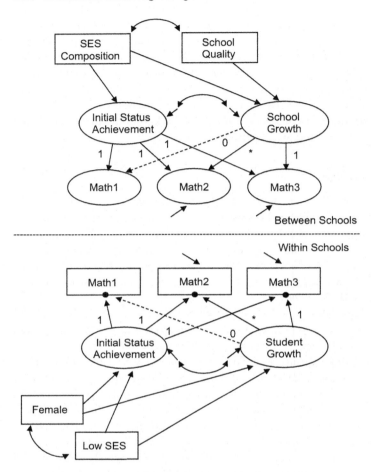

FIGURE 7.6 Proposed multilevel growth model of math outcomes.

which will result in estimating the growth rate over the period of the trend. In this example, we fix the errors for Math1 to zero (Math1@0;) within and between groups to facilitate the estimation of the model's parameters. Within groups, the model indicates 10 parameters to be estimated (i.e., one growth factor loading, two residuals in Θ, four beta coefficients, two factor residual variances, and one covariance). Between groups, the repeated measures are shown as ovals, indicating that they are continuous latent variables that vary across schools. There are 11 parameters to be estimated between groups (i.e., one factor loading, three regression coefficients, one level intercept, one shape intercept, two residual variances for math2 and math3, two factor residual variances, and one covariance). This makes a total of 21 parameters to estimate. We will change the direction of the coding of community SES using a "Define" statement, so that the effect of SES composition at the school level will be positive (i.e., higher community SES is related to higher math achievement). This change can be accomplished by using a "Define" command, specifying a new CSES variable (*ncses*), and multiplying the old variable (*cses*) by −1. Note that the new variable must be added as the last variable in the Usevariables line. Finally, we note that we needed to include a starting value for one of the covariates in the between-group latent shape factor (ncses*4) in order for the model to converge.

```
TITLE:      Two-level model of middle school math growth;
DATA:       FILE IS C:\mplus\ch7 ex2.txt;
            Format is 10f8.0,2f8.2;
VARIABLE:   Names are schcode math1 math2 math3
            female lowses slep sped middle notrans cses quality;
            Usevariables schcode math1 math2 math3
            female lowses quality ncses;
            within = female lowses;
            between = ncses quality;
            CLUSTER IS schcode;
define:     ncses = cses*(-1);
            center ncses quality (grandmean);
ANALYSIS:   TYPE = twolevel;
            Estimator is MLR;
Model:
            %BETWEEN%
            lb sb | math1@0 math2* math3@1;
            [math1-math3@0 lb sb];
            lb on ncses;
            sb on ncses*4 quality;
            math1@0;
            %WITHIN%
            sw lw |math1@0 math2* math3@1;
            sw lw on female lowses;
            math1@0;
OUTPUT:     sampstat standardized TECH1;
```

Model Output

The fit of the proposed model is summarized in Table 7.11 [χ^2 (6 *df*) = 16.589, $p = 0.011$, RMSEA = 0.016; CFI = 0.999; SRMR$_B$ = 0.053, SRMR$_W$ = 0.003]. Although the chi-square coefficient was significant ($p < 0.05$), with over 7,000 students in the sample, we can see that the fit of the model is quite good, given the other supporting indices.

TABLE 7.11 Selected Math Growth Model Fit Criteria

Number of Free Parameters	21
Chi-Square Test of Model Fit	
Value	16.589*
Degrees of Freedom	6
P-Value	0.0109
Scaling Correction Factor for MLR	0.8551
RMSEA (Root Mean Square Error of Approximation)	
Estimate	0.016
CFI/TLI	
CFI	0.999
SRMR (Standardized Root Mean Square Residual)	
Value for Within	0.003
Value for Between	0.053

The parameter estimates are summarized in Table 7.12. The school-level intercept for the initial status math factor is 600.751 and the average growth over the 3-year period is 82.665. Within schools, the free factor loading (*) is 0.983 (not tabled), suggesting little growth in the individual trajectories between T_2 and T_3. Between schools, the estimate is 0.711 (not tabled). This suggests the latent trajectories are curved rather than linear and have slightly different curved shapes for individuals and for schools.

Within schools, female ($\gamma = 1.716$, $p < 0.05$) is significantly related to the initial status factor. In particular, this suggests an initial achievement gap for males compared with their female peers. Regarding growth rate, females make significantly greater academic progress in math ($\gamma = 5.358$, $p < 0.001$), and low SES status is also significantly related to math growth ($\gamma = -18.086$, $p < 0.001$) but not to initial status ($\gamma = 1.294$, $p > 0.05$). Between schools, the table suggests that initial status means are higher in schools with higher student SES composition ($\gamma = 5.611$, $p < 0.001$). Both the perceived quality of school processes ($\gamma = 3.616$, $p < 0.01$) and SES composition ($\gamma = 2.663$, $p < 0.05$) affect growth over time. This can be interpreted as a standard deviation increase in perceptions about school quality and would yield an estimated 3.6 scaled-score increase in growth in achievement outcomes. Overall, SES composition and school quality account for about 17% of the growth in achievement between schools (not tabled). We could of course add various predictors to subsequent models.

Developing a Piecewise Growth Model

In the last section of the chapter, we extend our basic latent curve model to examine a piecewise growth model, which is useful in examining more than one growth trend over time. One design that is useful in examining trends is a time

TABLE 7.12 Mplus Math Growth Model Parameter Estimates

Fixed Effect	Coefficient	SE
Model for initial status,		
School intercept	600.751*	1.949
NCSES	5.611*	1.285
Between individuals		
Female	1.716*	0.598
Low SES	1.294	0.727
Model for learning rate		
School intercept	82.665*	1.294
NCSES	2.663*	1.183
Quality	3.616*	1.331
Between individuals		
Female	5.358*	0.871
Low SES	−18.086*	1.707
Model R-Square		
LW	0.002	0.001
SW	0.051*	0.008
LB	0.242*	0.108
SB	0.173	0.100

Note: *$p < 0.05$

series design. The essence of a time series design is the presence of periodic measurements and the introduction of an experimental change into the time series of measurements. In this case we examine a trend before and after a policy is introduced. Consider the case developed previously about institutions and their athletes' graduation rates. We examined whether the introduction of the policy resulted in graduation rate increases over time in a small random sample of institutions. A more thorough test of the policy's impact on changing graduation rates, however, would require the analyst to compare the trends in graduation rates several years before and after the policy was introduced.

Consider another example in which we examine the impact of a policy change to increase the academic skills of entering freshmen on resulting admissions rates in a random sample of colleges. In this example, we will compare the trends in percentage of freshman applicants admitted several years before and after the policy change was implemented. In a time series design, evidence of a treatment's effect is indicated by a discontinuity in the measurements recorded in the time series (Campbell & Stanley, 1966). In this example, the time series may be defined as follows:

$$O_1 O_2 O_3 X O_4 O_5 O_6 O_7 O_8 O_9,$$

where the three zeros preceding the X represent the yearly trend of percentage of freshman admitted before the introduction of the policy, and the six zeros afterward represent the trend in percentage of freshman admitted after the implementation of the policy to raise standards. The design is a sound quasi-experimental design, provided certain threats to internal validity can be successfully argued away (Campbell & Stanley, 1966).

The major threats to the single-group time series are instrumentation, testing, and history. Instrumentation and testing can be argued away more easily in this case because the data were collected utilizing the same variables and no repeated testing on individuals was done (i.e., as might be the case if the data were collected from individuals who received a treatment of some type). The determination of change is determined solely on the fluctuations in the institutional data over the years prior to the policy's implementation and the years following its implementation.

Threats due to history, however, could be a potential problem for this time series design. Rival explanations could include changes in the institutional norms within a set of schools (that may or may not correspond to the policy's instruction) or perhaps cyclical events. To deal with history as a rival explanation, it is important to specify in advance the expected relationship between the introduction of the policy and the manifestation of an effect. Importantly, as the time between implementation and resultant effect increases, the effects of extraneous events become more plausible. By raising admissions standards, it is likely the policy will result in a reduction of freshman admitted. If this is true, we would expect to observe a discontinuity of measurements (fewer freshmen admitted) after the policy was introduced.

Specifying the Piecewise Latent Curve Model

We can formulate a piecewise latent curve model to test these hypotheses against the data. Before the policy was introduced, we have available a policy trend covering 3 years (i.e., three 0s specified in the time series). After the introduction of the policy, we have a trend consisting of 6 years (six 0s specified) of data. To test the similarity of the trends, the idea is to fit one linear latent curve model segment to the data before the introduction of the policy and another linear latent curve model to describe the trend after policy introduction. The two separate slope trends can then be compared against each other. In this case, we propose that both the initial status (intercept) and slope trends will likely be affected by the introduction of the policy; therefore, we define two separate initial status intercept factors and two separate slope factors.

The complete model including a covariate (private versus public institution) is presented in Figure 7.7. Notice in the figure there are 3 years (Y1–Y3) comprising the first trend (before the policy was introduced) and 6 years (Y4–Y9) after its introduction. Each trend has an initial status factor and a growth factor and a covariance between the two latent factors. We eliminate some latent factor correlations from the figure (e.g., initial status1 and initial status2) to simplify the visual presentation of the model. The basic model specification also facilitates the

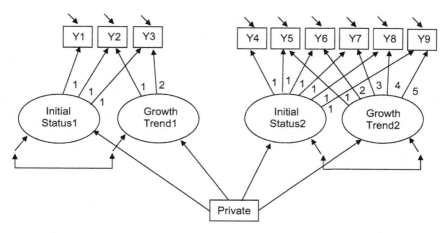

FIGURE 7.7 Proposed piecewise growth model of freshmen admitted before and after the introduction of the policy.

investigation of other possible models. For example, if the researcher thought a 1-year lag effect might exist, she or he could test the model in Figure 7.7 against a second model where Y4 (the year after the policy was first implemented) was included in the first trend. The fit of the two models could then be compared to determine which one fits the data better.

Model 1 Statements

We next provide the Mplus input statements for the initial model (Model 1). This model specifies the two growth trajectories (before and after policy implementation). Subsequently, we add a covariate (Model 2).

```
TITLE:       Model 1: Specifying the piecewise growth model;
DATA:        File is C:\mplus\ch7freshep.txt;
             format is 11f8.0,1f5.2,1f1.0;
VARIABLE:    Names are schid fresh1 fresh2 fresh3
             fresh4 fresh5 fresh6 fresh7 fresh8 fresh9
             private prestige hiprest;
             Usevariables are fresh1 fresh2 fresh3
             fresh4 fresh5 fresh6 fresh7 fresh8 fresh9;
ANALYSIS:    Type = general;
             Estimator is ML;
```

Model:

        I1 by fresh1@1 fresh2@1 fresh3@1;
        I2 by fresh4@1 fresh5@1 fresh6@1
        fresh7@1 fresh8@1 fresh9@1;
        S1 by fresh1@0 fresh2@1 fresh3@2;
        fresh1@0;
        S2 by fresh4@0 fresh5@1 fresh6@2 fresh7@3
        fresh8@4 fresh9@5;
        [fresh1-fresh9@0 I1 I2 S1 S2];
OUTPUT: Sampstat standardized;

Model 1 Output

We present the results of Model 1 and Model 2 in Table 7.13. For Model 1, the factor means are as follows: Initial Status 1, $M = 22.124$; Initial Status 2, $M = 20.325$; Growth trend 1, $M = -0.163$ ($p > 0.05$), Growth trend 2, $M = -0.478$ ($p < 0.001$). These results suggest the mean percentage of admitted freshmen in the first year of the study (22.124) is considerably higher than the mean percentage of freshmen admitted immediately after policy implementation (20.325). The trend of percentage of admitted freshmen is observed to be relatively stable before policy implementation (i.e., -0.163, $p > 0.05$). In the years after the policy implementation, however, the slope in percentage of freshmen admitted declines significantly (-0.478, $p < 0.001$), at about 0.5% per year. For Model 1, the supporting fit indices (not tabled) suggest that the proposed model fits the data reasonably well, with a small chi-square coefficient, χ^2 (32, $N = 105$) $= 46.305, p = 0.0489$) and RMSEA estimate (0.065) that is not statistically significant ($p = 0.258$). The first model, therefore, provides preliminary evidence that the policy has a statistically significant effect in reducing the percentage of freshman applicants admitted to the 105 institutions in the study.

Imposing Equality Constraints

At step 2, we can attempt to argue away the existence of separate trends by constraining the two initial status factors to be equal and the two growth factors to be equal. If the nested model with constraints provides a stronger fit to the data than the alternative model, it would provide evidence suggesting that the policy did not have any effect on the trends regarding the admission of freshmen. We next provide the necessary changes in the Model statements. We still fix the intercepts (fresh1-fresh9@0) but hold the latent factor intercepts and slopes to be equal using equality constraints.

TABLE 7.13 Piecewise Growth Model Estimates

	Estimate	S.E.	Est./S.E.	P-Value
Model 1 Factor Means				
I1	22.124	0.475	46.596	0.000
I2	20.326	0.402	50.602	0.000
S1	−0.163	0.269	−0.606	0.545
S2	−0.478	0.100	−4.798	0.000
Model 2 Factor Means				
I1	22.198	0.524	42.333	0.000
I2	20.396	0.441	46.212	0.000
S1	−0.297	0.295	−1.005	0.315
S2	−0.584	0.107	−5.477	0.000
Model 2 Coefficients				
I1 ON				
PRIVATE	−0.408	1.233	−0.331	0.741
I2 ON				
PRIVATE	−0.424	1.029	−0.412	0.680
S1 ON				
PRIVATE	0.740	0.695	1.066	0.287
S2 ON				
PRIVATE	0.597	0.249	2.403	0.016

```
[fresh1-fresh9@0];
[I1 I2] (1);
[S1 S2] (2);
```

For this nested model (with two more degrees of freedom), corresponding fit indices (not tabled) suggest that it is not a plausible model. For example, the chi-square coefficient is χ^2 (34, $N = 105$) $= 73.686, p < 0.001$). The RMSEA is also much larger and statistically significant (0.105, $p = 0.005$). The fit of the two models can also be compared by examining the change in chi-square coefficients for 2 degrees of freedom. The result (not tabled) is significant, χ^2 (2, $N = 105$) $= 27.381, p < 0.001$. The large chi-square coefficient also suggests that we should reject the hypothesis that the two models fit the data the same.

At step 3, we can constrain only the two intercepts to be equal (i.e., we remove the equality constraint on S1 and S2 in the model statements). This would imply the latent intercept factors are the same in year 1 (the beginning of the study) and year 4 (i.e., the year after policy implementation), but two change trends exist. The resulting fit indices (not tabled), however, indicate that this model resulted in a larger χ^2 coefficient than any of the previous models: $\chi^2 (35, N = 105) = 113.131$, $p < 0.001$. Because the change in the chi-square coefficient was even larger than in the previous test, the result suggests that restricting the intercepts to be equal would not provide as strong a representation of the data as the first model. Therefore, the conclusion is that two separate intercept and growth trends were most appropriate to describe the time series.

Model 2: Adding the Covariates

Finally, we can add one or more covariates to the model. In this case, we consider whether institutional type (private coded 1 and public coded 0) might affect the admission trends. We can continue to fix the intercepts for the repeated measures at zero, but we remove the equality constraints on the latent factor means as shown in the model statements.

Model 2 Statements

Given that models with equality constraints did not fit the data as well as the proposed with two trends, we continue with Model 1 and add the regression of the growth latent factors on the covariate (private versus public institution) as the last line of the model statements.

```
[fresh1-fresh9@0 I1 I2 S1 S2 ];
I1 I2 S1 S2 on private;
```

Model 2 Output

We now draw readers' attention to the parameter estimates for the covariate model (Model 2) in Table 7.13. In Model 2, the initial status 1 (I1) and initial status 2 (I2) means refer to the means in public institutions (coded 0). Institutional type does not affect I1 ($-0.408, p > 0.05$) nor growth rate (S1) before the policy is implemented ($0.740, p > 0.05$). After the policy is implemented, in the reference group of institutions (public institutions $= 0$), the results suggest mean percentage of freshmen admitted (S2) decreases by about 0.6% per year ($-0.584, p < 0.001$). In contrast, in private schools the yearly trend is significantly different from public institutions ($0.597, p < 0.05$). Model 2 also fits the data quite well (not tabled),

$\chi^2\,(37, N = 105) = 47.998, p = 0.1064)$. Moreover, the RMSEA is also not significant $(0.053, p = 0.423)$. Overall, our analysis suggests that the policy intervention has a significant effect on reducing the percentage of freshmen admitted across subsequent years in public institutions, with an unexpected differential effect in private institutions.

Summary

Longitudinal analysis represents a rapidly growing application of multilevel modeling techniques. Because they provide stronger ways for dealing with causal relationships between variables than cross-sectional analyses, they should continue to draw the increased attention of researchers. In this chapter, we introduced several basic types of individual change models that are very flexible for fitting a number of research purposes and designs (e.g., experimental, time series, nonexperimental). We suggest that analysts give careful thought to defining the time-related variable used to estimate individual growth (e.g., its coding such as the occasions of measurement or a variable such as age), as well as the specification of the model given the number of available measurement occasions. In addition, one should also consider the nature and extent of missing data in the data being employed to test the model. Often in longitudinal analyses it is reasonable to assume the data are missing at random. Mplus also provides the ability to incorporate different patterns of missingness into the analysis of individual growth. While the detailed programming of the example models was beyond the scope of this chapter, readers are encouraged to consult a number of introductory sources that provide overviews of the assumptions, uses, and programming of longitudinal, multilevel methods (e.g., Duncan et al., 2006; Muthén & Muthén, 1998–2006; Raudenbush et al., 2004; Raykov & Marcoulides, 2006; Singer & Willett, 2003). The *Mplus User's Guide* also offers a wide variety of introductory and more advanced examples.

Notes

1. For three repeated measures, the k–1 orthogonal contrasts would be $-1, 0, 1$ for the linear component and $1, -2, 1$ for the quadratic component. For four repeated measures, the k–1 orthogonal contrasts would be $-3, -1, 1, 3$ for the linear component; $1, -1, -1, 1$ for the quadratic component; and $-1, 3, -3, 1$ for the cubic component.
2. The measurement part of the model can therefore be specified as follows:

$$\begin{bmatrix} y_1 \\ y_2 \\ y_3 \\ y_4 \end{bmatrix} = \begin{bmatrix} 1 & 0 \\ 1 & 1 \\ 1 & 2 \\ 1 & 3 \end{bmatrix} \begin{bmatrix} \eta_0 \\ \eta_1 \end{bmatrix} + \begin{bmatrix} 0 & & & \\ 0 & \theta_{22} & & \\ 0 & 0 & \theta_{33} & \\ 0 & 0 & 0 & \theta_{44} \end{bmatrix}. \tag{A7.1}$$

3. The psi matrix corresponds to:

$$\Psi = \begin{bmatrix} \Psi_{11} & \\ \Psi_{21} & \Psi_{22} \end{bmatrix}.$$ (A7.2)

4. In the SEM matrix formulation, the growth factors (or other latent variables) may be regressed on each other using the Beta (B) matrix (B has zero diagonal elements and it assumed that I–B is nonsingular). For estimating the example model, this adds four parameters (the regression of the latent intercept on the two covariates and the regression of the latent slope on the two covariates). In this case, with two covariates, the B matrix is as follows:

$$B = \begin{bmatrix} 0 & 0 & B_{13} & B_{14} \\ 0 & 0 & B_{23} & B_{24} \\ 0 & 0 & 0 & 0 \\ 0 & 0 & 0 & 0 \end{bmatrix}.$$ (A7.3)

5. From the latent variable perspective, individual change can be examined as a multilevel process by redefining the three-level growth model (Muthén & Muthén, 2005). The Mplus framework supports models that decompose variables into their uncorrelated within- and between-cluster components, as well as models that examine randomly varying intercepts and slopes across groups. For a simple random-effects model involving students' linear growth in math, using multilevel regression terminology for convenience, at Level 1 the repeated math measurements (y_{ijt}) are a function of an intercept (η_{0ij}), a growth slope (η_{1ij}) describing the effect of a time-related variable such as successive grade levels (a_{tij}) on the outcomes, and time-specific errors of measurement (ε_{tij}) nested within individuals (i) and clusters (j):

$$y_{ijt} = \eta_{0ij} + \eta_{1ij} a_{tij} + \varepsilon_{tij}.$$ (A7.4)

The time scores enter into the Λ_t matrix within groups. Between-individual variation in achievement intercept (η_{0ic}), typically centered on their initial status, and growth (η_{1ic}), defined as the average yearly change in the measures of y_t, parameters can be expressed as

$$\eta_{0ij} = \alpha_{0j} + \gamma_{0j} x_{ij} + \zeta_{0ij},$$ (A7.5)

$$\eta_{1ij} = \alpha_{1j} + \gamma_{1j} x_{ij} + \zeta_{1ij}.$$ (A7.6)

It is assumed that η_{0ij} and η_{1ij} are normally distributed with means (adjusted for any covariates) equal to α_{0j} and α_{1j} respectively; γ_{0j} and γ_{1j} are structural parameters; x_{ij} refers to a time-invariant covariate such as student SES that affects the level of achievement and growth rate; and ζ_{0ij} and ζ_{1ij} are residuals with intercept and slope variances and covariances specified in in the within-groups covariance matrix Ψ_w. As suggested previously, in SEM formulations, the first two levels of the random-coefficients growth model can be contained in a within-groups measurement model [i.e., which relates the initial status and growth factors to the multiple observed indicators (y_t), with added subscript j representing clusters] and within-groups structural models representing covariates that affect the initial status and growth factors.

The between-groups portion of the model also contains a measurement model where the between-group latent change model is specified in (i.e., the time scores are entered as factor loadings). The model is identical to Equation A7.4 (except specified at the group level). If η_j then represents a vector of random effects, which include the mean initial level of achievement and mean school rate growth per year, the structural model can be specified as:

$$\eta_{0j} = \alpha_{0j} + \gamma_2 w_j + \zeta_{0j,} \qquad (A7.7)$$

$$\eta_{1j} = \alpha_{1j} + \gamma_3 w_j + \zeta_{1j}, \qquad (A7.8)$$

where each between-cluster equation has its own intercept (α_{0j} and α_{1j}), γ_2 and γ_3 are structural parameters relating a school-level covariate w_j (e.g., community SES) to the submodels to explain levels of initial school achievement and school growth rate, and ζ_{0j} and ζ_{1j} are residuals. Variances and covariances associated with the school achievement and growth factors are contained in Ψ_B.

References

Bryk, A. S. & Raudenbush, S. W. (1992). *Hierarchical linear models: Applications and data analysis methods*. Newbury Park, CA: Sage.

Campbell, D. T., & Stanley, J. C. (1966). *Experimental and quasi-experimental designs for research*. Chicago, IL: Rand McNally.

Dale, A., & Davies, R. B. (1994). *Analyzing social and political change: A casebook of methods*. Thousand Oaks, CA: Sage.

Davies, R. (1994). From cross-sectional to longitudinal analysis. In R. B. Davies & A. Dale (Eds.), *Analyzing social and political change: A casebook of methods* (pp. 20–40). Thousand Oaks, CA: Sage.

Duncan, T. E., Duncan, S. C., & Strycker, L. A. (2006). *An introduction to latent variable growth curve modeling: Concepts, issues, and applications* (2nd ed.). Mahwah, NJ: Lawrence Erlbaum.

Duncan, T. E., Duncan, S. C., Strycker, L. A., Li, F., & Alport, A. (1999). *An introduction to latent variable growth curve modeling: Concepts, issues, and applications*. Mahwah, NJ: Lawrence Erlbaum Associates.

Goldschmidt, P., Kilchan, C., & Martinez, F. (2004). *Using hierarchical growth models to monitor school performance over time: Comparing NCE to scale score results*. Los Angeles: University of California, Center for the Study of Evaluation, Report 618.

Heck, R. H., Thomas, S. L., & Tabata, L. N. (2013). *Multilevel and longitudinal modeling with IBM SPSS* (2nd ed.). New York: Routledge.

Hershberger, S. L., Molenaar, P. C., & Corneal, S. E. (1996). A hierarchy of univariate and multivariate time series models. In G. Marcoulides & R. Schumacker (Eds.), *Advanced structural equation modeling: Issues and techniques* (pp. 159–194). Mahwah, NJ: Lawrence Erlbaum.

Hox, J. J. (2010). *Multilevel analysis: Techniques and applications* (2nd ed.). New York: Routledge.

Marcoulides, G. A. & Hershberger, S. (1997). *Multivariate statistical methods: A first course*. Mahwah, NJ: Lawrence Erlbaum.

McArdle, J. J. (1988). Dynamic but structural equation modeling of repeated measures data. In J. R. Nesselroade & R. B. Cattell (Eds.), *The handbook of multivariate experimental psychology* (Vol. 2, pp. 561–614). New York: Plennum Press.

McArdle, J. J. & Anderson, E. T. (1990). Latent growth models for research on aging. In L. E. Birren & K. W. Schaie (Eds.), *Handbook of the psychology of aging* (3rd ed., pp. 21–44). San Francisco, CA: Academic Press.

Mehta, P. D. & Neale, M. C. (2005). People are variables too. Multilevel structural equations modeling. *Psychological Methods, 10*(3), 259–284.

Meredith, E. & Tisak, J. (1990). Latent curve modeling. *Psychometrika, 55*(1), 107–122.

Muthén, B. O. (1994). Multilevel covariance structure analysis. *Sociological Methods & Research, 22*(3), 376–398.

Muthén, B. O. (1998–2004). *Mplus technical indices*. Los Angeles, CA: Muthén & Muthén.

Muthén, B. O. (2002). Beyond SEM: General latent variable modeling. *Behaviormetrika, 29,* 81–118.

Muthén, B. O. & Asparouhov, T. (2003). *Advances in latent variable modeling, Part I: Integrating multilevel and structural equation modeling using Mplus*. Unpublished paper.

Muthén, B. O. & Muthén, L. (1998–2006). *Mplus user's guide*. Los Angeles, CA: Authors.

Muthén, L. K. & Muthén, B. O. (1998–2012). *Mplus user's guide* (7th ed.). Los Angeles, CA: Authors.

Muthén, L. & Muthén, B. O. (2005). *Growth modeling with latent variables*. Los Angeles: Authors. Retrieved from http://www.statmodel.com

Raudenbush, S. W. (2001). Comparing personal trajectories and drawing causal inferences from longitudinal data. *Annual Review of Psychology, 52,* 501–525.

Raudenbush, S. W. & Bryk, A. S. (2002). *Hierarchical linear models* (2nd ed.). Newbury Park, CA: Sage.

Raudenbush, S. W., Bryk, A. S., Cheong, Y. F., & Congdon, R. (2004). *HLM6: Hierarchical linear and nonlinear modeling*. Lincolnwood, IL: Scientific Software International.

Raykov, T. & Marcoulides, G. A. (2006). *A first course in structural equation modeling*. Mahwah, NJ: Lawrence Erlbaum Associates.

Seltzer, B., Frank, K., & Bryk, A. (1994). The metric matters: The sensitivity of conclusions about growth in student achievement to the choice of metric. *Educational Evaluation and Policy Analysis, 16,* 41–49.

Singer, J. & Willett, J. (2003). *Applied longitudinal data analysis: Modeling change and event occurrence*. New York: Oxford University Press.

Willett, J. & Sayer, A. (1996). Cross-domain analysis of change overtime: Combining growth modeling and covariance structure analysis. In G. Marcoulides & R. Schumacker (Eds.), *Advanced structural equation modeling: Issues and techniques* (pp. 125–158). Mahwah, NJ: Lawrence Erlbaum Associates.

8

MULTILEVEL MODELS WITH CATEGORICAL VARIABLES

Chapter Objectives

Our previous chapters have primarily focused on models with continuous outcomes. In this chapter we extend some of the previous models presented to consider a variety of modeling situations where categorical variables are present. We first develop several multilevel models with binary, ordinal, multinomial, and counts as the dependent variable. We then consider a multilevel factor model where the observed indicators are categorical (e.g., binary, ordinal).

Introduction

So far we have been working with data that are assumed to be continuous in developing measurement models. In this chapter we introduce readers to a range of multilevel models with categorical outcomes. Mplus also facilitates the analysis of factor models with dichotomous or ordinal items and models with ordinal, dichotomous, or multinomial outcomes. This ability to facilitate the analysis of various types of models with continuous and categorical indicators is one of the features that make Mplus such a flexible analytic program.

There are a number of important conceptual and mathematical differences between models with continuous and categorical outcomes. Categorical responses result from probability distributions other than the normal distribution and therefore require different types of underlying mathematical models. Ordinary least squares (OLS) estimation cannot be correctly applied to data where the outcome is dichotomous (e.g., two categories coded 0 and 1) or ordinal, since the range of responses is restricted and therefore the errors in predicting values of the dependent variable will not follow a normal distribution. For example, the distribution of the errors from predicting whether someone passes or fails, for example, will be nonrandom (since they can only have two values) and, therefore, they will not be normally distributed (i.e., violating a basic assumption of the linear model). Because categorical outcomes are almost always discrete rather than continuous, other types of probability distributions may better describe the specific populations from which they are obtained. **Discrete variables** take on a finite (or countable infinite) number of values and, therefore, are often best summarized as frequency and percentage distributions rather than as means and standard deviations. A frequency distribution provides a way of summarizing the probability that particular responses occur.

We often use the term **random variable** to describe the possible values that an outcome may have. Although we can calculate various descriptive statistics for categorical variables (means, standard deviations), we can no longer assume that a normal distribution is the mechanism that produces the observed response patterns. Similarly, the association between two categorical variables will be different from the typical Pearson correlation (r) because of the restricted range of observed values present in calculating the association and the particular measurement scale of each variable—that is, whether the two variables are both nominal, both ordinal, or one of each type. Because of these differences in the expected distributions of categorical outcomes, they can be more challenging to investigate than models with continuous outcomes.

Over the past few decades, analyses for statistical models with categorical outcomes have grown in sophistication. The generalized linear model (GLM), which provides a flexible framework for the investigation of categorical outcomes, consists of three components needed to specify the relationship between the categorical dependent variable Y and a set of independent X variables (McCullagh & Nelder, 1989). These include a dependent variable with an underlying random component that describes its sampling distribution (e.g., binomial, multinomial, Poisson), a structural model that refers to a linear combination of the independent variables that predicts expected values of the outcome, and a **link function**, which is required to transform the expected value of the outcome so that a linear model can be used to model the relationship between the predictors and transformed outcome (Hox, 2010). The probability distribution for the categorical outcome is linked to the explanatory model through a specific link function, which is a mathematical function that is used to transform the dependent outcome y so that it can be modeled as a linear function of a set of predictors (Azen & Walker, 2011). Because the outcome typically represents only a few response categories (e.g., yes or no; strongly agree, agree, neutral, disagree, strongly disagree), it is necessary to transform its expected values (e.g., using logit or probit transformations) into an underlying (or latent) variable that represents its predicted values, given the set of predictors. The predictive model is estimated through an iterative algorithm such as maximum likelihood.

As this introductory discussion implies, there are some added issues to consider in proposing and testing multilevel models with categorical outcomes. First, they can be harder to report about because the various link functions used produce the unstandardized coefficients are defined by different metrics (e.g., log odds coefficients and odds ratios, probit coefficients, event rates) from the unstandardized and standardized multiple regression coefficients with which most readers are already familiar. In some fields, such as health sciences, however, beginning researchers are more apt to encounter categorical outcomes routinely (e.g., the presence or absence of a particular disease) than in fields such as psychology, business, and education.

Second, with respect to multilevel modeling, models with categorical outcomes can be more difficult to estimate, since they require different estimation procedures because they result from probability distributions other than the normal distribution. A probability distribution may be considered as a mathematical model that links the actual outcome obtained from an empirical investigation to the probability of its occurrence (Azen & Walker, 2011). For example, for a binary, or dichotomous, variable, the predicted outcome can only take on two values (i.e., 0 or 1). Therefore, it cannot be normally distributed. Its sampling distribution is referred to as binomial, which represents the number of successes in a set of independent trials. Because a binary outcome is often expressed in terms of the probability that the event of interest occurs (e.g., having a particular health condition, obtaining a degree, failing a course), the predicted probability of its occurrence will approach but never exceed the boundaries of 0 and 1. The link function links the expected value of the random component of Y ($E(Y)$) to the deterministic component (i.e., the linear model). If we use a logit or probit link function to explain the probability that an event will occur, the predicted probabilities $y = 1$ result in an S-shaped function representing the effect of a predictor x on the predicted probabilities. In Figure 8.1, we provide a visual representation of the relationship between the predicted probability of students receiving a high school diploma and levels of their socioeconomic status. As the figure illustrates, the logit link function provides a more realistic model for the predicted probabilities between 0 and 1 than a linear model would provide, since if we imposed a linear function on the data, the predicted values for higher (or lower) values of SES would eventually exceed the boundaries of 0 and 1.

In Figure 8.2, we can also notice a characteristic of a logistic or probit function is that the SES slope is the steepest halfway between 0 and 1, which indicates the maximum effect of a unit change in SES on the probability $y = 1$. This value of x is sometimes referred to as the *median effective* level (Azen & Walker, 2011). Because the relationship between the probability $y = 1$ and the independent variable is nonlinear, the change in the predicted probability for a unit increase in x is not constant but instead varies depending on the level of x. Notice, for example, in the figure that the effect of a unit change in SES will lessen as the probability is closer to 1 or 0.

As we have noted previously, model estimation attempts to determine the extent to which a sample covariance matrix is a good approximation of the true population matrix. Because the outcomes are discrete rather than continuous, nonlinear link functions are required and therefore model estimation requires an

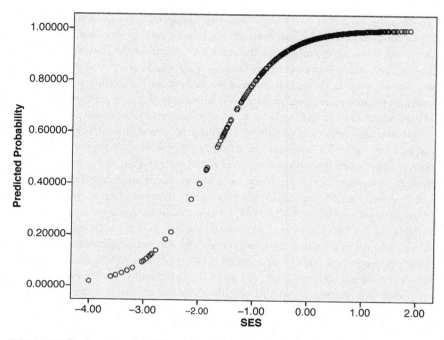

FIGURE 8.1 Predicted probabilities of student persistence for levels of SES.

iterative computational procedure to estimate the parameters correctly. Combining multilevel data structures and generalized linear models can lead to greater complexity in estimating model parameters and considerably more computer time in providing model convergence. Because the link functions estimated are nonlinear, one common approach is to approximate the nonlinear link by a nearly linear function and embed the multilevel estimation for that function in the generalized linear model (Hox, 2010). This approach represents a type of quasi-likelihood estimation relying on Taylor series expansion.

Mplus provides several ways to estimate models with discrete outcomes (e.g., maximum likelihood, weighted least squares, Bayesian estimation). For models with categorical outcomes and maximum likelihood estimation (ML), Mplus uses **numerical integration** for computing the likelihood function because the link function within groups is nonlinear (i.e., as shown by the S-shaped function in Figure 8.1). Numerical integration is an approach for estimating nonlinear functions, which maximizes the correct likelihood function (Schall, 1991; Wolfinger, 1993) through using approximate calculation methods. In general, numerical integration refers to a set of procedures that facilitate the estimation of an integral function (e.g., an approximation of the area of a curvilinear region) through expressing the area under the curve as a series of regularly spaced intervals using polynomials, exponentials, and trigonometric functions to interpolate the specific

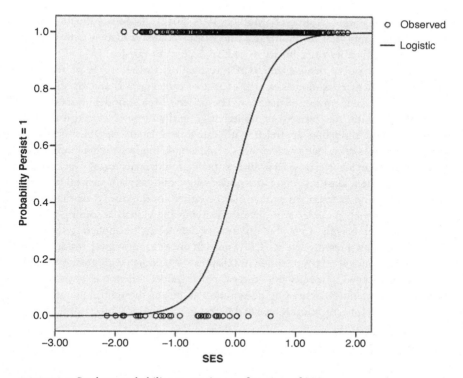

FIGURE 8.2 Student probability to persist as a function of SES.

curvilinear function under consideration. The function is typically evaluated at a series of points (referred to as quadrature points) and, generally, the more points, the less estimation error.

In Mplus, numerical integration is carried out with or without adaptive quadrature (i.e., where initial points are adapted over the estimation procedures) in combination with rectangular integration, Gauss-Hermite integration, or Monte Carlo integration (Muthén & Muthén, 1998–2012). Adding quadrature points can, however, require more estimation time, and as the model gets more complex (e.g., number of random effects, number of factors, larger sample size), this can add considerably more to the length of time it takes to obtain a solution, as well as whether the model actually converges. In some procedures (e.g., factor analysis with categorical indicators), to reduce computational time, the number of integration points can be decreased to provide an approximate solution. As Muthén and Muthén note, adaptive numerical integration often decreases the computation time but can lead to numerical instability under certain conditions, such as small cluster sizes. For models with categorical outcomes and many dimensions of integration, the weighted least squares estimator may improve computational speed, since it does not require numerical integration (Muthén & Muthén, 1998–2012). Bayesian estimation offers an alternative approach for estimating categorical multilevel models with random effects (i.e., with at least one binary or ordinal dependent variable).

Mplus also offers the capability of investigating various types of **mixture models** or latent class models, which consist of categorical latent variables representing emergent subsets of the data. The general Mplus modeling framework actually integrates the concept of underlying continuous and categorical latent variables. This modeling approach with categorical latent variables opens up many new types of modeling capabilities. An example might be where individuals belong to three latent classes according to their growth trajectories over time. In this type of latent class modeling, the underlying classes explain variability in the observed dependent variables, which may be either continuous (y) or categorical (u). The approach provides a means of classifying individuals according to their latent class membership. In Mplus, mixture modeling may be applied to the other types of models presented (e.g., CFA, growth models, multilevel models). We focus specifically on mixture models in Chapter 9. Of course with greater flexibility comes the need to specify how the particular model contributes to looking at a phenomenon in new ways. Our admonition about the thoughtful use of theory to guide model specification is repeated here.

Multilevel Models With Categorical Observed Outcomes

In Mplus, analyses can be conducted on outcomes that are censored, binary, ordinal, nominal (unordered categories), counts, or combinations of these categorical types. As we have stated, the GLM approach to categorical outcomes is to incorporate the necessary transformation and choice of error distribution directly into the statistical model (Hedeker, 2007; Hox, 2002). This approach makes it possible to extend standard single-level and multilevel regression models to a wider set of quantitative models including those with observed categorical outcomes and latent variables defined by categorical observed variables.

Specifying Models for Binary, Ordinal, and Nominal Outcomes

In this section, we outline the basic models for binary, ordinal, and nominal outcomes. Our approach is typical of the specification of generalized linear models that can be estimated with several basic statistical software programs. We then build a series of models using Mplus. Subsequently, we develop the model for count outcomes and build another series of models.

Binary Outcome

Categorical variables that follow a binomial distribution can take on only one of two values over a given number of n trials (such as flipping a coin). When y is dichotomous or a proportion, the probability distribution is specified as binomial (μ,n) with mean μ and the number of trials is represented as n. The mean can be interpreted as the probability of success. The focus is on determining the proportion of successes in the population (π) in a sequence of n independent trials or events. The expected value of y will then be

$$E(y \mid \pi) = n\pi, \tag{8.1}$$

and the variance will be

$$Var(y \mid \pi) = n\pi(1 - \pi). \tag{8.2}$$

A special case of the binomial distribution is the Bernoulli trial, which is defined as an experiment with only two possible outcomes and one trial or event (i.e., all $n = 1$). This type of distribution represents the most simplified probability distribution for categorical outcomes. From Equation 8.1, the expected value, or mean (μ), is then the population proportion $(\mu = \pi)$. The probability of success, that is, the event coded 1 $P(y = 1)$ occurs, is typically denoted by π in the population (and p in a sample). The probability the event coded 0 $P(y = 0)$ occurs is $1 - \pi$. The odds of the event occurring versus not occurring can be expressed as the following:

$$\frac{\pi}{1 - \pi}. \tag{8.3}$$

Logit Link Function

For proportions and dichotomous data, Mplus provides a logit link or probit link function. The logit link function is most often used because it represents a fairly easy transformation of the expected scores of y by using the natural logarithm (ln) of the probabilities of each event occurring. At Level 1, we take the natural logarithm[1] of the ratio of the probability of the two events occurring:

$$\eta_{ij} = \ln\left(\frac{\pi_{ij}}{1 - \pi_{ij}}\right), \tag{8.4}$$

where the logit coefficient η_{ij} is defined as the log of the odds of the event coded $y = 1$ as opposed to $y = 0$ for individual i in group j. Through taking the natural log of the ratio of the two events, therefore, the predicted value for the transformed outcome η_{ij} can take on any real value.

For example, let's say the proportion of students receiving a bachelor's degree is 0.60 and the proportion not receiving a degree is 0.40. Of course, we can state the relationship between receiving a degree versus not receiving a degree as a ratio in terms of raw odds as in Equation 8.3 ($0.6/0.4 = 1.5{:}1$). In terms of building a model to predicting the probability of receiving a receiving a degree, given one or more predictors, however, it is convenient to express the ratio in terms of a log odds coefficient, as Equation 8.4:

$$\eta_{ij} = \ln\left(\frac{0.6}{0.4}\right) = 0.405.$$

We obtain the log odds of 0.405 by taking the natural log of 1.5 ($0.6/0.4 = 1.5$). An associated advantage of working with log odds is that, for any predicted log odds, the probability $y = 1$ will always fall between 0 and 1. This will be useful later in estimating the probability of the event occurring or not for given values of a set of predictors. For now, we illustrate that we can use the following equation to obtain the probability of receiving a degree from the log odds coefficient (η):

$$P(y = 1) = \frac{1}{1 + e^{-(\eta)}},\tag{8.5}$$

where in this case η is the intercept log odds. We then can arrive back at the original probability of receiving a degree (0.60):

$$P(y = 1) = \frac{1}{1 + e^{-(\eta)}} = \frac{1}{1 + 2.71828^{-(0.405)}} = \frac{1}{1.667} = 0.60.$$

We note that Mplus uses thresholds instead of intercepts. A threshold is the same as an intercept but has the opposite sign. Thresholds are shown in Mplus output with a dollar sign.

Thresholds	Estimate
DEGREE$1	−0.405

To predict the probability $y = 1$, the analyst would first multiply the threshold by -1 [$(-0.405)(-1) = 0.405$] and then apply Equation 8.5.

Taking the log of the odds of success, as in Equation 8.4, provides a means of representing the additive effects of the set of predictors on the outcome. The level-1 structural model can then be expressed as a linear logit equation, where the log odds for the likelihood of individual i in school j being proficient in reading can be expressed in terms of the underlying variate (η_{ij}) as follows:

$$\eta_{ij} = \ln\left(\frac{\pi_{ij}}{1 - \pi_{ij}}\right) = \beta_{0j} + \beta_1 x_{1_{ij}} + \beta_2 x_{2_{ij}}, ..., \beta_p x_{pij}.\tag{8.6}$$

The intercept β_{0j} is the value of η_{ij} when the value of all independent variables is zero. Readers will note in Equation 8.6 that in the logit model the residual variance (e_{ij}) is not included in the level-1 model. This is because for a binomial distribution the residual variance is a function of the population proportion (π) and cannot be estimated separately (see Equation 8.2). Therefore, the residual term is typically fixed to a constant. The slope coefficient β_1 can be interpreted as the predicted change in the natural log of the odds that $y = 1$ (versus $y = 0$) for a one-unit increase in x_{1ij}. A key point to keep in mind is that equal intervals in logits are not equal in predicting the probability $y = 1$.

We often report the findings in terms of odds ratios, which is simply defined as the ratio of two odds (Azen & Walker, 2011). We can obtain the odds ratio from the logit coefficient by expressing it as e^β. In this case, if we raise the base of the natural log (e) to the power of the log odds coefficient $(2.71828^{0.405})$, we obtain 1.50, which, when there is only an intercept log odds, is also the original odds of the probability of the event occurring versus not occurring in Equation 8.3 $(0.6/0.4 = 1.50)$. Although the definition of the odds ratio is relatively simple, it can easily be confused with the simple odds of an event occurring versus not occurring (i.e., as defined in Equation 8.3). The odds ratio is typically expressed as the ratio of the odds of the event occurring versus not occurring for two groups, such as males and females, or for a one-unit increase in X. For example, if the odds of obtaining a degree is 0.80 for females and 0.40 for males, then the odds ratio for females versus males can be expressed as 2.0 $(0.80/0.40 = 2.0)$. This can be interpreted as the odds of obtaining a degree for females versus males are increased twofold.

Probit Link Function

The probit (or probability unit) model is another type of generalized linear model that extends the linear regression model by linking the range of real numbers to the 0–1 range of the probability $y = 1$. Whereas the logit link function for a dichotomous variable is based on the binomial version of the cumulative distribution function (CDF), which describes the distribution of the residuals, the probit link function is based on the normal CDF (i.e., which describes the normal distribution of residuals). The Greek capital letter phi (Φ) is used to represent the CDF of the normal distribution. For a binary outcome, the probability $y = 1$ in the population can be described as

$$P(y = 1) = \Phi(\eta), \tag{8.7}$$

where η is assumed to be underlying continuous variable (i.e., a z-score) with normally distributed residuals. For example, if $\eta = 0$ (i.e., a z-score of 0), then we can estimate the probability $y = 1$ as follows:

$$\Phi(\eta) = \Phi(0) = 0.50$$

because 50% of the normal distribution falls at or below a z-score of 0. Whereas the probability $y = 1$, given x, can be predicted as follows:

$$P(y = 1 \mid x) = \Phi(\beta_0 + \beta_1 x), \tag{8.8}$$

the function is nonlinear for values of x. This means that different levels of x will affect the probability $y = 1$ differentially; that is, a one-unit increase in x will change the probability $y = 1$ less at the boundaries of 0 or 1 than in the middle (0.5). Therefore, the probit link function makes use the inverse CDF $(\Phi)^{-1}$ to translate the predicted probability into a linear function:

$$\eta = \Phi^{-1}\left[P(y = 1 \mid x)\right] = \beta_0 + \beta_1 x. \tag{8.9}$$

This amounts to translating the predicted probability $y = 1$ into to a standard normal score (i.e., a z-score) of the underlying continuous predictor (referred to as η or as y^*). The predicted values of η range from $-\infty$ to $+\infty$. Therefore, while η can take on any real value, the predicted probability will be constrained to the boundaries of zero and one. For example, if the predicted probability $y = 1$ is 0.50, then this can be transformed into a z-score that corresponds to the population proportion in the cumulative normal distribution:

$$\Phi^{-1}(0.50) = 0.0,$$

where a z-score of 0.0 covers 50% of the normal distribution that is below 0 (or to the left of it on a normal curve).

Let's return to our previous example where the population proportion of students who receive a degree is 0.60. In this case, the estimated probit (or probability unit) score is

$$\Phi^{-1}(0.60) = 0.253.$$

If we consult a table of z-scores to find the area covered under the normal curve, we find for a z-score of 0.253, the area to the left under the normal curve is approximately 60% (0.5999). Conversely, if we see that if we multiple 0.252 by Φ, we would obtain the predicted probability $y = 1$.

$$0.60 = \Phi(0.253)$$

The level-1 linear model between the transformed outcome and one or more x predictors can then be defined as follows:

$$\eta_{ij} = \Phi^{-1}\left[P(y = 1 \mid x_{1ij}, x_{2ij}, \ldots, x_{qij})\right] = \beta_{0j} + \beta_1 x_{1ij}, \beta_1 x_{2ij} + \cdots + \beta_q x_{qij}. \tag{8.10}$$

A probit (probability unit) coefficient (β_q) describes a one-unit increase in a predictor (x_q) corresponding with a standard deviation increase in the probit score.

The logistic regression and probit regression models primarily differ in the scaling of the variance underlying the latent variable η in each link function. The standard logistic distribution has a variance of approximately 3.29, where in this case we are using $\pi \sim 3.14$ (Evans, Hastings, & Peacock, 2000). We note this within-group variance term can be used in estimating the proportion of variance in a dichotomous or ordinal outcome that lies between groups [i.e., referred to as the intraclass correlation (ICC)]:

$$ICC = \frac{\sigma^2_{Between}}{\sigma^2_{Between} + 3.29}. \qquad (8.11)$$

The probit variance at Level 1 is standardized at 1.0. The variance of the logistic distribution is therefore larger than the probit variance. This makes the standard deviation about 1.81 for the logistic distribution and 1.0 for the probit distribution, and this tends to make the regression coefficients and standard errors correspondingly larger in the logit model by about $1.6 - 1.8$ times (Hox, 2010). To illustrate, in our simple degree example (where $\pi = 0.6$), the resulting logit coefficient (0.405) is 1.6 times larger than the corresponding probit coefficient (0.253). For a probit model with no variables, an initial intraclass correlation (ICC) can therefore be estimated as follows:

$$ICC = \frac{\sigma^2_{Between}}{\sigma^2_{Between} + 1}. \qquad (8.12)$$

Ordinal Outcome

An ordinal outcome represents an ordered set of categories. The distribution is referred to as multinomial. The underlying assumption is that because the categories are ordered, the relationships between categories can be captured in one set of estimates. For example, a Likert scale implies the concept of "greater than" or "less than" but does not actually constitute continuous data. As we have noted previously, ordinal response patterns are often treated as if they were continuous, but there can be consequences resulting from assuming that such ordered categorical responses actually constitute continuous data (Olsson, 1979).

Because ordinal data are not continuous, using a linear modeling technique such as multiple regression can create bias in estimating the model's parameters, standard errors, and fit indices since the necessary assumptions may not be met when the observed data are discrete. The parameters may be underestimated and standard errors can be downwardly biased (Muthén & Kaplan, 1985; Muthén & Kaplan, 1992). The major issue to overcome with ordinal data is the calculation of a proper set of correlations for variables measured on ordinal scales, since the Pearson product-moment (r) correlation is not an optimal measure of association where there are only a few ordered categories. Currently, there are often better options for ordinal outcomes than assuming they are continuous.

For a logit link function, Mplus considers the cumulative (or proportional) odds model, where one considers the probability of the event of interest and all the events that precede it $[P(y \le c) = \pi_1 + \pi_2 + ...\pi_c]$. As a result, we only need to include the first $C - 1$ categories, since the cumulative probability must always be 1.0 for the set of all possible events. As with a binary outcome, what is predicted is not the observed values of the dependent variable but some transformation of it; that is, the ordered categories comprising the outcome are considered as comprising an underlying continuous predictor η_i. For the logistic link function, the odds of the cumulative probability are defined as the probability of being at or below the cth outcome category relative to being above the cth category, and the log odds for that ratio is as follows:

$$\eta_{ci} = \ln\left(\frac{P(\le c)}{P(y > c)}\right) = \ln\left(\frac{\pi_c}{1 - \pi_c}\right), \tag{8.13}$$

where $c = 1, \ldots, C - 1$.

For a response variable with three categories ($1 = $ left school early, $2 = $ still in school, $3 = $ graduated), for individual i the cumulative probabilities (which sum to 1) are then:

$$P(y_{1i} = 1) = P(c_i = 1) = \pi_{1i}$$
$$P(y_{2i} = 1) = P(c_i = 1) + P(c_i = 2) = \pi_{2i}$$
$$P(y_{3i} = 1) = P(c_i = 1) + P(c_i = 2) + P(c_i = 3) = 1. \tag{8.14}$$

As Equation 8.14 suggests, $P(y_3 = 1)$ is redundant, since once the probabilities of the first and second categories are estimated, the probability for the third category will follow by subtracting them from 1. The definition of the cumulative probability model allows us to compute the probabilities for a specific category as the difference between two adjacent probabilities.

It is important to keep in mind that in cumulative odds formulations, the probability of an event occurring is redefined in terms of cumulative probabilities; that is, ordinal regression models the odds of *cumulative counts*, not the odds of individual levels of the dependent variable. The key feature of the model is that it assumes a common slope between each set of odds modeled; that is, the effects of the predictors are specified to be constant across the categories of the outcomes (also referred to as a parallel regression model). The manner in which the outcome categories are coded determines the direction of the odds ratios as well as the signs of the β coefficients (Tabachnick & Fidell, 2007).

We note in passing that in many software programs, the last category is typically specified as the reference group. The model then represents the increase in log odds of falling into category c or *lower* (against being in the higher category) associated with a one-unit increase in x, while holding the other x variables constant. Therefore, a positive slope indicates a tendency for the response level to *decrease* as the level of x *decreases*. A negative slope indicates a tendency for the response level to *increase* as the level of x *decreases*. Because of the confusion that can result from the inverse relationship between the ordered outcome categories and the direction of the predictors in the linear model to predict η, Mplus simply multiplies the linear predictors $\beta_q x_q$ by -1 to restore the direction of the regression coefficients such that positive coefficients increase the likelihood of being in the highest category and negative coefficients decrease it (Hox, 2010).

For the level-1 structural model, for the log odds (logit), or log of the ratio of the two probabilities, each of these two events is a linear expression assuming proportional odds:

$$\eta_{cij} = \ln\left(\frac{\pi_{cij}}{1 - \pi_{cij}}\right) = \beta_{0j} + \sum_{q=1}^{Q} \beta_q X_{qij} + \sum_{c=2}^{C-1} \tau_c. \tag{8.15}$$

We note again that there is no separate residual variance term at Level 1. It is fixed to a constant (3.29) for model identification. Thresholds (τ_c), or cut points, at particular values of the latent continuous variable η_{cij} determine which categorical response is observed, with one less threshold than the number of ordered categories ($C - 1$) required to specify the predicted probabilities. The characteristic feature of the cumulative odds model is that the corresponding conditional probability curves expressed as functions of x are parallel and only differ due to the thresholds.

For three ordered categories, we have the following:

$$Y_i = \begin{cases} 0, \dots \dots if\, \eta_{ij} \leq \tau_1 \\ 1, \dots \dots if\, \tau_1 < \eta_{ij} \leq \tau_2 \\ 2, \dots \dots if\, \tau_2 < \eta_{ij} \end{cases}.$$

This suggests that if the value the continuous underlying predictor (η_{ij}) is less than the first threshold, we observe the lowest category of the outcome. If η_{ij} is greater than the first threshold, but less than or equal to the second threshold, we observe the second category. Finally, if η_{ij} is larger than the second threshold, then we observe the third category.

In the multilevel formulation, as in Equation 8.15, the lowest threshold becomes the intercept parameter (β_{0j}), which is allowed to vary across level-2 units (remembering that thresholds have opposite signs from intercepts). For model identification purposes, the other thresholds are fixed at the group level (so they do not have j subscripts in Equation 8.15). Otherwise, the assumption would be that there is no measurement equivalence between groups, since the thresholds would all be different for each ordered outcome category (Hox, 2010). The level-1 model is thus rewritten to accommodate an intercept, and the other thresholds are shifted. Thresholds are useful in determining predicted probabilities for the ordinal categories comprising the ordinal outcome (as they are fixed cut points), but they are not of substantive interest in interpreting the study's results, in that they are not influenced by the levels of the x predictors for individual cases in the sample.

We note that cumulative odds assumption underlying the model may not always hold empirically, so it is useful to check this assumption preliminarily. Mplus does not have a formal test of the validity of assuming an ordinal outcome model; however, the analyst can examine the distribution of the x predictors across ordered categories of y. For example, if x increases across the three categories of y, the proportional odds (or parallel regression) assumption would likely be met. If this assumption is generally met, then only one set of coefficients is needed. If the values of an interval predictor do not generally ascend or descend across the ordered categories, however, a different type of model (e.g., a multinomial logistic model for unordered categories) might provide a better fit to the data. As another preliminary examination, the analyst can also compare the predictor coefficients of the ordinal model with a reduced binary model. If the resulting coefficients in the two models generally have the same sign (see Table 8.3), then the parallel regression assumption likely holds. Various alternative formulations of ordinal outcomes are well known for single-level analyses, but they have currently not been widely implemented in multilevel software.

Ordered Probit Model

Alternatively, we can also define a probit model for ordered categorical outcomes. For an ordinal response variable y with C categories, the focus is on the probability that y falls in category c or *below* $P(y \leq c)$, where $c = 1, \ldots, C$. Once again, the inverse cumulative normal distribution function (Φ^{-1}) is used to transform the predicted probability $y = c$ into a z-score that represents its position on the cumulative normal distribution as follows:

$$\Phi^{-1}[P(y \leq c)] = \eta_{ij} \tag{8.16}$$

for $c = 1, \ldots, C - 1$, since the last category in the ordinal model is redundant. For example,

$$P(y \leq c) = 0.50$$

when $\eta_{ij} = 0$. For an outcome with three ordered categories we can describe the predicted probabilities in the same way as the previous logit regression model:

$$Y_i = \begin{cases} 0, ...if\, \eta_{ij} \leq \tau_1 \\ 1, ...if\, \tau_1 < \eta_{ij} \leq \tau_2 \\ 2, ...if\, \tau_2 < \eta_{ij} \end{cases}.$$

The level-1 structural model can be defined as

$$\eta_{cij} = \Phi^{-1}[\pi_{cij}] = \beta_{0j} + \sum_{q=1}^{Q} \beta_q X_{qij} + \sum_{c=2}^{C-1} \tau_c, \qquad (8.17)$$

where a set of thresholds (τ_c) specify the relationship between the underlying latent variable and the ordered categories of the outcome, with one less threshold than the number of categories of the outcome. The lowest threshold is the intercept β_{0j}, which varies randomly between groups at Level 2. As Equation 8.17 indicates, subsequent thresholds, beginning with the second threshold $(c = 2)$, are fixed at Level 2 for purposes of model identification. Since the underlying scale has a standard deviation of 1.0, the coefficient β_q has the interpretation that a unit increase in x_q corresponds to a change in the expected value of η_{cij} of β_q standard deviation units, controlling for other variables in the model. As in the logit proportional odds model, the slope effect β_q is same for predicting each ordered category of y_{ij}. As we noted previously, however, the effect on the predicted probability of the outcome depends on where one starts in terms of levels of x_q. The cumulative probit scale has a variance set to 1.0, so there is again no separate residual error term included in the model at Level 1. ML parameter estimates from cumulative logit models tend to be about 1.6 to 1.8 times larger than ML estimates from probit models.

Unordered Categorical (Nominal) Outcome

For nominal outcomes with C unordered categories $(c = 1, 2,. . .,C)$, the sampling distribution is referred to as multinomial, which represents an extension of the binomial distribution that assumes a set of counts in three or more categories (Agresti, 2007). In a multinomial distribution, the cumulative probabilities of each possible outcome $(\pi_1, \pi_2, . . . ,\pi_c)$ can be expressed such that their sum is 1.0. Unlike the proportional odds model (i.e., with one set of coefficients), for a nominal outcome a set of dummy variables is constructed such that $y_c = 1$ if $\pi = c$ and $y_c = 0$ otherwise. For a nominal variable with three categories, the predictors have different associations with the probabilities of individuals being in the three different categories of the response variable (y):

$$\text{Prob}(y_1 = 1) = \pi_1,$$
$$\text{Prob}(y_2 = 1) = \pi_2,$$
$$\text{Prob}(y_3 = 1) = \pi_3 = 1 - \pi_1 - \pi_2. \qquad (8.18)$$

Since $\pi_3 = 1 - \pi_1 - \pi_2$, the last category is redundant. In multinomial analyses, the last category typically becomes the reference category. Therefore, there are actually only $C - 1$ probabilities required to specify the nominal outcome. For example, in the case with three categories, then, there will be two probabilities required to specify the possible outcomes.

The most common link function for a multinomial outcome is a generalized logit link, where η_c is then the predicted log odds of being in category c ($c = 1,\ldots,C-1$) versus a reference category C (typically the last category):

$$\eta_c = \ln\left(\frac{\pi_c}{\pi_C}\right), \tag{8.19}$$

where $c = 1,\ldots,C-1$.

As we have noted, where the outcome is nominal, separate log odds coefficients are estimated for each response category of the dependent variable with the exception of the reference category, which is omitted from the analysis. In the case where y has three response categories, this amounts to equations for the probability that y is in category 1 versus category 3 (i.e., the reference group C), and the probability y is in category 2 versus category 3.

The level-1 structural model can then be defined to predict the odds of outcome c occurring relative to outcome C occurring for individual i in unit j as follows:

$$\eta_{cij} = \ln\left(\frac{\pi_{cij}}{\pi_{Cij}}\right) = \beta_{0(c)} + \sum_{q=1}^{Q}\beta_{q(c)}X_{qij} \tag{8.20}$$

for $c = 1,\ldots,C-1$ outcome categories. Beta coefficients $\beta_q(q = 1,2,\ldots,Q)$ can be interpreted as the increase in log odds of falling into category c versus category C resulting from a one-unit increase in the qth covariate, holding the other covariates constant. For three unordered categories, therefore, there will be two level-1 equations for η_{1ij} and η_{2ij} as follows:

$$\eta_1 = \beta_{0(1)} + \sum_{q=1}^{Q_1}\beta_{q(1)}X_q \text{ and}$$

$$\eta_2 = \beta_{0(2)} + \sum_{q=1}^{Q_2}\beta_{q(2)}X_q. \tag{8.21}$$

Mplus Latent Response Formulation

Mplus uses a latent linear model with a set of thresholds to incorporate categorical variables into the general modeling framework. The latent response formulation is similar to the probability curve formulation in the binary and ordinal cases but is based on the assumption that the observed categorical values result from an unobserved continuous latent response variable and a set of thresholds corresponding to cut points between observed categories (Curran, 2003; Flora & Curran, 2004; Grilli & Pratesi, 2004; Hedeker, 2007; Hox, 2002; Muthén, 1983; Muthén, 1998–2004). In the general Mplus modeling framework categorical dependent variables are referred to as u to distinguish them from continuous outcomes (y). The latent response distribution (u^*) for an observed dichotomous or ordered distribution for u is defined as

$$u = c, \text{if } \tau_c < u^* < \tau_{c+1}, \tag{8.22}$$

with thresholds (τ_c) defining the categories $c = 0, 1, 2, \ldots, C-1$, with $\tau_0 = -\infty$ and $\tau_C = \infty$. This suggests that the observed value of u changes when a threshold is exceeded on the latent response variable u^* (Muthén, 1998–2004). A threshold can be interpreted as the expected value of the latent variable at which an individual transitions from a value of 0 to 1 on the outcome when the continuous underlying latent variable's score is zero. For a binary variable, for example, the latent response formulation defines a threshold τ on u^* so that $u = 1$ when the threshold is exceeded, while if it is not exceeded $u = 0$. Although u^* focuses on changes in the values of the continuous underlying variable u^*, it can be used to derive changes in the probabilities of u.

Following Muthén and Muthén (2009), a linear regression equation is used to relate u^* to x,

$$u^* = \gamma x + \delta, \tag{8.23}$$

where γ is a slope and δ is a residual that is uncorrelated with x. An intercept is not needed because of the threshold τ. To identify the distribution of latent responses that yield the observed categorical outcome, as we have noted, it is necessary to fix the residual variance to some value, depending on the particular link function utilized. For the probit model, the residual is assumed to be normally distributed in the population $(0, V(\delta))$. Standardizing the variance $V(\delta)$ to equal 1.0 defines the model as a probit regression with intercept $(\beta_0) = -\tau$ and slope $(\beta_1) = \gamma$. Instead, if a logistic density is assumed for the residual δ $(0, \pi^2/3)$, the result will be the logistic distribution function $1/(1 + e^{-\delta})$. Hence, selecting a logit or probit link function will result in different parameters estimates but consistent substantive interpretation. Within groups, the coefficients are log odds for the logistic link function and probits (probability units) for the probit link function.

As a practical matter, the difference between the Mplus latent response formulation and other formulations is primarily in the between-groups portion of the model. Between groups, it is consistent with the continuous multilevel model to write the model for categorical outcomes in terms of unstandardized random effects, which are normally distributed in the population. Because the between-groups random effects are defined as latent continuous variables, the estimates in Mplus are linear regression coefficients as opposed to log odds coefficients reported in some other software. Changes in u^* due to predictors can be described by considering a standardized form of Equation 8.23 where the probability that $y = 1$ is standardized in terms of u^* and x [see McKelvey & Zavoina (1975) or Muthén (1998–2004) for further discussion]. This standardization is noted in Mplus output estimates as STDYX. If one chooses not to standardize the variance of a binary x predictor, the coefficient refers to a standard deviation change in u^* for a change in x from 0 to 1. Where standardized coefficients are requested on the Mplus OUTPUT statement (Output: standardized), an R^2 value for u^* can also be defined, but it is not quite the same as an R^2 for continuous variables because the residual variance is not a free parameter (Muthén, 1998–2004).[2]

As we noted earlier in this chapter, ML estimation with categorical outcomes in Mplus employs numerical integration (i.e., routines to approximate the solution of functions that cannot be found analytically) for computing the likelihood (because the link function within groups is nonlinear). There is a need to approximate the integrals using some approach (e.g., Monte Carlo, Laplace approximation). Mplus uses FIML estimation with numerical integration of the likelihood function with categorical data. As Hox (2010) notes, when FIML is used with numerical integration, the test procedures and goodness of fit indices based on the deviance are appropriate [i.e., provided the scaling factor is used that is part of the output with MLR estimation (Muthén & Muthén, 1998–2006)]. Estimation time and model convergence, however, can be problems with complex models. The *Mplus User's Guide* provides several options regarding methods of conducting the integration. The solutions are more challenging to approximate when there are larger samples and more random components in the model that may also result in convergence problems.

Explaining Student Persistence

In this first example, we compare estimates explaining student persistence produced with a dichotomous variable and similar ordinal outcome using logit and probit link functions. There are 12,900 students nested in 1,000 schools. In Table 8.1, Model 1 for the dichotomous and ordinal models is the null (no predictors) model. For Model 2, we can define a latent response variable (u^*) with single predictor (GPA) with groups as follows:

$$u^* = \beta_{0j} + \beta_1 GPA_{ij} + \varepsilon_{ij}, \tag{8.24}$$

and the between-groups equations can be defined as follows:

$$\beta_{0j} = \mu_0 + \zeta_0, \tag{8.25}$$

and, if x_{ij} is defined as randomly varying,

$$\beta_{1j} = \mu_1 + \zeta_1,$$ (8.26)

where μ and β are structural parameters, and ζ_{0j} and ζ_{1j} are between–group residual variances contained in Ψ_B. As noted previously, the residual variance within groups (ε_{ij}) is not estimated (because u^* is not observed) and is scaled slightly differently depending on the link function chosen (i.e., logit or probit). Hence, selecting logit or probit link function will result in different parameter estimates describing the probability $y = 1$ given x but consistent substantive interpretation.

Binary Outcome

In Table 8.1, we note that Model 1 is a null model (with no predictors). It is specified with a single BETWEEN statement (persist2;), since there is no within-group model (i.e., no intercept or variance). In Model 1, using a logit link (which is the default) and a probit link, we define a simple model with only a dichotomous outcome (graduated = 1, otherwise = 0). For Model 1, the logit threshold is estimated as -3.002 and the probit threshold is estimated as -1.661.

As we have noted previously, Mplus reports a threshold instead of an intercept. The two are the same except that they have opposite signs (so the intercept for the logit model would be 3.002). We can think of the threshold as representing the cut point on a latent response variable such that equal to or below -3.002, we would predict $y = 0$. If we take the negative of the threshold (3.002), we then can estimate probability of $y = 1$ as $1/(1 + e^{-(3.002)})$, which is equal to $1/1.050$, or 0.952. If we estimate the probability of falling at or below the threshold $[P(y = 0)]$, it will be $1/(1 + e^{-(-3.002)})$, or about 0.047 ($1/21.126 = 0.047$), with the slight difference due to rounding.

For the probit model we have a threshold of -1.661, which, if we take the negative of the threshold $[\Phi(1.661)]$, we also obtain the estimated probability $y = 1$ as 0.952. If we estimate the proportion falling at or below the threshold $[\Phi(-1.661)]$, we obtain 0.048 as the predicted probability $y = 0$.

If we wish to estimate the between-school variability (i.e., an ICC) for the logit model, it would be estimated as follows:

$$1.103/(1.103 + 3.29) = 1.103/4.393 = 0.251.$$

For the probit model, we would estimate the between-school variability as

$$0.284/(0.284 + 1) = 0.284/1.284 = 0.221.$$

TABLE 8.1 Mplus Outcomes for Dichotomous and Ordinal Persistence Model

	Model 1				Model 2			
	Logit	SE	Probit	SE	Logit	SE	Probit	SE
Dichotomous Model (PERSIST2)								
Within Level								
GPA					1.381	0.056	0.709	0.028
Between Level								
Thresholds								
PERSIST2$1	−3.002	0.068	−1.661	0.032	−3.307	0.071	−1.809	0.034
Variances								
PERSIST2	1.103	0.129	0.284	0.034	0.797	0.116	0.217	0.031
Ordinal Model (PERSIST3)								
Within Level								
GPA					1.499	0.053	0.780	0.027
Between Level								
Thresholds								
PERSIST3$1	−3.003	0.067	−1.671	0.032	0.623	0.119	0.229	0.064
PERSIST3$2	−2.663	0.062	−1.496	0.030	1.001	0.121	0.424	0.065
Variances								
PERSIST3	1.144	0.126	0.310	0.034	0.843	0.112	0.242	0.031

Model 2 Statements

For Model 2, we add student GPA. We provide the relevant VARIABLE, ANALYSIS, and Model statements for Model 2 with binary outcome next.

```
TITLE:      Model 2: Two-level binary persistence model (logit);
DATA:       FILE IS C:\mplus\ch8 ex1.dat;
            format is 4f8.0,2f8.2,3f8.0,5f8.2;
VARIABLE:   Names are schcode persist3 persist2 female
            ses gpa hiabsent public lowses teaqual
            panelwt hiabmean abteaq gpamean;
            usevariables are schcode persist2 gpa;
            CLUSTER IS schcode;
            categorical is persist2;
            within = gpa;
            between = ;
define:     center gpa(grand);
ANALYSIS:   TYPE = twolevel;
            Estimator is MLR;
            Link = logit;
```

Model:

%BETWEEN%

persist2;

%WITHIN%

persist2 on gpa;

OUTPUT: sampstat standardized Tech1;

For the logit model, the log odds coefficient is 1.381, and for the probit model, the probit coefficient is 0.709. The corresponding odds ratio for the logit model is e^β or 3.98 (not tabled). This suggests that for a one-unit increase in GPA (i.e., from the grand mean of 0), the odds of obtaining a degree will increase approximately fourfold (3.98 times). We can use the log odds to predict the probability of a student persisting for different levels of the predictor:

$$\pi = \frac{\exp(\beta_0 + \beta_1 x_1)}{1 + \exp(\beta_0 + \beta_1 x_1)}. \tag{8.27}$$

For example, if we want to know the probably of a student of average GPA receiving a degree, we need only the intercept log odds (β_0), since $\beta_1 x_1 = 0$ at the intercept (and any other variables in the model are also held constant at 0). In Table 8.1, for Model 2 the threshold is -3.307. Remembering that thresholds are the negative of intercepts in Mplus, we can estimate the probability $y = 1$ as follows

$$\pi = \frac{\exp[-(-3.307) + 0]}{1 + \exp[-(-3.307 + 0)} = \frac{27.303}{28.303} \approx 0.965 .$$

This suggests that the person on the grand mean for GPA has a predicted probability of graduating of about 96.5%. If an individual's GPA increases by one grade point from the grand mean (2.68), the predicted probability would be

$$\pi = \frac{\exp[-(-3.307) + 1.381]}{1[-(-3.307) + 1.381)} = \frac{108.635}{109.635} \approx 0.991 .$$

For the probit model, from Table 8.1 we can estimate the probability $y = 1$ for a person at the grand mean of GPA as

$$\pi = \Phi\left(-(\beta_0 + \beta_1 x_1)\right) . \tag{8.28}$$

In this case, for the individual at the grand mean for GPA, we would have the following:

$$\Phi\left(-(-1.809 + 0)\right) = \Phi\left(1.809\right) \approx 0.965.$$

For the individual who is one point above the grand mean in GPA, the probably of persisting would be as follows:

$$\Phi\left(-(-1.809 + 0.709 * 1)\right) = \Phi\left(2.518\right) \approx 0.994.$$

We note that while it is possible to interpret the probit coefficients as changes in z-scores, given x, it is typical to covert the z-scores to the corresponding probability $y = 1$. Because the probit function is based on the normal curve, an increase in the z-score does not affect the probability that $y = 1$ in a uniform way. If we consulted a table that translates z-scores into the corresponding area under the normal curve, we can see that at the mean (z-score $= 0$) a variable that increases the z-score one unit (from 0 to 1) would increase the probability of $y = 1$ from 0.5000 to 0.8413. In contrast, at a z-score of -2.0, a variable that the z-score by one unit (from -2 to -1) would increase the probably of $y = 1$ from 0.0228 to about 0.1587.

When we convert probit scores to the probability $y = 1$, given values of x, therefore, we must consider that a specific change in x cannot tell us the predicted change in the probability that $y = 1$, since the amount of change in the predicted probability depends on where we are beginning on the normal curve. In our example, we centered GPA on the sample mean of 2.68. If we had not, however, we would see that the predicted probability increase for a one-point increase in GPA will be different at different GPA levels. This presents the same problem for the logistic model as well; however, the coefficients are usually presented as odds ratios (which have a constant meaning for a one-unit change) rather than in terms of the probability $y = 1$.

Ordinal Outcome

In Table 8.1 for the ordinal model (Model 2), we can see that the impact of GPA is very similar to the binary model for the logistic model ($\gamma = 1.499, p < 0.01$) and the probit model ($0.780, p < 0.01$). We can also predict the probability for each ordered category of PERSIST3 (0 = dropped out, 1 = still in school, 2 = graduated) for levels of GPA. In this example, we did not center GPA on the sample mean, so the interpretation of the probit scores will be for change in GPA from 0 to 1.

Estimating Probabilities From Probit Coefficients

Following Muthén and Muthén (2009), for the probit coefficients, we can predict the probability for each ordered category as follows:

$$P(u = 0 \mid x) = \Phi(\tau1 - \gamma\, x),$$

$$P(u = 1 \mid x) = \Phi(\tau2 - \gamma\, x) - \Phi(\tau1 - \gamma\, x), \qquad\qquad (8.29)$$

$$P(u = 2 \mid x) = 1 - \Phi(\tau2 - \gamma\, x) = \Phi(-\tau2 + \gamma\, x).$$

In Table 8.1, for Model 2, the first threshold in the probit model is 0.229, and the second is 0.424. For the intercept (GPA $= 0$), the predicted intercept probability $y = 0$ (dropped out) will be 0.591:

$$\Phi(0.229 - 0) = 0.591.$$

The probability $y = 1$ (still in school) will be 0.073:

$$\Phi(0.424 - 0) - \Phi(0.229 - 0) = 0.664 - 0.591 = 0.073.$$

The probability $y = 2$ (persist) will then be 0.336:

$$1 - \Phi(0.424 - 0) = \Phi(-0.424 + 0) = 0.336.$$

For a one-point increase in GPA (i.e., from 0 to 1), for dropping out $[P(u = 0 \mid x)]$, the probability will estimated as

$$0.291\ [\Phi(0.229 - 0.780(\text{GPA})] = (\Phi)\text{--}0.\,551 = 0.291.$$

For being still in school $[P(u = 1 \mid x)]$, the estimated probability will be

$$\Phi[0.424 - 0.780(\text{GPA})] - \Phi[0.229 - 0.780(\text{GPA})]$$
$$= \Phi\ (-0.356) - \Phi(-0.551) = 0.070.$$

For graduating $[P(u = 2 \mid x)]$, the estimated probability is then

$$1 - \Phi(0.424 - 0.780) = \Phi(-0.424 + 0.780) = \Phi(0.356) = 0.639.$$

As a check, if we add these predicted probabilities, they should sum to 1.0 $(0.291 + 0.070 + 0.639 = 1.0)$.

Finally, we note, that for a one-point increase from GPA $= 1$ (D average) to GPA $= 2$, the probabilities will shift considerably in a probit model. For dropping out $[P(u = 0 \mid x)]$, the estimated probability is

$$\Phi(0.229 - 0.780(2) = (\Phi)\text{--}1.\,331 = 0.092.$$

For being still in school $[P(u = 1 \,|\, x)]$, the estimated probability is

$$\Phi[0.424 - 0.780(2)] - \Phi[0.229 - 0.780(2)] = \Phi\,(-1.136) - \Phi(-1.331) = 0.036.$$

For graduating $[P(u = 2 \,|\, x)]$, the estimated probability is

$$1 - \Phi(0.424 - 0.780(2) = \Phi[-0.424 + 0.780(2)] = \Phi(1.136) = 0.872.$$

As we noted, this illustrates that a point increase in GPA will have differing effects on the predicted probabilities in a probit model, depending on where we start on the x scale.

Estimating Probabilities From Logit Coefficients

We can also use the estimated log odds to predict the probabilities for the cumulative odds model in Table 8.1. For Model 2, the first threshold is 0.623 and the second threshold is 1.001. The coefficient for GPA is 1.499. For a one–unit increase in GPA, the log odds of the falling in the highest category of persist versus the combined middle and lower categories would be expected to increase by 1.499. The probability $y = 2$ can be expressed as

$$P(y = 2 \,|\, x) = \frac{1}{1 + e^{-(\tau_2 + \beta x)}}, \tag{8.30}$$

where we need to use the negative of the Mplus threshold.

$$\frac{1}{1 + e^{-(-1.001 + 1.499)}} = \frac{1}{1.608} = 0.622$$

The probably of being in category 1 or 2, given x, will then be the following:

$$P(y = 1 \text{ or } 2 \,|\, x) = \frac{1}{1 + e^{-(t_1 + \beta x)}}, \tag{8.31}$$

where we again use the negative of the Mplus threshold:

$$\frac{1}{1 + e^{-(-0.623 + 1.499)}} = \frac{1}{1.416} = 0.706 \,.$$

By subtraction, then, the predicted probability of students who are still in school would be 0.084 ($0.706 - 0.622 = 0.084$). The predicted probability of individuals who drop out early would then be 0.294 ($1 - 0.706 = 0.294$).

Adding Level-1 and Level-2 Predictors

We can add a set of level-1 and level-2 predictors to the preliminary models. Within groups, we could add a set of demographic indicators such as gender (coded male $= 0$, female $= 1$) and socioeconomic status (a composite with mean $= 0$, $SD = 1$). We also have a measure of students' grade point averages, and attendance (high absenteeism coded 1, else $= 0$). Between groups, we have school type (public $= 1$, private $= 0$), school SES (coded 50% or more on free/reduced lunch $= 1$, else 0), and mean teacher quality (defined as a factor score of students' perceptions of their teachers with mean $= 0$ and $SD = 1$).

Model Statements

The model statements for these types of models are provided below, using Model 1 as the template (i.e., with *persist2* as the dichotomous outcome). We will grand-mean center the predictors. The second model can be run using *persist3* (an ordinal variable) as the outcome.

```
TITLE:       Two-level binary persistence model with predictors (M1);
DATA:        FILE IS C:\mplus\ch8 ex1.dat;
             Format is 4f8.0,2f8.2,3f8.0,5f8.2;
VARIABLE:    Names are schcode persist3 persist2 female
             ses gpa hiabsent public lowses teaqual
             panelwt hiabmean abteaq gpamean;
             Usevariables schcode persist2 female ses gpa hiabsent
             public lowses teaqual;
             CLUSTER IS schcode;
             categorical is persist2;
             within = female ses gpa hiabsent;
             between = public lowses teaqual;
define:      center female ses gpa hiabsent public lowses
             teaqual (grandmean);
ANALYSIS:    TYPE = twolevel;
             Estimator is MLR;
Model:
             %BETWEEN%
             persist2 on public lowses teaqual;
             %WITHIN%
             persist2 on female ses gpa hiabsent;
OUTPUT:      sampstat tech1 tech8;
```

The output is summarized in Table 8.2. Within groups, for Model 1 (concerning the dichotomous *persist2* outcome), the results suggests that SES ($\beta = 0.929$, $p < 0.01$), GPA ($\beta = 1.131, p < 0.01$), and high absences (log odds $= -1.767$, $p < 0.01$) were all significant predictors of students' likelihood to persist. SES and GPA were positively associated with finishing high school. We can interpret this as for a one-unit increase in SES and GPA, the expected log odds increase by 0.929 and by 1.131, respectively, for the higher category of persist2. In terms of odds ratios, a one-point increase in GPA results in increasing the odds of persisting by about 3.1 times, holding other variables in the model constant. For students, a one-standard deviation $(1 - SD)$ increase in SES would increase the odds of persisting by a factor of approximately 2.53 (OR $= 2.533, p < 0.01$). We can obtain the percentage increase in odds by subtracting 1 from the odds ratio and multiplying by 100 $[(e^\beta - 1) \times 100]$. So in this case the percent increase over the mean for student SES (0) for a $1 - SD$ increase in student SES would be approximately 1.53×100 or a 153% increase in the odds of persisting.

Odds ratios less than 1.0 decrease the odds of higher levels of persistence. For example, for high absences (high absence), the odds ratio is 0.171. This means a one-unit increase in absenteeism (i.e., from low/average to high) decreases the odds of persisting by a factor of 0.171 (i.e., a bit less than 4/5). The percentage change in odds of persisting would decline by about 83% $[(0.17 - 1.0) = -0.83 \times 100]$. To

TABLE 8.2 Estimates for Dichotomous and Ordinal Persistence Outcome

	Model 1 (dichotomous)			Model 2 (ordinal)		
	Estimates	S.E.	Odds Ratio	Estimates	S.E.	Odds Ratio
Within Level Model to Explain Persistence						
Female	−0.011	0.082	0.989	0.171**	0.073	1.186
SES	0.929***	0.065	2.533	0.868***	0.058	2.383
GPA	1.131***	0.061	3.099	1.255***	0.056	3.509
High Absence	−1.767***	0.130	0.171	−1.741***	0.125	0.175
Between Level Model to Explain Persistence						
Public	−2.339***	0.474		−1.190***	0.301	
Low SES	−0.346***	0.128		−0.414***	0.137	
Teacher Quality	0.205*	0.108		0.128	0.098	
Residual Variances						
Persist2	0.443***	0.096				
Persist3				0.511***	0.092	
Thresholds						
Persist2$1	−3.808***	0.096				
Persist3$1				−3.722***	0.076	
Persist3$2				−3.316***	0.071	

Notes: *$p < 0.10$, **$p < 0.05$, ***$p < 0.01$

interpret odds ratios for values less than 1.0, it is sometimes easier to use the reciprocal value. More specifically, an odds ratio of 0.171 for graduating is equivalent
to an odds ratio of 5.85 (or 1.0/0.171) for dropping out. To compute the percentage change, we can first subtract 1 from the reciprocal of the odds ratio and then
multiply by 100 $\{[(1/e^{\beta}) - 1] \times 100\}$. Thus, the percentage change in the odds
ratio for dropping out (5.85) is 485% [calculated as $(1/0.171) - 1 = 5.85 - 1 =
4.85 \times 100 = 485\%$].

Between groups, students in public high schools are less likely to persist compared with their peers in private schools ($\beta = -2.339, p < 0.01$). Students in
schools with larger percentages of students in free/reduced lunch programs are
less likely to persist ($\beta = -0.346, p < 0.01$) than students in schools with lower
percentages of students on free/reduced lunch programs. There is also some initial
evidence that average teacher quality is related to student persistence ($\beta = 0.205,
p < 0.10$). Keep in mind that between groups, the coefficients are unstandardized
regression coefficients.

Overall, the ordinal results for Model 2 are consistent with the results for the
binary persistence outcome (i.e., persist = 1, else = 0). Within groups, the only
difference is that *female* is significant in the second model ($\beta = 0.171, p < 0.05$)
but not in the first model. This suggests that females are more likely to persist,
or still be in school, compared with their male peers. Between groups, average
teacher quality is unrelated to persistence ($\beta = 0.128, p > 0.10$). The probit results
are very similar, so we do not report them here.

Our ordinal formulation of processes leading to persistence allows us to capture
the impact of the independent variables on the outcome with one set of parameter estimates (i.e., as opposed to one set less than the number of categories). The
consistency in the direction of the predictors for the binary and ordinal persistence
outcomes suggest the parallel regression assumption likely holds for the ordinal
model. Procedures for specifying ordinal models are very similar to multinomial
models. The models could also be evaluated with multinomial regression. It is
important to note, however, that multinomial logistic regression requires the use
of two sets of coefficients, which can result in less efficiency due to many more
parameters being estimated (and, hence, the possible inflation of Type I errors).
It also results in a loss of information because the ordering of the categories is
ignored [i.e., each category is only compared to the reference category and not to
adjacent categories (1 to 0 and 2 to 0, but not 2 to 1)].

Ordinal regression works well when its assumptions are met (e.g., the means
of the predictors vary from low to high across the categories of the dependent
variable in a consistent manner). For example, in this case, student SES levels
increase from dropouts (−0.68) to students still in school (−0.51) to graduates
(0.02). Student GPA similarly increases across categories (2.03, 2.07, 2.70), while
the percentage of students with high absenteeism decreases across the same categories (i.e., 0.22, 0.15, 0.06). If this is not the case, then multinomial logistic
regression will be a preferable choice.

Examining a Cross-Level Interaction

What might happen if we consider a **cross-level interaction** in the model? When the focus of the analysis is on cross-level interactions, group-mean centering is often preferred, as it results in a mean that is unadjusted for within-group predictors (Hofmann & Gavin, 1998). In this example, we will group-mean center the level-1 predictors. This allows researchers to focus on individuals' relational positions within units and how other variables might moderate those positions. In this example, we will use the ordinal persistence outcome (*persist3*) again. In examining outcomes like students' likelihood to persist versus fall behind peers or drop out, the consequences of within-school relationships regarding persistence are likely to be moderated (i.e., enhanced or diminished) by school contexts, structures, and processes. For example, we might hypothesize that students who are absent many times early in their high school years will be more likely to drop out early. If this is the case, we should anticipate school settings where the impact of this behavior has greater or lesser consequences for student persistence.

To test this proposition, we will propose there will be a stronger negative relationship between high absenteeism and likelihood to graduate in situations where the overall quality of teaching is rated as lower. In contrast, we propose that there will be weaker consequences in schools where the overall teaching quality is rated higher. We can test by designating the slope within schools to be randomly varying in the model statement (S | persist3 on hiabsent;). In the between-group intercept model, we will also include the group-level mean for high absenteeism (*hiabmean*) and create an interaction term for high absenteeism and teacher quality (*hiateaq*) between schools. As Hofmann and Gavin (1998) suggest, this type of group-mean formulation will allow us to detect the difference between the presence of a cross-level interaction (i.e., teacher quality moderating the slope of high absenteeism on students' likelihood to persist) and the presence of a between-group interaction (i.e., *mean absenteeism × mean teacher quality*).

It is important to note that where an interaction is included at the group or individual level, the two direct effects from which the interaction is produced should also be included in the model, even if they are not significant (Hox, 2010). The metric of the predictors is important to consider, so that the interaction can be interpreted more easily. In this case, because teacher quality is standardized and high absenteeism is the mean percentage of students who have high absenteeism (and both are grand-mean centered since they are between-school variables), we can interpret the interaction as the change in effect of mean absenteeism on persistence when teacher quality changes by one standard deviation.

Within groups, we have defined a few demographic indicators (*female*, SES) and academic orientation (GPA), in addition to the randomly varying slope of high absenteeism *hiabsent*) on persistence. Within schools, we might also wish to include an interaction term. For example, we will propose that females' likelihood to persist is contingent on their SES levels (*female × SES*). As this type of model specification suggests, investigating within-level and cross-level (moderating) interactions within a multilevel model can greatly expand understanding of the data by encouraging the testing of more refined hypotheses about how individual and group processes mutually affect outcomes.

Model Statements

The Mplus model statements for this model are next presented. We will create two needed interactons using "define" statements:

femses = female * ses;
hiateaq = hiabmean * teaqual;

and for Model 1 we will add *femses* at the end of the Usevariables list in the VARIABLE model statements. We do not need to add *hiateaq* to the Usevariables list yet, since for Model 1, between groups we will only examine the effect of teacher quality on the random intercept and slope. We will add *hiateaq* when we specify Model 2.

TITLE:	Two-level ordinal persistence model with predictors (M1);
DATA:	FILE IS C:\mplus\ch8 ex1.dat;
	Format is 4f8.0,2f8.2,3f8.0,5f8.2;
VARIABLE:	Names are schcode persist3 persist2 female ses gpa hiabsent
	public lowses teaqual hiabmean abteaq gpamean;
	Usevariables schcode persist3 female ses gpa hiabsent
	teaqual femses;
	CLUSTER IS schcode;
	categorical is persist3;
	within = female ses gpa hiabsent femses;
	between = teaqual;
define:	femses = female*ses;
	hiateaq = hiabmean*teaqual;
	center female ses gpa hiabsent femses (groupmean);
	center teaqual (grandmean);
ANALYSIS:	TYPE = twolevel random;
	Estimator is MLR;
Model:	
	%BETWEEN%
	S persist3 on teaqual;
	%WITHIN%
	persist3 on female ses femses gpa;
	S | persist3 on hiabsent;
OUTPUT:	Sampstat tech1 tech8;

For Model 2, we need only add the more complete set of predictors in the Between portion of the model as follows:

Between = teaqual gpamean hiabmean hiateaq;

We then change the %Between% part of the model as follows:

S persist3 on teaqual gpamean hiabmean hiateaq;

We compare the estimates for two models in Table 8.3. Model 1 includes the effect of teacher quality only on the level-2 intercept and random slope (i.e., high absenteeism-persistence). As shown in Table 8.3, teacher quality is positively related to persistence ($\beta = 0.909, p < 0.01$). We also note that the mean absenteeism-persistence slope is statistically significant between schools ($\beta = -1.791\ p < 0.01$). Notice in the table that the mean slope is referred to in the between-groups portion of the model, since it is conceived as an underlying (latent) continuous variable. Teacher quality, however, is not significantly related to the high absence-persistence slope ($\beta = 0.418, p > 0.10$) in Model 1.

In the second model, after we reentered the between-group mean for high absences into the model as a compositional effect (Hofmann & Gavin, 1998), the size relationship between teacher quality and the slope increases ($\beta = 0.916$, $p < 0.10$). This suggests that in schools where teacher quality is higher on average, the negative relationship between individuals' high absenteeism and persistence is diminished. The second model is also useful in detecting whether there might be a significant between-group interaction between mean teacher quality and mean absenteeism (*hiateaq*). The unobserved presence of this type of relationship could confuse our ability to detect a significant cross-level inter-action (Hofmann & Gavin, 1998). In this case, however, the model-2 results indicate that the interaction is not significant in either the intercept model or the slope model.

The pattern of findings in Model 2 therefore provides some preliminary evidence (at $p < 0.10$) supporting the initial proposition that higher perceived teacher quality reduces the negative relationship between high student absenteeism and persistence. Formulating the model in this way allows the analyst to detect the presence of either interaction and therefore provides a more complete test of the proposed relationships than Model 1, which specified the between-groups model incorrectly. In doing so, it obscured the potential cross-level relationship between teacher quality and the level-1 slope and also overestimated the average coefficient of the random slope.

TABLE 8.3 Mplus Outcomes for Ordinal Persistence Model

	Model 1			Model 2		
	Estimates	*SE*	*Odds Ratio*	*Estimates*	*SE*	*Odds Ratio*
Within Level						
PERSIST3 ON						
FEMALE	0.157	0.082	1.171	0.164*	0.084	1.179
SES	0.798***	0.079	2.222	0.806***	0.079	2.239
FEMSES	0.015	0.103	1.015	0.023	0.105	1.023
GPA	1.309***	0.065	3.702	1.305***	0.065	3.688
Between Level						
PERSIST3 ON						
TEAQUAL	0.909***	0.122		0.424***	0.113	
HIABMEAN				−2.000***	0.452	
GPAMEAN				1.881***	0.147	
HIATEAQ				−0.038	0.542	
Slope ON						
TEAQUAL	0.418	0.367		0.916*	0.524	
HIABMEAN				−1.534	1.020	
GPAMEAN				0.796	0.487	
HIATEAQ				−1.979	1.372	
Mean Slope	−1.791***	0.178		−1.306***	0.241	
Thresholds						
PERSIST3$1	−3.705***	0.083		−3.713***	0.078	
PERSIST3$2	−3.285***	0.077		−3.294***	0.072	
Residual Variances						
PERSIST3	1.504***	0.170		0.939***	0.125	
Slope	2.595***	0.771		2.157***	0.657	

* $p < 0.10$, **$p < 0.05$, ***$p < 0.01$

Count Data

Count outcomes represent situations where the values of Y are nonnegative integers $(0, 1, 2, . . ., N)$. Data values that are less than 0, or missing, will not be used in the analysis. If one has data that are bunched near zero, we can specify a model for counts. For count outcomes in Mplus, Poisson and negative binomial regression models can be used. When the counts represent relatively rare events, a Poisson distribution is often used. The Poisson distribution can be thought of as an approximation to the binomial distribution for rare events where the probability of π is very small and the number of observations (N) is relatively large. Counts in such distributions are likely to be positively skewed, since they may have many zeros and considerably more low values than high values. The period of time for which the counts are observed must be specified to occur within a fixed interval (or exposure), with the events occurring at a constant rate (Hox, 2010).

To illustrate the analysis of count data, we will develop an example to investigate variables that explain how many courses students fail during their ninth-grade year in high school. In this example, there are 9,956 individuals nested in 44 high schools. A considerable number of students might not fail any courses during this period. In our example, we will assume y is the number of courses individual i in school j fails during ninth-grade year, such that the time interval $n = 1$. The exposure, however, does not have to be time related. We refer to y as having a Poisson distribution with exposure n and event rate λ:

$$y \mid \lambda \sim P(n, \lambda) . \tag{8.32}$$

The expected number of events for an individual then is the following:

$$E(y \mid \lambda) = n\lambda . \tag{8.33}$$

The variance is then the mean of the $n\lambda$ parameter:

$$\mathrm{Var}(y \mid \lambda) = n\lambda . \tag{8.34}$$

Because the exposure is the same for every individual in a Poisson distribution (i.e., the number of courses failed during a 1-year period for each person in each group), n is fixed to 1. The expected value of y then is just the event rate λ. The Poisson distribution therefore has only one parameter—the event rate λ. This suggests that as the expected value of y increases, so does the expected variability of the event occurring. Due to the presence of zeros, often the variance is greater than the mean, however, which is referred to as **overdispersion**.

The link function for the Poisson distribution is the log link $[(\eta = \log_e(\mu)]$. We can represent this at Level 1 as follows:

$$\eta = \ln(\lambda) . \tag{8.35}$$

Since the log of $\lambda = 1$ is 0, when the event rate is less than 1, the log will be negative, and when the event rate is greater than 1, the log will be positive. Using its inverse link function, the predicted log rate can be converted to the expected mean event rate as follows:

$$\lambda = e^{\eta}. \tag{8.36}$$

In our course failure example, the mean failure event rate for the student sample is 0.60 (not tabled). If we estimate a simple single-level model to determine the event rate, the estimated natural log of the expected count of failing a course during freshman year is -0.508. If we then exponentiate the logged count ($e^{-0.508}$), we obtain the expected event count ($\lambda = 0.60$). Once we know the expected incident, or event, rate (λ), we can determine the probability of failing a given number of courses in the population. We substitute the expected rate into the following equation to obtain the predicted probability of a count of c events:

$$P(Y = c) = \frac{e^{-\lambda}\lambda^c}{c!}. \tag{8.37}$$

In this case, the probability of not failing a course ($c = 0$) can be calculated as

$$P(Y = c) = \frac{e^{-(0.6)}0.6^0}{0!} = \frac{0.549(1)}{1} = 0.549.$$

Using the above formula, the probability of failing one course will be 0.330 and two courses will be 0.099.

One assumption of the Poisson model is that the mean and variance of the outcome are approximately equal. As we noted, when the conditional variance exceeds the conditional mean (which frequently occurs in practice), overdispersion can result in the tendency for standard errors to be underestimated. This, in turn, can lead to more significant findings than would be expected, since significance tests are based on the ratio of the parameter estimate to its standard error. An alternative is the negative binomial model, which adds an unobserved heterogeneity estimate (ε_i) for each of the outcomes (Hilbe, 2011; Long, 1997). Where the dispersion parameter is zero, the two models are the same. A second important assumption of the Poisson distribution is that the events are independent and have a constant mean rate (Hox, 2010). In our course failure example, therefore, we would have to assume that failing a math class is independent from failing an English or social studies class. If there is some tendency for events not to be independent for subjects, the data may not follow the theoretical distribution very closely.

It is also possible to estimate zero-inflated Poisson and negative binomial models. Zero-inflated models refer to the tendency to have more zero counts in the data set than expected by the Poisson sampling distribution. This type of model assumes that some of the zeros are part of the event count and are assumed to follow a Poisson or negative binomial distribution (Hox, 2010). Other zeros are part of the event taking place or not—that is, a binary process modeled by a binomial process. In this case, this portion of the model is related to structural zeros, indicating that the event never takes place. An example might be a portion of the population that never exhibits a particular behavior being studied, like texting while driving. The other portion of the population sometimes exhibits this behavior but does not over the length of time their behavior is studied. With a zero-inflated Poisson model, two regressions are estimated. The first is the Poisson regression of the count part. The second describes the logistic regression of the binary latent inflation variable, which predicts the probability of being unable to assume any value except zero.

Building a Level-1 and Level-2 Model

In the Mplus formulation, the level-1 and level-2 structural model that produces an underlying latent response variable u^* is the same as in Equations 8.24–8.26. We will use four individual-level predictors. Student socioeconomic status (SES) is coded 0 = average or high SES and 1 = low SES. For gender, male is coded 1 and female is coded 0. We use a standardized state math test to describe students' achievement during grade 8. Age is the number of years old the student was at the time she or he started ninth grade.

The general model can be described at Level 1 as follows:

$$\eta_{ij} = \ln(\lambda) = \beta_{0j} + \beta_1 SES_{ij} + \beta_2 male_{ij} + \beta_3 math_{ij} + \beta_4 age_{ij} + \varepsilon_{ij}, \tag{8.38}$$

where η_{ij} (or u^* in Mplus terminology) is the log of the event rate λ_i. We note that in a Poisson distribution the level-1 error term is fixed (because u^* is not observed) and scaled slightly differently depending on the link function chosen. For demonstration purposes, at Level 2, we will add two predictors (teachers' average experience in years and the proportion of teachers at the school who are fully licensed). We could, of course, add a more complete set of context and process variables:

$$\beta_{0j} = \alpha_0 + \beta_5 avetexp_j + \beta_6 licper_j + \zeta_{0j}, \tag{8.39}$$

where α_0 and β are structural parameters and ζ_{0j} is the residual variance at Level 2, which is contained in Ψ_B. We will treat the level-1 predictors as fixed at level 2.

Model Statements

We first developed a model with only within-group predictors. The second model adds the between-group predictors. We next present the model statements for Model 2.

TITLE:	Model 2: Two-level course failure model with predictors;
DATA:	FILE IS C:\mplus\ch8ex1c.dat;
	Format is 5f8.0,3f8.2;

```
VARIABLE:    Names are schcode lowses male math fail
             avetexp licper age;
             Usevariables schcode fail male lowses math
             age avetexp licper;
             within = male lowses math age;
             between = licper avetexp;
             CLUSTER IS schcode;
             count is fail;
define:      center math age licper avetexp(grandmean);
ANALYSIS:    TYPE = twolevel;
             Estimator is MLR;
Model:
             %BETWEEN%
             fail on avetexp licper;
             fail;
             %WITHIN%
             fail on male lowses math age;
OUTPUT:      SAMPSTAT STANDARDIZED TECH1 TECH8;
```

Level-1 and Level-2 Model Output

We present the results for two models in Table 8.4. We first estimated a null model in order to obtain the logged event rate at the school level (not tabled), which was −0.701 (not tabled). This implies that the event rate at the school level is 0.496 ($e^{-0.701} = 0.496$). For demonstration purposes, the first model in Table 8.4 considers only the level-1 predictors. The second model then adds the level-2 predictors.

For Model 1, the results suggest that adjusted logged event rate is −1.070. The intercept is the expected logged event rate when all the predictors are 0. Given the coding of the variables, this would be the expected failure rate for a female of high/average SES, who is at the grand mean for math achievement and age. The expected event rate for this individual would be 0.343 ($e^{-1.070}$). We could calculate this individual's probability of failing one course ($c = 1$) as follows:

$$P(Y = c) = \frac{e^{-(0.343)}0.343^1}{1!} = \frac{(0.710)(0.343)}{1} = 0.244$$

When there are a number of variables in a model, our primary focus is on the predictors. The first model suggests all the level-1 predictors are significantly related to students' probability of failing a course. The ratio of the difference in expected event rates between low SES and average/high SES students can be expressed as 1.346, which can be calculated from the log of the event rate in the table for low SES ($e^{0.297} = 1.346$).

TABLE 8.4 Variables Explaining Course Failure (Poisson Distribution)

	Model 1			Model 2		
	Estimates	S.E.	Rate Ratio	Estimates	S.E.	Rate Ratio
Within Level						
Model to Explain						
Course Failure						
Male	0.165***	0.032	1.179	0.165***	0.032	1.179
Low SES	0.297***	0.057	1.346	0.297***	0.057	1.346
Math	−0.007***	0.000	0.993	−0.007***	0.000	0.993
Age	0.197***	0.045	1.218	0.197***	0.045	1.218
Between Level						
Model to Explain						
Course Failure						
Teacher Exp				0.086*	0.029	
License Prop				−1.152	1.106	
Mean						
Fail	−1.070***	0.098		−1.032***	0.088	
Residual Variance						
Fail	0.236***	0.070		0.207***	0.055	
Model Fit						
AIC	21048.597			21046.478		
Parameters	6			8		

Notes: $*p < 0.10$, $**p < 0.05$, $***p < 0.01$

In Model 2, we can see the level-2 mean logged event rate is slightly different (−1.032), after adjusting for average teacher experience and the proportion of teachers that are fully credentialed. Only the level-1 estimate for age is slightly different from Model 1. At the school level, we can see some evidence that schools with higher average teacher experience are settings where students are more likely to fail courses (0.086, $p < 0.10$). Keep in mind that at the unit level, the outcomes are continuous latent variables. At the school level, the unstandardized coefficients can be interpreted as a unit change in the predictor (i.e., 1 year of increased staff experience) produces a 0.086 increase in the underlying latent response variable. We also note that the proportion of fully licensed teachers was unrelated course failures ($p > 0.10$).

Negative Binomial Results

We note that if we suspect the variance is larger than expected in the Poisson model, we can add an overdispersion parameter by switching to a negative binomial (NB) model. We can change to negative binomial by adding NB in parentheses after the specifying the outcome as count.

---

count is fail (nb);

We note in passing that sometimes for a particular model to converge, it may be necessary to use starting values from a recent set of estimates (e.g., from the Poisson model) in order for obtaining model convergence. These can be added with asterisks (e.g., avetexp*0.08) if needed.

When we estimated this model, we obtain an overdispersion estimate of 1.442 in the output ($p < 0.01$) for Model 1 (see Table 8.5). The negative binomial model appears to fit the data better than the Poisson regression model. For example, the AIC is considerably lower (19,487.818 with nine parameters estimated) compared

TABLE 8.5 Variables Explaining Course Failure (Negative Binomial Distribution)

	Model 1		Model 2	
	Estimates	S.E.	Estimates	S.E.
Within Level				
Model to Explain				
Course Failure				
Male	0.200***	0.036	0.200***	0.032
Low SES	0.337***	0.058		
Math	−0.009***	0.001	−0.009***	0.001
Age	0.229***	0.052	0.228***	0.051
Dispersion				
Fail	1.442***	0.149	1.425***	0.152
Between Level				
Model to Explain				
Course Failure				
Teacher Exp	0.086***	0.031	0.092***	0.034
License Prop	−1.147	1.142	−1.112	1.240
Intercept/Means				
Fail	−1.087***	0.090	−1.098***	0.091
S			0.343***	0.057
Variances				
S			0.044	0.029
Residual Variance				
Fail	0.211***	0.057	0.217***	0.055
Model Fit				
AIC	19487.818		19481.566	
Parameters	9		10	

Notes: *$p < 0.10$, **$p < 0.05$, ***$p < 0.01$

to the final Poisson model in Table 8.4 (AIC = 21,046.478, with eight parameters estimated). As we have suggested, adding the dispersion parameter can improve the model's fit and provide more accurate estimates of the standard errors. In this case, the standard errors for Model 1 in Table 8.5 are a bit larger than those for similar parameters in Model 2 of Table 8.4. Making this adjustment can therefore result in more accurate hypothesis tests when overdispersion is present. So in this case we might accept the NB link function as providing a slightly better way of representing the course failure data.

Finally, we might also investigate a random slope (e.g., fail on lowSES;). We illustrate the necessary changes in the model statements. Since we will define a random slope within groups (S | fail on lowses;), we also have to change the Analysis statement (Type = Twolevel random). This will increase the length of time the model takes to estimate compared to the first model, due to the addition of another random effect. We altered the %Between% model as follows:

```
%BETWEEN%
fail on avetexp licper;
S;
%WITHIN%
fail on male math age;
S | fail on lowses;
```

The results for Model 2 in Table 8.5 suggest most of the parameters are very similar to Model 1 with the fixed *lowSES-fail* slope. Since the variance parameter for the random slope is not significant $(0.044, p > 0.10)$, it suggests that we may wish to keep this parameter fixed.

We will end our presentation of categorical observed outcomes here. We hope we have succeeded in illustrating some possible multilevel models with observed categorical outcomes and their interpretation. As we noted previously, one of the primary challenges is getting used to reporting results in the diverse metrics used to summarize the effects of a set of predictors on the different types of categorical outcomes.

Multilevel CFA With Ordinal Observed Indicators

Many instances of where we wish to use observed indicators to define latent constructs involve items that have been measured on binary or ordinal scales. There are a number of potential problems to consider in measuring underlying constructs with ordinal items. When statistical methods that are designed to measure continuous constructs are applied to ordinal data, there is a potential for a mismatch between the assumptions underlying the statistical model and the empirical characteristics of the data (Flora & Curran, 2004). Common is the situation where individuals are bunched at the top or the bottom of an ordinal scale (e.g., a five-point, Likert-type scale). This potential measurement bias can call into question the validity of a particular proposed factor model. Although with ordinal data from five-point scales, acceptable solutions can be generated where the data do not depart too much from normality (Boomsma, 1987; Rigdon, 1998), there are other options for dealing with binary or ordinal indicators of latent factors.

The major problem that must be overcome is the calculation of a covariance matrix for the observed indicators measured on binary or ordinal scales. Using Pearson Product Moment correlations would be inefficient, since the individual items are not measured on interval or ratio scales. Hence, the calculation of the correlations would have to take into consideration the binary or ordinal nature of the items used to define the latent factors. Because the indicators are not interval, a set of probabilities must be modeled. Although the observed variables may be categorical, the latent factors are assumed to be continuous. Models where the latent variables themselves are conceived of as being categorical [or are defined by a binary or ordered class indicator (designated as u in the *Mplus User's Guide*)] may be defined as *mixture* models using Mplus (see Chapter 9).

For single-level CFA models, Flora and Curran (2004) found ordinal data to be robust to moderate levels of nonnormality in the latent response variables. Bias in correlation estimates contributes to modest overestimation of CFA model parameters but has little effect on chi-square test statistics or standard errors of parameters. Grilli and Rampichini (2007) provided a recent illustration of the multilevel CFA for ordinal variables, addressing issues in defining, estimating, and interpreting models.

The categorical option in the Mplus model statements can be used to specify the binary or ordered categorical indicators. The program will determine how many categories there are for each indicator. For factor indicators that are binary or ordered categories, maximum likelihood with robust standard errors and a chi-square test statistic is adjusted for nonnormality and non-independence of observations is the default (referred to as MLR). MLF estimation, which produces standard errors approximated by first-order derivatives and a conventional chi-square statistic, is also available for categorical indicators (Muthén & Muthén, 1998–2012) but may not perform as well in some situations as MLR. As we have noted previously, with categorical data, ML estimation requires a numerical integration algorithm. As Muthén and Muthén (1998–2012) indicate, the likelihood function is minimized with numerical integration carried out with or without adaptive quadrature in combination with rectangular integration, Gauss-Hermite integration, or Monte Carlo integration. It is important to keep in mind that numerical integration can become increasingly complex as the number of factors and sample size increase. Thus, it can take considerable computer time to arrive at a solution.

Weighted least squares (WLS) estimation provides another option for estimating two-level models with binary and ordered categorical outcomes, which does not require numerical integration, provided there are no random slopes. For models with random slopes, in addition to the ML estimators, Bayesian estimation is also available. For two-level models with censored, unordered categorical, or count dependent variables, only ML, MLR, and MLF are available for two-level models with or without random slopes. For three-level models, there are currently fewer estimation options (readers can examine the users' manual for further information).

Developing a CFA Model

In this example, 650 employees in 105 organizations rated their managers' leadership in 36 areas. We will concentrate on a subset of the data—six items that we propose define two latent leadership factors within and between groups. The goal of the multilevel analysis is to summarize the within- and between-group variation in this CFA model and establish whether the same individual-level model holds at the organizational level. It is likely that there may be differences in the quality of measurement of items defining the factors that result from the multilevel nature of the data. For example, we may reasonably expect that employees within each organization differ to some extent in their assessments of a manager's performance with respect to these two leadership dimensions. The within-groups model addresses the portion of variance in the factors that result from variation among individuals. Similarly, we can expect that there are also differences in managers' leadership performance across the organizations (i.e., between-organization variance).

The proposed multilevel factor model is presented in Figure 8.3. Within groups, the two latent leadership factors (i.e., which we will call decision-making style and evaluation procedures) are enclosed in ovals. Each factor is defined by arrows leading to the three observed indicators (enclosed in rectangles) and their corresponding unique factors (i.e., with short arrows representing measurement error). Within groups, the decision-making factor consists of three observed indicators indicating extent to which the manager involves employees in shared decision making (*Shdec*), encourages the involvement of clients in policymaking (*Invcli*), and uses a team approach for decision making internally (*Team*). The evaluation factor consists of the extent to which the manager evaluates programs and procedures that are implemented (*Evprog*), uses and systematic assessment procedures (*Sysas*), and develops evaluation standards for assessing employee performance (*Evstan*). The dots at the ends of the arrows from the latent variables to the observed categorical indicators within groups indicate that the intercepts vary across groups. The analyst may also decide whether the factors are specified to covary. In some cases, we might specify the strength of the relationships for certain parameters (e.g., loadings, factor variances, and covariances) ahead of time and test whether these proposed estimates fit the actual data. We note that within-groups, because the items are defined as ordered categories, there are no error terms.

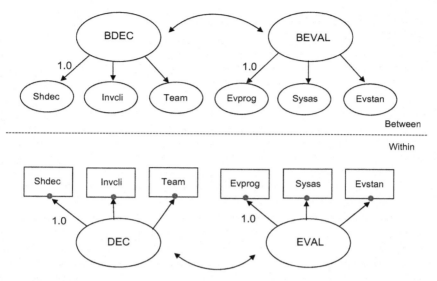

FIGURE 8.3 Proposed multilevel factor model with ordinal indicators using MLR estimation.

The between-groups model addresses across-group variation rather than across-individual variation. Hence, we hypothesize that the same two-factor model holds across organizations, but that there may be likely differences in the measurement quality of the items used to define the two leadership factors. In the between-groups portion of the model, observed indicators are shown as ovals because they are latent variables. Because the residuals of the latent variable indicators are fixed to 0.0 between groups, there are no arrows in the figure indicating the presence of residuals associated with the observed variables that define the factors. Because the measurement level of the indicators is ordinal (five-point scales) and the group sizes are unbalanced, we will use MLR to analyze the data and designate the factor indicators as categorical.

In Table 8.6, we provide the univariate distributions for the items used to define the two latent factors. The data generally show that the scores are likely to be negatively skewed (i.e., more responses in categories 4 and 5). Skewness ranged from −0.90 to −0.44, and kurtosis ranges from −0.43 to 0.14. We would therefore expect some bias in calculating correlations if we used Pearson Product Moment correlations as input for the analysis. For comparative purposes, in Table 8.7 we provide Pearson Product Moment correlations and correlations based on a latent response model (in parentheses). The latent response formulation represents more of a mathematical convenience that is of little practical importance when latent response variables are slightly or moderately nonnormal (Flora & Curran, 2004). Still, it is likely that skewness and kurtosis of observed ordinal variables can make a

TABLE 8.6 Univariate Distributions of Ordinal Indicators of Latent Factors Across Categories*

Variable	1	2	3	4	5
Shdec	2.8	8.2	17.1	34.6	37.4
Incli	1.1	2.6	13.2	40.5	42.6
Syass	1.2	9.5	20.0	32.6	36.6
Evprog	1.4	6.3	30.0	40.4	22.3
Team	4.8	12.6	24.8	37.1	20.8
Evstan	4.8	9.4	21.4	32.3	32.2
TOTAL	2.7	8.1	21.1	36.3	32.0

*Row totals do not add to 100% due to rounding.

TABLE 8.7 Pearson Product Correlations and Latent Response Correlations (in Parentheses)

Variable	1	2	3	4	5	6
1. Shdec	1.00					
	(1.00)					
2. Incli	.452	1.00				
	(.521)	(1.00)				
3. Syass	.506	.422	1.00			
	(.557)	(.501)	(1.00)			
4. Evprog	.457	.407	.639	1.00		
	(.516)	(.483)	(.717)	(1.00)		
5. Team	.495	.417	.440	.495	1.00	
	(.549)	(.474)	(.495)	(.543)	(1.00)	
6. Evstan	.454	.367	.604	.605	.555	1.00
	(.449)	(.421)	(.668)	(.674)	(.599)	(1.00)

difference (even when they are within normal limits), which has some observable effect on the estimation of the correlations in Table 8.7.

For a two-level CFA model, the total covariance matrix can be decomposed into its between- and within-organization covariance matrices and restrictions placed on each matrix to test the proposed model against the data. We will propose that the first three items define a type of decision-making factor (*dec*) and the last three items define an evaluation factor (*eval*).[3] In some cases, we might propose that a somewhat different factor model exists within and between groups. For example, we might hypothesize that one general leadership factor is sufficient to account for the variation in leadership between organizations. As suggested previously, confirming these hypothesized relationships helps establish a model's construct validity. Of course, there are many additional possibilities to consider when multi-level factor models are conceptualized and tested. We could, for example, consider a situation where one latent factor has a within-groups and a between-groups portion, while another factor may only exist within groups or between groups.

Model Statements

We next provide the Mplus model statements. In this example, the six factor indicators are defined as categorical variables rather than continuous variables. The Categorical option is used to specify which dependent variables are treated as binary or ordered categorical (ordinal) variables in the model. In this example all six factor indicators are ordinal since they are all measured on five-point scales. The program can determine the number of categories for each binary or ordinal indicator. The default estimator for this type of analysis is maximum likelihood with robust standard errors using a numerical integration algorithm. Weighted least squares estimation provides an alternative means of estimating the model's parameters, which does not require numerical integration (Muthén & Muthén, 1998–2012).

Each within-group factor is measured by three observed variables. Once again, this is specified using the BY statement, which is short for "measured by." By default, Mplus fixes the first observed indicator specified for each factor at 1.0, which provides a reference item to define a metric for each latent factor. We chose to constrain each pair of within- and between-group item loadings to be equal across levels to provide a common metric between levels. This is specified by placing the same number in parentheses after the parameters that are fixed to be equal [e.g., Involcl (1), Team (2), Evprog (3), Evstan (4)]. The first item pair is automatically fixed at 1.0 within and between groups to provide a metric for defining each factor. This allows the factor variance within and between groups to be defined with the same metric. This type of specification is not required, however, for multilevel latent variable models. Keep in mind, however, that if the residuals are fixed between groups, a full decomposition of variance across levels will not be possible (Grilli & Rampichini, 2007). If this type of analysis is desired, the between-group residuals should be estimated (e.g., using WLS estimation).

```
Title:       Multilevel CFA for two constructs with ordinal items;
Data:        File is C:\mplus\ch7CFA.dat;
             Format is 7f8.0;
Variable:    Names are orgcode shdec incli team sysas evprog evstan;
             Usevariables are orgcode shdec-evstan;
             categorical are shdec-evstan;
             cluster is orgcode;
```

```
Analysis:    Type = general twolevel;
             Estimator is MLR;
             link = logit;
             algorithm = integration;
             integration = montecarlo;
Model:       %Between%
             bdec by shdec
             incli(1)
             team(2);
             beval by evprog
             sysas(3)
             evstan(4);
             %Within%
             dec by shdec
             incli(1)
             team (2);
             eval by evprog
             sysas(3)
             evstan(4);
Output:      standardized tech1 tech8;
```

Users can look at the TECH1 output to determine how the model is specified. Within groups, the six items loading on the two factors are specified in the
Λ_W matrix. Thresholds (τ) and errors are fixed parameters within groups. Factor variances and covariances are defined in Ψ_B (i.e., with two factor variances
Ψ_{11} and Ψ_{22} and covariance Ψ_{21} estimated). Readers should keep in mind that for
categorical outcomes within-group residual variances are not estimated (because
the continuous latent response variable defined by each ordinal indicator is unobserved), so the usual formula for calculating intraclass correlations for observed
indicators of factors (i.e., between-group variance divided by within variance plus
between variance) does not apply. As Grilli and Rampichini (2007) note, it is possible to fit a series of univariate ordinal probit variance component models, one for
each item, as a preliminary analysis. If β_{0c} is fixed to zero and $Var(\varepsilon_{ic}) = 1$ for each
item (which assumes an error normal distribution as implied in a probit link), the
estimable parameters are the thresholds and the between-groups residual variance
(as in Equation 8.12), from which an ICC can be obtained [$Var(\delta_{0c})/Var(\delta_{0c}) + 1$].
This can provide some indication of whether a multilevel analysis would be
needed (i.e., these ICC coefficients ranged from about 0.12 to 0.31).

In the between-groups portion of the model, each leadership factor is similarly
defined by three observed items. The items defining the factors are continuous
latent response indicators, which we noted are shown as ovals between groups
in Figure 8.3 because they are latent variables that vary randomly across groups.

Items defining the two latent factors are contained in the Λ_B matrix with loadings on each factor specified to be the same as the within-groups portion of the model. Factor variances and covariances are contained in Ψ_B. Factor variances within and between groups may be directly compared if a common metric has been established within and between groups (Muthén & Muthén, 1998–2012). A vector of thresholds (τ) is estimated, with four thresholds for each item (since the items are measured on five-point scales). Between groups, the residual variances of the random intercepts are fixed at zero by default. These are fixed because the residual variances are generally very small and because two-level models with categorical indicators require numerical integration when MLR is used. Each residual contributes one integration dimension and lengthens the time it takes the model to run (Muthén & Muthén, 1998–2012). This can become a computational burden with complex factor structures between groups.

The algorithm option is used to indicate the optimization method used to obtain the ML estimates. There are a number of integration options (see the *Mplus User's Guide* for further discussion). Monte Carlo uses randomly generated integration points with a default of 500 total integration points (Muthén & Muthén, 1998–2012). This can substantially reduce the amount of time it takes to generate a solution to the model by reducing the required numerical integration. If TECH8 is requested as an output statement, the optimization history is printed to the screen during the computations, which helps determine how long the analysis takes.

Model Output

The output information is similar to a CFA with continuous outcomes except that a summary of the proportions of individuals in each category of the categorical indicators is provided and threshold information is produced for each ordinal variable. For any ordinal variable with C levels, Mplus will output $C - 1$ thresholds. For example, in this case since the indicators are measured on five-point Likert scales, there are four threshold values. If standardized estimates are requested (OUTPUT = standardized), the output will include standardized parameter estimates and squared multiple correlations of the observed variables on the factors.

In Table 8.8, for comparative purposes, we provide the relevant parameter estimates from both a logit (the default) and probit link function. Within groups, the observed indicators using either approach can be seen to load substantively on the factors (with standardized loadings ranging from 0.59 to 0.83). Between groups, the standardized loadings are all 1.0 (since there are no residuals). This prevents a complete decomposition of the variance across levels, but this is generally not the primary interest in estimating multilevel factor models. The interpretation of the factor structures is unaffected (Grilli & Rampichini, 2007). In this particular CFA model, the correlation between the latent factors is somewhat stronger within groups than between groups.

TABLE 8.8 Mplus Logit and Probit Coefficients for Two-Level CFA With Ordinal Items

	Logit Link			Probit Link		
	Estimates	S.E.	StdYX	Estimates	S.E.	StdYX
Within Level						
DEC BY						
SHDEC	1.000	0.000	0.723	1.000	0.000	0.736
INCLI	0.698*	0.096	0.590	0.687*	0.103	0.599
TEAM	0.899*	0.115	0.685	0.892*	0.136	0.696
EVAL BY						
EVPROG	1.000	0.000	0.819	1.000	0.000	0.825
SYSAS	0.923*	0.100	0.797	0.924*	0.093	0.803
EVSTAN	0.829*	0.086	0.764	0.825*	0.082	0.769
EVAL WITH						
DEC	4.471*	0.803	0.909	1.454*	0.259	0.916
Variances						
DEC	3.603*	0.707	1.000	1.183*	0.261	1.000
EVAL	6.717*	1.369	1.000	2.128*	0.433	1.000
Between Level						
BDEC BY						
SHDEC	1.000	0.000	1.000	1.000	0.000	1.000
INCLI	0.698*	0.096	1.000	0.687*	0.103	1.000
TEAM	0.899*	0.115	1.000	0.892*	0.136	1.000
BEVAL BY						
EVPROG	1.000	0.000	1.000	1.000	0.000	1.000
SYSAS	0.923*	0.100	1.000	0.924*	0.093	1.000
EVSTAN	0.829*	0.086	1.000	0.825*	0.082	1.000
BEVAL WITH						
BDEC	1.125*	0.464	0.784	0.315*	0.159	0.717
Variances						
BDEC	1.575*	0.653	1.000	0.537*	0.270	1.000
BEVAL	1.309	0.778	1.000	0.360	0.232	1.000

Note: * $p < 0.05$

In Table 8.9, we provide an alternative specification using WLS estimation. When WLSMV is specified, a robust weighted least squares estimator using a diagonal weight matrix with standard errors and mean- and variance-adjusted chi-square test statistic that uses a full weight matrix will be used to estimate the model (Muthén & Muthén, 1998–2012). This estimator is useful in improving computational speed with many dimensions of integration and categorical indicators. It also provides a way to estimate the between-group residuals in

TABLE 8.9 Two-Level CFA Model Using WLSMV Estimation

	Estimates	S.E.	StdYX
Within Level			
DEC BY			
SHDEC	1.000	0.000	0.736
INCLI	0.767*	0.080	0.641
TEAM	0.963*	0.095	0.724
EVAL BY			
EVPROG	1.000	0.000	0.802
SYSAS	0.990*	0.123	0.799
EVSTAN	0.878*	0.089	0.762
EVAL WITH			
DEC	1.282*	0.159	0.878
Variances			
DEC	1.185*	0.190	1.000
EVAL	1.799*	0.300	1.000
Between Level			
BDEC BY			
SHDEC	1.000	0.000	0.621
INCLI	0.767*	0.080	0.714
TEAM	0.963*	0.095	1.000
BEVAL BY			
EVPROG	1.000	0.000	1.000
SYSAS	0.990*	0.124	0.958
EVSTAN	0.878*	0.095	0.888
BEVAL WITH			
BDEC	0.440*	0.131	0.871
Variances			
BDEC	0.345*	0.111	1.000
BEVAL	0.740*	0.217	1.000
Residual Variances			
SHDEC	0.550*	0.209	0.614
INCLI	0.195	0.111	0.490
TEAM	0.000	0.000	0.000
SYSAS	0.064	0.135	0.081
EVPROG	0.000	0.000	0.000
EVSTAN	0.154	0.147	0.212

Note: * $p < 0.05$

the two-level CFA model with categorical observed indicators. In estimating the final model summarized in Table 8.9, we needed to fix two between-group errors to 0 (as they were slightly negative). We can see the estimates in Tables 8.8 and 8.9 are similar using either estimation approach. For example, one can confirm this by examining the standardized estimates in each table. The WLSMV approach also provides a full range of fit indices (e.g., RMSEA = 0.039, CFI = 0.988).

Overall, we can conclude that our proposed two-factor leadership model fits the data reasonably well (e.g., substantial standardized loadings), both at the individual and group levels. The support of the proposed model tends to enhance its construct validity; that is, the items define the factors fairly well, and the two factors are related to each other in a manner that we might expect (i.e., a moderate to strong positive correlation). In most instances, we would probably use more items to ensure that we have defined the factors adequately from a theoretical standpoint. The multilevel CFA, therefore, has given us valuable information about the psychometric properties of the measures as well as the validity of our proposed model. Of course, unanswered from this part of the analysis is what individual and organizational variables might account for this variation in perceptions about leadership.

The basic multilevel CFA model with either ordinal indicators or continuous indicators can be extended to include models where there are covariates (e.g., see Kaplan, 2009) and random slopes indicating the regression of a latent factor on a covariate. Variation in the latent slopes and the between-groups portion of the latent factors can be explained as a function of between-groups covariates.

Summary

In this chapter we provided an introduction to specifying and testing multilevel models for observed categorical outcomes. We also developed a multilevel factor model with ordinal observed indicators used to define latent variables. Mplus provides considerable flexibility in specifying a wide variety of measurement and structural models with both categorical and continuous indicators. In the next chapter, we look more closely at mixture models, where categorical latent variables can be used to define emergent subgroups within a population.

Notes

1. The base (e) for the natural logarithm is approximately 2.71828.
2. $R^2 (y^*) = \gamma^2 V (x)/(\gamma^2 V (x) + c)$, where $c = 1$ for probit and $\pi^2/3$ for logit (McKelvey & Zavoina, 1975).
3. The respective matrices are specified as follows:

$$\Sigma_W = \Lambda_W \Psi_W \Lambda_W' + \Theta_W \tag{A8.1}$$

$$\Sigma_B = \Lambda_B \Psi_B \Lambda_B' + \Theta_B . \tag{A8.2}$$

Model restrictions can then be placed on the respective covariance matrices in terms of specifying which items define which factors, whether or not the factors are correlated, as well as how the errors may be defined. We can define the within-groups factor model as

$$y_{ij} = \Lambda_W \eta_{W_{ij}} + \varepsilon_{W_{ij}},\tag{A8.3}$$

with the factor loadings on the latent variables defined as follows:

$$\Lambda_W = \begin{bmatrix} 1 & 0 \\ \lambda_{21} & 0 \\ \lambda_{31} & 0 \\ 0 & \lambda_{42} \\ 0 & 1 \\ 0 & \lambda_{62} \end{bmatrix},\tag{A8.4}$$

and residuals are typically defined in on the diagonals in Θ_w. We note that one item defining each factor is fixed at 1.0 to provide a metric for the factor. Mplus automatically sets the first item to 1.0 as the default (i.e., *shdec*). For the second factor, we set item 5 (*evprog*) to 1.0 by defining it as the first item measuring the latent factor in the model statement (*eval by evprog*). Factor variances and covariances are contained in Ψ_w. Covariances between residuals can be defined as off-diagonal elements in Θ_w. For models with categorical indicators, the residuals are not defined within groups. The between-groups measurement model can be defined as

$$\nu_j^* = \nu_B + \Lambda_B \eta_{B_j} + \varepsilon_{B_j},\tag{A8.5}$$

with factor loadings defined in Λ_B (as in A8.4), factor variances and covariances defined in Ψ_B and residuals for observed items in Θ_B. For models with categorical indicators, residuals are often fixed to 0.0 to reduce the required numerical integration demands.

References

Agresti, A. (2007). *An introduction to categorical data analysis.* Hoboken, NJ: John Wiley & Sons, Inc.

Azen, R., & Walker, C. M. (2011). *Categorical data analysis for the behavioral and social sciences.* New York: Routledge.

Boomsma, A. (1987). The robustness of maximum likelihood estimation in structural equation models. In P. Cuttance & R. Ecobe (Eds.), *Structural modeling by example* (pp. 160–188). Cambridge: Cambridge University Press.

Curran, P. J. (2003). Have multilevel models been structural equation models all along? *Multivariate Behavioral Research, 38*, 529–569.

Evans, M., Hastings, N., & Peacock, B. (2000). *Statistical distributions.* New York: Wiley.

Flora, D. B. & Curran, P. J (2004). An empirical evaluation of alternative methods of estimation for confirmatory factor analysis with ordinal data. *Psychological Methods, 9*(4), 466–491.

Grilli, L. & Pratesi, M. (2004). Weighted estimation in multilevel ordinal and binary models in the presence of informative sampling designs. *Survey Methodology, 30*(1), 93–103.

Grilli, L. & Rampichini, C. (2007). Multilevel factor models for ordinal variables. *Structural Equation Modeling: A Multidisciplinary Journal, 41*(1), 1–25.

Hedeker, D. (2007). Multilevel models for ordinal and nominal variables. In J. de Leeuw & E. Meijer (Eds.), *Handbook of multilevel analysis* (pp. 241–276). New York: Springer.

Hilbe, J. M. (2011). *Negative binomial regression* (2nd ed.). New York: Cambridge University Press.

Hofmann, D., & Gavin, M. (1998). Centering decisions in hierarchical models. Theoretical and methodological decisions for organizational science. *Journal of Management, 24,* 623–644.

Hox, J. (2002). *Multilevel analysis: Techniques and applications.* Mahwah, NJ: Lawrence Erlbaum.

Hox, J. J. (2010). *Multilevel analysis: Techniques and applications* (2nd ed.). New York: Routledge.

Long, J. S. (1997). *Regression models for categorical and limited dependent variables.* Newbury Park, CA: Sage.

McCullagh, P. & Nelder, J. A. (1989). *Generalized linear models* (2nd ed.). London: Chapman & Hall.

McKelvey, R., & Zavoina, W. (1975). A statistical model for the analysis of ordinal level dependent variables. *Journal of Mathematical Sociology, 4,* 103–120.

Muthén, B. O. (1983). Latent variable structural equation modeling with categorical data. *Journal of Econometrics, 22,* 43–65.

Muthén, B. O. (1998–2004). *Mplus technical indices.* Los Angeles, CA: Muthén & Muthén.

Muthén, B. O. & Kaplan, D. (1985). A comparison of some methodologies for the factor-analysis of non-normal Likert variables. *British Journal of Mathematical and Statistical Psychology, 38,* 171–180.

Muthén, B. O. & Kaplan, D. (1992). A comparison of some methodologies for the factor-analysis of non-normal Likert variables: A note on the size of the model. *British Journal of Mathematical and Statistical Psychology, 45,* 19–30.

Muthén, B. O. & Muthén, L. (1998–2006). *Mplus user's guide.* Los Angeles, CA: Authors.

Muthén, L. K. & Muthén, B. O. (1998–2012). *Mplus user's guide* (7th ed.). Los Angeles, CA: Authors.

Muthén, L. & Muthén, B. (2009). *Regression analysis, exploratory factor analysis, confirmatory factor analysis, and structural equation modeling for categorical, censored, and count outcomes. Mplus Short Courses (Topic 2).* Los Angeles: Authors.

Olsson, U. (1979). On the robustness of factor analysis against crude classification of the observations. *Multivariate Behavioral Research, 14,* 485–500.

Rigdon, E. (1998). Structural equation models. In G. A. Marcoulides (Ed.), *Modern methods for business research* (pp. 251–294). Mahwah, NJ: Lawrence Erlbaum Associates.

Schall, R. (1991). Estimation in generalized linear models with random effects. *Biometrika, 78,* 719–727.

Tabachnick, B. G. & Fidell, L. S. (2007). *Using multivariate statistics* (5th ed). Boston, MA: Allyn & Bacon.

Wolfinger, R. W. (1993). Laplace's approximation for nonlinear mixed models. *Biometrka, 80,* 791–805.

9

MULTILEVEL MIXTURE MODELS

Chapter Objectives

In this chapter, we present an overview of latent mixture modeling. Mixture models are a special type of quantitative model in which latent variables can be used to represent mixtures of subpopulations or classes where population membership is not known but, rather, is inferred from the data. Mixture modeling is used to assign individuals to their most likely latent class and to obtain parameter estimates that explain differences between the classes identified. Mixtures can be identified among individuals within organizational units as well as among organizational units. The approach can be applied to both cross-sectional and longitudinal models and can enrich our understanding of heterogeneity among both individuals and groups. In this chapter, we provide several examples where mixture models might be applied to typical multilevel models. We then illustrate how choices of analytic method can impact the optimal investigation of the data. This overview provides some basics for further development of these issues and models.

Introduction

Latent categorical mixture modeling is an emerging methodology for cross-sectional, multilevel, and longitudinal data structures with a number of related techniques that use latent classes including **latent class analysis**, latent profile analysis, latent class growth analysis, latent transition analysis, mixture regression analysis, and growth mixture modeling (Muthén, 2001, 2008; Muthén & Muthén, 1998–2012). These new approaches recognize that there can be inconsistencies in the results obtained from cross-sectional, longitudinal, and multilevel analyses that incorrectly assume population homogeneity when, in fact, heterogeneity may be present among individuals or groups sampled from a population (Marcoulides &

Heck, 2013). Mixture models generally refer to quantitative models with a categorical latent variable that represents mixtures of subpopulations where population membership is not known but, rather, is inferred from the data (Muthén, 2001). Some types of mixture modeling treat possible within-class variation as fixed (i.e., the same model is presented within each class but outcome means may differ across classes), while other types support examining variation among individuals within each identified latent class. The purpose of this type of analysis is to estimate the number and size of the latent classes in the mixture, estimate the response probabilities for each indicator given the latent class, and assign membership in the latent classes to individuals in the population (Duncan et al., 2006). Although the general mixture model can be extended to include continuous latent variables used to classify individuals, in this chapter we will focus only on analyses involving categorical latent variables [for additional details, see Muthén (2002)].

In the Mplus latent variable framework, mixture models can be combined with various other types of quantitative models we have presented including multilevel regression models, factor models, structural models with continuous latent variables, and latent growth curve models. The *Mplus User's Guide* provides numerous examples of the wide variety of types of single-level and multilevel mixture models that can be investigated with Mplus (Muthén & Muthén, 1998–2012). In this chapter we provide several introductory examples. Readers should keep in mind that the common thread running through the latent class modeling techniques is that the underlying classes explain variability in the observed dependent variables (y) and that the overall approach provides a means of classifying individuals according to their latent class membership (Marcoulides & Heck, 2013).

Defining Latent Classes

The general latent variable mixture modeling framework has two basic parts (Muthén, 1998–2004). The first part focuses on measurement, articulating the relationship between the set of observed dependent variables and one or more categorical latent variables, commonly labeled simply as (c). As a simple example, consider individuals distributed on an outcome variable, an example being job satisfaction. We would expect them to be distributed from relatively low job satisfaction to relatively high job satisfaction. Within this larger population of individuals measured on job satisfaction, there may be two latent classes ($c = 0$ and $c = 1$), each with a separate mean. As summarized in Figure 9.1, we can refer to this heterogeneity as a latent categorical variable that is responsible for the observed heterogeneity in y. The relationship can be extended to include multiple y variables, which are considered as multiple indicators of c. This type of analysis is referred to as latent profile analysis (LPA) for continuous outcomes and latent class analysis (LCA) for categorical outcomes (Muthén, 2001). For mixture analysis, the measurement model is a multivariate regression model that describes the relationships between a set of observed dependent variables and one or more categorical latent variables.

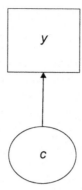

FIGURE 9.1 Representing a mixture.

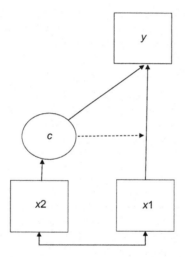

FIGURE 9.2 Proposed mixture model with structural relationships.

The second part is the set of structural relationships between categorical latent variables, observed variables, and between latent categorical (c) variables and observed variables that are not latent class indicators (Muthén & Muthén, 1998–2012). The specific form of the structural equations depends on the measurement properties of the variables. In Figure 9.2, we illustrate a simple regression mixture model. Besides the arrow from c to y, which indicates that the intercept of y varies across classes of c, the dotted line from c to the regression of y on x_1 indicates that the slope coefficient is hypothesized to differ across the latent classes. The arrow from x_2 to c defines a multinomial logistic regression of c on x_2, which implies that x_2 explains differences in the probability of latent class membership.

For some basic types of mixture models, such as LPA and LCA, the proposed structural model is defined to be the same for each class; however, the means for continuous y outcomes, or the probabilities for binary outcomes, are assumed to be different across classes. At their most basic level, LPA and LCA operate much in the same way as any structural equation model (e.g., a CFA model) whereby a latent variable is measured via a number of manifest or indicator variables. Often it is assumed that the manifest variables correspond to the distributional characteristics of a single sample or that group membership can be readily defined based on an observable variable. An example is where the sample consists of explicitly identifiable groups such as males and females or experimental and control groups (Marcoulides & Heck, 2013). Other times, however, group membership may not be known beforehand. In this latter situation, the groups are commonly called latent classes (i.e., membership is not observable but latent).

In order to conduct a mixture analysis of one or more y outcomes, an explicit model that divides the sample into various mutually exclusive latent classes must be posited. Following Muthén (2001), the general model relates the categorical latent variable c to a vector of x covariates by multinomial logistic regression. The latent categorical variable is defined as consisting of K classes, $c_i = (c_{i1}, c_{i2}, \ldots, c_{iK})'$, where $c_{ik} = 1$ if individual i belongs to Class k and $c_{ik} = 0$ otherwise. The multinomial regression of c on the x covariates uses a $K - 1$ dimensional parameter vector of logit intercepts (defined as a_c) and the $(K - 1) \times q$ parameter matrix of logit slopes Γc, where for $k = 1, 2, \ldots, K$

$$P(c_{ik} = 1 \mid x_i) = \frac{\exp(\alpha_d + \gamma_d' x_i)}{\sum_{k=1}^{K} \exp(\alpha_d + \gamma_d' x_i)}, \tag{9.1}$$

where the last class is the reference class with coefficients standardized to 0 (i.e., $\alpha_c = 0, \gamma_d = 0$).

A corresponding measurement model relating observed indicators to latent factors can be specified, where conditional on Class k,

$$y_i = \nu_k + \Lambda_k \eta_i + K_k x_i + \varepsilon_i, \tag{9.2}$$

where for any class k, an individual's response y_i is a vector of observed scores, ν_k is a mean vector, Λk is a matrix of factor loadings, η_i is a vector of factor scores, K is a logit parameter matrix, and ε_i is a vector of residual errors that are normally distributed $(0, \Theta_k)$ and assumed to be uncorrelated with other variables. The structural model can be specified as follows:

$$\eta_i = \alpha_k + B_i \eta_{ik} + \Gamma_k x_i + \zeta_i, \tag{9.3}$$

where the residual vector ζ_i is normally distributed $(0, \Psi_k)$ and assumed to be unrelated to other variables. Equations 9.1–9.3 are defined slightly differently for using an underlying latent response variable and thresholds for categorical outcomes [see Muthén (2001) for further discussion]. Equation 9.3 can easily be simplified in the case where there are only observed variables, one example being a regression mixture model.

We can also extend the basic mixture model framework to a two-level model. This will allow us to account for mixtures within groups and between groups. The basic mixture model can be adapted to various multilevel models for two types of outcome variables—categorical and normally distributed continuous variables. Following Asparouhov and Muthén (2008), we will let y_{pij} be the pth observed dependent variable for individual i in cluster j. We will assume that there is a latent categorical variable C_{ij} for individual i in cluster j with k classes, which takes on values $1,\ldots,K$. As Muthén (1984) notes, we can define a structural model for categorical outcome variables by defining an underlying normally distributed latent variable y^*_{pij} such that for a set of parameters τ_{ck}

$$\left[y_{pij} = k \mid C_{ij} = c \right] \Leftrightarrow \tau_{ck} < y^*_{pij} < \tau_{ck+1}. \tag{9.4}$$

A linear regression for the latent response variable y^*_{pij} is equivalent to a probit regression for y_{pij}, or if a logistic distribution for y^*_{pij} is assumed, a linear regression for y^*_{pij} will translate to a logistic regression for y_{pij} (Asparouhov & Muthén, 2008). We note that for continuous variables, $y^*_{pij} = y_{pij}$. Following Asparouhov and Muthén, dependent variables in a proposed model can then be defined as the vector y^*_{ij} and x_{ij} can be defined as a vector of all covariates. The structural model (specified as single level in Equations 9.1–9.3) is then represented by the following, conditional on Class c:

$$\left[y^*_{ij} \mid C_{ij} = c \right] = v_{cj} + \Lambda_{cj}\eta_{ij} + \varepsilon_{ij} \tag{9.5}$$

$$\left[\eta_{ij} \mid C_{ij} = c \right] = \mu_{cj} + \beta_{cj}\eta_{ij} + \Gamma_{cj}x_{ij} + \zeta_{ij} \tag{9.6}$$

$$P(C_{ij} = c) = \frac{\exp(\alpha_{cj} + \beta_{cj}x_{ij})}{\sum_{c=1}^{C}\exp(\alpha_{cj} + \beta_{cj}x_{ij})}, \tag{9.7}$$

where η_{ij} are normally distributed latent variables, and ε_{ij} and ζ_{ij} are normally distributed residuals with zero means. Equation 9.7 considers a covariate, where the probability that individual i falls in Class c of the latent variable C_{ij} is represented through a multinomial logistic regression equation. For Equation 9.7, as noted previously, at Level 1 the residual variance is fixed for identification purposes for categorical variables, such that $\alpha_{cj} = \beta_{cj} = 0$ so that $\exp^0 = 1$ (Asparouhov &

Muthén, 2008), which implies that the log odds comparing Class c to the last Class C (i.e., the reference group), given x_{ij}, is as follows:

$$\ln\left(\frac{P(C_{ij} = c \mid x_{ij})}{P(C_{ij} = C \mid x_{ij})}\right) = \alpha_{cj} + \beta_{cj} x_{ij}. \tag{9.8}$$

Between groups, the intercepts, slopes, or loading parameters in the previously defined model can be specified as fixed or randomly varying across clusters. Following Asparouhov and Muthén (2008), the random effects can be collected in a η_j vector and x_j can be defined as a vector of group-level covariates. The between-level model is then

$$\eta_j = \mu + \beta \eta_j + \Gamma x_j + \zeta_j, \tag{9.10}$$

where μ, β, and Γ are structural parameters and ζ_i is a vector of normally distributed residuals contained in Ψ_B. Clearly, this basic mixture framework can be extended in various ways (e.g., multiple latent categorical variables, growth mixture models) within the Mplus latent variable framework [e.g., see Asparouhov & Muthén (2008); Duncan et al. (2006); Muthén (2001), (2002), (2007) for further examples].

An Example Latent Profile Analysis

We will begin with a simple, single-level mixture model. In our first analysis, we assume we have cross-sectional data with a vector of continuous items $(y_1, y_2, y_3)'$ assumed to represent a latent class variable (Muthén, 2001). Since the items are continuous, this is an example of a LPA. Both LPA and LCA have features similar to factor analysis, in that it is assumed that the latent categorical variable (c) is responsible for the association between the observed y variables. The goal is to identify items that indicate the classes well, estimate the class probabilities, identify covariates that explain class membership, and classify individuals properly within each latent class. In this simple example, we have 120 individuals who we think may be distributed on their achievement scores (i.e., reading, math, and language standardized test scores) across three classes. The assumption is that the specified relationship is due to the mixing of several classes of individuals, each having unrelated outcomes (Muthén, 2001).

We specify the model in Figure 9.3. The arrow from c to reading, math, and language suggests that the means vary across the latent classes. Each outcome has a variance that is specified as the same across classes. There are $k - 1$ means associated with the c latent classes, with the last class serving as the reference group. For LPA, the mean of the outcome changes across classes, and for LCA, the probability of the outcome changes across classes.

Several criteria can be used to establish the fit of models with different numbers of latent classes. We discuss these in more detail as we present a series of examples

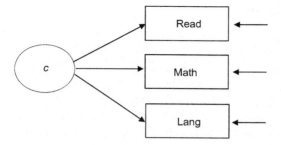

FIGURE 9.3 Proposed latent profile analysis of achievement.

in this chapter. Similar to deciding on the optimal number of factors in an exploratory factor analysis, it can be challenging to decide on the optimal number of latent classes. One commonly used criterion is the BIC (Schwartz, 1978). The BIC favors smaller coefficients despite the number of parameters estimated. In our example, for a model consisting of two latent classes, the BIC is 3,495.204. For three latent classes, the BIC is considerably smaller at 3,434.903. For four latent classes, the BIC was almost the same as the three-class model.

The quality of a mixture model selected can also be evaluated based on its classification of individuals. The likelihood of an individual's membership in a particular latent class is related to posterior probabilities of belonging to each of the latent classes in the analysis. The distribution of the categorical latent variable is represented by the probabilities of being a member of any particular latent class. We can examine the estimated posterior probabilities of each individual's membership in each class. These probabilities are used to classify each individual into the class that she or he most likely belongs (Muthén, 2001). Similar to discriminant analysis, for a proposed mixture model, the average probability of belonging to the most likely class should be high, and the average probability of belonging to the other classes should be low. Given these criteria, we selected the three-class model, which had class proportions of 0.27 in Class 1, 0.24 in Class 2, and 0.49 in Class 3 (not tabled). Table 9.1 provides the average posterior probabilities from the three-class model. The correct classification was well above 90% in each class (i.e., 96%, 94%, 92%, respectively).

TABLE 9.1 Average Classification Probabilities for the Three-Class Model

	1	2	3
1	0.958	0.000	0.042
2	0.000	0.938	0.062
3	0.045	0.035	0.920

Model Statements

We next provide the model statements. Our primary goal is to specify the proposed number of latent classes in the model. Using the CLASSES option on the model statements, the user can designate the number of latent classes in the model for each categorical latent variable. We will use c to designate the classes. The means and variances of the latent class indicators and the mean of the categorical latent variable are estimated as the default. We note that the variances are held equal across classes as the default and the covariances among the latent class indicators are fixed at zero as the default.

The default estimator for mixture modeling is maximum likelihood with robust standard errors (MLR) using a numerical integration algorithm. As Muthén and Muthén (1998–2012) note, some parameter starting values may result in local solutions that do not represent the global maximum of the likelihood function. To facilitate optimal model estimation, therefore, different sets of starting values are automatically produced, and the solution with the best likelihood is reported. More specifically, initially several random sets are created (i.e., 10 is the default). Optimization is carried out for 10 iterations for each of the 10 sets of starting values. The ending values of this initial stage of estimation are used as starting values in the final optimization stage. In the model statements for our example, the actual input lines describing the proposed model do not need to be included if automatic starting values are used (as well as **random starts**). In the Mplus model statements, we simply refer to the number of proposed latent classes (i.e., three in this case) and specify the ANALYSIS as TYPE = Mixture. Sometimes, however, providing estimated starting values for model parameters (and sometimes start values for particular parameters within a particular latent class) can greatly facilitate model estimation. We return to this point in our subsequent examples.

TITLE:	Example LPA Model;
DATA:	FILE IS C:\mplus\ch9ex1.dat;
	Format is 1f4.0,3f4.0,2f4.2,4f4.0;
VARIABLE:	Names are schcode read math lang ess cses femalelowses lgsch age ncses;
	Usevariables are read math lang;
	classes = c(3);
ANALYSIS:	TYPE = mixture;
OUTPUT:	TECH1;

Model Output

The output is summarized in Table 9.2. We can see there are three definite achievement profiles. Class 1 is the lowest-achieving class in all three subjects tested. Class 2 is the highest-achieving class, and Class 3 is somewhere in the middle. We can

TABLE 9.2 Single-Level LPA Results

	Estimate	S.E.	Est./S.E.	Two-Tailed P-Value
Residual Variances				
READ	338.189	46.418	7.286	0.000
MATH	574.090	120.051	4.782	0.000
LANG	269.901	47.620	5.668	0.000
Latent Class 1				
Means				
READ	608.736	6.755	90.121	0.000
MATH	616.731	4.452	138.517	0.000
LANG	608.884	5.008	121.590	0.000
Latent Class 2				
Means				
READ	688.966	6.095	113.043	0.000
MATH	721.504	8.038	89.765	0.000
LANG	682.488	4.581	148.996	0.000
Latent Class 3				
Means				
Means				
READ	648.381	3.860	167.983	0.000
MATH	668.817	6.844	97.726	0.000
LANG	647.536	4.672	138.592	0.000
Categorical *Latent Variable*				
Means				
C#1	−0.601	0.341	−1.763	0.078
C#2	−0.735	0.309	−2.379	0.017

also observe that the variances are fixed across classes. We note that in this example we formulated the latent profiles without student demographics. As a follow-up step, we could add one or more covariates (e.g., gender, student SES) that could explain differences in latent class membership. Of course, if we utilized student background information in forming the latent classes, they might have somewhat different membership.

Examining Heterogeneity in Intercepts

In the next example, we assume that employees' workplace satisfaction is positively related to their job performance. This is similar to the basic type of random-coefficients or multilevel regression model we presented in Chapter 3. Instead of just a simple regression model at Level 1, however, we will assume that there are

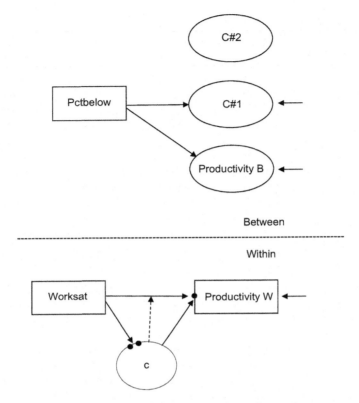

FIGURE 9.4 Proposed two-level mixture model with three latent classes.

three latent classes of individuals with intercepts that vary across the latent classes. In Figure 9.4 we provide a visual representation of the proposed model.

In the within-groups part of the model, the filled ovals at the end of the arrows from workplace satisfaction (*worksat*) to *productivity* and from *worksat* to *c* represent random intercepts, which are referred to as *C#1*, *C#2*, and *productivity B* in the between-groups part of the model. We note that for a categorical latent variable there can be one less random intercept than the number of latent classes ($k - 1$). As Muthén and Muthén (1998–2012) note, this corresponds to the regression of y on a set of dummy variables representing the categories of c.

For the categorical latent variable, the arrow from c to *productivity* indicates that its intercept varies across the classes of c. The broken arrow from c to the arrow from *worksat* to *productivity* indicates that the slope in the linear regression of productivity on workplace satisfaction varies across the classes of c. The residual variances are fixed for each latent class. Between groups, the random intercepts are shown in ovals because they are continuous latent variables that vary across groups. We will propose that an organizational covariate referring to the distribution of individuals below the organizational mean in workplace satisfaction (*pctbelow*) affects both the *productivity* intercept and the latent *C#*1 intercept (i.e., since we initially found it did not affect the *C#*2 intercept).

We note that as a practical matter the covariates can have some influence over class membership (Asparouhov & Muthén, 2013; Bolck, Croon, & Hagenaars, 2004; Vermunt, 2010). In certain situations, as in our first example, one might wish to explore generating the latent classes initially (i.e., the measurement part of the mixture model) without the covariate or covariates used to predict class membership. The resulting class memberships with and without covariates can then be compared initially to see whether they are broadly consistent. We emphasize this is a type of conceptual issue as well as a technical one. More specifically, one might ask:

- Do I think the covariates are important in forming the classes and so they should be included in the class formulation stage?
- Conversely, do I want a sort of "generic" set of latent classes formulated that I subsequently wish to differentiate with the covariates?

If desired, the AUXILIARY option can be used to specify variables that are not part of generating the latent classes but are used subsequently as important predictors of latent classes using a three-step approach (Asparouhov & Muthén, 2013; Vermunt, 2010). In this case, the probabilities of class membership and assignments of individuals to a latent class can be saved and then used in the multinomial regression part of the analysis to explain differences in membership between classes. Where latent class separation is clear, simulation studies suggest the one-step (simultaneous) approach and a three-step approach (i.e., where latent classes are formed initially, saved, and then used in subsequent analyses of differences between classes) work with equal efficiency (Asparouhov & Muthén, 2013). In principle, the one-step approach can be used in practical applications as well, such that the analyst need not generally compare one-step and three-step solutions (L. Muthén, personal communication, 2014). In LCA-type situations, where substantial direct effects of covariates are found, those covariates should be included in the measurement model for defining the latent class variable even with the three-step approach (Asparouhov & Muthén, 2013).

Model Statements

In this example, we will designate three latent classes. In the MODEL portion of the statements, we first specify the model as multilevel (%WITHIN% and %BETWEEN%). For a mixture model, there is an overall model statement designated as %OVERALL%. The statements under this heading describe relationships that are common to all latent classes in the model.

In the %WITHIN% portion of the proposed model, in the %OVERALL% model, the first ON statement describes the linear regression of productivity on individuals' workplace satisfaction (*worksat*). The second ON statement describes the multinomial logistic regression of the categorical latent variable *c* on the individual-level covariate *worksat* when comparing Class 1 to Class 3 and Class 2 to Class 3. The intercept in the regression of *c* on *worksat* is estimated as the default. The classes of a categorical latent variable are referred to by adding to the name of the categorical latent variable the number sign (#) followed by the number of the class (%c#1%). We can also refer to separate models for a particular class such as Class 1 (%c#1%). For example, in the %WITHIN% portion of the model we freed the regression of *product* on *worksat* to be freely estimated in the three latent classes (product on worksat;), by referring to Class 1 and Class 2 separately in the MODEL statements.

```
%c#1%
product on worksat;
%c#2%
product on worksat;
```

The residual variance of *y* is fixed within classes as the default; however, if it is mentioned for one of the specific classes, this indicates that it is not held equal for that class.

```
%c#1%
product;
```

For example, we could free the variance in Class 1 by referring to the variance within that latent class.

In the %BETWEEN% portion of the %OVERALL% model, we specified the relationship of c#1 on *pctbelow*. When we initially estimated the model, we found that the effect of *pctbelow* was not significant for Class 2 versus Class 3 (*c#2 on pctbelow;*), so we subsequently removed that path in the %OVERALL% model. We also specified the means of the latent classes to be different across groups by referring to it in the %c#1% portion of the %BETWEEN% model as follows:

```
%c#1%
[product];
```

The default estimator for the analysis is MLR, using a numerical integration algorithm. We note that numerical integration becomes increasingly more computationally demanding as the number of factors and the sample size increase.

There is considerable flexibility in providing more thorough investigation (e.g., varying the random starts, the number of iterations used, the number of optimizations carried out, estimation algorithms). As we noted, because some model starting values can generate a likelihood function with several local maxima, we reiterate the importance of exploring a given model with different optimizations that are carried out with various sets of starting values (Muthén, 2002). For preliminary solutions, one can turn off the random starts command (Starts = 0;) on the ANALYSIS command. Such solutions should be considered as tentative, however. We used this as a beginning step and subsequently re-estimated the model several times using differing numbers of random starts.

```
TITLE:       Two-level mixture model with latent intercept classes;
DATA:        FILE IS C:\mplus\ch9ex2.dat;
VARIABLE:    Names are orgid worksat female hiexp product pctbelow;
             Usevariables are product worksat pctbelow;
             classes = c(3);
             within = worksat;
             between = pctbelow;
             CLUSTER IS orgid;
define:      center worksat pctbelow(grandmean);
ANALYSIS:    TYPE = twolevel mixture;
             Starts = 0;
Model:       %Between%
             %Overall%
             product on pctbelow;
             c#1 on pctbelow;
             %c#1%
             [product];
             %Within%
             %Overall%
             product on worksat;
             c on worksat;
               %c#1%
               product on worksat;
               %c#2%   product on worksat;
OUTPUT:      SAMPSTAT TECH1 TECH11;
```

Model Output

The output on the mixed model with three latent classes is presented in Table 9.3. Model 1 in Table 9.3 represents a typical multilevel regression model with a random intercept and fixed slope within units. We can see for this

TABLE 9.3 Estimates for Multilevel Regression and Multilevel Mixture Model With Continuous Outcome

Model 1			Model 2 (3 Classes)	
	Estimates	*S.E.*	*Estimates*	*S.E.*
Within Level				
Performance on				
Worksat	12.173**	0.142		
Residual Variance	1778.627**	29.193		
Latent Class 1				
Worksat			5.529**	0.535
Residual Variance			963.640**	48.419
Latent Class 2				
Worksat			7.108**	0.682
Residual Variance			963.640**	48.419
Latent Class 3				
Worksat			7.419**	0.793
Residual Variance			963.640**	48.419
Between Level				
Performance on				
Pctbelow	−0.282**	0.072		
Intercept	262.763**	1.088		
Residual Variance	165.361**	21.233		
Latent Class 1				
Pctbelow			−0.162*	0.076
Intercept			197.621**	3.138
Residual Variance			167.852**	22.049
Latent Class 2				
Pctbelow			−0.162*	0.076
Intercept			261.307**	2.607
Residual Variance			167.852**	22.049
Latent Class 3				
Pctbelow			−0.162*	0.076
Intercept			304.996**	4.091
Residual Variance			167.852**	22.049
Categorical Latent Within Level				
C#1 on Worksat			−0.653**	0.109
C#2 on Worksat			−0.263**	0.072
Intercept (C#1)			−0.810*	0.473
Intercept (C#2)			1.041**	0.176
Between Level				
C#1 on Pctbelow			0.016**	0.003
Model Fit				
Bayesian (BIC)	136514.853		136357.195	
Entropy			0.526	
Adj LRT (2 vs 3)				
83.720 (p < 0.05)				

Notes: *p < 0.05, **p < 0.01

baseline model that workplace satisfaction affects individual performance positively ($12.173, p < 0.01$). Between groups, the percentage of individuals below the unit mean in terms of their workplace satisfaction affects organizational productivity negatively ($-0.282, p < 0.01$). Although this is a viable model, it is possible that there is additional heterogeneity within groups in terms of subgroups of individuals.

For Model 2, our primary goal is the identification of possible latent classes within groups. We propose that there may be two or more latent classes of individuals within groups who have similar mean performance outcomes. We also propose that the means of these latent classes vary across level-2 units and specify separate *worksat-productivity* slopes between the latent classes but hold the residual variances constant.

Determining the number of latent classes for the categorical latent variable can be challenging. At present, there is no certain way of determining the number of latent classes that may exist in the population. Similar to exploratory factor analysis, a series of models is sometimes fit using different numbers of classes (e.g., 2, 3, 4, 5). Preliminarily, we investigated models with two, three, and four classes. Several criteria can be used to establish the fit of models proposed with differing numbers of latent classes. We suggest first, however, that the solution should make substantive sense. It is unlikely that the classes will be the same size, but they should serve to differentiate sizable subgroups of similar individuals. In this case, for our three-class model, the proportions based on estimated posterior probabilities are 0.18, 0.55, and 0.27, respectively, which are certainly reasonably sized classes.

Posterior probabilities of class membership for each individual can also be used to determine how well the categories define groups of individuals. Similar to individual classification in discriminant analysis or logistic regression, high diagonal proportions and low off-diagonal proportions are indicators of good classification. We can think of the diagonal proportions as correctly classified individuals and the off-diagonal proportions as errors in classifying individuals into their most likely classes. Lubke and Muthén (2007) found better classification is related to separation of classes (e.g., due to intercepts, increasing covariate effects). **Entropy**, which is closely related to average class probabilities, can suggest how problematic class assignment is (Ramaswamy, DeSarbo, Reibstein, & Robinson, 1993). Lubke and Muthén noted that entropy below 0.60 is related to misclassifying approximately 20% of the subjects, while entropy of 0.80 suggests upward of 90% are correctly classified. In this case, the entropy coefficient for Model 2 was approximately 0.53, with diagonal classification probabilities for the three classes of 74%, 84%, and 63%, which indicates some misspecification, especially in Class 3.

There are several steps that analysts can take to increase confidence in selecting the optimal number of latent classes. One possibility is to make use of the Vuong-Lo-Mendell-Rubin Likelihood Ratio Test (LRT) for examining whether adding another latent class is supported (Lo, Mendell, & Rubin, 2001). This test is available if TECH11 is requested on the OUTPUT statement. For example, we first compared a solution with one (H_0) versus two classes (H_1), and found the two-class model to fit the data better. The LRT difference was 193.056 ($p < 0.0001$), which suggests that the model with two classes fit the data better than the model with one class (not tabled). Another possibility makes use of an adjusted likelihood that is provided (Lo et al., 2001). The likelihood ratio test for the one- versus two-class model (189.070, $p < 0.0001$) was also significant (not tabled). The comparison is obtained by deleting the first class in the estimated model. Because of this, Muthén and Muthén (1998–2012) recommend that when using starting values they be chosen so that the last class is the largest class.

For the model with three latent classes (compared against two classes), the LRT coefficient was 85.486 ($p < 0.0001$), for a difference of five parameters, and the adjusted LRT was 83.721 ($p < 0.0001$). We do caution, however, that using likelihood ratio goodness-of-fit tests to evaluate model fit is optimal in cases where there are not large numbers of sparse cells (Nylund, Asparouhov, & Muthén, 2007).

We replicated the three-class results by removing the random starts line (starts = 0), and when TECH11 is requested, the default will generate 20 initial stage random starts and four final stage optimizations.

Random Starts Specifications for the $k - 1$ Class Analysis Model
Number of initial stage random starts   20
Number of final stage optimizations   4

This can be overridden. For this model, the adjusted LRT test was again significant (83.419, $p < 0.0001$). Mplus will generate the following message:

THE BEST LOGLIKELIHOOD VALUE HAS BEEN REPLICATED. RERUN WITH AT LEAST TWICE THE RANDOM STARTS TO CHECK THAT THE BEST LOGLIKELIHOOD IS STILL OBTAINED AND REPLICATED.

We again re-estimated the model after doubling the random starts and received confirmation that the log-likelihood value had again been replicated.

Model-fitting criteria (e.g., BIC) can also be used that reward better-fitting models with fewer parameters (Muthén, 2002). BIC is useful because it provides an ideal way to examine the relative fit of any proposed latent class model against the model for just one class (i.e., the case for which the considered sample is homogeneous with respect to the model considered). The BIC values for the various alternative or competing models can be compared, and the model with the smallest value is considered the preferred model (Marcoulides & Heck, 2013). For the baseline model (Model 1) in Table 9.3, with one set of within-group estimates, the BIC was 136,514.849 (for five estimated parameters). For the comparison model with two only latent classes (and 10 estimated parameters) the BIC was 136,367.916 (not tabled). Subsequently, we found that a model with three classes (with 14 estimated parameters) fit better than the model with two classes. The BIC for this model (Model 2) in Table 9.3 was 136,357.195. We also investigated four latent classes, but the BIC index of 1366,395.164 (not tabled) indicated it did not fit the data as well as the three-class model.

In this case, all of the evaluation criteria point toward the model with three latent classes. In Table 9.3, we provide the results of the final model as tested. Within groups, the effect of workplace satisfaction on productivity is 5.529 ($p < 0.01$) in Class 1, 7.108 ($p < 0.01$) in Class 2, and 7.419 ($p < 0.01$) in Class 3. We note that the strength of the slope effect increases across latent classes. For the multinomial logistic regression of c on *worksat*, we can see that the log odds for Class 1 (-0.653, $p < 0.05$) and Class 2 (-0.263, $p < 0.01$) suggest that higher standing on workplace satisfaction is related to lower probability of being in the first two productivity classes relative to the reference class (Class 3). These effects weaken from Class 1 to Class 2.

Between organizations, we can also see the latent class means increase across the three classes (i.e., Class1 M = 197.621 Class2 M = 261.307; Class3 M = 304.996). The fixed effect of *pctbelow* on organizational performance is negative and significant (-0.162, $p < 0.05$). Finally, at the organizational level, the effect of *pctbelow* is significantly and positively associated with being in Class 1 versus Class 3 (0.016, $p < 0.01$). As this basic mixture model formulation suggests, the random latent class effects provide information about the existence of latent classes within groups, as well as the possible influence of the organizational context on the probability of latent class membership.

Investigating Latent Classes for Random Slopes at Level 2

In our next example, we specify a categorical latent variable between groups. In this case, we examine whether there might be level-1 slopes whose means vary across classes of a categorical latent variable (*cb*) defined at the organizational level. Between organizations, the random organizational productivity intercept and the identified class means of a categorical latent variable *cb* are regressed on an organizational covariate (*pctbelow*). This type of multilevel mixture model facilitates the investigation of population heterogeneity that is due to group-level variables. This means that latent classes are formed for organizations rather than for individuals. To investigate this type of organizational latent class model, a modification is made to accommodate a between-level latent categorical variable:

$$C_{ij} = C_j . \tag{9.11}$$

The other change is that Equation 9.7, for the multinomial regression within groups, becomes the following:

$$P(C_j = c) = \frac{\exp(\alpha_c + \beta_c x_j)}{\sum_{c=1}^{C} \exp(\alpha_c + \beta_c x_j)}, \tag{9.12}$$

which implies that only between-level covariates can be used as latent class predictors (Asparouhov & Muthén, 2008). For the between-groups latent class model, the latent class intercepts and slopes in Equation 9.12 are not randomly varying. However, this type of model facilitates the investigation of sets of organizations that may have similar relationships in terms of productivity means and slope means. As Asparouhov and Muthén indicate, in the between-organization part of the structural model, all parameters (including the residual covariance matrix) can be class specific:

$$\eta_j = \mu_c + \beta_c \eta_j + \Gamma_c x_j + \zeta_j. \tag{9.13}$$

As they caution, however, it is not always clear whether between-group heterogeneity is feasible to estimate in some practical applications—for example, if there is a small between-group sample size. As they note, the key issue is whether the within-group variables (e.g., workplace satisfaction, employee experience) can be used to identify the group-level latent classes. In such cases, models that identify class-varying fixed or random effects with large variation across classes (and small variation across clusters) can be considered as reliable. When the between-group sample is small, it is probably best to consider the results as preliminary.

The between-level categorical latent variable is defined using the CLASSES and BETWEEN options of the VARIABLE command. We draw attention to the need to specify cb on the BETWEEN variable command (between = cb), so the categorical latent variable is properly specified only at that level. Otherwise, if it is not specified as a between-group variable, it will be defined at both levels. In this example, we will assume there are two latent classes of random slopes between units. We will also define a second within-group predictor *high experience* (i.e., a binary variable coded 1 = 5 years or more experience with the company, 0 = less than 5 years).

In Figure 9.5, the random effects for the productivity intercept, *worksat-productivity* slope (β_1), and *high experience-productivityslope* (β_2) are shown in ovals in the between part of the model because they are continuous latent variables that vary across clusters. The arrows from cb to *productivity* and Slope(β_1) and Slope(β_2) indicate that the *productivity* intercept and the slope means vary across the classes of cb. In addition, the random *productivity* intercept and the categorical latent variable cb are regressed on a cluster-level covariate (*pctbelow*). For this example, between

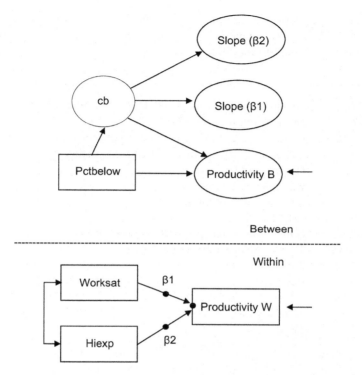

FIGURE 9.5 Two-level mixture regression model with level-2 categorical latent variable.

groups we will specify the random slopes as having no within-class variance, which reduces the numerical integration demands. Only their means vary across the classes of *cb*. This implies that the distribution of the slopes can be thought of as nonparametric representations rather than normal distributions (Aitkin, 1999; Muthén & Asparouhov, 2009).

Model Statements

In the OVERALL subcommand of the within-groups part of the model, we specify two random slopes that describe the relationships between workplace satisfaction (*worksat*) and productivity and between high employee experience (*hiexp*) and productivity. Between groups, in the %OVERALL% portion of the model, the ON (for regressed on) statement describes the regression of the productivity intercept and the categorical latent variable *cb* on the cluster-level covariate (*pctbelow*). Between groups, we specify separate slope means (S1 and S2) for each latent class (%c#1% and %c#2%). We also specify separate variances between groups and starting values based on earlier versions of the model that fit the data reasonably well. This was because for presenting our final model, we had to use a considerable number of random starts (250) in order to obtain a viable solution which replicated the best log-likelihood value.

```
TITLE:       Two-level mixture model with latent classes at level 2;
DATA:        FILE IS C:\mplus\ch9ex2.dat;
VARIABLE:    Names are orgid worksat female hiexp product pctbelow;
             Usevariables are product worksat hiexp pctbelow;
             classes = cb(2);
             within = worksat hiexp;
             between = cb pctbelow;
             CLUSTER IS orgid;
define:      center worksat hiexp pctbelow(grandmean);
ANALYSIS:    TYPE = twolevel mixture random;
             Estimator is mlr;
             starts 250 4;
Model:
             %Between%
             %Overall%
             product cb on pctbelow*-.5;
             s1@0 s2@0;
             %cb#1%
             [s1*11 s2*7];
             Product*170;
              %cb#2%
             [s1*12 s2*13];
             %Within%
             %Overall%
             s1 | product on worksat;
             s2 | product on hiexp;
OUTPUT:      SAMPSTAT TECH1;
```

Model Output

Once again, Model 1 in Table 9.4 provides the typical multilevel regression model with a random slope at Level 2 (12.172, $p < 0.01$). The random intercept is 262.756 ($p < 0.05$). We can also see that the level-2 covariate (*pctbelow*) is negatively related to organizational performance (−0.282, $p < 0.05$). It is

TABLE 9.4 Estimates for Random Slope Multilevel Regression and Multilevel Mixture Model With Continuous Outcome

	Model 1		Model 2 (2 Classes)	
	Estimates	S.E.	Estimates	S.E.
Within Level				
Performance				
Residual Variance	1778.260**	29.179		
C1 Residual Variance			1753.300**	28.481
C2 Residual Variance			1753.300**	28.481
Between Level				
Performance on				
Pctbelow	−0.282**	0.072		
Intercept	262.756**	1.088		
Slope(worksat)	12.172**	0.142		
Slope Variance	0.000	0.000		
Residual Variance	165.359**	21.230		
Latent Class 1				
Pctbelow			−0.359**	0.120
Intercept			261.318**	1.709
Slope1 (Worksat)			11.743**	0.291
Slope2 (Hiexp)			7.695**	1.140
Slope1 Variance			0.000	0.000
Slope2 Variance			0.000	0.000
Residual Variance			163.588**	32.162
Latent Class 2				
Pctbelow			−0.359**	0.120
Intercept			271.759**	8.936
Slope1 (Worksat)			13.177**	0.435
Slope2 (Hiexp)			15.935**	4.619
Slope1 Variance			0.000	0.000
Slope2 Variance			0.000	0.000
Residual Variance			156.617**	68.479
Categorical Latent				
Between Level				
C#1 on Pctbelow			−0.069*	0.040
Intercept (C#1)			1.955	1.608
Model Fit				
Bayesian (BIC)	136514.849		136424.747	
Entropy			0.655	

Notes: *$p < 0.10$, **$p < 0.05$ (final class counts 0.82 and 0.18)

possible, however, that there may be heterogeneity in the slope means across the between-group latent classes. This would suggest, for example, that workplace satisfaction has a differential effect on performance in these different organizational subgroups. Hence, investigating latent classes at the organizational level provides a means of examining differing contextual effects on organizational relationships.

In the table, we can see that the BIC for Model 2 (136,424.747) favors the model with two classes over Model 1. Given the favorable BIC, we report results based on two latent classes. The final class counts indicate that the first latent class includes 82% of the units and the second class includes 18% (with classification probabilities of 92% and 77% for the two classes, respectively). For Class 1, the productivity intercept is 261.318, *worksat-productivity* slope is 11.743, and the *hiexp-productivity* slope is 7.695. Both slopes are statistically significant ($p < 0.05$). For Class 2, the productivity intercept is 271.759 and the *worksat-productivity* slope is 13.177 ($p < 0.05$). This suggests that the relationship between workplace satisfaction and organizational performance is more consequential (i.e., a larger slope) for individuals in higher-producing organizations (Class 2) than for their peers in lower-producing organizations (Class 1). Similarly, in Class 2, the slope for *hiexp* is 15.935 ($p < 0.05$), which also suggests that higher experience was more strongly related to productivity for individuals in higher-producing organizations than for individuals in lower-producing organizations. For demonstration purposes, this supports our initial supposition that there may be latent classes of organizations with similar workplace relationships.

The next part of our analysis then investigates what organizational variables might affect those relationships. In this case, the results provide preliminary support for the view that the distribution of individuals regarding workplace satisfaction (*pctbelow*) has a negative relationship to membership in Class 1 (−0.069, $p < 0.10$) compared with the reference class (Class 2); that is, a higher percentage of individuals below the mean in workplace satisfaction is related to membership in Class 1.

Alternative Model Specification

Following is an alternative specification of the MODEL command that is simplified when the model has many covariates and when the variances of the random slopes are zero. In this specification, instead of the random slope statements used at Level 1 (e.g., S1|product on worksat;), the random slopes are represented as class-varying slopes in the class-specific parts of the level-1 model (Muthén & Muthén, 1998–2012). This specification makes it unnecessary to refer to the means and variances of the random slopes in the between-groups part of the model.

```
Model:
        %Between%
        %Overall%
        product cb on pctbelow;
        %Within%
        %Overall%
        product on worksat
        %cb#1%
        product on worksat;
        %cb#2%
        product on worksat;
```

Defining a Two-Level Mixture Model for Math

In this third example, within schools we have a continuous dependent variable y (a math test score) that is explained by two within-group covariates (i.e., *male* coded 1, female = 0) and *academic program* (coded academic = 1, and other = 0). Between schools are two covariates, *public school* (i.e., coded = 1, and other = 0) and *academic school* (coded academic = 1, else = 0). Even with a few variables, there are a considerable number of possible relationships that can be modeled.

The proposed model is summarized in Figure 9.6. First, in the within-group part of the model, the two random intercepts are shown as filled dots at the ends of the arrows that point to the dependent variable *math* and the categorical latent variable c. These relationships suggest that the intercepts of math and c vary across clusters in the between-groups portion of the model, where they are defined as continuous latent variables. Each latent class has a random intercept except the last class (i.e., $c\#2$ is the reference class). In this case, we will posit the existence of two latent classes. Second, the arrow from c to math indicates the math intercept varies across the classes of c. This relationship corresponds to the regression of math on a set of dummy variables representing the classes of c. The prediction of class membership is based on the logistic regression of c on the covariates. It is often useful to check the proposed model against the specifications in the TECH1 output. The specification indicates 13 parameters to be estimated in the model as it is proposed in Figure 9.6. Within groups, there are a total of six parameters. In the Beta matrix, we can see two structural parameters within groups representing the regression of *math* on *male* and *acadprog*. There is also a residual variance for math. These parameters are proposed to be the same in each latent class. We can also see an intercept for C#1 (in the alpha matrix

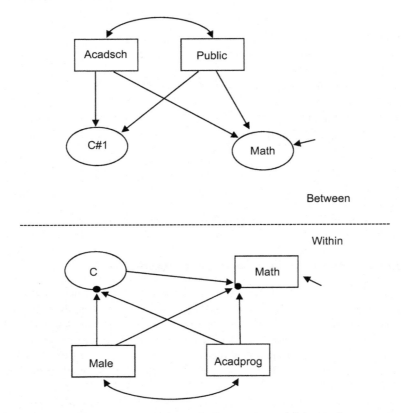

FIGURE 9.6 Proposed cross-sectional two-level mixture model for math.

as parameter 11) and the regression of C#1 on *male* and *acadprog* (in the gamma matrix as parameters 11 and 12).

Third, between groups, the variability of the random effects is explained by the between-groups covariates *public school* and *academic school*. For the dependent variable (*math*), it describes the linear regression of the random intercept on the between-group covariates. For *c*, it describes the linear regression of the latent variable *c* on the covariates. The random intercept of *math* is a continuous latent variable. We reiterate that each latent class of *c* has a random intercept except the last class. In this example, since there are only two latent classes, there is only one random intercept. This part of the model relates the random effects (e.g., the latent math intercept and *c* intercept) to the explanatory variables at two levels, as is typical in multilevel models. Between groups, there are seven parameters to be estimated. These include four beta parameters relating the covariates to the latent factors, one residual variance for math, and two latent class intercepts for math.

TECH1 OUTPUT
Within Groups
Latent Class#1 BETA

	C#1	MATH	ACPROG	MALE	PUBLIC	ACADSCH
C#1	0	0	0	0	0	0
MATH	0	0	1	2	0	0
ACPROG	0	0	0	0	0	0
MALE	0	0	0	0	0	0
PUBLIC	0	0	0	0	0	0
ACADSCH	0	0	0	0	0	0

Latent Class#2 BETA

	C#1	MATH	ACPROG	MALE	PUBLIC	ACADSCH
C#1	0	0	0	0	0	0
MATH	0	0	1	2	0	0
ACPROG	0	0	0	0	0	0
MALE	0	0	0	0	0	0
PUBLIC	0	0	0	0	0	0
ACADSCH	0	0	0	0	0	0

Latent Class #1 PSI

	C#1	MATH	ACPROG	MALE	PUBLIC	ACADSCH
C#1	0	0	0	0	0	0
MATH	0	3	0	0	0	0
ACPROG	0	0	0	0	0	0
MALE	0	0	0	0	0	0
PUBLIC	0	0	0	0	0	0
ACADSCH	0	0	0	0	0	0

Latent Class #2 PSI

	C#1	MATH	ACPROG	MALE	PUBLIC	ACADSCH
C#1	0	0	0	0	0	0
MATH	0	3	0	0	0	0
ACPROG	0	0	0	0	0	0
MALE	0	0	0	0	0	0
PUBLIC	0	0	0	0	0	0
ACADSCH	0	0	0	0	0	0

Between Groups
Latent Class#1 ALPHA

C#1	MATH	ACPROG	MALE	PUBLIC	ACADSCH
0	4	0	0	0	0

Latent Class#2 ALPHA

C#1	MATH	ACPROG	MALE	PUBLIC	ACADSCH
0	10	0	0	0	0

(*Continued*)

Latent Class#1 BETA

	C#1	MATH	ACPROG	MALE	PUBLIC	ACADSCH
C#1	0	0	0	0	5	0
MATH	0	0	1	2	7	0
ACPROG	0	0	0	0	0	0
MALE	0	0	0	0	0	0
PUBLIC	0	0	0	0	0	0
ACADSCH	0	0	0	0	0	0

Latent Class#2 BETA

	C#1	MATH	ACPROG	MALE	PUBLIC	ACADSCH
C#1	0	0	0	0	5	6
MATH	0	0	1	2	7	8
ACPROG	0	0	0	0	0	0
MALE	0	0	0	0	0	0
PUBLIC	0	0	0	0	0	0
ACADSCH	0	0	0	0	0	0

Latent Class #1 PSI

	C#1	MATH	ACPROG	MALE	PUBLIC	ACADSCH
C#1	0	0	0	0	0	0
MATH	0	9	0	0	0	0
ACPROG	0	0	0	0	0	0
MALE	0	0	0	0	0	0
PUBLIC	0	0	0	0	0	0
ACADSCH	0	0	0	0	0	0

Latent Class #2 PSI

	C#1	MATH	ACPROG	MALE	PUBLIC	ACADSCH
C#1	0	0	0	0	0	0
MATH	0	9	0	0	0	0
ACPROG	0	0	0	0	0	0
MALE	0	0	0	0	0	0
PUBLIC	0	0	0	0	0	0
ACADSCH	0	0	0	0	0	0

PARAMETER SPECIFICATION FOR LATENT CLASS REGRESSION MODEL PART

ALPHA(C)

	C#1	C#2
	11	0

GAMMA(C)

	C#1	MATH	ACPROG	MALE	PUBLIC	ACADSCH
C#1	0	0	12	13	0	0
C#2	0	0	0	0	0	0

A number of other possible parameters could be estimated if some of the constraints were removed across the latent classes. As a general modeling strategy, however, it is probably best to start with a basic model and then alter it to test specific hypotheses about individual classes. For example, we could hypothesize that the relationship between *gender* and *math* is different across categories of c (which would be shown by a dotted arrow from c to the path between the covariate and *math*).

Model Statements

The model statements for Figure 9.6 are next described. If desired, a single-level model could be examined initially. Parts that are specific to one latent class (e.g., Class 2) can be designated as %c#2%. For example, we could specify that one regression relationship (e.g., the regression of *math* on *gender*) is varied across classes. Perhaps the relationship does not matter in one class but does in the other. We might also specify the residual variance of math in each class to be different. If the residual variance is mentioned (math;), it will not be constrained across classes. In this model, however, we designate the same model to hold across both classes. In the between part of the model, the %OVERALL% statement describes the regression of the latent variables (defined as η_1 and η_2) on the school-level covariates.

```
TITLE:       Two-level mixture model math achievement;
DATA:        FILE IS C:\mplus\ch8 ex3.dat;
             Format is 2f8.0,5f8.2,7f8.0;
VARIABLE:    Names are schcode heldback ses math sci attprob
             gpa acprog moved lowses smallsch male public acadsch;
             Usevariables schcode math acprog male public acadsch;
             classes = c(2);
             within = acprog male;
             between = public acadsch;
             cluster = schcode;
define:      center acprog male public acadsch(grandmean);
ANALYSIS:    TYPE = twolevel mixture;
             Estimator is MLR;
             starts = 0;
Model:

             %Within%
             %Overall%
             math on acprog male;
```

```
            c#1 on acprog male;
            %Between%
            %Overall%
            math on public acadsch;
            c#1 on public acadsch;
OUTPUT:     SAMPSTAT STANDARDIZED TECH1 TECH8 TECH11;
```

Model Output

For the proposed model in Figure 9.6, the final class counts based on estimated posterior probabilities are 18% in Class 1 and 82% in Class 2. The output is summarized in Table 9.5. In this model, the covariate effects and residual variances are proposed to be equal across latent classes. Within groups, regarding math achievement, as we might expect, being in a college-oriented curricular program is related to higher math achievement ($\beta = 1.721$, $p < 0.01$). Moreover, males' math achievement level is slightly higher than females' achievement level ($\beta = 0.558$, $p < 0.01$). Between groups, being in a public school is negatively related to achievement ($\beta = -1.722$, $p < 0.01$) and being in an academic school (i.e., a school having advanced course work) is positively related to achievement ($\beta = 0.562$, $p < 0.01$). Between groups the estimated latent class intercepts describing math achievement (which are allowed to vary as the default) are 44.769 for Class 1 and 60.338 for Class 2.

The last part of the output addresses the model to explain membership in the latent classes. Within groups, being in an academic (i.e., college preparatory) program (log odds $= -0.621$, $p < 0.01$) and being male (log odds $= -0.150$, $p < 0.05$) are significantly related to class membership. The negative log odds coefficient for academic program suggests that students in college preparatory curricular programs are less likely to be in Class 1 (i.e., the latent class with lower math achievement). Similarly, males are less likely to be members of Class 1 than females. Between schools, students in academic schools are less likely to be in Class 1 ($\beta = -0.249$, $p < 0.01$), and students in public schools are more likely to be in Class 1 ($\beta = 1.05$, $p < 0.01$).

In the model presented, the entropy was 0.825, suggesting that it classified individuals fairly well. The BIC was 88,293.409 and the LRT for two classes (compared to one class) was 1,861.184 ($p < 0.0001$) and the adjusted LRT being 1,828.982 ($p < 0.0001$). We were able to replicate the best log-likelihood value of this model with 20 random starts and four final stage optimizations. In the example presented, defining three latent classes was unnecessary. The third class did not result in sufficient separation from the other two classes to classify individuals. More specifically, for the proposed three-class model, the BIC was 88,312.413 and entropy was only 0.377 (not tabled).

TABLE 9.5 Output From Two-Level Math Mixture Model

	Estimates	S.E.	Est./S.E.	StdYX
Model for math				
Within Level				
Latent Class 1				
MATH ON				
ACPROG	1.721**	0.160	10.723	0.159
MALE	0.558**	0.135	4.122	0.054
Residual Var				
MATH	25.619**	0.603	42.490	0.972
Latent Class 2				
MATH ON				
ACPROG	1.721**	0.160	10.723	0.134
MALE	0.558**	0.135	4.122	0.054
Residual Var				
MATH	25.619**	0.603	42.490	0.980
Between Level				
Latent Class 1				
MATH ON				
PUBLIC	−1.722**	0.241	−7.140	−0.341
ACADSCH	0.562**	0.201	2.803	0.126
Intercept				
MATH	44.769**	0.183	244.147	24.391
Residual Var				
MATH	2.897**	0.331	8.762	0.860
Latent Class 2				
MATH ON				
PUBLIC	−1.722**	0.241	−7.140	−0.341
ACADSCH	0.562**	0.201	2.803	0.126
Intercept				
MATH	60.338**	0.085	711.940	32.873
Residual Var				
MATH	2.897**	0.331	8.762	0.860
Model for C				
Within Level				
C#1 on				
ACPROG	−0.621**	0.074	−8.417	
MALE	−0.150*	0.062	−2.432	
Intercept				
C#1	−1.575**	0.046	−34.040	
Between Level				
MATH ON				
PUBLIC	1.050**	0.193	5.444	
ACADSCH	−0.249**	0.092	−2.715	

Note: $*p < 0.05$, $**p < 0.01$

Model Modifications

We also investigated two model modifications as suggested earlier. We specified part of the model within groups to be specific to Class 2 (i.e., math on male; math;). This allowed the regression of math on male to be different across classes and the math residual variance to vary across classes.

```
%Within%
%Overall%
math on acprog male;
c#1 on acprog male;
%c#2%
math on male;
math;
```

We highlight these results briefly (not tabled). When the effect of gender is allowed to vary across classes, the advantage for males versus females is not statistically significant in the higher-achieving latent class (Class 2), but it is significant in the lower-achieving latent class (Class 1). For two more estimated parameters, the BIC index indicates this is an improved model (75,580.456). Similarly, in this model the entropy increases to 0.894.

Two-Level CFA Mixture Model With Continuous Indicators

We will next illustrate a two-level CFA mixture model with continuous indicators. Using a mixture model, we could also consider situations where individuals are members of subpopulations (or latent classes) that differ in the parameters of the individual factor model (Marcouides & Heck, 2013). There may be a situation where we propose a set of subpopulations (or latent classes) that differ in the parameter values of the measurement model defined for individuals. In this case, the mixture factor model is something like a multiple-group factor analysis, where individuals belong to latent classes differing with respect to the measurement model.

In this example, we have 2,720 employees nested in 148 organizations. They are measured on six items defining two factors. We may believe there are several latent classes of employees, as defined by their perceptions of the workplace. In this case, we will assume that there are two latent classes.

We present the proposed model in Figure 9.7. In the within-groups part of the model, the filled dots at the end of the arrows from the within factors (F1 and F2) to the set of items represent random intercepts that vary across organizations. The arrow from c to the latent factors indicates that their means are allowed to vary across the latent classes of c. The filled dot on the latent categorical variable

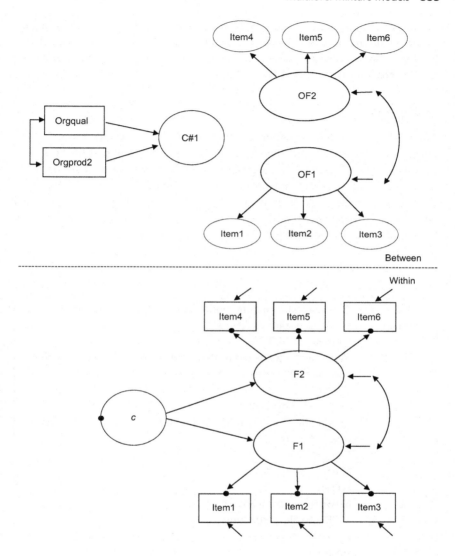

FIGURE 9.7 Two-level CFA mixture model.

c represents a random mean that varies across clusters. In the between part of the model, the random item intercepts and mean for c (referred to as C#1) are shown as ovals because they are continuous latent variables that vary across units. The between-group factors add O (for organizational level) to differentiate them from the within-group factors (F1 and F2). The between-group item residual variances are fixed to zero as the default, since they are often very small and increase the demands on integration (Muthén & Muthén, 1998–2012). We note that in this case, the random mean of C#1 and the latent factors are specified as uncorrelated. Finally, we specify that two organizational covariates (i.e., quality and productivity) are related to latent class membership.

Model Statements

The CFA model is defined within and between groups with three items measuring each factor. We specified two latent classes. In the overall part of the model, the ON statement describes the regression of random intercept of C#1 on organizational quality (*orgqual*) and organizational productivity (*orgprod2*). We fixed the variance of the random mean of C#1 to 1.0 (c#1@1;) to facilitate model estimation. This proposed model takes several minutes to run because of the heavy numerical integration demands.

```
TITLE:       Two-level CFA mixture model with continuous indicators;
DATA:        FILE IS C:\mplus\3LCFA.dat;
             Format is 11f8.0,7f8.2;
VARIABLE:    Names are orgcode deptid item1 item2 item3 item4 item5 item6
             age female deptsize dept_m orgsize empstab orgdemos
             orgqual
             orgprod1 orgprod2;
             Usevariables are orgcode item1 item2 item3 item4 item5 item6
             orgqual orgprod2;
             Classes = c(2);
             cluster is orgcode;
             Within = ;
             Between = orgqual orgprod2;
ANALYSIS:    TYPE = twolevel mixture;
             Estimator is MLR;
             starts = 0;
Model:
             %Between%
             %Overall%
             OF1 by item1 item2 item3;
             OF2 by item4 item5 item6;
             c#1 on orgqual orgprod2;
             c#1@1;
             %c#1%
             [OF1*5 OF2*8];
```

```
                 %Within%
                 %Overall%
                 F1 by item1 item2 item3;
                 F2 by item4 item5 item6;
      Output:    sampstat standardized TECH1;
```

Model Output

The correct classification for the two classes is 95% and 89%, indicating very good individual classification (with entropy of 0.758). We note in passing that this model fits better than a three-class model (i.e., where entropy was only 0.68 and the BIC was considerably larger than for the two-class model).

The estimates are summarized in Table 9.6. The factor model is specified to be the same in both groups—however, the means in latent Class 1 are both significantly higher than the reference latent class (i.e., OF1 mean = 5.839; OF2 mean = 13.672). For the regression of $C\#1$ on the organizational covariates, organizational quality (0.489 $p < 0.001$) and organizational productivity ($0.629, p < 0.05$) are significant predictors of stronger mean perceptions of workplace processes in explaining membership in Class 1 (accounting for about 22% of the variance in the random $C\#1$ intercept).

TABLE 9.6 Two-Level CFA Mixture Model

	Two-Tailed			
	Estimate	*S.E.*	*Est./S.E.*	*P-Value*
Factor Model				
Within Level (STDYX)				
F1 BY				
ITEM1	0.848	0.012	72.125	0.000
ITEM2	0.856	0.016	54.661	0.000
ITEM3	0.912	0.032	28.636	0.000
F2 BY				
ITEM4	0.768	0.025	30.369	0.000
ITEM5	0.693	0.023	29.532	0.000
ITEM6	0.641	0.025	26.070	0.000
F2 WITH F1	0.894	0.025	36.119	0.000
Variances				
F1	1.000	0.000	999.000	999.000
F2	1.000	0.000	999.000	999.000

(Continued)

| | Two-Tailed | | | |
	Estimate	S.E.	Est./S.E.	P-Value
Residual Variances				
ITEM1	0.281	0.020	14.089	0.000
ITEM2	0.267	0.027	9.950	0.000
ITEM3	0.168	0.058	2.889	0.004
ITEM4	0.411	0.039	10.583	0.000
ITEM5	0.519	0.033	15.964	0.000
ITEM6	0.589	0.032	18.711	0.000
Between Level (STDYX)				
OF1 BY				
ITEM1	1.000	0.000	999.000	999.000
ITEM2	1.000	0.000	999.000	999.000
ITEM3	1.000	0.000	999.000	999.000
OF2 BY				
ITEM4	1.000	0.000	999.000	999.000
ITEM5	1.000	0.000	999.000	999.000
ITEM6	1.000	0.000	999.000	999.000
OF2 WITH OF1	0.862	0.042	20.591	0.000
Latent Class 1				
Means (Unstandardized)				
OF1	5.839	0.320	18.226	0.000
OF2	13.672	0.373	36.634	0.000
Latent Class 2				
Means (Unstandardized)				
OF1	0.000	0.000	999.000	999.000
OF2	0.000	0.000	999.000	999.000
Categorical Latent Variable				
Within (Unstandardized)				
Intercepts				
C#1	0.729	0.109	6.695	0.000
Between Unstandardized)				
C#1 ON				
ORGQUAL	0.489	0.109	4.476	0.000
ORGPROD2	0.629	0.315	2.001	0.045
Residual Variances				
C#1	1.000	0.000	999.000	999.000
R-Square C#1	0.223	0.076	2.933	0.003

Latent Growth Mixture Models

The next example considers **latent growth mixture modeling** of repeated measures of y. Latent curve modeling (see Chapter 7) uses continuous latent variables to describe random effects (i.e., intercepts and slopes). The continuous latent variables describe unobserved heterogeneity in individual differences in change over time (Marcoulides & Heck, 2013). Most commonly considered growth models usually assume that all individuals in a given sample come from a single population with one mean growth (change) pattern, and the variability around that mean growth is captured by the variance of the growth factors.

Latent growth mixture modeling (LGMM) represents an extension of the traditional growth model that permits the consideration of latent classes with differing developmental trajectories. LGMM thereby permits more than one mean growth rate pattern, often assuming unique mean growth patterns for each apparently existing unobserved subpopulation (Marcoulides & Heck, 2013). In LGMM, heterogeneity in y over time is captured by both continuous and categorical latent variables. Growth mixture models propose that latent intercept (e.g., initial status, end status) and latent growth rate factors are different for different classes of individuals. More specifically, each class may have a different random effect growth model (Muthén, 2001). The random intercept and slopes are continuous latent variables, while the trajectories classes can be represented as a categorical latent variable.

The classes of a categorical latent variable (c) can be proposed to represent latent trajectory classes, which classify individuals into sets of exclusive categories (Clogg, 1995). The multiple indicators of the latent classes correspond to repeated measures over time (Muthén, 2002). Within-class variation is permitted for the latent trajectory classes (Muthén & Muthén, 1998–2012). This variation is also represented by random effects that influence the outcomes at all time points. Covariates can be added to the model, both to describe the formation of the latent classes if desired and how they may be differentially measured by the repeated measures (Asparouhov & Muthén, 2013). As in previous examples, the prediction of latent class membership is by the multinomial logistic regression of c on x.

We note that various measurement concerns in defining the latent growth trajectories, as well as the type of model one is conducting (e.g., growth mixture model, latent transition analysis), may be considerations in whether to define the latent classes initially before covariates are added. Specifying the nature of individual growth trajectories within latent classes is a measurement issue (Marcoulides & Heck, 2013). With respect to latent transition analyses, Asparouhov and Muthén (2013) note that the three-step estimation approach may be "very desirable in the LTA context because the 1-step approach has the drawback where an observed measurement at one point in time affects the definition of the latent class variable at another point in time" (p. 19).

Latent growth mixture models can also be thought of as having two basic parts. The first part of the model is the general latent factor growth model for continuous and normally distributed y variables as specified in Chapter 7. In this case we will define y_{it} as a vector of science outcomes at time $(y_{i1}, y_{i2}, \ldots, y_{iT})'$ for individual i at time t, as follows

$$y_{it} = \nu_t + \Lambda_t \eta_i + K x_i + \varepsilon_{it}, \tag{9.14}$$

where ν_t is a vector of measurement intercepts, Λ_t is a $p \times m$ design matrix representing the growth process, η_i is an m-dimensional vector of latent variables $(\eta_0, \eta_1)'$, K is a $p \times q$ parameter matrix of regression slopes relating x_i $(x_{1i}, x_{2i}, \ldots, x_{pi})'$ to the latent factors, and ε_{it} represents time-specific errors contained in Θ. The factor loadings for the latent factors (i.e., in this case, η_{0i} and η_{1i}) are contained in the Λ_t factor-loading matrix, as in the following:

$$\Lambda = \begin{bmatrix} 1 & 0 \\ 1 & 1 \\ 1 & 2 \end{bmatrix}. \tag{9.15}$$

We can define an initial status factor (η_0) by fixing the first time score measurement to zero. Assuming linear growth, we then define the second time score as 1 and the third time score as 2. With equidistant observations, we therefore have $x_0 = 0, 1, 2$. Fixing the loadings of each assessment occasion on the first factor (i.e., the intercept factor) to a value of 1 in Equation 9.15 ensures that it is interpreted as an initial true status factor (i.e., as a baseline point of the underlying developmental process under investigation). Specifying the change trajectory in increments of years on the second factor (the slope factor) also ensures that the correlation between the intercept and slope factors reflects the relationship between the initial point and the slope of the proposed linear trajectory (Marcoulides & Heck, 2013). By fixing the factor loadings to a particular pattern ($t = 0$, 1, 2), the hypothesized growth shape may then be tested against the actual data and its fit determined by examining various SEM fit indices. Of course, it is possible to incorporate more complex patterns of change into the model, especially when there are more repeated measures.

Variation in the latent growth factors may be expressed as the following:

$$\eta_{0i} = \alpha_0 + \gamma_0 w_i + \zeta_{0i} \tag{9.16}$$

$$\eta_{1i} = \alpha_1 + \gamma_1 w_i + \zeta_{1i}, \tag{9.17}$$

where alpha (α) parameters are intercept and slope mean parameters, respectively, and ζ are residuals with zero means and covariance matrix Ψ.

The second part of the LGMM (i.e., the latent class part) extends the basic growth model to a growth mixture model for K latent trajectory classes, which describes individuals with similar development over time (i.e., similar growth trajectories) and relates these latent classes to covariates x_i (Muthén & Muthén, 1998–2012). Of interest are the class-varying means for the $k - 1$ classes. Because the growth factor means can change over the latent classes, this can result in different trajectory shapes (Muthén, 2002).

Examining Latent Classes in Students' Growth in Science

In this example, we will first examine a single-level LGMM for individuals' science achievement and growth ($N = 6,623$) using two within-school covariates. Students are observed on three occasions (with means of 46.94, 51.64, and 55.76, respectively). In this example, the mean grade point average (GPA) and student socioeconomic status (SES) were standardized ($M = 0$, $SD = 1$). The proposed model is summarized in Figure 9.8.

We propose that GPA and SES will affect students' initial status (i) and growth rate (s) in science. A covariance is also specified between the initial status and slope factors. Because c is a categorical latent variable, the arrows from c to the latent growth factors indicate the intercepts of the regressions of the growth factors on the covariates vary across the classes of c. This corresponds to the regressions of i and s on a set of dummy-coded variables representing the categories of c (Muthén & Muthén, 1998–2012). The arrows from student SES and GPA to c represent the multinomial logistic regressions of c on the covariates (x).

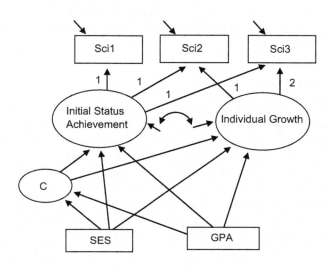

FIGURE 9.8 Proposed single-level growth mixture model for science.

The latent growth mixture model combines a continuous latent growth variable for science (represented as η_i, which consists of an intercept and slope factor) and a categorical latent variable (c) with K classes, $C_i = (c_1, c_2, \ldots, c_K)'$, where x_i, if individual i belongs to class k, and zero otherwise. We can extend the basic latent growth model just described to a latent growth mixture model for K latent trajectory classes, where in Class k ($k = 1, 2, \ldots, K$)

$$\eta_{0i} = \alpha_{0k} + \gamma_{0k} w_i + \zeta_{0i} \tag{9.18}$$

$$\eta_{1i} = \alpha_{1k} + \gamma_{1k} + w_i + \zeta_{1i}, \tag{9.19}$$

where the α parameters vary across the classes, γ are structural parameters relating a vector of covariates (w_i) to the random effects such that the influence of w can vary across latent classes, ζ_{0i} and ζ_{1i} are vectors of residuals assumed to be normally distributed, uncorrelated with other variables, and with means of zero. If there are no covariates, the alphas are the means of the growth factors (Muthén, 2001). Residuals have a 2×2 covariance matrix (Ψ_k) that may vary across the latent classes (Muthén, 2002).

The LGMM formulation provides considerable flexibility for defining across-class parameter differences. The different shapes of the latent trajectory classes can be characterized by class-varying intercept parameters, holding Λ_k invariant across latent classes. Some classes may require class-specific variances in Θ_k and Ψ_k (Muthén, 2002). Moreover, different classes may have different relations to the covariate, corresponding to class-varying γ_k coefficients (Muthén, 2002). More technical descriptions of extensions of basic growth mixture models (e.g., with categorical repeated measures) can be found in Muthén (2002), Duncan et al. (2006), and the technical appendices of Mplus (Muthén, 1998–2004).

Model Statements

For purposes of presentation, we will restrict the student growth trajectory model to be the same across latent classes by defining the same model (i.e., using %OVERALL% statement without specifying differences for particular classes). However, we will specify the predictors explaining class membership to be different for the classes. In the model statements, the individual classes of c are referred to by adding to the name of the categorical latent variable the number sign (#) followed by the number of the class (with one less regression equation than the number of classes specified). For example, we refer to the multinomial regression of the first three classes (c #1 to c #3) on GPA and SES.

When a linear growth model is specified, there are no free parameters in the Λ_k matrix. For the rest of the model, there are 26 free parameters to be estimated.

These include four regression equations from the covariates to the intercept and slope factors, one covariance between intercept and slope factors, eight intercepts (i.e., one initial status intercept and one growth slope for each class), four residual variances (i.e., two for observed indicators and one for initial status and one for the slope), six logistic regressions of c on the covariates, and three latent class intercepts (i.e., since there are four latent classes). The specification of the model can be verified in the TECH1 information if requested as output. We also plot the trajectories.

```
TITLE:       Latent growth mixture model for science achievement;
DATA:        FILE IS C:\mplus\ch9ex4.dat;
             Format is 1f8.0,5f8.2,3f8.0;
VARIABLE:    Names are schcode ses gpa sci1 sci2 sci3
             moved lowses acadsch;
             Usevariables sci1 sci2 sci3 gpa ses;
             classes = c(4);
ANALYSIS:    TYPE = mixture;
             Estimator is MLR;
             starts = 100 4;
Model:
             %Overall%
             i s |sci1@0 sci2@1 sci3@2;
             sci1@0;
             i on gpa ses;
             s on gpa ses;
             c#1 on gpa ses;
             c#2 on gpa ses;
             c#3 on gpa ses;
Plot:        TYPE IS PLOT3;
             SERIES IS sci1-sci3(*);
OUTPUT:      SAMPSTAT STANDARDIZED TECH11 TECH14;
```

Model Output

We investigated a number of different preliminary models with different numbers of latent classes before settling on four classes, relying primarily on the BIC associated with each model. The TECH11 option can also be used in conjunction with TYPE = MIXTURE to request the Vuong-Lo-Mendell-Rubin test, which compares the model with k classes (i.e., four) to a model with $k - 1$ classes (i.e., three classes). A low p-value favors the current model. For the four- versus

TABLE 9.7 Average Classification Probabilities for the Four-Class Model

	1	2	3	4
1	0.845	0.000	0.040	0.114
2	0.000	0.880	0.000	0.120
3	0.157	0.000	0.842	0.000
4	0.027	0.015	0.000	0.958

three-class model, the Vuong-Lo-Mendell-Rubin test is 486.830 ($p < 0.0001$) and the Lo-Mendell-Rubin adjusted LRT test is 476.009 ($p < 0.0001$). Similarly, the bootstrapped parametric likelihood ratio test (TECH14) has a p value < 0.0001. All three tests suggest that four classes fit better than three classes.

Classes 1 to 4 have class probabilities of 0.186, 0.106, 0.063, and 0.645, respectively (not tabled). We note in passing that the estimation process may result in changing the order of the categories across different random starts and final optimizations. Table 9.7 provides the average posterior probabilities from the four-class model. Entropy is 0.864, indicating excellent classification (i.e., with correct classification of 85%, 88%, 84%, and 96% for Classes 1–4, respectively).

Model estimates are summarized in Table 9.8. We do not include the definition of the linear growth model within each since there are no free parameters. First, the table suggests that students with higher GPAs and higher SES have significantly higher initial status intercepts than their peers with lower GPAs ($0.374, p < 0.001$) and SES ($0.500, p < 0.001$). Moreover, students with higher GPAs ($0.831, p < 0.001$) and SES ($0.981, p < 0.001$) make significantly greater growth over time than their peers with lower GPAs and lower SES. For the latent class portion of the model, initial status means and growth rate means differ across the four latent classes. Initial status intercepts are 40.213 for Class 1, 58.095 for Class 2, 32.539 for Class 3, and 48.468 for Class 4. Corresponding growth rates are 3.729 for Class 1, 2.240 for Class 2, 6.870 for Class 3, and 4.783 for Class 4. These coefficients suggest considerable differences in students' starting knowledge in science and in their growth rates over the period of the study.

For the multinomial regressions of C#1, C#2, and C#3 on GPA and SES (with Class 4 serving as the reference group), the results suggest considerable variability across the latent classes. For C#1 the coefficients are −0.302 for GPA and −0.502 for SES (with $p < 0.001$). For C#2, the GPA coefficient is 0.744 and the SES coefficient is 0.501 (with $p < 0.001$). For C#3, the GPA coefficient is −0.401 and the SES coefficient is −0.756 (with $p < 0.001$). This suggests that both student GPA and SES background are useful in explaining their latent class membership with respect to their initial status and growth rate. The estimated

TABLE 9.8 Growth Mixture Model Results

| | Two-Tailed | | | |
	Estimate	S.E.	Est./S.E.	P-Value
Overall Growth Model				
I ON				
GPA	0.374	0.057	6.533	0.000
SES	0.500	0.074	6.738	0.000
S ON				
GPA	0.831	0.046	18.238	0.000
SES	0.981	0.058	16.814	0.000
S WITH I	−1.482	0.345	−4.299	0.000
Residual Variances				
SCI1	0.000	0.000	999.000	999.000
SCI2	22.560	0.630	35.807	0.000
SCI3	8.602	1.099	7.829	0.000
I	7.506	0.318	23.588	0.000
S	8.222	0.332	24.737	0.000
Latent Class 1				
Intercepts				
I	40.213	0.222	180.850	0.000
S	3.729	0.149	25.081	0.000
Latent Class 2				
Intercepts				
I	58.095	0.229	253.821	0.000
S	2.240	0.182	12.293	0.000
Latent Class 3				
Intercepts				
I	32.539	0.295	110.421	0.000
S	6.870	0.284	24.172	0.000
Latent Class 4				
I	48.468	0.070	688.463	0.000
S	4.783	0.053	90.132	0.000
Categorical Latent Variable				
C#1 ON				
GPA	−0.302	0.039	−7.735	0.000
SES	−0.502	0.059	−8.529	0.000
C#2 ON				
GPA	0.744	0.070	10.667	0.000
SES	0.501	0.071	7.014	0.000
C#3 ON				
GPA	−0.401	0.055	−7.319	0.000
SES	−0.756	0.089	−8.456	0.000
Intercepts				
C#1	-1.364	0.052	−26.296	0.000
C#2	-2.227	0.090	−24.850	0.000
C#3	-2.586	0.095	−27.241	0.000

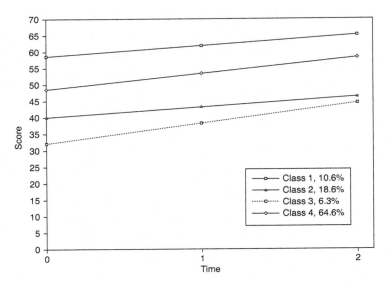

FIGURE 9.9 Estimated latent class means and growth trajectories for growth mixture model.

means for each of the four latent classes over the three measurement occasions are plotted in Figure 9.9.

As part of our model development, we also investigated a three-step model for developing the latent classes to compare the results against the one-step approach as outlined. In this case, we first developed the latent classes without covariates and saved the latent class probabilities and assignment of individuals to most their likely latent classes. Our analysis confirmed a four-class latent class model (e.g., using BIC as a criterion); however, we noted that the proportional sizes of the classes identified differed to some extent (i.e., primarily the two smallest classes). In addition, as we might expect, the correct classification rate for individuals was not as strong (entropy = 0.733) as in the one-step model presented previously. In the multinomial regression part of the analysis, we found that the GPA and SES covariates still differentiated between-class membership, even if they were not used in defining the initial latent classes.

Two-Level LGMM

The previous model provides a preliminary indication of different classes of latent growth trajectories. We can also add a school level to the model (N = 779). In this example, we will examine the possible effects of a school-level variable—the *student composition* (i.e., defined as schools with 50% or more students identified as participating in the federal free/reduced lunch program coded 1 versus others coded 0) on the level of schools' initial status in science achievement and their growth rate. Additionally, we can determine whether *student composition* explains membership in the latent trajectory classes. Within schools, we will use student grade point average (GPA) and individual SES as covariates.

The two-level LGMM specification defines growth models within and between groups and extends the growth model to K latent classes. The two-level LGMM formulation corresponds to a three-level growth modeling approach as we specified in Chapter 7 [e.g., see Muthén & Asparouhov (2011) for further discussion]. This is because in the two-level LGMM the repeated measures of y are represented by a multivariate vector $y = (y_1, y_2, ..., y_T)'$, which reduces the two lower levels of the three-level growth model (i.e., measurements within students, between students) to one within-group level. In the LGMM formulation, to define growth within and between groups, we can fit measurement models at two levels and impose constraints on the corresponding within-group and between-group covariance matrices. Similarly, the matrices defining the growth parameters can be split into their between- and within-groups matrices (i.e., Λ, B, Ψ, Θ).

The two-level LGMM is illustrated in Figure 9.10. In the student part of the model, the initial achievement and growth factors are defined by the observed

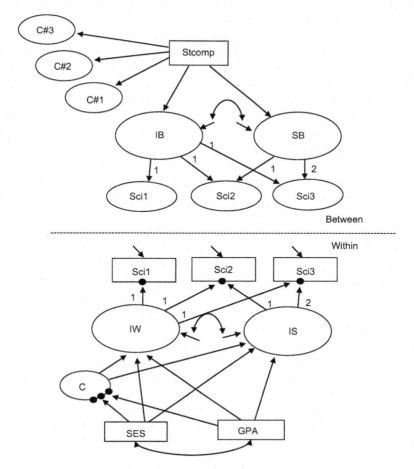

FIGURE 9.10 Proposed two-level growth mixture model.

indicators *sci1*, *sci2*, and *sci3*. The filled dots at the end of the arrows from the within growth factors *iw* and *sw* to *sci1*, *sci2*, and *sci3* represent random intercepts that vary across clusters. The filled dots at the end of the arrow from *x* to *c* indicate random intercepts for the latent classes. In this case, since there are four latent classes specified, three random intercepts for *c* can vary across level-2 units (schools). In the between-groups part of the model, the random intercepts are referred to as *sci1*, *sci2*, *sci3*, *c#1*, *c#2*, and *c#3*, which are shown as ovals because they are continuous latent variables. The arrow from *c* to the growth factors indicates that the means of the growth factors vary across the latent classes of *c*. The residual variances of the outcome variables are estimated and allowed to be different across time and the residuals are not correlated as the default (Muthén & Muthén, 1998–2012).

Model Statements

We again specify a four-class model since we found previously this worked for the single-level model. We note in passing that it can be more difficult to fit a multilevel LGMM to the data than a single-level model, given that there is a level-2 sample that may have its own idiosyncratic nature (e.g., sample size, distribution of units, how they were selected, etc.). The multilevel case can require some changes in the numerical integration process used to estimate the model (see the *Mplus User's Guide* for further discussion of these options). Keep in mind that the choices made in estimating multilevel models with categorical outcomes (e.g., method of integration, choice of the number of random starts) can have a considerable effect on the final estimates and the time it takes to generate a solution. At present, therefore, it is probably best to consider such results as preliminary. For purposes of initial investigation, users may wish to set random starts to 0 (starts = 0;). We eventually present a solution with 300 starts and four final stage optimizations, which replicates the best log-likelihood value.

In the within-groups portion, for the %OVERALL% model, the BY statements define the growth factors as linear. The first ON statements represent the regression of the intercept and growth factors (*iw*, *sw*) on the individual-level covariates (SES, GPA). They can also be defined in one statement (iw sw on gpa ses;) The residual variances of the growth factors are free to be estimated as the default. The second ON statements describe the logistic regression of the categorical latent variable *c* on the individual-level covariates when comparing Class 1 (*C#1*), Class 2 (*C#2*), and Class 3 (*C#3*) to Class 4 (the reference group).

Between groups, in the %OVERALL% model, the BY statements define the between-groups growth model as linear. The first ON statement defines the regression of the intercept and growth factors on school student composition context (*stcomp*). The second ON statement describes the regression of C#1, C#2, and C#3 on school SES. We note that the residual variance of the growth factor (*sb*) is free to be estimated as the default. We fix its residual variance to zero (sb@0;), however, since it is often small and each residual variance requires one dimension of numerical integration. Because the slope growth factor residual variance is fixed at zero, the covariance between *ib* and *sb* is automatically fixed at zero (although we show it as fixed at 0 in the model statements).

```
TITLE:        Two-level latent growth mixture model for science;
DATA:         FILE IS C:\mplus\ch9ex4.dat;
              Format is 1f8.0,5f8.2,3f8.0;
VARIABLE:     Names are schcode ses gpa sci1 sci2 sci3
              moved lowses acadsch;
              Usevariables sci1 sci2 sci3 gpa ses lowses;
              classes = c(4);
              within = gpa ses;
              between = lowses;
              CLUSTER IS schcode;
define:       center SES GPA lowses(grandmean);
ANALYSIS:     TYPE = twolevel mixture;
              Estimator is MLR;
              starts= 300 4;
Model:
              %Within%
              %Overall%
              iw by sci1@1 sci2@1 sci3@1;
              sw by sci1@0 sci2@1 sci3@2;
              iw on gpa*1.8 ses*1.2;
              sw on gpa*.6 ses*.6;
              c#1 c#2 c#3 on gpa*.1 ses*.1;
              %Between%
              %Overall%
              ib by sci1@1 sci2@1 sci3@1;
              sb by sci1@0 sci2@1 sci3@2;
              [ib sb];
              sb@0;
              sb with ib@0;
              ib sb on lowses;
              c#1 c#2 c#3 on lowses*-.3;
OUTPUT:       SAMPSTAT STANDARDIZED TECH1 TECH11;
```

Model Output

Regarding model fit criteria (not tabled), for our proposed four-class model (34 estimated parameters), the BIC is 125,412.427). For the three-class model, the BIC is 125,773.885. For a difference of six parameters, the adjusted LRT for a four-class versus three-class model is 403.371 ($p < 0.018$). The final proportions for the four classes are 0.189, 0.105, 0.069, and 0.637 with corresponding proportions correctly classified of 0.844, 0.878, 0.814, and 0.957. For the four-class model entropy is 0.858. This result is consistent with the single-level analysis (entropy = 0.858). We conclude that this model fits the data quite well.

Table 9.9 presents the results of the model tested. Regarding the overall growth model, within groups, we can see that GPA (0.279) and SES (0.359) affect initial

TABLE 9.9 Multilevel Growth Mixture Model

	Two–Tailed			
	Estimate	S.E.	Est./S.E.	P–Value
Within Groups Model				
IW ON GPA	0.279	0.077	3.617	0.000
IW ON SES	0.359	0.100	3.583	0.000
SW ON GPA	0.777	0.055	14.113	0.000
SW ON SES	0.874	0.074	11.734	0.000
S WITH I	0.032	0.781	0.041	0.967
Residual Variances				
SCI1	5.872	2.783	2.110	0.035
SCI2	19.932	1.349	14.780	0.000
SCI3	12.912	2.407	5.365	0.000
IW	1.904	2.236	0.852	0.395
SW	5.921	1.176	5.035	0.000
Between Groups Model				
IB ON Stcomp	0.071	0.231	0.309	0.757
SB ON stcomp	−0.470	0.155	−3.035	0.002
IB WITH SB	0.000	0.000	999.000	999.000
Residual Variances				
IB	0.753	0.175	4.307	0.000
SB	0.000	0.000	999.000	999.000
Latent Class 1				
Intercepts				
IB	−7.801	0.310	−25.149	0.000
SB	−1.363	0.247	−5.515	0.000
Latent Class 2				
Intercepts				
IB	9.696	0.208	46.681	0.000
SB	−1.921	0.305	−6.291	0.000
Latent Class 3				
Intercepts				
IB	−15.383	0.399	−38.527	0.000
SB	1.243	0.563	2.208	0.027

	Two–Tailed			
	Estimate	S.E.	Est./S.E.	P–Value
Latent Class 4				
Intercepts				
IB	0.000	0.000	999.000	999.000
SB	0.000	0.000	999.000	999.000
Categorical Latent Variable				
Within Level				
C#1 ON				
GPA	−0.297	0.041	−7.209	0.000
SES	−0.485	0.059	−8.213	0.000
C#2 ON				
GPA	0.873	0.089	9.765	0.000
SES	0.509	0.081	6.307	0.000
C#3 ON				
GPA	−0.446	0.058	−7.704	0.000
SES	−0.787	0.106	−7.428	0.000
Intercepts				
C#1	−1.312	0.054	−24.251	0.000
C#2	−2.344	0.097	−24.149	0.000
C#3	−2.505	0.109	−22.878	0.000
Between Level				
C#1 ON Stcomp	0.229	0.120	1.901	0.057
C#2 ON Stcomp	−0.860	0.340	−2.526	0.012
C#3 ON Stcomp	0.456	0.201	2.271	0.023

status ($p < 0.001$). Similarly, GPA (0.777) and SES (0.874) also affect growth significantly ($p < 0.001$). Between schools, student composition does not affect initial status ($0.071, p > 0.10$) but does affect growth in science significantly ($−0.470, p < 0.01$). We can also observe that the latent classes have different growth trajectories. Relative to Class 4 (the reference class and the largest class), Class 1 had lower initial status (−7.801) and growth per year (−1.363); Class 2 had higher initial status (9.696) and lower growth per year (−1.921); and Class 3 had lower initial status (−15.283) but positive growth per year (1.243).

Regarding the multinomial regressions of *C*#1, *C*#2, and *C*#3 on GPA and SES (with coefficients in log odds metrics), we can see that lower GPA (−0.297, $p < 0.001$) and SES (−0.495, $p < 0.001$) increase the odds of membership in *C*#1 versus the reference group. Regarding *C*#2, higher GPA (0.873, $p < 0.001$) and SES (0.509, $p < 0.001$) increase the probability of membership in *C*#2 versus the reference group. Regarding *C*#3, lower GPA (−0.446, $p < 0.001$) and SES (−0.787, $p < 0.001$) increase the probability of being in *C*#3 versus the reference class.

Finally, between groups (where coefficients are unstandardized betas), we can see that low student SES composition positively predicts membership in C#1 versus the reference class ($0.229, p < 0.06$), negatively predicts membership in C#2 ($-0.860, p < 0.05$), and positively predicts membership in C#3 ($0.456, p < 0.05$). The results are therefore consistent with the theoretical propositions that student achievement background (GPA) and SES are related to different latent classes of science growth within schools and that student composition is associated with different latent classes of school science growth between schools.

Summary

Models with categorical observed and latent variables greatly increase the range of multilevel models that can be examined. There are a number of types of mixture models that can be conducted using the SEM framework (e.g., growth mixture models, latent transition analyses, latent variable hybrid models). These models expand ways that we can think about how individuals' shared environments affect their individual outcomes (Asparouhov & Muthén, 2008). These models can vary considerably in their complexity and demands on estimation time. They offer exciting possibilities to conduct research that establishes the usefulness of these types of models for answering questions related to substantive theories.

References

Aitkin, M. (1999). A general maximum likelihood analysis of variance components in generalized linear models. *Biometrics, 55*, 117–128.

Asparouhov, T. & Muthén, B. (2008). Multilevel mixture models. In G. R. Hancock & K. M. Samuelsen (Eds.), *Advances in latent variable mixture models* (pp. 27–51). Charlotte, NC: Information Age Publishing, Inc.

Asparouhov, T. & Muthén, B. O. (February 2013). Auxiliary variables in mixture modeling: A 3-step approach using Mplus. *Mplus Web Notes (No. 15)*. Retrieved from www.statmodel.com

Bolck, A., Croon M. A., & Hagenaars, J. A. (2004). Estimating latent structure models with categorical variables: One-step versus three-step estimators. *Political Analysis, 12*, 3–27.

Clogg, C. C. (1995). Latent class models. In Arminger, C. C. Clogg, & M. E. Sobel (Eds.), *Handbook of statistical modeling for the social and behavioral science* (pp. 311–359). New York: Plenum.

Duncan, T. E., Duncan, S. C., & Strycker, L. A. (2006). *An introduction to latent variable growth curve modeling: Concepts, issues, and applications* (2nd ed.). Mahwah, NJ: Lawrence Erlbaum.

Lo, Y., Mendell, N. R., & Rubin, D. B. (2001). Testing the number of components in a normal mixture. *Biometrika, 88*, 767–778.

Lubke, G. & Muthén, B. (2007). Performance of factor mixture models as a function of model size, covariate effects, and class-specific parameters. *Structural Equation Modeling, 14*(1), 26–47.

Marcoulides, G. A. & Heck, R. H. (2013). Mixture models in education. In T. Teo (Ed.), *Handbook of quantitative methods for educational research* (pp. 347–366). Rotterdam, Netherlands: Sense Publishers.

Muthén, B. O. (1984). A general structural equation model with dichotomous ordered categorical and continuous latent variable indicators. *Psychometrica, 49*, 115–132.

Muthén, B. O. (1998–2004). *Mplus technical indices.* Los Angeles, CA: Muthén & Muthén.

Muthén, B. O. (2001). Latent variable mixture modeling. In G. A. Marcoulides & R. E. Schumacker (Eds.), *New developments and techniques in structural equation modeling* (pp. 1–33). Mahwah, NJ: Lawrence Erlbaum Associates.

Muthén, B. O. (2002). Beyond SEM: General latent variable modeling. *Behaviormetrika, 29,* 81–118.

Muthén, B. O. (2008). Latent variable hybrids: Overview of old and new models. In G. R. Hancock & K. M. Samuelson (Eds.), *Advances in latent variable mixture models* (pp. 1–24). Charlotte, NC: Information Age Publishing.

Muthén, B. & Asparouhov, T. (2009). Growth mixture modeling: Analysis with non-Gaussian random effects. In G. Fitzmaurice, M. Davidian, G. Verbeke, & G. Molenberghs (Eds.), *Longitudinal data analysis* (pp. 143–165). Boca Raton: Chapman & Hall/CRC Press.

Muthén, B. & Asparouhov, T. (2011). Beyond multilevel regression modeling: Multilevel analysis in a general latent variable framework. In J. Hox & J. K. Roberts (Eds.), *Handbook of advanced multilevel analysis* (pp. 15–40). New York: Taylor and Francis.

Muthén, L. K. & Muthén, B.O. (1998–2012). *Mplus user's guide* (7th ed.). Los Angeles, CA: Authors.

Nylund, K. L., Asparouhov, T., & Muthén, B. O. (2007). Deciding on the number of classes in latent class analysis and growth mixture modeling: A Monte Carlo simulation study. *Structural Equation Modeling, 14,* 535–569.

Ramaswamy, V., DeSarbo, W., Reibstein, D., & Robinson, W. (1993). An empirical pooling approach for estimating marketing mix elasticities with PIMS data. *Marketing Science, 12,* 103–124.

Schwartz, G. E. (1978). Estimating the dimension of a model. *Annals of Statistics, 6*(2), 461–464.

10

DATA CONSIDERATIONS IN EXAMINING MULTILEVEL MODELS

Chapter Objectives

In this chapter, we present an overview of several data-related issues associated with modeling individual and group processes embedded in hierarchical data structures. We first provide an introductory discussion of the application of **sample weights**, focusing in particular on their potential impact at the group level of the study. Second, we turn our attention to issues related to sample size requirements in multilevel models and corresponding statistical **power** to detect hypothesized effects. Third, we discuss some common issues related to missing data. Finally, we conclude with some further thoughts about multilevel modeling.

Introduction

In this final chapter we provide some further data considerations in developing and testing multilevel models. To some extent, these are considerations present in any example study we have presented—sometimes more apparent and sometimes less so. In many ways, the quality of the data we can bring to bear on a particular research problem is the key issue regarding the credibility of our results and the extent to which they will contribute to knowledge building. In this chapter we address import ancillary considerations that include sample weights, general sample size requirements, and corresponding statistical power to observe hypothesized effects, as well as working with missing data.

Complex Samples, Design Effects, and Sample Weights

In recent years, research in many fields has benefited tremendously from the increased availability of high-quality, survey-based, **secondary data** sets germane to our varied interests. The ease of availability of these data, often combined with well-publicized financial incentives for their use, and the increasingly sophisticated technology that permits powerful analyses of large data sets have led many to rightfully view such data as an exciting research opportunity. Throughout the book we have developed analyses where the results were unweighted. This implies that every individual had an equal chance of being included in the sample—an assumption of simple random sampling. Importantly, the responses of the individuals were assumed to be weighted equality (i.e., the presence of unweighted responses assumes that each response is weighted as 1.0). Of course, this assumption about the unequal weighting of individuals may not hold in many existing data sets. The sampling scheme is often ignored in the level-2 part of the analysis as well (Pfeffermann, Skinner, Holmes, Goldstein, & Rasbash, 1998). As Pfeffermann et al. note, an argument supporting this practice is that the multilevel model can incorporate covariates with certain characteristics of strata and cluster indicators in the sampling design (i.e., covariates that capture the dimensions on which the sample is stratified or disproportional to the population). This may be inadequate, however, when units are selected with unequal probabilities in ways that are not accounted for by the model.

Belying the ease of use implied by the increasing accessibility of sample weights, there are a few critical issues to consider in making use of secondary databases in multilevel analyses. Among these issues are considerations around the correct application of sample weights that may be present in the data set to ensure the representativeness of the samples analyzed and the correct assessment of population variances that form the basis for the identification of statistical effects and hypothesis testing. When working with secondary data sets, applying sample weights is important to correct the estimates for features of the sampling design (e.g., probability of selection at multiple levels of the data hierarchy) and data collection problems (Thomas & Heck, 2001). We note, however, that while sample weights over the years have been more related to correcting for various types of sampling strategies, multilevel analysis has raised a number of issues about the correct application of weights in different situations. Weights may be available only at the individual level (Level 1), the group level (Level 2), or they may be available at both levels. We often have to decide which among several weights included in the data set to use. Here one can consult accompanying documentation.

Cluster sampling (or **two–stage cluster sampling**) refers to the common practice of first drawing a sample at a higher level—organizations, for example—and then within each organization drawing a sample of lower-level units—employees, for example. This is often done since the researcher may not have immediate access to individuals without first selecting their higher-level groupings (e.g., colleges/universities, schools, hospitals, businesses). The units may or may not be drawn proportionate to their presence in the larger population. To illustrate this point, if one were to sample organizations by rural or urban location for some reason related to the study's purposes, it might be desirable to oversample rural organizations to ensure inclusion of a sufficient number organizations located in less populated rural areas. Such oversampling results in a disproportionate number of rural organizations relative to their representation in the broader population. This must be accounted for at the analysis stage to ensure that the estimates accurately represent to population of interest.

In some cases, statistical weights are provided to account for design effects and disproportionate sampling in a single-level analysis. The consideration of sample weights and design effects is vitally important in analyses using disproportionate sampling and multistage cluster samples. In most data sets, typically sample weights are developed to produce correct results for single-level models by incorporating information about design effects and disproportionate sampling. Weighting for unequal selection is well established for single-level analyses. Sampling weights adjust the parameter estimates (e.g., fixed effects, standard errors) for both disproportionate sampling and cluster sampling. In the single-level context, this is the appropriate way to analyze data collected through complex sample designs. In this type of approach (referred to as a design-based approach), similarities among individuals due to clustering are treated as "noise," which is adjusted out of the analysis. In contrast, MLM incorporates this design feature as a central focus of the analysis. In this latter situation (referred to as a model-based approach), it is well known that departures from simple random sampling, which assumes each individual is randomly selected and independent of other individuals, can affect the estimation of coefficients, standard errors, and associated significance tests.

To illustrate, we may be interested in various subgroups within the overall population. We may use stratified sampling with proportional sampling. Sampling members of subgroups proportionally, however, often results in too few sample members to allow meaningful analyses. We therefore may use disproportionate sampling, or oversampling of subjects from smaller but important subpopulations to ensure their sufficient numbers in the final sample. Disproportionate sampling is often found in multistage cluster samples. We might wish to sample individuals disproportionately by race/ethnicity, religious affiliation, geographical location, organizational role, or work experience, to use some common examples. As a result, disproportionate sampling, while ensuring sufficient numbers for analysis, will lead to samples that overrepresent certain segments of the populations of interest.

A *design effect* (*deff*) quantifies the extent to which the sampling error present in sampling individuals in a sampling design departs from the sampling error that would be expected under simple random sampling (i.e., where each individual has the same chance of being selected). For example, to the degree that the observations within each of the higher-order clusters are more similar to each other, there will be a design effect present that biases the estimated standard errors downward. Because hypothesis tests are based on the ratio of the estimate to its standard error, having standard errors that are too small will lead to a greater propensity to commit a Type I error (i.e., falsely concluding that an effect is statistically significant when it is not) than if the sample were drawn through a simple random sampling procedure.

The design effect is defined as the ratio of the biased standard error to the standard error that would be estimated under a true random sample design. For example, if we know that the true standard error is 1.5, but the biased standard error estimated from the data collected through the multistage cluster sample is 1.2, the calculated design effect would be $1.5/1.2 = 1.25$. A design effect of 2.0 would suggest that sample would have to be twice as large to yield the same sampling variability found in a simple random sample. Incorporating design effects provides one way to adjust the standard errors of the model's regression coefficients for features of the sampling design. While design effects are often approximated for the whole sample, they actually differ from variable to variable depending on the intraclass correlation (ICC), also referred to as rho (ρ). The amount of clustering present determines the extent to which the standard errors are underestimated. The *deff* effect is defined in terms of rho as $1 + \rho\,(n - 1)$. Therefore, the larger ρ is, the larger will be the design effect. Hox (2010) notes that ρ can also be viewed as the degree of correlation within clusters; that is, a ρ of 0.165, which suggests that 16.5% of the variance in the outcome exists *between* clusters, can also be viewed as an indication that one might expect a within-cluster correlation of 0.165 on an outcome between any two selected individuals. This conceptual connection between ρ and within-cluster correlation is important in understanding design effects. In short, the greater the between-cluster variance in the individual-level outcome, the more homogenous will be the individual observations within each of the clusters. To the extent that there exist within-cluster similarities, estimates of the level-1 variances will be smaller than they would be if the sample were collected through a simple random sample design (where such clustering would be irrelevant to the variance structure). The implication central to our interests is that ignoring the clustering that is part of the sample design will yield downwardly biased estimates of standard errors.

In contrast to the previous issues related to sample selection in order to maintain a single-level analysis, modeling multilevel processes with secondary data sets introduces some additional issues to consider in examining data in the presence of sample weights. We note that the sample weight provides a means of representing the population strata correctly and is determined by the sampling design and any adjustments for nonresponse or other sample characteristics (Stapleton, 2013). By design, multilevel models capitalize on the clustered (or hierarchical) nature of data, which is an issue separate from the manner in which the within-group and between-group samples were obtained. Standard two-level models typically result from two-stage cluster sampling designs (i.e., where units are sampled and then individuals within those units), rather than the basic simple random or stratified samples, which comprise the majority of single-level analyses. Because individuals sampled from the same cluster may be more similar than two individuals sampled at random between clusters, the resulting standard errors will be lower than would be found in a simple random selection process.

Although multilevel models capitalize on the clustered nature of the data, they do not necessarily address disproportionate sampling, and, without proper weighting, they will produce incorrect parameter estimates. Often multilevel models are developed from large-scale survey data that have been collected through complex sample designs. One common problem is where there are sample weights provided for individuals (Level 1), but no weights are provided for the organizational level (Level 2). As we have noted, in most existing data sets, adjustments are made for the sampling strategies employed (i.e., stratified random sampling, two-stage random sampling of individuals within units) with the expectation that analyses are conducted at the individual level. For multi-stage samples involving disproportionate sampling at multiple levels, some data sets will include the level-2 unit weights, which can be used for multilevel analyses (Stapleton, 2013). If level-2 weights are available, one would want to be sure to adjust for this at the organizational level by using a level-2 (organizational) weight in the same fashion that the level-1 individual weight discussed previously was used. Hence, there can be sampling weights for each level of the data, although we note that many currently available data sets do not include weights at multiple levels of the data hierarchy. If the available sampling weights are ignored at either level, the parameter estimates can be substantially biased (Asparouhov, 2006).

Currently, there are no commonly established procedures for applying weights in multilevel analyses, although a considerable number of different approaches have been proposed (e.g., Asparouhov, 2005, 2006; Grilli & Pratesi, 2004; Jia, Stokes, Harris, & Wang, 2011; Pfeffermann et al., 1998; Stapleton, 2002, 2013). Research in this area is ongoing, and important advances have been made over the past decade. Mplus includes weighting options that incorporate statistical weights that combine information on clustering, the degree of intraclass correlation, and disproportionate sampling to create a set of scaled weights that will produce accurate estimates at each level of analysis.

A number of factors can influence the estimation of model parameters. These factors include the method of scaling the weights at Level 1 (i.e., how weights are scaled within the clusters), the size of the clusters, the relative invariance of the probability selection method applied to clusters (referred to as informativeness), the presence of missing data, and the size of the ICC (Asparouhov, 2006). In particular, the bias of the estimates increases as the ICC decreases. The scaling of level-1 sample weights is very important in the multilevel context, helping to improve efficiency and decrease bias in estimation (Pfefferman et al., 1998; Skinner, 2005). Asparouhov explains that the scaling of the weights at Level 1 involves multiplying the weights by a scaling constant, so that the sum of the weights is equal to some kind of characteristic of the higher-level unit (e.g., the cluster size). We note in passing that where the selection probabilities referred to by the sample weights are not related to the outcome variable of interest, a sample weight may not be required (Stapleton, 2013).

Where sample weights exist at only one level, Asparouhov (2006) has provided some guidance for obtaining proper parameter estimates. First, he suggests that when weights are only present at Level 2 (i.e., where clusters have been sampled with unequal probability), we can identify this situation as being within the framework of single-level weighted modeling, and methods available for single-level weighted analysis can be applied with consistent estimations regardless of the size of the clusters. Although the model is multilevel, the nature of the weighting is not. Of course, if sample weights are also provided at Level 1, this will change. Second, Asparouhov cautions that the situation is different when weights are provided only at Level 1, as the unequal probability of selection is applied to dependent units and, therefore, the assumptions of the single-level method of analysis will be violated. This issue may be even more severe when estimating models with categorical outcomes (Rabe-Hesketh & Skrondal, 2006). If sample weights are present at Level 1 but are not present for the group-level portion of the analysis, the best strategy may be to use a weighted single-level analysis (Asparouhov, 2006). Asparouhov's cautions imply that it is desirable to have weights available at both levels for optimal estimation of model parameters in situations where groups and individuals have been selected with known probabilities. Unfortunately, at present most available secondary data sets do not have sample weights available for multiple levels of the data hierarchy.

Mplus provides two approaches for dealing with the analysis of complex survey data (Muthén & Muthén, 1998–2012). The first approach (a design-based approach) is to compute standard errors and a chi-square test of model fit by taking into consideration stratification, non-independence of observations due to cluster sampling, and/or unequal probability of selection. Subpopulation analysis is also available. This approach can be obtained by specifying TYPE=COMPLEX in the ANALYSIS command in conjunction with the STRATIFICATION, CLUSTER, WEIGHT, and/or SUBPOPULATION options of the VARIABLE command.

The second approach (the model-based approach) is to specify a model for each level of the multilevel data thereby modeling the non-independence of observations due to cluster sampling. The use of sampling weights in the estimation of parameters, standard errors, and the chi-square test of model fit is allowed. Both individual- and cluster-level weights can be used. Users should, however, make sure the sample weights were designed for multilevel analysis (Asparouhov, 2006). For models with weights at two levels, Mplus permits the estimation of models when the data are obtained from a multistage stratified sampling design and the units sampled at each level are selected with unequal probability of selection (Asparouhov & Muthén, 2007). This model-based approach can be obtained for two-level data by specifying TYPE=TWOLEVEL in the ANALYSIS command in conjunction with the CLUSTER, WEIGHT, WTSCALE, BWEIGHT, and/or BWTSCALE options of the VARIABLE command. Observed outcome variables can be continuous, censored, binary, nominal, ordinal, counts, or combinations of these variable types. This approach is also available for three-level data with continuous outcomes but presently is not available for categorical outcomes (Muthén & Muthén, 1998–2012). As Muthén and Muthén note, these two approaches can also be combined by specifying TYPE=COMPLEX TWOLEVEL in the ANALYSIS command. Interested readers can consult the *Mplus User's Guide* (Chapter 9).

An Example Using Multilevel Weights

The efficacy of various weighting schemes used in different software programs is an issue that needs further research. Applying or not applying sample weights can change model estimates of standard errors considerably. Failure to take clustering into account by applying the appropriate weights can bias estimates of standard errors downward. Because standard errors are used in determining hypothesis tests about individual parameters, downward-biased estimates can lead to more findings of significance than should be the case. In this section, we provide an example of a two-level model using TYPE=TWOLEVEL, which incorporates level-1 and level-2 sample weights. Weights are typically constructed such that the level-2 weight is 1/probability of selecting cluster *j*, and the within-cluster weight is 1/probability of the *i*th observation being selected, if cluster *j* is selected (Asparouhov, 2006). We also provide the unweighted estimates for comparative purposes. In the example, there are 5,952 students nested in 185 schools with a continuous outcome.

Model Statements

For model-based approaches, Mplus offers considerable flexibility in applying sample weights to multilevel models. The specification of a multilevel model facilitates addressing the non-independence of observations due to cluster sampling. The use of sampling weights in the estimation of parameters, standard errors, and the chi-square test of model fit is allowed at both the individual level and cluster level. With sampling weights, parameters are estimated by maximizing a weighted log-likelihood function. Standard error computations use a sandwich estimator (Muthén & Muthén, 1998–2012). We next provide the model statements.

```
TITLE:      Two-level model with sample weights;
DATA:       FILE IS C:\mplus\ch10wt.dat;
            Format is 2f8.0,3f8.2,1f8.0,3f8.2,2f8.0,f8.2,2f8.0,f8.2;
VARIABLE:   Names are schcode tutorm ses math gmpv1math female
            gminterSES
            stwgt sSES private academic gmrankm city lcity schwt;
            Usevariables schcode tutorm math ses female
```

```
            sSES private academic city Icity;
            within = ses female tutorm;
            between = sSES private academic city Icity;
            CLUSTER IS schcode;
            weight is stwgt;
            wtscale = cluster;
            bweight = schwt;
            bwtscale = sample;
define:     center sSES (grandmean);
ANALYSIS:   TYPE = Twolevel Random;
            Estimator is MLR;
Model:

            %BETWEEN%
            math on sSES private academic city Icity;
            S on sSES;
            %WITHIN%
            math on ses female;
            S | math on tutorm;
OUTPUT:     SAMPSTAT TECH1;
```

For two-level models with a random slope, we can specify TYPE=TWOLEVEL RANDOM in the ANALYSIS command if there is a random slope included in the analysis. The WEIGHT option is used to identify the variable that contains sampling weight information for Level 1 (*stwgt*). We note that the sampling weight values must be non-negative real numbers. Using the unscaled within-level weights in the estimation method can lead to bias in the parameter estimates (Aparrouhov, 2006). We can rescale the original sample weights, however, before the model is estimated. The scaling modification methods adjust the level-1 weights across clusters so that the total weight of the cluster is equal to some cluster characteristic (Asparouhov, 2006).

The WTSCALE option is used with TYPE=TWOLEVEL to adjust the weight variable named using the WEIGHT option (i.e., the WEIGHT option identifies the within-group sampling weight information). The following options are available: Unscaled, Cluster (the default), and Ecluster. The Unscaled option provides within-group weights with no adjustment. The Cluster setting scales the within-group weights so that they sum to the sample size in each cluster. The Ecluster setting scales the within-group weights so that they sum to the effective cluster sample size (Pothoff, Woodbury, & Manton, 1992).

Asparouhov (2006) has provided some guidance for selecting scaling at Level 1. The unscaled setting should only be used in situations where the scaling is done outside of Mplus prior to the analysis. In general, if the random effects in the model are conditionally independent, given all model covariates, it is likely the probability of selection at Level 1 is invariant across clusters. Individuals may have been selected through simple random sampling or through some method of stratified sampling such that the probability of selection is unequal. We are primarily interesting in the situation where individuals are not selected through simple random sampling at Level 1. For example, if low-SES individuals were selected at two times the rate of average- or high-SES individuals, this would indicate invariance with respect to clusters. If the selection is invariant, the analyst can rescale the within-group weights so that they sum to the sample size in each cluster. Asparouhov refers to this as scaling method A. We note in passing that if the selection process is not invariant across level-2 units, then the weights within each cluster could be on different scales and direct comparison between the weights might become problematic. In most situations, however, simulation studies (e.g., Asparouhov, 2006; Pfefferman et al., 1998) conclude that scaling to cluster sample size tends to have the most robust performance with varied cluster sizes, selection probabilities, and weight informativeness. As Asparouhov notes, where the concern is with accurate variance and covariance parameters in particular, users may select ecluster rather than the default cluster method. This is referred to as scaling method B (Asparouhov, 2006).

In general, it is often a good idea to consider both the weighted and unweighted results, as well as the different methods of scaling to understand the possible implications of the choices for the level-1 weight scaling (Stapleton, 2013). For example, users can also use the unweighted and weighted estimates to compute an a measure of the level of informativeness of the selection method for the dependent variables Y in the model [see Asparouhov (2006) or Pfeffermann et al. (1998) for further discussion for computing the informative index]. This refers to whether the method of selecting individuals with different selection probabilities at Level 1 results in a sample weight that is informative and, as a result, should be included in the analysis. The mean of Y is usually the most sensitive to selection bias (Asparouhov, 2006). If the analyst determines that the sample weight is not informative (i.e., the probability of selection is related to one or more covariates but not to Y itself) or only slightly informative, it should not be included in the analysis, as it may actually contribute to a loss of precision. As a general guideline, Asparouhov suggests that where the informative index is less than 0.2 for Y, scaling the level-1 weights to sum to the cluster sample size (scaling method A) will work with any sample size. If the index is between 0.2 and 0.3 or the average sample size is larger than 10, the weighted parameter estimates should be trustworthy for various types of multilevel models.

The BWEIGHT option is used with TYPE=TWOLEVEL to identify the variable that contains between-level sampling weight information (*schwt*). The scaling of the between-level weights generally does not affect the parameter estimates and standard errors, but it does influence the log-likelihood value and resulting fit indices that depend on the log-likelihood (Asparouhov, 2006; Muthén & Muthén,

1998–2012). BWTSCALE has the options of Unscaled and Sample. Unscaled uses the between-group weight from the data set with no adjustment (i.e., where the scaling is done prior to the Mplus analysis), whereas Sample (the default) adjusts the between-group weight so that the product of the between-group and the within-group weights sums to the total sample size (Muthén & Muthén, 1998–2012). This will generally produce accurate fit indices for the model.

Sampling weights can be used for all analysis types and most common estimators (e.g., MLR, WLS, WLSM, WLSMV). However, they are not available for WLS when all dependent variables are continuous (Muthén & Muthén, 1998–2012). In addition to modeling the non-independence of observations due to cluster sampling, standard errors and a chi-square test of model fit are computed by taking into account stratification, non-independence of observations due to cluster sampling, and unequal probability of selection. Moreover, where there may be clustering due to both primary and secondary sampling stages, the standard errors and chi-square test are computed by taking into consideration the clustering due to the primary sampling stage and clustering due to the secondary sampling stage is modeled (Muthén & Muthén, 1998–2012).

Readers can consult the *Mplus User's Guide* for more detailed information about availability of other estimators under various types of modeling conditions.

Model Output

In Table 10.1, we provide the unweighted versus weighted estimates for the within- and between-group variables. For this analysis, the level-1 weights were scaled within level-2 units such that the sum of these weights equals the size of the respective level-2 unit (Asparouhov, 2006).

The results suggest that providing proper weights can affect the size of the estimated coefficients as well as the calculation of the standard errors at both Level 1 and Level 2. First, the unweighted and weighted estimates of average school achievement are quite different. For example, the unweighted estimate of the adjusted level of school math achievement was considerably higher ($\bar{X} = 542.99$) than the weighted estimate, which takes into consideration the proper representation of the schools in the stratified sample drawn from the population ($\bar{X} = 515.94$). As we might expect, the unweighted standard error was somewhat smaller than the weighted estimate (7.56 to 7.79, respectively). Second, at the school level, we can observe a difference in the pattern of hypothesis testing. Because hypothesis tests are based on the ratio of the estimate to its standard error, on many occasions we can note differences in significance testing of unweighted versus weighted estimates. In the model with unweighted estimates, school SES and school type (i.e., private or public) were the only significant predictors of math scores. In the weighted solution, however, there is some evidence that that the school's curriculum orientation (*academic*) may also affect math outcomes ($12.80, p < 0.10$).

TABLE 10.1 Unweighted and Weighted Two-Level Estimates

	Unweighted		Weighted	
	Estimates	SE	Estimates	SE
School Model				
Intercept	542.99**	7.56	515.94**	7.79
SchSES	141.82**	9.88	131.36**	11.87
Private	−57.11**	6.75	−55.57**	6.90
Academic	10.41	7.25	12.80*	7.78
City	−2.30	7.07	5.23	8.82
Large City	6.82	8.03	8.40	9.23
Individual				
SES	7.76**	1.54	6.87**	2.08
Female	−16.41**	1.96	−14.04**	2.66
Slope Model				
Tutoring	−17.41**	2.96	−23.97**	4.58
Tutoring*SchSES	31.11**	7.56	42.63**	8.40
Random Effects				
Residual	3,692.37**	89.86	3,849.39**	128.23
Level 2(I)	1,413.14**	166.13	1,360.18**	195.48
Level 2(S)	158.05	109.05	283.94	223.21

$*p < 0.10; **p < 0.05$

Third, regarding the slope model, we can see that students who received outside tutoring had significantly lower math scores in both the unweighted and weighted solutions. There was, however, a considerable difference in the average size of the coefficient regarding students who received outside tutoring in math. More specifically, the unweighted estimate was approximately −17.41, while the weighted estimate was −23.97. Similarly, the cross-level interaction (*tutoring* * *School SES*) was also different; that is, approximately 31.11 in the unweighted solution and 42.63 in the weighted solution. These results suggest that students who were likely to obtain outside tutoring in high-SES school settings were more highly achieving than their peers in schools at the grand mean of school achievement. For example, at $1 - SD$ above the grand mean, the advantage would be about 18.66 points in the standardized math test ($-23.97 + 42.63 = 18.66$).

Finally, we note considerable differences in calculating the variance components in the weighted and unweighted models in Table 10.1. Despite these differences, however, in both models, after accounting for school SES, we can see that there was not significant random variance in slopes remaining to explain between schools

($p > 0.10$). We emphasize that no definitive conclusions should be drawn from this one simple comparison of unweighted and weighted multilevel results. Our analysis was only to make the point that using sample weights, and using them correctly, does make a difference in the accuracy of the estimates obtained and certainly can affect the associated hypothesis tests in multilevel analyses.

Parameter Bias and Statistical Power

We have mentioned several times that multilevel models can be quite demanding of data, and the analyst should be very aware of the limitations that exist as model specification becomes more complicated. For example, we have found that small data sets (e.g., 20 to 30 individuals per unit nested within 25 or 30 units) are often adequate to identify variability in random intercepts across groups; however, when we wish to estimate random slopes, we often need considerably more units in order to observe statistically significant variability across groups (e.g., often requiring 20 to 30 individuals within groups and 100 or more groups). This gave us pause to consider that many published multilevel studies may report nonsignificant results due primarily to making Type II errors (i.e., failure to reject the null hypothesis due to not having adequate data ahead of time to detect the effects). This suggests the failure may not always be the proposed conceptual model but, rather, the various shortcomings of the sample data and, perhaps, the measurement reliability of key variables.

In designing multilevel studies, therefore, researchers need to give attention to a number of issues regarding necessary sample sizes (e.g., number of units) and the distribution of individuals within units on variables of interest. Tests of statistical significance were designed to help the researcher assess the evidence with respect to the probability of an event having arisen because of sampling error, assuming that the hypothesis being tested is true (Pedhazur & Schmelkin, 1991). These issues typically arise though questions about the appropriate (or minimum) sample size needed for various types of multilevel analyses. Such questions are implicitly after a determination of two things: the sample size required to ensure that estimates of fixed effects and variances are unbiased, and the sample size required to ensure that an effect would be detected if, in fact, it existed (i.e., power). Readers can consult Scherbaum and Ferreter (2009), Snijders and Bosker (1999), and Snijders (2005) for further discussion of issues related to power.

Bias

The bulk of the research examining the potential parameter bias and sample size suggests that the number of clusters in the study is typically the primary concern. Mok's (1995) simulations suggest that when using smaller samples ($N_i < 800$, with perhaps up to 20 students in each of 40 schools), level-1 fixed estimates are less biased when the number of groups is increased at the expense of the number of observations within each group, as opposed to the other way around. When thinking about precision, a temptation might be to ensure better representation by increasing the size of the groups. Maas and Hox (2002), however, found that while regression coefficients and variance components are unbiased under a range of realistic conditions (i.e., within-groups sizes, number of groups, and realistic intraclass correlations), estimates of standard errors of level-2 variances tend to be biased downward when there are 30 or fewer level-2 units. This suggests that the group-level sample size is typically more important than the individual-level sample size when estimating individual-level fixed effects. They also noted that although the regression coefficients and level-1 variance components are generally unbiased with smaller numbers of groups, the bias in group-level variance components is simply too great when using 20 or fewer groups, regardless of within-group sample sizes and level of the intraclass correlation.

For most multilevel studies, therefore, the greater concern is having enough groups available to ensure accurate estimation of group-level parameters, as well as sufficient ability to detect between-group effects. Where group-level sample sizes are a concern for estimating parameters accurately, researchers can consider reducing the complexity of the group portion of the model (e.g., reducing the number of structural paths, fixing various error parameters in a covariance structure model). They can also use the Monte Carlo procedure in Mplus to examine the accuracy of the estimated parameters (and their corresponding power in detecting effects) over repeated sampling (Muthén & Muthén, 1998–2012).

Power

The ability to detect an effect if it exists is understood as power; that is, the probability of rejecting the null hypothesis of no difference between groups when it is not true. The power of a test is related to the significance level (α), the sample size (N), and the population effect size (ES). In general, power increases with a higher alpha level (e.g., $\alpha = 0.05$ versus $\alpha = 0.01$), with larger sample sizes, and with larger effect sizes (e.g., a 0.5 standard deviation difference between group means versus a 0.2 standard deviation difference). It can be challenging to determine sample requirements ahead of time because our model may be multivariate (with many parameters and their associated standard errors), have different sample sizes at each level, and, therefore, include decisions about how many individuals to have within groups as well as how many groups to have (given that there may be cost considerations as well). We can use information about alpha, power, and population effect size to estimate the required sample size to obtain a desired level of statistical power in a proposed study (*a priori* power analysis), or to determine what the power to detect a particular effect would be, given a particular effect size, sample size, and significance level for conducting our hypothesis test (*post hoc* power analysis).

An Example

Suppose we have approximately 520 students who are assigned to classes taught by 52 randomly selected teachers (10 students per class) participating in a study. We have assigned teachers to treatment and control groups based on evaluations of their performance during the previous year, with the treatment group comprised of teachers who were in the top 50% of the population in terms of their performance scores and the control group comprised of teachers in the lower 50% of the population. For demonstration purposes, we wish to test the null hypothesis (H_0) that the population means for student math scores in the following year are equal, in order to determine whether student learning is at least in part due to the quality of their teachers:

$$H_0: \mu_1 = \mu_2. \tag{10.1}$$

This is the same as saying that the difference in treatment and control means is 0. A familiar measure of effect size is Cohen's (1988) *d*, which is defined differently for various experimental designs (Cohen, 1988). For example, in a two-group design with a single dependent variable (i.e., using an independent samples *t*-test), Cohen defined the population effect size as follows:

$$d = (\mu_1 - \mu_2)/\sigma, \tag{10.2}$$

where σ is the assumed common population standard deviation. We can observe, therefore, that the effect size can be referred to as the number of standard deviation units separating the two means. For a *t*-test, Cohen referred to a standard deviation effect size of 0.20 as small, 0.50 as medium, and 0.80 as large.

If we were to test this difference in means using a *t*-test, there would be a required *t*-ratio coefficient for a given alpha (or error rate) that we might choose. By convention, the error rate is often set at $\alpha = 0.05$ (for a 5% error rate) or $\alpha = 0.01$ (for a 1% error rate). Because alpha levels will be inflated in the presence of small group samples (e.g., Barcikowski, 1981), one possibility to guard against wrongly rejecting the null hypothesis is to consider using a lower alpha level (e.g., from 0.05 to 0.01) for hypothesis tests. Another possibility is to use the Monte Carlo feature of Mplus to save the parameter estimates from the study and to compare them with data generated by a Monte Carlo simulation study (Muthén & Muthén, 1998–2006). This can provide information about how well the parameters and standard errors are estimated. The point is that we generally want a relatively small error rate in order to feel confident that we have not made a mistake (i.e., a Type I error) in rejecting the null hypothesis of no difference between the means.

The other type of error we could make is a Type II error (which is denoted as β). This is the error of accepting the null hypothesis when it should, in fact, be rejected. It turns out that the types of error are inversely related; that is, when we lower the alpha rate (from 0.05 to 0.01) to guard against making a Type I error, we are increasing the likelihood that we make a Type II error by increasing the possibility of failing to find a difference between the groups when one actually does exist. The power of a statistical test (defined to as $1 - \beta$) is defined as the probability of making a correct decision, that is, deciding the groups are not the same when they are in fact not the same. Power is often ideally set as 0.80, but as we reiterate, the power to detect an effect actually depends on the significance level adopted, the sample size, and the size of an effect one intends to observe (e.g., small, medium, large). All things equal, for example, it would take a larger sample size to detect a smaller effect in the population. As this discussion suggests, the amount of error the researcher is willing to accept in falsely rejecting or failing to reject the null hypothesis is an important consideration in determining whether a treatment effect may exist.

Since power is defined as the probability of finding a significant effect if it indeed exists, power is closely tied to hypothesis testing. More specifically, if we have smaller groups, all things being equal, we will have less power to detect possible significant differences in the standard deviation units between the treatment- and control-group means. Of course, in the multilevel setting, we have to take into consideration the level at which the treatment is implemented (e.g., students randomly assigned to treatment and control groups within teachers' classes, students randomly assigned to either treatment-group or control-group teachers), as well as the possibility that the treatment and control groups are not balanced.

In the multilevel setting, we also need to consider the size of the intraclass correlation in determining the power to detect effects in a proposed study. Although the impact of sample size at each level might be more immediately intuitive, the role of the intraclass correlation deserves further explanation. Recall that rho (ρ) is the correlation between outcomes for any two individuals in a group. A ρ coefficient of zero would suggest there is no correlation between scores—that is, each individual's score is independent of others' scores within the group (i.e., an assumption of a simple random sample). As we noted earlier, holding group size constant, as ρ increases, the design effect increases. What this means is that as the groups become more internally homogeneous, little added information will be gained from additional individuals within each group. Typically, the number of individuals at Level 1 is not a particular problem in estimating level-1 fixed effects. For example, when sample sizes of subgroups of individuals at Level 1 (e.g., gender) are 100 or more, power will not be an issue in detecting a difference in means between the subgroups. The typical multilevel sample of 50–60 groups might therefore have somewhere between 500 (i.e., 10 individuals per group) and 1,200 (i.e., 20 individuals per group). This relatively large sample will generally be sufficient to detect level-1 effects where $\rho = 0.10$–0.20). In situations where there are small within-group sample sizes, and where there is a high ρ coefficient (e.g., ρ

= 0.30), the power to detect level-1 effects will be lower than if ρ were low, holding sample size constant at each level. This is because as the groups become more homogeneous, the number of groups in the study will become more relevant in determining the power to detect an effect.

As might be expected, the power to detect level-2 effects is much more sensitive to the number of groups in the sample than the number of observations within groups. As research designs become more complex, the need for larger samples at both levels increases. For example, Bassiri (1988) suggested that the power necessary to detect cross-level interactions (e.g., an organizational effect at Level 2 on a level-1 slope) might require at least 30 groups with 30 within each group ($N = 900$). The group-level variance in the random intercept can be expressed as its proportion of the total variance, that is, the intraclass correlation $[\sigma_B^2 / (\sigma_B^2 + \sigma_W^2)]$. This suggests that the more similar the individuals within groups are, the more variance there will be between groups. We can test the proposition about the variance at Level 2 in terms of ρ as follows:

$$H_0: \rho = 0 \tag{10.3}$$

We can estimate the power of the statistical test conducted to reject the null hypothesis that $\rho = 0$, by setting the desired alpha level (0.05), and specifying the sample size within groups (10 students per teacher), the sample size between groups (52 teachers), and the intraclass correlation (i.e., 0.10). Following Liu (2014), the power $(1 - \beta)$ for testing the between-group variance component, defined as $\rho = 0$, uses the central F distribution under the alternative hypothesis, which can be expressed as follows:

$$1 - \beta = 1 - P\left[F < F_{1-\alpha, J-1, J(n-1)} \frac{1-\rho}{n\rho + (1-\rho)}\right]. \tag{10.4}$$

In Table 10.2, we provide an example of looking at the power to detect variance in intercepts across classes, given different numbers of classes and individuals within those classes, and different ρ coefficients. We present ρ correlations from 0.10 to 0.30 (increasing by 0.05), numbers of classes ranging from 10 to 50, and different numbers of individuals within classes (i.e., 10, 15, and 20). For example, for looking at variability in student math scores in our example, we can see that with 10 students per class and 10 classes, the power for rejecting the null hypothesis of no variability in scores between classes would be only 0.49. With 30 classes the power would be 0.86, and in our study with slightly over 50 classes, the power to detect variability in class means if it existed would be 0.97 (i.e., considerably above the required power of 0.80).

We can also see that with higher ρ coefficients, which suggest more variability in class means, we would need fewer classes to have sufficient power to

TABLE 10.2 Power for Testing Variability in Level-2 Means With Different ICCs by Number of Units and Individuals Within Units

	ICC = 0.10			ICC = 0.15			ICC = 0.20			ICC = 0.25			ICC = 0.30		
I =	10	15	20	10	15	20	10	15	20	10	15	20	10	15	20
J = 10	.49	.68	.80	.69	.85	.92	.82	.93	.97	.90	.97	.99	.94	.98	.99
20	.73	.90	.96	.91	.98	.99	.97	1.0	1.0	.99	1.0	1.0	1.0	1.0	1.0
30	.86	.97	.99	.97	1.0	1.0	1.0	1.0	1.0	1.0	1.0	1.0	1.0	1.0	1.0
40	.93	.99	1.0	.99	1.0	1.0	1.0	1.0	1.0	1.0	1.0	1.0	1.0	1.0	1.0
50	.97	1.0	1.0	1.0	1.0	1.0	1.0	1.0	1.0	1.0	1.0	1.0	1.0	1.0	1.0

reject the null hypothesis. For example, with $\rho = 0.30$, with 10 classes and 10 students per class we would have power of 0.94, rather than power of 0.49 if we had $\rho = 0.10$, holding the numbers of classrooms and students constant. Table 10.2 also suggests that adding students within classrooms would increase power, such that we could find similar power with different combinations. For example, with $\rho = 0.10$ and 20 students per class, we could obtain similar power of 0.96 for rejecting the null hypothesis with only 20 classrooms. Of course, this might not be as desirable in terms of detecting a treatment effect. As we have mentioned previously, at some point, adding classes will be more efficient than adding students within classes.

We can conclude from this example that in estimating power for multilevel studies, many assumptions need to be made regarding the variances of random effects, intraclass correlations, and effect sizes. This precludes any simple rule of thumb for multilevel studies regarding sample size. For simple variability in intercepts, however, we can see that even with a ρ coefficient of 0.10, 50 groups with 10 individuals sampled from each class would be adequate for determining variability in an outcome across classes if it existed. Of course, model complexity (e.g., random effects, multiple types of parameters of interest) could increase these initial requirements as we noted previously.

Anticipated Effect Size and Power

After considering the number of units that might be required to determine whether the variability in intercepts is not equal to 0, a second issue we may consider is the anticipated magnitude of a proposed treatment effect. We note that the larger the effect size (ES) considered meaningful in one's research, the greater the power of the statistical test. This should make sense because larger effects should be easier to detect than smaller effects in a population. The researcher can use previous theory as a guide on what anticipated effect size might be realistic. Characteristics of the anticipated effects in a proposed model therefore are typically considered in the sampling strategy underlying the data collection process for the secondary dataset.

There are a number of different ways to consider effect sizes. One common approach is Cohen's (1988) d values regarding standard deviation differences of 0.2, 0.5, and 0.8 (small, medium, and large, respectively) in evaluating treatment effects, which correspond to correlations of 0.10, 0.30, and 0.50 (Hox, 2010). As Hox (2010) suggests, it is often convenient to work with standardized coefficients in estimating power in a multilevel model, in order to avoid differences in scale metrics. For example, correlations can also be used as a reference point for describing standardized regression coefficients with continuous variables as roughly equal to $\sqrt{R^2 / (1 - R^2)}$ (Hox, 2010). So, for example, if the correlation (R) were 0.3, the corresponding standardized beta would be estimated as $\sqrt{0.09 / (.91)} = 0.314$. Using standardized coefficients makes various effect sizes easier to think about. We would expect relatively small effects (0.1–0.2) in any of these types of effect size outlined to be more difficult to detect in studies with fewer than 50 or 60 groups.

We will now return to our study consisting of 52 teachers (i.e., with 26 termed as "high quality" and 26 termed average/low quality) and 520 students nested within their classrooms. In examining power, Liu (2014) proposes standardizing the variance in the outcome to 1.0. When we standardize the outcome, we obtain estimates of the variance of 0.081 at Level 2 and 0.917 at Level 1. The proportion of variance between groups (ρ) is then estimated as $0.081/(0.081 + 0.917) = 0.081$. Since the study is conceived as a treatment implemented at Level 2, and we assume equal numbers of teachers in the treatment and control groups, it is convenient to use grand-mean centering for the treatment variable (i.e., treatment group coded 0.5, control group coded −0.5). The difference between the treatment and control groups can then be referred to in terms of Cohen's (1988) d, which we can obtain since the effect is in standard deviation units (i.e., the difference between the averaged cluster man in the treatment and the average cluster mean in the control group).

We next add the fixed treatment effect. Our concern is whether there is a significant difference in treatment and control means, as well as the estimated power to detect this effect should it exist. Following Liu (2014), the test for the treatment effect uses a t-test with degrees of freedom equal to $j - 2$:

$$T = \frac{\hat{\gamma}_{01}}{\sqrt{Var(\hat{\gamma}_{01})}}. \tag{10.5}$$

When the null hypothesis is true (i.e., that $\gamma_{01} = 0$), the test statistic T follows a central t distribution (Liu, 2014). When the alternative hypothesis is true (i.e., that $\gamma_{01} \neq 0$), the test statistic has a noncentral t distribution (T') with $j - 2$ degrees of freedom and noncentrality parameter λ (Liu, 2014, p. 173). The variance of the treatment main effect can be derived from the variance of the cluster mean of the treatment and control groups, which are independent of each other and have a common variance, which is the pooled sum of squares of the cluster means divided by the pooled degrees of freedom (Liu, 2014). As Liu notes, replacing the sample estimates in the test statistic T with their population parameters yields the noncentrality parameter:

$$\lambda = \frac{\gamma_{01}}{\sqrt{\frac{4(\sigma_W^2 / n + \sigma_B^2)}{j}}}. \tag{10.6}$$

Following Liu (2014), we can then estimate the power for a two-sided test of the treatment as

$$1 - \beta = 1 - P[T'(j-2, \lambda) < t_0] + P[T'(j-2, \lambda) \leq -t_0], \tag{10.7}$$

where the critical value is a t quantile ($t_0 = t_{1-\alpha/2, j-2}$). We can first compute the noncentrality parameter and then examine power for different combinations of group sizes. We also make use of the intraclass correlation coefficient ρ in determining how correlated the outcomes of individuals within each teacher are. Note that covariates can be added to multilevel models to reduce error variance and improve statistical power (Liu, 2014). While it can be more difficult to estimate power with adjustments for covariates, Cohen (1988) suggested simply replacing the dependent variable with the adjusted dependent variable, which implies that the group sample sizes are sufficiently large. One can also make an adjustment to the degrees of freedom at Level 2 if the covariate is added (since it will use 1 degree of freedom). The presence of a covariate will generally reduce the error variance, which can produce higher statistical power than in the model without the covariate (Liu, 2014). As Liu cautions, however, where the number of clusters is small, covariance adjustment may create an imbalance in the level-2 units, which may distort the treatment effect. Of course, one can compare model estimates without and with the covariate and observe the corresponding changes in model parameters.

In Table 10.3 we provide the estimates of the model parameters. When we add the pretest and treatment to the model, we obtain slightly different estimates of the variance components since the predictors will reduce variance at each level. We can make use of the variance components at Level 1 (0.908) and Level 2 (0.056) as well as the effect size of the treatment (0.244) in estimating the power to detect the effect for different numbers of level-2 units, where we are assuming 10 individuals within each unit and a ρ coefficient of 0.06.

We summarize this in Figure 10.1. The estimated power for 52 groups with a treatment effect of 0.244 was 0.63. It turns out that 75 groups would provide a power estimate of 0.80, while 100 groups would provide a power estimate of 0.89.

TABLE 10.3 Mplus Estimates for Treatment Effect at Level 2

	Two-Tailed			
	Estimate	*S.E.*	*Est./S.E.*	*P-Value*
Within Level				
ZREAD ON				
PRETEST	0.019	0.005	3.692	0.000
Residual Variances				
ZREAD	0.908	0.062	14.538	0.000
Between Level				
ZREAD ON				
TREAT	0.244	0.107	2.287	0.022
Intercepts				
ZREAD	−0.001	0.054	−0.025	0.980
Residual Variances				
ZREAD	0.056	0.028	2.035	0.042

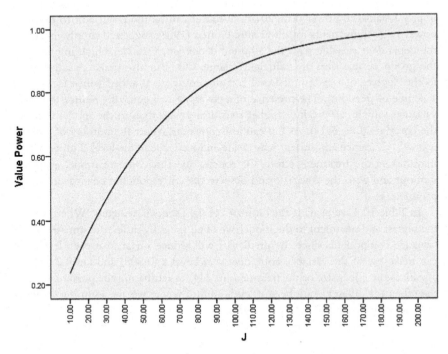

FIGURE 10.1 Estimated power to detect the effect (effect size = 0.244), given different numbers of groups.

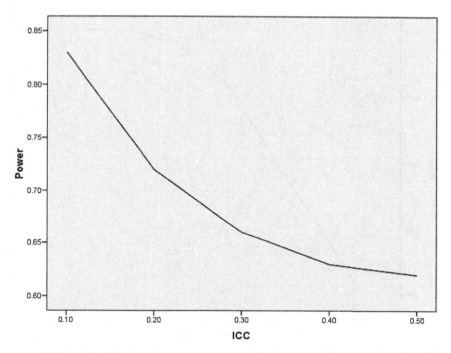

FIGURE 10.2 Effect of intraclass correlation (ICC) on power to detect treatment effect (Groups $= 100, N = 10$, Treatment Effect $= 0.244$).

We can also examine the effect of the size of ρ on the ability to detect the treatment effect. For example, holding group size constant at 100, the treatment effect at 0.244, and the number of students within classes at 10, we can see in Figure 10.2 that as ρ increases, power will decrease.

We can also look at how the effect size of the treatment might affect power. Holding the number of classes constant at 100 and individuals within classes at 10, with a ρ coefficient of 0.10, we can see in Figure 10.3 that increasing the effect size we expect to observe will increase the power to detect the effect.

Mplus Monte Carlo Study

An alternative approach is to use the Monte Carlo capability of Mplus to estimate the power of individual parameters in a variety of multilevel cross-sectional and growth models. For example, we can specify a model that contains all variables and parameters of interest. We estimate the model using their assumed population values (supplied by the model estimation using MLR and saved as a new data set). We can then select a number of replications (e.g., 500 replications) in order to obtain estimates regarding the extent to which the assumed population model

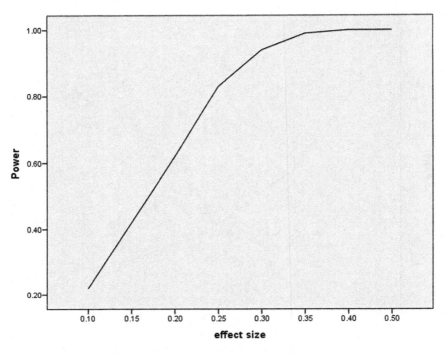

FIGURE 10.3 Power by effect sizes (100 groups, 10 individuals, ICC $= 0.10$).

is covered. If we use real data, at step 1, the estimates are saved in an external file, and then at step 2, the saved estimates are employed as population parameter values for use in data generation and coverage in a subsequent internal Monte Carlo simulation study using the POPULATION and COVERAGE options of the MONTECARLO command. The POPULATION option is used to name the data set that contains the population parameter values to be used in data generation. The COVERAGE option is used to name the data set that contains the parameter values to be used for computing coverage and are printed in the first column of the output labeled *Population* (Muthén & Muthén, 1998–2012).

This Monte Carlo simulation study can be used to estimate the power to detect that the binary cluster-level treatment variable has a significant effect on the cluster intercept. The NCSIZES option is used to specify the number of unique cluster sizes to be used in data generation. In our example, there is only one unique cluster size (10). The CSIZES option is used to specify the number of clusters (52) and the sizes of the clusters to be used in data generation (10). The WITHIN option is used to identify the variables in the data set that are measured on the individual level and modeled only on the within level. They are specified to have no variance in the between-groups part of the model. The variable *pretest* is an individual-level covariate. The BETWEEN option is used to identify the variables in the data set that are measured on the cluster level and modeled only on the between–group level. The variable *treat* is a cluster–level variable.

Model Statements

The first step estimates the models and saves the results in external data files. These can be analyzed separately.

```
TITLE:        Two-level power model (Step1);
              !this is an example of a real data analysis
              where the parameter estimates are saved and then
              used in Monte Carlo simulation study!
DATA:         FILE IS C:\mplus\ch10p.dat;
              Format is 4f8.0 1f8.5;
VARIABLE:     Names are teacode nread treat pretest zread;
              Usevariables teacode zread treat pretest;
              within = pretest;
              between = treat;
              CLUSTER IS teacode;
define:       center treat pretest (grandmean);
ANALYSIS:     TYPE = twolevel;
              Estimator is MLR;
Model:

              %BETWEEN%
              zread on treat;
              %WITHIN%
              zread on pretest;
Output:       Sampstat standardized tech1;
SAVEDATA:     ESTIMATES = ch10power.dat;
```

The second step then provides the Monte Carlo study.

```
TITLE:        Two-level power model (Step 2);
              !External estimates used to estimate power of detecting effects;
MONTECARLO:
              NAMES ARE treat pretest zread;
              NOBSERVATIONS = 520;
              NREPS = 500;
              SEED = 45335;
              POPULATION = ch10power.dat;
```

```
             COVERAGE = ch10power.dat;
             NCSIZES = 1;
             CSIZES = 52 (10);
             WITHIN = pretest;
             BETWEEN = treat;
             MODEL POPULATION:
             %BETWEEN%
             zread on treat;
             %WITHIN%
             zread on pretest;
ANALYSIS:    TYPE = TWOLEVEL;
             Estimator is MLR;
MODEL:
             %BETWEEN%
             zread on treat;
             %WITHIN%
             zread on pretest;
OUTPUT:      TECH9;
```

Model Output

Regarding the output, the results in Table 10.4 include the population value for each parameter, the average of the parameter estimates across replications, the standard deviation of the parameter estimates across replications, the average of the estimated standard errors across replications, the mean square error for each parameter (MSE), 95% coverage, and the proportion of replications for which the null hypothesis that a parameter is equal to zero is rejected at the 0.05 level (Muthén & Muthén, 1998–2012). In this case, we used 500 replications, assuming a consistent number of clusters (52) with 10 individuals per cluster.

The column labeled *Population* gives the population parameter values that are given in the MODEL command, the MODEL COVERAGE command, or using the COVERAGE option of the MONTECARLO command (Muthén & Muthén, 1998–2012). The column labeled *Average* gives the average of the parameter estimates across the replications of the Monte Carlo simulation study. These two values are used to evaluate parameter bias. To determine the percentage of parameter bias, subtract the population parameter value from the average parameter value, divide this number by the population parameter value, and multiply by 100.

In Table 10.4, the column labeled *95% Cover* provides the proportion of replications for which the 95% confidence interval contains the population parameter value. This gives the coverage and indicates how well the parameters and their standard errors are estimated. In this output, all coverage values are close to the correct value of 0.95. For parameters with population values different from zero,

TABLE 10.4 Estimates From Monte Carlo Study (500 Replications)

	ESTIMATES			S. E.		M. S. E.		
	Population	Average	Std. Dev.	Average	Cover 95%	Coeff %	Sig
Within Level								
ZREAD ON								
PRETEST	0.019	0.0187	0.0065	0.0061	0.0000	0.924	0.850
Residual Variances								
ZREAD	0.908	0.9013	0.0620	0.0578	0.0039	0.920	1.000
Between Level								
ZREAD ON								
TREAT	0.244	0.2445	0.1129	0.1043	0.0127	0.926	0.630
Intercepts								
ZREAD	−0.001	−0.0033	0.0538	0.0522	0.0029	0.940	0.062
Residual Variances								
ZREAD	0.056	0.0506	0.0270	0.0271	0.0008	0.922	0.410

this value is an estimate of power with respect to a single parameter, that is, the probability of rejecting the null hypothesis when it is false (Muthén & Muthén, 1998–2012). In contrast, for those parameters with population values equal to zero, this represents an estimate of Type I error, that is, the probability of rejecting the null hypothesis when it is true (Muthén & Muthén, 1998–2012). In this case, the power to reject null hypothesis that the treatment slope is zero is estimated as 0.63, which is below the optimal standard of 0.80 power. We can also run a Monte Carlo model changing the number of groups. For example, holding everything else constant, with 100 groups, the estimated power to detect the difference in means due to the treatment would be 0.87.

We note in passing that the approach we outlined will work well for a continuous variable, assuming it is normally distributed. More specifically, when we used a z-score of a continuous teacher quality indicator, the level-2 estimate was 0.107 and the standard error was 0.044 (not tabled). With a similar Mplus Monte Carlo study (again with 500 replications), the power estimate for the continuous teacher quality effect was estimated as 0.65 for our sample of 52 classes consisting of 10 students per class. This is similar to the power (0.63) of the treatment effect estimated with a dichotomous teacher quality (treatment) variable.

Snijders (2005) also provides a convenient formula for estimating the power to detect an effect if we know three of the following four parameters:

$$Effect \ / \ SE \approx (Z_{1-\alpha} + Z_{1-\beta}) \tag{10.8}$$

In the above equation, it is convenient to consider power as a consequence of the ratio of the estimated effect to its standard error. We may wish to test whether a parameter is equal to 0. For a one-tailed test that the parameter is 0 (at alpha of 0.05), we can use an estimate of 1.645 for $Z_{1-\alpha}$. For a one-tailed test, 1.645 covers 0.95 of the area under the curve (i.e., the alpha at this this z-score level would be 0.05). The power of the test is the probability of exceeding the critical value of 1.645. For a $Z_{1-\beta}$ score of positive 0.84, the associated area under the curve (or power) is 0.80. This suggests that the ratio of the estimate of the effect to its standard error, which can be tested with a t-test if the sample is large enough, should be approximately equal to $1.645 + 0.840$ or 2.485. If we know the standard error of the parameter, we can easily estimate the power.

As Snijders (2005) indicates, for a two-tailed test (i.e., using $Z_{1-\alpha/2}$, or 1.96), the previous formula holds only if the power is not too small (e.g., $1 - \beta \geq 0.3$) or, equivalently, the effect size is not too small. In this case, using this formula, for a two-sided test, we estimated power as about 0.66, using an estimate of 0.107 and a replicated value for the SE from our Monte Carlo study of 0.045. The resulting ratio was 2.38 ($2.38 = 1.96 + Z_{1-\beta}$). This calculation of power was consistent with our Monte Carlo power estimate presented previously.

We note that we could also re-estimate the population coefficients to estimate variability in a level-1 random slope. It turns out in this case, however, there is very little variance between units in the *pretest* effect on student outcomes (indicating it should be considered as fixed at Level 2). With our 52 classes, the power to detect the size of the pretest effect was 0.84 (not tabled). In contrast, however, since the variance component for the slope was so small (0.0002, not tabled), there was no appreciable power to detect the effect.

Design Complexity

As designs become more complex, the need for larger samples at both levels increases. Once again, we note that it is often more efficient to add higher-level units than to add individuals within groups, since this former approach generally reduces that need for sizable samples within the groups and tends to be more efficient in estimating random effects. For example, in a given sample of individuals within groups, slopes in some units may be less reliably estimated than intercepts because, while intercepts depend only on the average level (mean) of a variable within each group, slope estimates depend both on the levels of an outcome and a particular covariate, as well as the variability of their covariance among individuals within each group (Mehta & Neale, 2005).

This means that estimating variability in random slopes across units generally requires larger sample sizes for more stable estimates than simply estimating random intercepts. Complications can also arise due to correlations between random effects and the investigation of cross-level interactions (Raudenbush & Bryk, 2002). As this suggests, a number of considerations go into assessing potential bias and estimating power in various types of multilevel designs. Of course, the best situation is to have large numbers of observations per unit, relatively large numbers of units, appropriate sample weights at each level, and little or no missing data. Changes in any one of these conditions affect the completeness of our knowledge.

Missing Data

Another issue to consider in thinking about multilevel analyses is the presence of missing data. It is often the case that the weakest point of a study is the quality of the data that can be brought to bear on the research problem. Missing data can affect multilevel analyses, depending on the sampling design underlying the data set, the extent to which the data are missing at each level, and whether or not the data can be assumed to be missing at random. As we noted earlier, where sample weights are available, they may correct for individuals who did not respond (e.g., nonparticipant in a particular wave of a longitudinal study). The more the analyst can find out about why the data are "as they are," the more she or he can develop a case about the patterns of missing data, as well as a rationale about why the patterns may or may not matter.

Researchers should consider data preparation and data analysis as two separate steps. In preparing the data for analysis, it is often useful first to determine the amount of missing data present, as well as the number of missing data patterns (e.g., for which variables do missing values occur? Are there specific patterns of missing data?). It is important to keep in mind that the reality is that there is no real way to get back data that are missing (short of actually following up with subjects in a study). In a sense, then, we are generally dealing with the problem of missing information to some extent when we use actual data. The quality of our analysis depends on assumptions we make about the patterns of missing responses present and what is reasonable to conclude about those patterns in relation to the study's design (e.g., experimental or quasi-experimental, survey) and data collection (e.g., cross-sectional, longitudinal).

What we do about the missing data we have becomes a more pressing concern. There are a number of available options for dealing with missing data. It helps to know what the defaults and options are for handling missing data in the software programs that we are considering to use in each given research situation. Typically used approaches for handling missing data such as listwise or pairwise deletion, mean substitution, or simple imputation using regression-based techniques (e.g., estimating outcomes with dummy-coded missing data flags to determine whether there were differences in outcomes associated with individuals with missing versus complete data) lead to biased results in most situations (Acock, 2005; Allison, 2002; Larsen, 2011; Peugh & Enders, 2004). Currently, for single-level models, acceptable approaches include full information maximum likelihood (FIML) estimation with the partial data included and **multiple imputation** (MI) of plausible values (Asparouhov, 2006; Enders, 2011; Enders & Bandalos, 2001; Peugh & Enders, 2004). Additionally, as Enders notes, inverse probability weighting methods are also gaining attention in the statistics literature (e.g., Little & Rubin, 2002; Robins & Rotnitzky, 1995). It is important to note that few studies have examined the use of these commonly accepted, single-level approaches with multilevel data structures [e.g., see Larsen (2011); van Buuren (2011)].

Handling missing data in an appropriate manner depends on one's knowledge of the data set and why particular values may be missing. In general, there are three main types of missing data: MCAR, MAR, and NIM [see Hox (2010) or Little & Rubin (2002) for further discussion]. Rubin (1976) introduced the notion of the distribution of "missingness" as a way to classify the probability conditions under which missing data can be ignored. These include data that are missing completely at random (MCAR), missing at random (MAR), and non-ignorable missing (NIM), which is also referred to as missing not at random (MNAR). For data to be MCAR, strong assumptions must hold. The missing data on a given outcome should be unrelated to either a subject's standing on the outcome or to other observed data or unobserved (missing) data in the analysis. This is the assumption underlying listwise deletion. Typically, this assumption is only met when the data are missing by design, as in the situation where we draw a random sample of the studied population.

In contrast, if the probability of data being missing on the outcome is related to missing data on a covariate, but not to subjects' standing on the outcome, then the data are MAR (Little & Rubin, 2002). This is important, since keeping participants with partial data is important for justifying the MAR assumption (Hox, 2010). It is reasonable to assume that there will be some relationships between data that are missing on two or more variables in a study. For example, if students have missing data on attendance for a number of different reasons such as changing schools, having a health condition, or living in a particular region, they may also have missing data on math outcomes. These other variables provide a mechanism for explaining the missing values present. The MAR assumption underlies the MI and FIML approaches to dealing with missing data. Although it is often reasonable to assume that data are MAR, under some circumstances, this assumption may not hold (Enders, 2011).

More problematic is the situation where the probability of missing data on the outcome is related to standing on the outcome for individuals with the *same* value on a covariate. For example, if there is more missing low-math data than missing average- and high-math data among students with the same attendance level, then the data are NIM. Suppose we have 500 students who take a test, but 150 have missing data. If these missing individuals also tend to have relatively high absenteeism (e.g., 20 or more days), then we might have to acknowledge that there is some bias present. Suppose ⅔ of the missing data are students who are in the high absenteeism group and low math achievement group. It will now be hard to argue that the missing data on the student absenteeism predictor will not affect the estimation of students' math test scores for the population. This latter type of missing data can produce more bias during model estimation than either of the other situations because the missing data on math achievement are related to actual values of individual achievement for those subjects who do not take the test. We would prefer to be able to say the pattern of missing data on student outcomes is relatively similar for students with high, average, and low absenteeism. This would then indicate data that are likely MAR.

Other techniques have been developed for data that are NIM. Enders (2011) demonstrates the usefulness of two of the NIM approaches for longitudinal data (i.e., selection models and pattern mixture models) and demonstrates their use on a real data set. More specifically, selection models for longitudinal data combine a substantive model (i.e., a growth curve model) with a set of regression equations that predict missingness, while a pattern mixture analysis stratifies the sample into subgroups that share the same missing data pattern and estimates a growth model separately within each pattern. Interested readers can consult Hedeker and Gibbons (1997, 2006) for one example of a pattern mixture modeling approach that uses the missing data pattern (represented by one or more dummy variables) as a predictor in the growth model. Choosing an approach for handling missing data (whether assuming MAR or NIM) is a matter of choosing among competing assumptions. As Enders (2011) concludes, "[R]esearchers should choose a model with the most defensible set of assumptions, and they should provide a logical argument that supports this choice" (p. 15).

A first step in formulating a strategy for dealing with missing data is to assess the degree to which data are missing on each variable that will be included in the model. Even with 5% or less per variable, in some situations, listwise deletion can result in a tremendous loss of data and biased parameter estimation. The traditional solutions provided in most software programs are listwise or pairwise deletion or mean substitution of missing data. In most situations none of these would be considered as optimal (or acceptable) approaches (Enders & Bandalos, 2001; Puegh & Enders, 2004). For example, listwise deletion leads to inflated standard errors when the data are MCAR and biased parameter estimates when the data are MAR (Allison, 2002; Larsen, 2011). Mean substitution treats individuals with missing data as if they were on the "grand mean" (MCAR), which is also likely to introduce bias in most situations (e.g., by reducing variance).

Mplus provides a set of multiple imputation (MI) data procedures, where patterns of missing data can first be identified and then plausible values can be imputed using the EM algorithm. EM is a common method for obtaining ML estimates with incomplete data and has been shown to reduce bias due to missing data (Peugh & Enders, 2004). Obtaining estimates involves an iterative, two-step process where missing values are first imputed and then a covariance matrix and mean vector are estimated. This repeats until the difference between covariance matrices from adjacent iterations differs by a trivial amount [see Peugh & Enders (2004) for further discussion]. The imputed data sets can be saved as separate data sets and then analyzed. It is often the case, for example, that even with 25–35% missing data, the analyst can impute a number of "random" plausible values for individuals in order to generate a number of new data sets that can be saved for further analysis.

One of the advantages of this approach is that other variables can also be used to supply information about missing data (referred to as *auxiliary* variables), but they need not be included into the actual model estimation. This approach to missing data is recommended when the assumption that the data are MAR is plausible. The analyst can generate a relatively large number of imputed data sets (Bodner, 2008) and then analyze the complete data sets and report the mean estimates and standard errors across the several imputed data sets. The values imputed through MI represent draws from a distribution; in other words, they inherently contain some variation. This parameter variation across multiple imputations is important for creating reasonable distributions of plausible values for variables with missing values. If we assume some degree of normality, we can average the parameter estimates over the imputed data sets. Our practical experience with MI approaches suggests that they do pretty well at estimating the total data set where missing values are randomly dispersed across a sizable number of individuals (100–200 or more) found in most published studies.

For multilevel data, there is less guidance available from previous research (e.g., Daniels & Hogan, 2008; Larsen, 2011; van Buuren, 2011). Larsen (2011) recently conducted a study comparing MI and FIML approaches in situations where there were individuals nested within groups. He found that both approaches were relatively similar in handling level-1 estimates under the different conditions he examined. But he also found that as missing data increased at Level 2, the estimates of the level-2 predictor from imputed data sets displayed increased parameter bias and decreased standard errors compared to the estimates estimated from the full data set. For level-2 estimation, Larsen found FIML estimation with the missing data performed much better than the MI approach. This is because the MI procedure used in his study did not account for random effects. The key takeaway from this is that the bias results from the assumption that the student-level data (Level 1) were assumed to be randomly sampled from the same population (i.e., in this case, a classroom), rather than from different classrooms (Larsen, 2011).

Van Buuren (2011) presented an introduction to a number of different missing data situations encountered with multilevel data. Where data are missing for level-2 predictors (e.g., as for a school covariate), some software programs that default to listwise deletion would drop all the individuals within those units. These individuals may not have any missing data on the outcome or the level-1 predictors, and this strategy could decimate an otherwise rich data set and also complicate the estimate of group-level effects (van Buuren, 2011). Fortunately, this is not the approach used in Mplus. We reiterate that the sampling frame through which the data were generated may have an impact on assumptions we make about the distribution of the data at each level. This implies that the nature of missing data at Level 2 in relation to the manner in which the units were selected—whether units themselves were randomly sampled from a population of units or were just an unspecified collection of available units—can further complicate the interpretation of the level-1 results. As van Buuren noted, although ML methods are quite good at estimating repeated measures values of Y in longitudinal studies, no generally acceptable approach has developed for handing missing values on level-1 and level-2 predictors (i.e., since the data are assumed to be MAR). If MAR is correct, van Buuren cautioned that the variables governing the probability of the missing data should be included in the analysis, in order not to bias the estimate, for example, of a treatment effect.

Much of our discussion about missing data suggests that dealing with missing data is not so much about "How much missing data is allowable?" but, rather, is more about how to develop a process to deal with the missing data. We favor a strategy of triangulating our results with different approaches that are currently recommended for examining missing data. One possible approach is to do something like the following. First, one can try running the model using listwise deletion (which assumes MCAR). This data set will likely be considerably smaller than the "partially complete" data, but it gives the analyst a baseline view (albeit likely a biased one) for comparing subsequent results. The results with listwise deletion should match the results of the existing (partially complete) data set, since the variables with missing values are listwise deleted, unless the data are vertically arranged as in a growth model.

Second, if there is not too much missing data per variable, the listwise results can be compared against a number of complete data sets generated using the MI program in Mplus, since it can be applied to hierarchical data structures. We emphasize that single-level MI programs, which ignore the grouping structure in multilevel data, will be likely to underestimate standard errors (Cheung, 2007; Gibson & Olejnik, 2003). Analysts may wish to keep in mind the cautions we have mentioned about estimating plausible values when individuals are nested within groups. There are a number of sources that can be consulted for dealing with missing data under MAR and NIM in growth modeling studies (e.g., see Enders, 2011; Muthén & Muthén, 1998–2012). We also note that van Buuren (2011) examined several types of missing multilevel data situations and found the multilevel multiple imputation used (i.e., which generated multiple imputations from prior distributions of the parameters using the Gibbs sampler) worked generally the best of several approaches compared (e.g., listwise, single-level MI, MI with separate groups), but it was not optimal in all situations with respect to recovering true values by 95% confidence intervals across different cluster sizes and numbers of individuals within clusters.

Third, the model can be estimated with FIML with the cases with partial data included in the analysis and then compared with the MI results produced. If sample weights are available in existing data sets, users should check whether they include adjustments for nonresponse. If so, making use of sample weights at two levels will facilitate accurate estimation. We contrast some of these techniques briefly in the next section with a short example where missing data are encountered at Level 2.

Missing Data at Level 2

It is clear that more work needs to be done on the use of multiple imputation procedures for hierarchical data structures (Larsen, 2011; van Buuren, 2011). We next provide a simple two-level analysis to illustrate the potential effects of missing data at Level 2 on the analysis. In this case, we started with a complete sample of 1,000 students randomly selected from within 139 schools, which were randomly selected from some 180 schools in the database. We specified a two-level simple model with one predictor at each level and a random intercept.

Model Statements

There are several options for the estimation of models with missing data in Mplus (Muthén & Muthén, 1998–2012). Mplus provides ML estimation under MCAR (missing completely at random), MAR (missing at random), and NMAR (not missing at random) for continuous, censored, binary, ordered categorical (ordinal), unordered categorical (nominal), counts, or combinations of these variable types (Little & Rubin, 2002). MAR suggests that missingness can be a function of observed covariates and observed outcomes. Non-ignorable missing data (NMAR) modeling is possible using maximum likelihood estimation where categorical outcomes are indicators of missingness and where missingness can be predicted by continuous and categorical latent variables (Muthén, Asparouhov, Hunter, & Leuchter, 2011; Muthén, Jo, & Brown, 2003). For censored and categorical outcomes using WLS estimation, missingness is allowed to be a function of the observed covariates but not the observed outcomes (Asparouhov & Muthén, 2010).

We next provide the input statement for the model with missing data. The default is to estimate the model under missing data theory using all available data. The LISTWISE option of the DATA command can be used to delete all observations from the analysis that have missing values on one or more of the analysis variables. The MISSING option is used to identify the values or symbols in the analysis data set that will be treated as missing or invalid. We are estimating with the default, which is missing data present. In this case, we referred to the missing data in the analysis as MISSING = CSES(–999), since MISSING=BLANK) will create a listwise deletion.

TITLE:	Level 2 missing covariate;
DATA:	FILE IS C:\mplus\ch10miss2.dat;
	Format is 5f8.0,4f8.2;
VARIABLE:	Names are schcode female lowses read math CSES
	read_m math_m lowses_m;
	Usevariables schcode read lowses CSES;
	Cluster = schcode;
	MISSING = CSES(–999) ;
	between = CSES;
	within = lowses;
ANALYSIS:	Type = twolevel;
	Estimator = MLR;
Model:	
	%Between%
	read on CSES;
	%Within%
	read on lowses;
OUTPUT:	TECH1;

Initial Summary Output

This output provides an initial summary of the missing data across variables to be used in the model.

SUMMARY OF DATA
Number of missing data patterns   1
    Number of clusters   139
    Average cluster size   7.194

COVARIANCE COVERAGE OF DATA
Minimum covariance coverage value   0.100

PROPORTION OF DATA PRESENT
Covariance   Coverage

	READ	LOWSES	CSES
READ	1.000		
LOWSES	1.000	1.000	
CSES	1.000	1.000	1.000

We can see in this example that all of the original individual-level cases are present in the analysis, since the missing data is limited to the school SES covariate (CSES) at Level 2.

Imputation File

Multiple data sets generated using multiple imputation can be analyzed using a special feature of Mplus. The default is five new data sets that can be saved for further analyses. Parameter estimates are averaged over the set of analyses, and standard errors are computed using the average of the standard errors over the set of analyses and the between analysis parameter estimate variation (Rubin, 1987; Schafer, 1997). A chi–square test of overall model fit is provided (Asparouhov & Muthén, 2008; Enders, 2010).

```
TITLE:       Multiple imputation of missing level-2 covariate;
DATA:        FILE IS C:\mplus\ch10miss2.dat;
             Format is 5f8.0,4f8.2;
VARIABLE:    Names are schcode female lowses read math CSES
             read_m math_m lowses_m;
             Usevariables schcode read lowses CSES;
             Cluster = schcode;
             MISSING = CSES(–999);
             between = CSES;
             within = lowses;
ANALYSIS:    Type = twolevel;
             Estimator = MLR;
Model:
             %Between%
             read on CSES;
             %Within%
             read on lowses;
DATA IMPUTATION:
             IMPUTE = CSES;
             SAVE = ch10bimpMLR*.dat;
OUTPUT:      TECH8;
```

For the imputed data set for CSES, we have the following summary information provided in the output.

SUMMARY OF MISSING DATA PATTERNS FOR THE FIRST DATA SET
MISSING DATA PATTERNS (x = not missing)

	1
READ	x
LOWSES	x
CSES	x

MISSING DATA PATTERN FREQUENCIES
Pattern   Frequency
      1   1000

COVARIANCE COVERAGE OF DATA FOR THE FIRST DATA SET
Minimum covariance coverage value 0.100

PROPORTION OF DATA PRESENT
Covariance Coverage

	READ	LOWSES	CSES
READ	1.000		
LOWSES	1.000	1.000	
CSES	1.000	1.000	1.000

The second step then reads the saved data and provides an analysis of the five imputed data sets with averaged results.

TITLE:	Estimation of model with missing level-2 covariate using multiple imputation data sets;
DATA:	FILE IS ch1imp9MLRlist.dat;
	TYPE = IMPUTATION;
VARIABLE:	NAMES ARE read lowses CSES schcode;
	Cluster = schcode;
	between = CSES;
	within = lowses;
ANALYSIS:	Type = twolevel;
	Estimator = MLR;
Model:	
	%Between%
	read on CSES;
	%Within%
	read on lowses;
OUTPUT:	TECH8;

Model Estimates

Model Output

We provide the comparisons in Table 10.5. The coefficients in Column 4 (Complete) suggest that community SES (*CSES*), which was reverse coded, and *lowses* were statistically significant ($p < 0.05$) in explaining students' reading scores. In

TABLE 10.5 Comparison of Approaches for Dealing With Missing Data

Variable	MLR	Impute(MLR)	Listwise	Complete
Between Schools				
Intercept	642.05*	641.88*	641.91*	642.60*
CSES	−7.39*	−6.05*	−7.69*	−6.06*
Within Schools				
Low SES	−12.16*	−12.49*	−10.48*	−12.26*
Variance Components				
Level-2 Intercept	52.54	49.82	51.89	39.79
Level-1 Residual	1643.28*	1645.73*	1628.77*	1652.93*
Sample Size				
Level-2 Schools	139	139	115	139
Level-1 Students	1000	1000	711	1000

Columns 1–3 we illustrate several possible approaches for dealing with missing data. In this example, we eliminated data regarding school SES composition in 24 of the 139 schools (17.3%). To simplify matters, at the individual level, there was no missing data. Because of the missing data on the level-2 covariate, however, we lose nearly 29% of the level-1 student data if we use listwise deletion (i.e., $289/1000 = 28.9\%$). We assume the school-level data are MAR. In Column 1, we used FIML estimation to deal with the missing level-2 data. In Column 2, we present the results of five data imputations using Mplus. We can see that both analyses in Column 1 and Column 2 retain the original number of students ($N = 1,000$) and schools ($n = 139$). In Column 3, we present the listwise results, which indicate there were 711 students nested within 115 schools.

In Column 3, we can see the listwise results indicate that both *CSES* and *lowses* affect students' reading scores ($p < 0.05$); however, with nearly 20% missing data at Level 2 and a resulting 29% missing data at Level 1, the listwise analysis appears to be a bit further away from the original estimates than the two approaches in estimating the both the *CSES* and *low SES* parameters. We suspect this is due to the effect of the missing data on the school SES variable, which we can see may influence both level-2 and level-1 estimates. We note that listwise results will typically produce the largest errors in estimating the parameters (since the sample size may be severely reduced), as well as reduced power, which can both lead to errors in interpreting the results.

In Column 1, we present the results of FIML estimation with missing data (estimated with MLR), which appears to do a reasonable job of recapturing the original estimates in the complete data set presented in Column 4. In addition to the intercept, the FIML approach accurately estimates *low SES*. In contrast, however, the estimate for the *CSES* covariate (−7.39), is not as close to the estimate in Column 2 (multiple imputation) or Column 4 (complete), since it was generated from nearly 20% missing data on the covariate at Level 2. In this specific example, we suspect this estimate is a bit stronger because we noted in preliminary analyses that the reverse-coded mean *CSES* of the missing schools was about 0.37 of a standard deviation higher than the data set of schools with complete data on this covariate. What this means is that there were higher percentages of students participating in the federal free/reduced lunch program in those schools. This would overattend to the schools where there are lower percentages of low-income students in generating the school-level estimate.

In Column 2, we report results using five imputed data sets to estimate plausible values for the CSES covariate. The estimates in Column 2 represent the averaged output from the data imputations (Muthén & Muthén, 1998–2012). We can see the average estimate for *CSES* is quite close to the actual estimate with the complete data. Imputing values into the level-2 data set is likely viable if we know the process through which units were selected at Level 2 (e.g., simple random sample, stratified random sample). A common problem, however, is that in many multilevel studies the number of level-2 units available tends to be considerably smaller and, therefore, less likely to represent a "randomly sampled" population of units. We therefore need to keep in mind the likely distribution of level-2 units, since our assumption about the nature of the level-2 units will certainly affect estimates that might be generated. If we can assume the data at Level 2 are MCAR (or more likely MAR), we may be able to provide reasonable estimates for missing data on one or more covariates.

We reiterate the point that the MI approach has the advantage of incorporating some variability in the level-2 estimates that are saved into separate data sets. Readers should keep in mind that imputing values at Level 2 may not adequately deal with the nature of random effects present. Again, this relates back to assumptions about the sampling process through which units and individuals were selected. Even in this simple case, we noted considerable variation in the size of the estimates, their standard errors, and their statistical significance. We suspect that in many situations, it is probably reasonable to consider the level-2 units as comprising a random sample of a population (i.e., each unit has an equal probability of being selected), even if in practice this assumption may be violated, which can lead to some underestimation of sampling variance (Kish, 1987). Sample weights at Level 2 are created to deal with these types of selection probability issues, but they are not available in many multilevel data sets.

Our practical experience with imputing plausible values suggests that this problem can become more important where there are small numbers of level-2 units available for analysis, or where there are only a few individuals within each unit. Accurately estimating variance parameters typically takes much more data than estimating fixed effects. Using MI procedures in some fashion would certainly require imputing a sizeable number of level-2 sets of estimates (perhaps 30 or more) where there is 20% or so missing data (e.g., see Bodner, 2008; Larsen, 2011). This would provide a broader distribution of values. This might be a reasonable approach for level-2 data, where there are a relatively large number of units in the study (as in our example) and the assumption of MAR can be made.

No definitive conclusion should be drawn from this simple illustration in Table 10.5. Our point is simply to suggest that missing data can have a considerable influence on the credibility of our modeling results. It is a problem that should be addressed in preparing the data for analysis. From this preliminary analysis, if we were preparing the data for further analysis, we would likely conclude that the data are MAR instead of MCAR, since the listwise results were different substantively. We might choose either the MI or FIML estimation with missing data as viable approaches to use in examining these data. Monte Carlo simulations can also be used to study missing data patterns further and to generate new data sets under various sampling conditions for subsequent analysis. As we have shown in the previous section, this latter approach can also be useful in conducting various power analyses. We hope that the illustration alerts readers to a few of the possible ways in which missing data may influence model results.

Concluding Thoughts

Our treatment in this book has focused on an expanded application of multilevel techniques. This has been facilitated by an array of statistical, computational, and software advances as well as an evolution in the world of data collection and management that has provided researchers with an abundance of data through which these models can be brought to life. Simultaneously, we have attempted to illustrate the significant value of this class of models for the more complete specification of complex theoretical and conceptual models that give rise to new forms of research questions. Indicative of the growing use of multilevel models, in the 15 years between our first volume on multilevel modeling using multilevel regression and SEM and our current effort, all mainstream statistical software programs (e.g., Stata, SAS, SPSS, etc.) now include some form of multilevel modeling capability. In this volume, we have illustrated how multilevel modeling approaches can be subsumed under a general modeling framework focusing on latent variables and simultaneous equations provided in the Mplus statistical package. This type of modeling framework can incorporate multilevel regression modeling, structure equation modeling, and finite mixture modeling (Muthén & Asparouhov, 2011). While we note above that all mainline statistical packages now provide some form of multilevel modeling capabilities, we have chosen to use Mplus in this book because of its extraordinary modeling flexibility (within and across the MLM and SEM frameworks) and the intellectual energy its authors have channeled into the development and continued evolution of the computational aspects of these models.

Although multilevel modeling (MLM) and SEM have evolved from different conceptual traditions, the strengths of each approach can be used to address a wide range of theoretical models. We expect that the expansion of methods available to address increasingly complex theoretical models will continue in the near future. One of the attractive features of the various multilevel techniques we presented in this book is the adaptability in accommodating a wide range of theoretical models, data structures, simulations (e.g., various mixture models, three-level models, cross-classified and longitudinal data structures, models with categorical observed variables, data with various missing data structures). These analyses help researchers to address a variety of methodological problems and research interests, including, for example, multiple units of analysis, the incorporation of measurement error, the impact of missing data on model parameters, the investigation of the differential impact of predictors across units, and evolving temporal relationships between parallel change processes.

We hope readers can see that there is a considerable similarity in the methods we demonstrated to investigate hierarchical data structures. The MLM approach allows considerable flexibility in examining data structures with random coefficients (Raudenbush, 1998), while the SEM approach (i.e., emphasizing continuous and categorical latent variables, separate model components within and between groups, reciprocal causation) offers an expanded set of possibilities to investigate a wide variety of models with various cross-sectional, cross-classified, and longitudinal data structures. As Raudenbush notes, a more complete view for understanding the advantages of each type of formulation centers on determining the research design (e.g., research questions, data structure, scale of outcome variables) before considering the estimation and algorithms appropriate for various designs and data, and finally considering the type of model formulation that would be optimal in conducting the analyses.

In Chapter 1, we presented a general framework for considering alternative quantitative analyses. The framework was based on the type of theoretical model to be investigated (e.g., the number of outcome variables, the data structure present, and the overall goals of the analysis. It is important to keep in mind that statistical models are mathematical representations of hypothesized processes of interest among subjects in a population—but they are not the processes themselves. We fit the proposed mathematical model against the data to determine whether its theoretical assumptions have empirical coherence. Harvey (1989) suggested a number of useful criteria that can be adapted to evaluate the suitability of multilevel models. He suggested that a model should (1) be *parsimonious*, that is, it should describe the data using relatively few parameters; (2) be *consistent with prior knowledge*—or should tend to confirm accepted theory and prior knowledge; (3) have *data admissibility*, that is, it should not have impossible values for the data; (4) have *structured stability*, or fit across the context (or times) tested; and (5) be *encompassing*—it should encompass competing models by explaining aspects of the data accounted for by competing models and should provide additional explanation.

Of course, the bottom line is whether or not we gain new substantive insights by employing these analytic tools. Scholarship in the social and health sciences has benefitted over the past several decades from improvements in the application of both theory and methodology. Over the past 25 years, multilevel regression models have certainly heightened our understanding of how organizational processes impact outcomes of interest. Compared with the widespread use of these models, there are fewer empirical examples of multilevel SEM analyses in the literature—a problem related to the more limited software that can be used to conduct the analyses as well as the demands placed on the data structures analyzed. As we note above, we chose to illustrate multilevel analyses using the Mplus software because we find it adaptable to a wide variety of theoretical models, data structures, and variable measurement. In our latter chapters, we illustrated longitudinal modes and mixture models. We see longitudinal analysis being used with great frequency in today's applied research as data sets become more available. Because most theoretical models imply some type of temporal sequence among variables, longitudinal analysis can provide a stronger basis for making inferences about explanatory variables and outcomes than cross-sectional data structures.

Previous organizational and social research has not as frequently addressed the problem of modeling change using dynamic organizational indicators (at least in sufficient detail). It is more challenging to define and measure changing organizational and social processes and to describe their corresponding changes in outcomes over time. We have tried to provide a number of illustrations of how multilevel modeling techniques can be used examine changes over time. Longitudinal data collection can help with the proper time ordering of variables so that processes that are assumed to be dynamic can be incorporated into multilevel models. Multilevel models with categorical outcomes represent another important and evolving area of quantitative modeling (e.g., factor models with categorical observed indicators, categorical observed outcomes, categorical latent variables). In particular, mixture models (e.g., latent class analysis, latent profile analysis) represent a relatively new area for applied researchers and hold tremendous promise as tools in social, behavioral, organizational, and health-related research.

Mixture models represent special cases of a general latent variable framework that provide a unifying view of a wide range of theoretical models (Muthén, 2001). These go far beyond typical multilevel models that have become popular in the past few decades. These models can focus on unobserved heterogeneity in a sample by identifying individuals who belong to different subpopulations, with membership derived from the data through categorical latent variables. They can involve single-level and multilevel data that are either cross-sectional or longitudinal in nature. For example, in a growth mixture model, heterogeneity in an outcome over time can be captured by both continuous and categorical latent variables. Identified classes can have a different random-effect growth model (Muthén, 2001). Mixture models can involve categorical latent variables and hybrids of continuous and categorical latent variables. A categorical latent variable can be a within-level variable, a between-level variable, or a within-and between-level variable.

Multilevel modeling techniques provide us with a powerful and more refined means for investigating the types of processes embedded within our theories.

From this standpoint, they allow us to create and test more complex models. Although the models presented in this book were simplified for demonstrating the techniques, complexity can be added by increasing the number of observed variables, the number of latent variables, the cross-level interactions, combinations of continuous and latent variables, and so forth. Although remembering that any statistical model is not a substitute for reality, and in many cases can actually be a severe reduction of reality (e.g., when key processes are omitted), we are optimistic that progress will continue to be made where it is simultaneously defined on both theoretical and methodological fronts.

References

Acock, A. C. (2005). Working with missing values. *Journal of Marriage and Family, 67*, 1012–1028.

Allison, P. (2002). *Missing data.* Thousand Oaks, CA: Sage.

Asparouhov, T. (2005). Sampling weights in latent variable modeling. *Structural Equation Modeling, 12*(3), 411–434.

Asparouhov, T. (2006). General multilevel modeling with sampling weights. *Communications in Statistics: Theory and Methods, 35*, 439–460.

Asparouhov, T. & Muthén, B. O. (2007). *Computationally efficient estimation of multilevel high-dimensional latent variable models.* Proceedings of the 2007 JSM meeting in Salt Lake City.

Asparouhov, T. & Muthén, B. (2008). Multilevel mixture models. In G. R. Hancock & K. M. Samuelsen (Eds.), *Advances in latent variable mixture models* (pp. 27–51). Charlotte, NC: Information Age Publishing, Inc.

Asparouhov, T. & Muthén, B. (2010). Weighted least squares estimation with missing data. Retrieved from www.statmodel.com/download/GstrucMissingRevision.pdf

Barcikowski, R. (1981). Statistical power with group mean as the unit of analysis. *Journal of Educational Statistics, 6*(3), 267–285.

Bassiri, D. (1988). *Large and small sample properties of maximum likelihood estimates for the hierarchical model.* Unpublished doctoral dissertation, Michigan State University.

Bodner, T. E. (2008). What improves with missing data imputations? *Structural Equation Modeling, 15*, 651–675.

Cheung, M. W. L. (2007). Comparison of methods of handling missing time-invariant covariates in latent growth models under the assumption of missing completely at random. *Organizational Research Methods, 10*, 609–634.

Cohen, J. (1988). *Statistical power analysis for the behavioral sciences* (2nd ed.). Hillsdale, NJ: Lawrence Erlbaum.

Daniels, M. J. & Hogan, J. W. (2008). *Missing data in longitudinal studies. Strategies for Bayesian modeling and sensitivity analysis.* Boca Raton, FL: Chapman & Hall/CRS.

Enders, C. K. (2010). *Applied missing data analysis.* New York: Guilford Press.

Enders, C. K. (2011). Missing not at random models for latent growth curve analyses. *Psychological Methods, 16*(1), 1–16.

Enders, C. K. & Bandalos, D. (2001). The relative performance of full information maximum likelihood estimation for missing data in structural equation models. *Structural Equation Modeling, 8*, 430–457.

Gibson, N. M. & Olejnik, S. (2003). Treatment of missing data at the second level of hierarchical models. *Educational and Psychological Measurement, 63*, 204–238.

Grilli, L. & Pratesi, M. (2004). Weighted estimation in multilevel ordinal and binary models in the presence of informative sampling designs. *Survey Methodology, 30*(1), 93–103.

Harvey, A. (1989). *Forecasting, structural time series models and the Kalman filter.* Cambridge, MA: Cambridge University Press.

Hedeker, D. & Gibbons, R. D. (1997). Application of random-effects pattern-mixture models for missing data in longitudinal studies. *Psychological Methods, 2,* 64–78.

Hedeker, D. & Gibbons, R. D. (2006). *Longitudinal data analysis.* Hoboken, NJ: Wiley.

Hox, J. J. (2010). *Multilevel analysis: Techniques and applications* (2nd ed.). New York: Routledge.

Jia, Y., Stokes, L., Harris, I., & Wang, Y. (April 2011). *The evaluation of bias of the weighted random effects model estimators* (ETS RR-11–13). Princeton, NJ: Educational Testing Service.

Kish, L. (1987). *Statistical design for research.* New York: Wiley.

Larsen, R. (2011). Missing data imputation versus full information maximum likelihood with second-level dependencies. *Structural Equation Modeling, 18*(4), 649–662.

Little, R. & Rubin, D. B. (2002). *Statistical analysis with missing data* (2nd ed.). Hoboken, NJ: Wiley.

Liu, X. S. (2014). *Statistical power analysis for the social and behavioral sciences: Basic and advanced techniques.* New York: Routledge.

Maas C. J. M. & Hox, J. J. (2002). Sample sizes for multilevel modeling. In J. Blasius, J. Hox, E. de Leeuw, & P. Schmidt (Eds.), *Social science methodology in the new millennium. Proceedings of the fifth international conference on logic and methodology.* Opladen, RG: Leske + Budrich Verlag (CD ROM).

Mehta, P. D. & Neale, M. C. (2005). People are variables too. Multilevel structural equations modeling. *Psychological Methods, 10*(3), 259–284.

Mok, M. (1995). *Sample size requirements for 2-level designs in educational research.* Sydney, Australia: Macquarie University.

Muthén, B. O. (2001). Latent variable mixture modeling. In G. A. Marcoulides & R. E. Schumacker (Eds.), *New developments and techniques in structural equation modeling* (pp. 1–33). Mahwah, NJ: Lawrence Erlbaum Associates.

Muthén, B. & Asparouhov, T. (2011). Beyond multilevel regression modeling: Multilevel analysis in a general latent variable framework. In J. Hox & J. K. Roberts (Eds.), *Handbook of advanced multilevel analysis* (pp. 15–40). New York: Taylor and Francis.

Muthén, B., Asparouhov, T., Hunter, A., & Leuchter, A. (2011). Growth modeling with nonignorable dropout: Alternative analyses of the STARD antidepressant trial. *Psychological Methods, 16,* 17–33.

Muthén, B., Jo, B., & Brown, H. (2003). Comment on the Barnard, Frangakis, Hill, & Rubin article. Principal stratification approach to broken randomized experiments: A case study of school choice vouchers in New York City. *Journal of the American Statistical Association, 98,* 311–314.

Muthén, B. O. & Muthén, L. (1998–2006). *Mplus user's guide.* Los Angeles, CA: Authors.

Muthén, L. K. & Muthén, B. O. (1998–2012). *Mplus user's guide* (7th ed.). Los Angeles, CA: Authors.

Pedhazur, E. & Schmelkin, L. (1991). *Measurement, design, and analysis: An integrated approach.* Hillsdale, NJ: Lawrence Erlbaum.

Peugh, J. A. & Enders, C. K. (2004). Missing data in educational research: A review of reporting practices and suggestions for improvement. *Review of Educational Research, 74*(4), 525–556.

Pfeffermann, D., Skinner, C. J., Holmes, D. J., Goldstein, H., & Rasbash, J. (1998). Weighting for unequal selection probabilities in multilevel models. *Journal of the Royal Statistical Society: Series B (Statistical Methodology), 60*(1), 23–40.

Pothoff, R. F., Woodbury, M. A., & Manton, K. G. (1992). "Equivalent sample size" and "equivalent degrees of freedom" refinements for inference using survey weights under superpopulation models. *Journal of the American Statistical Association, 87*, 383–396.

Rabe-Hesketh, S., & Skrondal, A. (2006). Multilevel modelling of complex survey data. *Journal of the Royal Statistical Society: Series A, 169*, 805–827.

Raudenbush, S. W. (October 1998). *Toward a coherent framework for comparing trajectories of individual change*. Paper presented for the conference New Methods for the Analysis of Change, Pennsylvania State University.

Raudenbush, S. W. & Bryk, A. S. (2002). *Hierarchical linear models* (2nd ed.). Newbury Park, CA: Sage.

Robins, J. M., & Rotnitzky, A. (1995). Semiparametric efficiency in multivariate regression models with missing data. *Journal of the American Statistical Association, 90*, 122–129.

Rubin, D. B. (1976). Inference and missing data. *Biometrika, 63*, 581–592.

Rubin, D. B. (1987). *Multiple imputation for nonresponse in surveys*. New York: John Wiley & Sons.

Schafer, J. L. (1997). *Analysis of incomplete multivariate data*. London: Chapman & Hall.

Scherbaum, C. A., & Ferreter, J. M. (2009). Estimating statistical power and sample size requirement for organizational research using hierarchical linear models. *Organizational Research Methods, 12*, 347–367.

Skinner, C. J. (May 2005). *The use of survey weights in multilevel modeling*. Paper presented at the Workshop on Latent Variable Models and Survey Data for Social Science Research, Montreal, Canada.

Snijders, T. A. (2005). Power and sample size in multilevel linear models. In B. S. Everitt & D. C. Howell (Eds.), *Encyclopedia of statistics in behavioral sciences* (Vol. 3, pp. 1570–1573). New York: Wiley.

Snijders, T. & Bosker, R. (1999). *Multilevel analysis: An introduction to basic and advanced multilevel modeling*. Newbury Park, CA: Sage.

Stapleton, L. M. (2002). The incorporation of sample weights into multilevel structural equation models. *Structural Equation Modeling, 9*(4), 475–502.

Stapleton, L. M. (2013). Incorporating sampling weights into single- and multi-level models. In L. Rutkowski, M. von Davier, & D. Rutkowski (Eds.), *A handbook of international large-scale assessment* (pp. 353–388). London: Chapman Hall/CRC Press.

Thomas, S. L. & Heck, R. H. (2001). Analysis of large-scale secondary data in higher education research: Potential perils associated with complex sampling designs. *Research in Higher Education, 42*(5), 517–550.

van Buuren, S. (2011). Multiple imputation of multilevel data. In J. J. Hox & J. K. Roberts (Eds.), *Handbook of advanced multilevel analysis* (pp. 173–196). New York: Routledge.

GLOSSARY

Aggregation/Disaggregation. Aggregation refers to combining varying levels of an individual-level predictor within a group to a single group mean. Disaggregation refers to assigning a group-level mean to all the individuals within the group.

Bayesian estimation. Bayesian estimation provides a contrasting approach to ML for estimating model parameters. Bayesian estimation involves the incorporation of information about uncertainty from prior knowledge of the distributions of variables. Because Bayesian estimation is not conditional on the accuracy of the specific point estimates of variances and covariances from the sample data, it can correct the tendency for ML methods to underestimate variance and covariance parameters in small (or nonrandom) group samples.

Centering. Predictors in multilevel models are often centered on some value in the sample to facilitate the meaning of the intercept at Level 2. For example, if X (education) is entered in its raw metric, the meaning of the intercept is the level of Y when education is zero. It would be very unlikely, however, that anyone in the data set would have zero years of education. We could therefore choose to center education on its grand mean (i.e., the overall mean of the education for the sample) or its group mean (i.e., the mean for education within the group in which the individual resides).

Clustered data/Hierarchical data. This describes data that consists of successive groupings of individuals within groups or repeated measurements of individuals. Clustering can result in similarities between the members of each group (e.g., socialization processes, attitudes).

Confirmatory factor analysis (CFA). Confirmatory factor analysis (CFA) often represents the first part of an SEM analysis, since it focuses on defining a smaller set of latent variables through their observed indicators. In the CFA approach, the proposed relationships are specified first and then examined against the data to see whether the hypothesized model is confirmed. CFA models are also referred to as measurement models given their focus on defining a set of constructs through examining the quality of their observed indicators in measuring each factor.

Construct validation. Construct validation refers to an ongoing process of defining and checking to see whether the defined construct is useful within a larger system of theoretical relations among the constructs. The first part refers to having the right set of items to measure the construct (as opposed to other items that might not measure the construct as well). The second part refers to examining whether the defined construct is useful in explaining some other theoretical process among several constructs of interest. One example would be defining job satisfaction through several items thought to be observed manifestations of job satisfaction and then testing whether the job satisfaction construct as defined is positively related to employees' actual staying (versus leaving) the organization over time.

Covariance matrix. Covariance measures the degree to which two variables change or vary together (i.e., covary). These relationships between pairs of variables are often summarized in a variance-covariance matrix, which is a symmetric matrix where the diagonal elements represent the variances of individual variables and the off-diagonal elements represent the covariances between pairs of row and column variables. Covariance matrices represent variances and covariances between variables expressed in their original metrics. A correlation matrix can be described as the covariance matrix of normalized, or standardized (i.e., mean of 0.0 and standard deviation of 1.0), random variables. Covariances and correlations have two properties of interest—their magnitude and the sign (which tells whether the relationship is positive or negative). A positive relationship suggests that as the first variable increases, so does the second, and vice versa. In contrast, a negative relationship suggests that as the first variable increases, the second decreases, and vice versa. Unlike a covariance coefficient, the correlation coefficient has a mathematical lower boundary of −1.0 and an upper bound of 1.0. This property permits correlation coefficients to be compared, while ordinary covariances usually cannot be compared.

Cross-level interaction. A cross-level interaction is a moderating effect of a higher-level variable on a slope relationship at a lower level. For example, organizational size may have a moderating effect on the relationship between employee job satisfaction and productivity.

Design effect. Design effect provides an estimate of the extent to which the sample in a multilevel study deviates from simple random sampling. The design effect is a function of both the intraclass correlation and the average cluster size. Where approximate design effects are less than 2.0, there is little systematic variation between groups, and one could retain a single-level analysis of the data.

Determinant. The determinant is a summary measure of the variation that exists within a square matrix (e.g., 2×2, 3×3). It represents measures of generalized variance in the matrix after removing covariance. The determinant is useful in finding the nature of solution of the system of linear equations defined by a covariance or correlation matrix.

Direct and indirect relationships. A direct effect of X on Y describes how a one-unit change in X will affect Y, holding all other variables constant. It may be, however, that another variable is part of the causal mechanism between X and Y. An indirect effect is defined as an effect of a predictor X on an outcome Y through a mediator (M), that is, a variable between the predictor and outcome. We assume a recursive (or unidirectional) path model. The total effect (or correlation) of X and Y may be defined as the sum of the direct and indirect effects. The total effect of X on Y can therefore be described as the sum of the contribution of all the pathways through which the two variables are connected. When a mediator is present between X and Y, the strength of each of these contributing pathways is calculated as the product of the standardized path coefficients along that pathway.

Discrete variables. Discrete (or categorical) variables have a finite (or countable infinite) number of values and therefore are often presented as frequencies and percentages rather than means and standard deviations. A frequency distribution is a means of summarizing the probability that particular responses occur.

Entropy. Entropy is useful in determining how well a mixture model classifies individuals into their most likely latent classes. Higher entropy coefficients suggest stronger classification, with a coefficient of 0.60 describing roughly 80% correctly classified and 0.80 suggesting that more than 90% are correctly classified.

Exogenous and endogenous variables. In path models, exogenous variables are variables whose variability is determined by variables outside of the model being examined. Such variables are sometimes referred to as independent variables. Endogenous variables are variables whose variability is determined by other variables in the proposed model. They can be either mediating variables or outcomes in a proposed model. For example, in the proposed model $A \rightarrow B \rightarrow C$, A would be an exogenous variable (since its variability is determined by a variable outside of the causal model), while B and C would be endogenous variables, since their variability is determined by other variables in the model.

Fixed effects. The notion of "fixed effects" originally is terminology used in analysis of variance designs, where it is assumed that a factor (categorical predictor) can be either fixed or random. A fixed effect implies that data has been gathered from all levels of a factor that are of interest. An example might be an experiment where the treatment includes three levels of a drug dosage; however, there are certainly many other levels of dosage that could be investigated. A random effect, on the other hand, is viewed as representing a random draw from a probability distribution of such effects. In mixed effects and multilevel modeling, fixed effects often refer to estimates that are defined as nonvarying across higher-order units. The effects are seen as fixed to be the same within the entire sample of individuals. In contrast, a random effect is assumed to vary across the higher-level units. For example, we might see the mean of salary as varying across different organizations. In a multilevel model, the random effects are therefore the variance and covariance parameters at the group level, which may be seen to have varied effects across the sample of groups.

Full information maximum likelihood (FIML). Model estimation refers to various approaches used for estimating the values of parameters based on the sample data. There are a variety of methods for developing estimators; maximum likelihood estimation is often the default in estimating multilevel models. For example, if we assume that the dependent variable is normally distributed with some unknown mean and variance, these parameters can be estimated using maximum likelihood by knowing information drawn from a sample of the overall population. The estimation proceeds by taking the mean and variance as parameters and finding particular parametric values that make the observed results the most probable in the population given the proposed model. More specifically, maximum likelihood estimation selects the set of values of the model parameters that maximizes the likelihood function (or minimizes the discrepancy function). What this means is that the set of estimates obtained maximize the "agreement" of the selected model with the observed data.

Interaction. Interaction terms are introduced to investigate whether the effect of one predictor on an outcome is dependent on the level of a second predictor. Interaction terms can be interpreted as the amount of change in the slope of Y with respect to X when Z changes by one unit. In this case, the second predictor may be said to moderate (enhance, diminish, or wash out) the effect of the first predictor.

Intercept and slope (IS) model. The primary assumption of the IS model is that change occurs in a specific type of trajectory (i.e., linear, quadratic, or cubic trajectories). Part of the individual growth may be summarized as am intercept factor (e.g., initial status), which summarizes the relative standing of a particular individual with respect to his or her peers at a particular point in time, and the growth trend can be summarized as one or more factors that describe its slope (e.g., a linear, quadratic) or change per some unit of time.

Intraclass correlation. The intraclass correlation (ICC or *rho*) refers to the portion of variance that lies between groups, which will be a subset of the total variance in the outcome to be explained. The intraclass correlation can also be interpreted as the expected correlation between any two randomly chosen individuals in the same group.

Latent class analysis. Latent class analysis is a type of mixture model where a categorical latent variable is assumed to be responsible for observed heterogeneity in categorical observed dependent variables.

Latent curve analysis. Latent curve analysis (LCA) is applicable to all cases in which the analyst is interested in studying change over time, including those cases with a more complex pattern of change such as growth followed by decline or vice versa In the LCA approach, individual growth is captured as latent variables that are measured by the repeated observations of y.

Latent growth mixture model. Latent growth mixture models (LGMM) propose that latent intercept (e.g., initial status, end status) and latent growth rate factors are different for different subsets (or latent classes) of individuals. For example, each proposed latent class may have a different random effect growth model.

Latent variables. A latent variable is an underlying or unobserved variable that is not directly observed but is assumed to be responsible for the covariation observed among a set of observed variables. They often refer to abstract concepts such as motivation or job satisfaction. Since latent variables such as job satisfaction cannot be directly observed, they must be defined through a series of observations or observed items. It is assumed that the observed variables used to define a latent construct should correlate substantially with each other (a concept often referred to as shared (or common) variance between the underlying construct and each observed indicator. A unique error term is used to define the portion of the variance that is not shared between the construct and observed indicator. In a factor analysis a covariance matrix can be rearranged into a matrix of factor loadings, a matrix of factor variances and covariances, and a matrix of error terms.

Level and shape (LS) model. The LS model is less restrictive in terms of describing the shape of the change trajectory compared with the IS model. The LS model does not impose a specific type of change trajectory upon the pattern of change ahead of testing the model. Because of this, it will generally be expected to fit the data better than the IS model. The primary difference between the two approaches is in the manner in which the loadings on the growth factor are specified.

Link function. A link function is required to transform the expected value of a discrete outcome so that a linear model can be used to model the relationship between the predictors and transformed outcome. Since the observed outcome represents only a few categories (e.g., binary, ordinal), it is necessary to transform its expected values to an underlying latent (continuous) variable that represents predicted values of the outcome through using some type of nonlinear transformation (e.g., logit or probit transformation). Using such a transformation for a dichotomous outcome, for example, provides a type of s-shaped function representing the effect of a predictor x on the outcome.

Matrix. A matrix is a rectangular arrangement of numbers arranged in rows and columns for which operations such as addition, multiplication, and transformation are defined. Matrices are useful in storing information as well as in writing and working with multiple linear equations. The size of the matrix is defined by its number of rows and columns. For example, a 3×2 matrix has three rows and two columns. A square matrix has the same number of rows and columns.

Maximum likelihood (ML) estimation. ML estimation provides a means for estimating unknown model parameters in a proposed model by finding optimal values for the unknown parameters (e.g., means, regression parameters, variances) using a likelihood function that is based on the underlying sampling distribution of the outcome. Obtaining a set of model estimates involves an iterative process that determines a set of weights for random parameters in the model in order to maximize the likelihood function. For multiparameter models, the fit of the model to the data can also be expressed as the relative discrepancy between the sample covariance matrix and a model-implied covariance matrix, with a smaller discrepancy implying a stronger fit of the proposed model to the data. Full information maximum likelihood (FIML) estimation represents an approach based on the raw data (i.e., individual-level data) in the sample, rather than just the sample covariance matrix. FIML takes advantage of all *available* data on individuals (including where some individuals may have only partial data), which makes it useful in estimating a variety of multilevel regression and structural equation models.

Measurement error. Measurement error refers to the difference between the actual (or true score) value of a quantity and the observed value obtained by a measurement.

Measurement model. Generally the first submodel of a structural equation model where observed items are used to define latent (or underlying) constructs. This part of the model is also referred to as confirmatory factor analysis (CFA), since it involves decomposing the observed covariance matrix into a matrix of factor loadings, a matrix of latent factors, and a matrix of residual errors in defining the factors through their observed items. This allows the incorporation of measurement error into the definition of the constructs.

Missing data. Patterns of missing data can bias model parameters. Typical approaches such as listwise deletion (where a case with missing data is eliminated from the analysis) can result in biased model estimates. It is important to examine data for patterns of missing responses and to devise a strategy for dealing with missing data. Mplus can provide ML estimation under various conditions of missing data including MCAR (missing completely at random), MAR (missing at random), and NMAR (not missing at random) for categorical and continuous outcomes.

Mixture model. Mixture models are used to refer to a wide variety of models (e.g., latent class, latent profile, growth mixture models) where categorical latent variables are proposed to represent emergent subsets of the data. For example, in a latent growth mixture analysis, the underlying classes may explain variability among subsets of individuals with respect to their growth trajectories.

Model estimation. Model estimation provides a means of determining the values of a model's unknown population parameters from the sample data. Two broad approaches are referred to as frequentist versus Bayesian. For frequentists, the concern is often the distribution of specific observed data and its likely distribution over repeated sampling under similar conditions in the future. For Bayesians, the concern is how probability theory may be used to make statements about uncertain events beyond any specific instance of observed data. Bayesian computations begin with an explicit statement about a phenomenon's probable occurrence, often by referring to a prior distribution.

Model fit indices. Model fit indices are useful in determining how well the constraints implied in a proposed model conform to the actual data. Available fit indices (e.g., chi-square coefficient, comparative fit index, standardized root-mean-square residual) describe the fit of the proposed model to the data in different ways.

Model identification. Model identification refers to having sufficient information to solve for unknown values in the model-implied equations. If a model is underidentified, it would be possible to find an infinite number of values for the parameters in the proposed model. Model estimation assumes there is just enough information available to solve for the unknown parameters (a just-identified model) or there is more than enough information available to solve for the model unknowns (an overidentified model). Overidentified models are desirable because they produce positive degrees of freedom; that is, fewer parameters are estimated than could be estimated.

Model syntax file. An Mplus syntax file consists of a series of input statements regarding the TITLE, DATA, VARIABLES, ANALYSIS, and OUTPUT.

Multilevel regression modeling. This type of modeling is referred to by a variety of names including random coefficients models, mixed effects models, and hierarchical linear models. Such models have a primary concern with the decomposition of variance generally in a single outcome and the explanation of this variance by sets of explanatory variables, which are located in different strata of the data hierarchy.

Multilevel structural equation modeling (SEM). The SEM framework represents a generalization of both multiple regression and factor analysis and subsumes most linear modeling methods as special cases. This approach can be used to address two basic concerns in sample data: development of latent (or underlying) variables through a set of observed indicators and the adjustments for measurement error in estimating the latent variables. Adjusting latent constructs for measurement errors results in more accurate estimates of relationships between the latent constructs.

Multiple imputation. Multiple imputation (MI) is an approach to handing missing data where patterns of missing data are first identified and then random plausible values are imputed using the EM (expectation maximization) algorithm. Obtaining estimates involves an iterative, two-step process where missing values are first imputed and then a covariance matrix and mean vector are estimated. This process repeats until the difference between covariance matrices from adjacent iterations differs by a trivial amount.

Nested models. A nested model is one that can be derived from a more general model by removing parameters from the general model. The fit of two alternative models can be compared by examining the difference in deviance (or $-2 \times \log$ likelihood) between the two models. The deviance has a chi-square distribution with degrees of freedom equal to the difference in number of parameters estimated in each model.

Numerical integration. For curvilinear functions, numerical integration involves a family of algorithms used for finding the approximate of an integral, which is often referred to as quadrature (or calculating area). The problem is often approached by constructing interpolating polynomial functions that are easy to integrate. The most simplified numerical approximation (a polynomial function of degree 0) is at the midpoint of the interval. A more accurate approximation can be obtained by partitioning the interval of interest into a number of sub-intervals, calculating an approximation for each, and adding up the results. More complex multidimensional integration problems require Monte Carlo integration methods (e.g., Markov chain Monte Carlo algorithms). Numerical integration can become increasingly complex as the number of factors, random effects, and sample size increase. Thus, it can take considerable computer time to arrive at a solution.

One-way ANOVA model. A preliminary model to estimate the variance in the outcome within and between groups with no predictors included in the model. The one-way ANOVA (or no predictors) model provides a means of decomposing the variance into within- and between-group proportions.

Ordinary least squares (OLS) regression. OLS regression is an estimation approach focused on minimizing the squared distances of each observed value from the predicted value that rests on the regression line. The distance from the actual line to the estimated regression line is referred to as the error or residual since it expresses the inaccuracy of the predicted model. The line that minimizes the sum of these squared distances is said to fit the data best. Key assumptions of the single-level multiple regression (or OLS regression) model include independent sampling (i.e., random sampling) and independent errors with mean of zero and some variance. These assumptions are often violated in hierarchical data sets because individuals within groups may be similar on many important variables. One adjustment that must be made is the addition of a more complex error term since individuals within groups are no longer independent.

Overdispersion or underdispersion. One assumption of the Poisson model is that the mean and variance of the outcome are approximately equal. When the conditional variance exceeds the conditional mean, which frequently occurs in practice, it is referred to as *overdispersion* (with the opposite referred to as *underdispersion*). This can lead to some inaccuracy in estimating the model's standard errors.

Path model. Path analysis is a form of statistical analysis used to evaluate causal models by examining the relationships between a dependent variable and two or more independent variables. Path models require the analyst to specify relationships among all of the independent variables, which can result in a model specifying both direct and indirect effects of predictors on a dependent variable.

Piecewise growth model. This is a type of growth model where more than one trend may be modeled. For example, there may be one trend defined before the introduction of a treatment and another trend after its introduction.

Polynomial curves. A linear trajectory will fit any two time points in a longitudinal study. Higher-order polynomials are often used to fit growth curves that are not linear. For example, if the order of the equation is increased to a second degree polynomial, it will fit a curve with three time points exactly. Similarly, a third degree polynomial will fit four time points exactly.

Power. Power concerns the ability to detect an effect if it actually exists in the population, that is, the probability of rejecting the null hypothesis of no difference between groups when it is not true. The power of a test is related to the significance level (α), the sample size (N), and the population effect size (ES). We can use the concept of power to estimate the required sample size needed in a proposed study (a priori power analysis) as well as to determine what the power to detect a particular effect would be if it existed in the population, given a particular observed effect size, sample size, and significance level from our study (post hoc power analysis).

Random effects. When some effect in a statistical model is modeled as being random, we mean that we wish to draw conclusions about the population from which the observed units were drawn, rather than about these particular units themselves. Random effects modeling puts a focus on the variance of an effect across the population from which the units were sampled, rather than assuming the effect being fixed to one value in the population.

Random intercept. This is a model where the level of the outcome mean is allowed to vary across the units in the sample. Differences in the levels of the means may be explained by unit-level predictors.

Random slope. This is a model where the size of the level-1 slope summarizing the regression of Y on X is allowed to vary across units in the sample. Differences in the strength of the level-1 slopes may be explained by unit-level predictors.

Random starts. In models with categorical outcomes and numerical integration (e.g., mixture models), some parameter starting values may result in local solutions that do not represent the global maximum of the likelihood function. To facilitate optimal model estimation, initially, different random sets of starting values are automatically produced (i.e., the default number is 10), and the solution with the best likelihood is reported. Users can set random starts to 0 initially but should only treat this initial solution as preliminary solution. It can be important when exploring a given mixture model with different optimizations that are carried out with various sets of starting values.

Random variable. We often use the term *random variable* to describe possible values that a variable may have (i.e., its sampling distribution). In addition to the normal distribution that underlies continuous variables, discrete variables may have underlying sampling distributions such as binomial (e.g., binary variable), multinomial (nominal or ordinal variable), or Poisson (count) sampling distributions.

Reciprocal effects. Reciprocal-effect (or nonrecursive) models propose that relationships between two or more variables are bi-directional. This implies that the variables may be both a cause and an effect of each other. An example might be that motivation increases productivity and, in turn, productivity increases motivation. These relationships are sometimes referred to as mutual-influence relationships or as feedback loops.

Recursive and nonrecursive relationships. In a recursive model, the causal-chain system flows in one direction. In a nonrecursive model, the possibility of reciprocal effects between two or more variables in a causal chain is considered (i.e., where X causes Y and Y causes X). Reciprocal effects between variables can indicate a mutually reinforcing set of relationships over time. This approach requires methods that can deal with correlated residuals between the variables in the reciprocal relationship. SEM offers an ideal methodological framework for investigating such complex relationships because of its flexibility in estimating direct, indirect, and reciprocal effects within a single model.

Reliability. The reliability of the sample mean for any level-2 unit as an estimate for its population mean can also be estimated from the variance components and its sample size.

Residuals. Residuals represent random errors in predicting an outcome from one or more predictors. In a single-level model, residuals are assumed to be independent and normally distributed. In a multilevel model, random error is more complex. The individual-level residuals are dependent within each unit because they are common to every individual within that unit.

Sample weights. Sample weights are used to ensure the representativeness of the sample analyzed and the correct assessment of population variances that form the basis for the identification of statistical effects and hypothesis testing. When working with secondary data sets, applying sample weights is important to correct the analyses for features of the sampling design.

Secondary data. Secondary data sets refer to data sets that have been developed for wide use by researchers. Because they are often created with large, disproportionate cluster samples, they offer a number of advantages in generating knowledge about important substantive and policy issues. Of course, the downside is that the analyst is limited by the range of variables included in the data collection and other problems that may surface (e.g., missing data, correct application of available sample weights).

Structural equation modeling (SEM). SEM is a modeling approach that combines measurement error in defining latent variables through their observed indicators (referred to as the measurement model or confirmatory factor analysis) and facilitates the examination of direct, indirect, or reciprocal relationships between constructs (referred to as the structural model).

Structural model. Generally, this is the second submodel of an SEM analysis that is used to specify relationships between latent constructs or between a set of observed predictors and the latent constructs.

Sums of squares and cross products (SSCP) matrix. A sum of squares and cross products (SSCP) matrix results from the multiplication of a data matrix by its transpose. This provides a convenient way of storing information about the variance of each variable in a matrix and the covariances between pairs of variables. The diagonals in the matrix are the sums of squares of each variable, and the cross products are the multiplication of the individual deviations from the mean for each of the variable pairs. We can obtain the sample variance-covariance matrix by dividing the sum of squares for each diagonal element by $N - 1$ (which provides the variance of each variable), and dividing the cross products elements by $N - 1$ (which provides the covariances between variables).

Two-stage cluster sample. Units are selected first and then individuals are selected within the units. These are typical two-level data sets. The analyst should check to make sure that weights are available at both levels of the two-stage sample if attempting a multilevel analysis.

Unconditional model. The unconditional model is a model with only level-1 predictors; that is, it is unconditional at Level 2.

Univariate/multivariate models. Univariate models have a single dependent variable that may be explained by one or more predictors. Multivariate models have two or more dependent variables that may be explained by a set of predictors.

Vector. A k-dimensional vector of y is an ordered collection of real numbers $y_1, y_2, \ldots y_k$, which may be written as $y = (y_1, y_2, \ldots, y_k)$. The numbers are referred to as components of the vector. A matrix with only one column is called a column vector, while a matrix with only one row is called a row vector.

Weighted least squares (WLS) estimation. WLS is an estimation approach that minimizes a weighted sum of the squared residuals. WLS estimation is useful in handling binary, ordered categories, multinomial, and count outcomes, as well as combinations of continuous and categorical outcomes.

AUTHOR INDEX

SUBJECT INDEX